ROWLATT ON
THE LAW OF PRINCIPAL AND SURETY

AUSTRALIA
The Law Book Company Ltd.
Sydney : Melbourne : Brisbane

CANADA AND U.S.A.
Oceana Publications Inc.
New York

INDIA
N.M. Tripathi Private Ltd.
Bombay
and
Eastern Law House Private Ltd.
Calcutta and Delhi
M.P.P. House
Bangalore

ISRAEL
Steimatzky's Agency Ltd.
Jerusalem : Tel Aviv : Haifa

MALAYSIA : SINGAPORE : BRUNEI
Malayan Law Journal (Pte.) Ltd.
Singapore

NEW ZEALAND
Sweet & Maxwell (N.Z.) Ltd.
Auckland

PAKISTAN
Pakistan Law House
Karachi

Sir Sidney Rowlatt
1862–1945

ROWLATT
ON
THE LAW OF
PRINCIPAL AND SURETY

by

DAVID G. M. MARKS, M.A. (OXON.), B.C.L.

of Gray's Inn, Barrister
Member of the Illinois Bar

and

GABRIEL S. MOSS, M.A. (OXON.), B.C.L.

of Lincoln's Inn, Barrister
Sometime Eldon Scholar in the University of Oxford

With a Foreword by
THE HONOURABLE SIR ALAN MOCATTA

FOURTH EDITION

LONDON
SWEET & MAXWELL
1982

First Edition	(1898)	By S. A. T. Rowlatt
Second Edition	(1926)	By J. Rowlatt
Third Edition	(1936)	By A. A. Mocatta
Fourth Edition	(1982)	By D. G. M. Marks and G. S. Moss

Published in 1982 by
Sweet & Maxwell Limited of
11 New Fetter Lane, London
and printed in Scotland
Thomson Litho Limited,
East Kilbride

British Library Cataloguing in Publication Data

Rowlatt, *Sir* Sidney Arthur Taylor
   Rowlatt on the law of principal and surety.—4th ed.
   1. Suretyship and guaranty—England
   I. Title   II. Marks, David G.M.
   III. Moss, Gabriel S.
   344.203'74   KD1752

ISBN 0-421-26240-0

©
SWEET & MAXWELL
1982

FOREWORD

The subject dealt with in this book is an important one in everyday life as well as in the more complex fields of commercial dealings. The relevant law has never been found easy; even the very able author in his Preface to the First Edition admitted that he had found the subject a difficult one.

It is a long time now since the publication of the third edition in 1936 and copies have been increasingly difficult to obtain for consultation, a matter which has not infrequently come to my notice in recent years.

I, therefore, welcome the publication of the present fourth edition of this work, which I have no doubt will meet a real need. As can be seen from the Preface, Contents and Appendices, the editors have had to cover a somewhat wider ground than in the earlier editions and the various standard and sample forms contained in the appendices are bound to prove helpful.

I have no doubt that the high standard of legal scholarship displayed in the first edition has been maintained in the present one.

Alan A. Mocatta

PREFACE TO THE FOURTH EDITION

In his Preface to the Third Edition in 1936 Sir Alan Mocatta was able to say that he had not found it necessary to make any extensive alterations to the previous edition in 1926. Such a long period has elapsed however since the third edition that the mere passage of time and inevitable flow of decisions have necessitated a number of changes throughout the book. There has still been no general legislation on the subject, although a draft Directive from the E.E.C. Commission is in circulation aimed at harmonising the community laws on the subject. Nevertheless a number of modern statutes impinge upon the law of suretyship, *e.g.* the Consumer Credit Act 1974, the Unfair Contract Terms Act 1977 and the Civil Liability (Contribution) Act 1978.

In the Commonwealth, the subject of guarantees has come under considerable review and examination from various law reform bodies and reference is made in this edition to changes suggested by the relevant bodies in British Columbia and South Australia and it may be hoped that the Law Commission in England will soon take an interest in thoroughly reviewing the subject. We have therefore taken note of some of the more important Commonwealth and United States decisions particularly where there is a dearth of English authority.

Some of the more significant English decisions which are included in this edition include the question of unequal bargaining power in entering guarantees: *Lloyds Bank* v. *Bundy* [1975] Q.B. 326, the effect on a guarantee obligation of the rescission of the principal contract: *Moschi* v. *Lep Air Services* [1973] A.C. 331 together with the question of whether in such a situation there can be a set-off of the principal's counterclaim: *The Hyundai Cases* [1978] 2 Lloyd's Rep. 502 and [1980] 1 S.L.R. 1129, the question of whether a mortgagee or a receiver of a mortgaged property owes any duty of care to a surety: *Barclays Bank Ltd* v. *Thienel* (1978) 247 E.G. 385, *Latchford* v. *Beirne* [1981] 3 All E.R. 705, the general problem of whether a surety is discharged by variation of a principal obligation: *National Bank of Nigeria Limited* v. *Awolesi* [1964] 1 W.L.R. 1311, the question of *quia timet* relief to a surety who has terminated his guarantee but has not yet been called on to pay: *Thomas* v. *Nottingham Football Club Limited* [1972] Ch. 596 and the question of marshalling in favour of relatives and spouses of bankrupts standing in positions analogous to that of a surety: *Re Marley* [1976] 1 W.L.R. 952.

It is a fact of life in the field of guarantees that many suretyship relationships, especially with institutional lending organisations, are governed by standard form documents which exclude many of the rules dealt with in this work. It will be interesting to see what limited effect, if any, provisions of the Unfair Contract Terms Act 1977 will have in invalidating clauses which avoid liability for negligence. In order to assist the reader we reproduce some standard form guarantees in Appendix 1.

The rewriting of much of the work has necessitated a rearrangement of the subject matter and new chapters now appear concerning consumer credit, bills of exchange and the increasingly important area of performance bonds although strictly speaking the latter does not fall within the classical definition of guarantees. There is also a specimen set of performance and related bonds contained in Appendix 1. For the sake of greater clarity and convenience we have added chapters on the special effect of suretyship law on such subjects as landlord and tenant and building contracts.

In view of the many judicial expressions of approval and even praise given to the previous editions of this work in England and the Commonwealth, we can only hope that in updating and modernising this work we have retained the best features of the old whilst adding what is needed from the new.

Warmest thanks are extended for the courtesy and help offered by Eric Woods LL.M., Principal of the Solicitors and Legal Department of the Midland Bank Limited, and his colleagues and to our publishers, Sweet and Maxwell.

The responsibility for any errors appearing in this work is that of the editors alone.

3 Paper Buildings   D.G.M.M.
The Temple.   G.M.
December 1, 1981

HISTORICAL NOTE

Sir Sydney Arthur Taylor Rowlatt was born on July 20, 1862 in Cairo, the eldest son of the manager of the Bank of Egypt. After education at Fettes and Kings College Cambridge, where he was placed in the first class in both parts of the classical tripos he became for a while an assistant master at Eton where according to his obituary in The Times in 1945, "his cheery and boyish ways made him a popular teacher." He was subsequently elected Fellow of his college and then was called to the Bar by the Inner Temple becoming first a pupil of (Sir) F. A. Bosanquet and afterwards of Abel John Ram. On becoming a devil for R. B. (later Viscount) Finlay, he began a friendship which was to last until the latter's death. The two frequently used to walk home to Kensington after work in the Temple, translating English poetry into Latin on the way. It was Finlay who, as Attorney-General in 1900, nominated Rowlatt for the appointment of junior counsel to the Board of Inland Revenue. According to The Times obituary "Rowlatt had brought to bear upon his task a vigour to which the Treasury staff was not accustomed." In 1905 he became junior counsel to the Treasury on the common law side which resulted in his being offered a judgeship in 1912 by Lord Haldane, to replace Sir J. A. Hamilton, later Viscount Sumner.

Although the range of cases Rowlatt dealt with as a judge was extremely varied ranging from Old Bailey and circuit work to the commercial list, he was predominantly associated with revenue cases. He himself at the time of his retirement in 1932 admitted that during his period as a revenue judge he had neither been "disturbed by much sensation nor fatigued by acute controversy, it having been to some extent a family party." His qualities and combination of a scholarly precision, clear reasoning and lack of pomposity can be seen in such cases as *Cape Brandy Syndicate* v. *IRC* [1921] 1 K.B. 64. It may be that his failure to attain promotion was attributable to his working in a specialised field as well as an innate modesty and courtesy.

Rowlatt did however conduct various significant public committees and inquiries including chairing the committee on criminal conspiracies in India in 1917 which led to the passing of the so-called Rowlatt Act in 1919 and which aided the Government in dealing with revolutionary crime. Later in 1932 he was appointed chairman of the Royal Commission on Lotteries and

Betting. During the Second World War he was chairman of the general claims tribunal under the Compensation (Defence) Act of 1939. *The Law of Principal and Surety* was published in 1898 and his third son, Sir John Rowlatt who became first parliamentary counsel to the Treasury in 1953 and who died in 1956, was responsible for the second edition published in 1926. Rowlatt himself died at his home at Bagnor Manor, Newbury in Berkshire on March 1, 1945.

D.G.M.M.

CONTENTS

xiii

TABLE OF CASES

XV

TABLE OF STATUTES

SELECT BIBLIOGRAPHY

English and Commonwealth

Burge, W., *Commentaries on the Law of Suretyship and of obligations in solido, under laws of England, Scotland, other European States and the United States etc.* (Boston, 1847).

De Colyar, H.A., *A Treatise on the Law of Guarantees and of Principal and Surety* (3rd edition, 1897).

Eddis, A.C., *The Rule in ex parte Waring* (1876).

Fell, W.W., *A Treatise on the Law of Mercantile Guaranties and Engagements in the nature of Guarantie* (2nd edition, 1820).

Hartley, T.C., *Law of Suretyship and Indemnity in United Kingdom of Great Britain and Northern Ireland and Ireland* (EEC Studies: Competition: Approximation of Legislation Series, Vol. 28, 1974).

Hewitson, T., *Suretyship: Its Origin and History in Outline* (Sydney, 1927).

Kiralfy, A., *History of Law of Personal Guarantees in England since 1500* (Société Jean Bodin, Vol. 29, p. 395).

Pitman, E.D., *Law of Principal and Surety* (1840).

Theobald, W., *Law of Principal and Surety* (1832).

Ventris, F.M., *Bankers' Documentary Credits* (Lloyds, 1980), Chap. 11.

Williams, G.L., *Joint Obligations* (London, 1949).

Wood, P., *Law and Practice of International Finance* (1980).

39th Report of the Law Reform Committee of South Australia (1976).

Law Commission Report No. 79, *Contribution*, Cmnd. 9721 (1977).

Law Reform Commission of British Columbia, Report on Guarantees of Consumer Debts (1979).

American

Arant, H.W., *Handbook of the Law of Suretyship and Guaranty* (St. Paul, 1931).

Arant, H.W., *Cases in Law of Suretyship* (2nd edition, Chicago, 1931).

Brandt, G.W., *The Law of Suretyship and Guarantee* (3rd edition, Chicago, 1905).

Cardozo, B.N., *Law and Literature* (1931).

Cardozo, B.N., *Nature of the Judicial Process* (1928).

Hagendorn, W.V., *The Law of Surety and Guaranty* (New York, 1938).

Osborne, G.E., *Cases and Materials in the Law of Suretyship* (1966).

Pingrey, D.H., *A Treatise on the Law of Suretyship and Guarantee* (2nd edition, New York, 1913).

Simpson, L.P., *Handbook of the Law of Suretyship* (St. Paul, 1950). [This is based largely on Arant's earlier, work *supra*]

Stearns, A.A., *The Law Suretyship* (5th edition by James L. Elder, Cincinnati, 1951).

American Law Institute, *The Restatement of the Law of Security* (1941), Chaps. 3 to 6 inclusive.

ARTICLES

Blair, M.C., *The Conversion of Guarantee Contracts* (1966) 29 M.L.R. 522.

Böhlhoff, Dr. K., *Letters of Responsibility* (1978) *International Business Lawyer* 288

Cohn, E.J., *The Form of Contracts of Guarantee in Comparative Law* (1938) 54 L.Q.R. 220.

Cohn, E.J., *Validity of Guarantees for Debts of Minors* (1947) 10 M.L.R. 40.

Else Mitchell, R., *Is a Surety's Liability Co-extensive with that of Principal Debtor?* (1947) 63 L.Q.R. 355.

Furmston, M.P., *Infants' Contracts—La Nouvelle Vague?* (1961) 24 M.L.R. 644.

Partlett, D., *The Right of Subrogation in Accommodation Bills of Exchange* (1970) 53 A.L.J. 694.

Steyn, J., *The Co-extensiveness Principle* (1974) 90 L.Q.R. 246.

Williams, K.P., *On Demand and Conditional Performance Bonds* (1981) *Journal of Business Law* 8.

CHAPTER 1

SCOPE OF THE LAW OF PRINCIPAL AND SURETY

Definition

A surety may be defined as one who contracts with an actual or possible creditor of another to be responsible to him by way of security, additional to that other, for the whole or part of the debt.

The obligation of a surety is thus necessarily a collateral obligation, postulating the principal liability of another, the principal debtor.[1] A person is not, therefore, a surety who either (a) in order to procure an advantage for another becomes bound upon any other basis than that that other shall also become liable,[2] or (b) becomes bound instead of a person already bound who is released by the substitution.[3]

---

[1] See *Re Royal Albert Life Assurance Company* (1870) L.R.11 Eq.164 at 177.*Cf. Nicholas* v. *Ridley* [1904] 1 Ch. 192 at 209, 210. If the promisor has himself an interest in the transaction, the proper inference is often that he is more than a surety and is a principal debtor: *Huggard* v. *Representative Church Body* [1916] 1 I.R.1 at 13. *Cf. post*, pp.32 *et seq.* and the cases there cited.

[2] See *Mountstephen* v. *Lakeman* (1871) L.R.5 Q.B.613; 7 Q.B.196; 7 H.L.17; and see *post* p.23.

[3] Despite the definition in the text, there have been occasional judicial comments to the effect that "collateral" does not sufficiently convey the accessory character of suretyship see, *e.g. National Telephone Co.* v. *I.R.C.* [1899] 1 Q.B.250, 258 *per* A.L. Smith L.J. affd. [1900] A.C.1 but see later discussion at pp.21 *et seq. Cf. Re Athill, Athill* v. *Athill* (1880) 16 Ch.D.211 at 222. The definition and discussion contained in the 2nd edition of this work was cited in *Re Conley* [1938] 2 All E.R.127 where Lord Greene M.R. saw no distinction between the giving of personal credit and the giving of a pledge or security for the purpose of rendering the giver a surety. Usage of the term "guarantee" has broadened considerably dependent upon the context. It has come to mean a warranty as employed in the Sale of Goods Act 1979, or a retailer's obligation to undertake repairs, whether free or not (see, *e.g. Adams* v. *Richardson and Starling Ltd.* [1969] 1 W.L.R.1645) or even a contract conferring rights upon a buyer against a manufacturer in return for giving up some or all of his rights against a seller. None of these meanings are considered in this work. Nor is any mention made of the law of bail in which the concept of suretyship is also employed, and as to which reference should be made to the various textbooks on criminal law. See also *Heisler* v. *Anglo—Dal Ltd.* [1954] 1 W.L.R.1273, where on the construction of the contract there involved, an undertaking by a party to furnish a guarantee was held satisfied by his personal guarantee. For a modern illustration of rights analogous to those of a surety, see *Re Downer Enterprises Ltd.* [1974] 1 W.L.R.1460 and *infra*, p.5. One of the leading current American treatises on principal and surety, Simpson, *Handbook on the Law of Suretyship* (West Publishing Co., 1950) makes a further distinction between suretyship, which in its narrow sense entails a primary, though still accessory obligation on the part of the surety, and guarantee, which is entirely secondary in nature (see pp. 6 to 11 and 16 to 23 inclusive). For an American judicial discussion see *W. T. Rawleigh Co.* v. *Overstreet* 32 S.E. 2d 574, 71 Ga.App. 873 (1944). For judicial and practical illustrations of the differences between guarantees and indemnities see, *e.g. Yeoman Credit Ltd.* v. *Latter* [1961] 1 W.L.R. 828; *Unity Finance Ltd.* v. *Woodcock* [1963] 1 W.L.R. 455; *Goulston Discount Co. Ltd.* v. *Clark* [1967] 2 Q.B. 493; *Stadium Finance Co. Ltd.* v. *Helm* (1965) 109 S.J.471; *Goulston Discount Co. Ltd.* v. *Sims* (1967) 111 S.J.682; *Ralli Brothers Ltd.* v. *Cooper* (1968) 112 S.J.67. See also *Argo Caribbean* v. *Lewis* [1976] 2 Lloyd's Rep. 288 at p.296. So-called "letters of comfort" or "letters of respectability" which are often given by a parent company to reassure a lender to its subsidiary of the parent's commitment to maintain interest and support in the subsidiary, are not guarantees in a legally binding sense and are not dealt with further in this work. See generally Wood, *Law and Practice of International Finance* (1980) and (1978) 8 *International Business Lawyer* 288.

Principal under disability

In view of the necessity of a principal debtor a difficulty arises where a person purports to become surety for one who is under disability. It seems clear that this does not prevent the so-called surety from being liable to the creditor where there is no fraud or misrepresentation. In nearly every instance it will be found that the proper inference from the facts is that the intention of the parties was that the so-called surety should be liable as principal, *i.e.* whether the principal could be liable or not.[4] Thus, although a promise that a company or corporation shall do something beyond its legal powers is void,[5] a surety for the repayment of money borrowed by a company *ultra vires* may be liable on his guarantee if the transaction was entered into in good faith.[6] However, in the case of a loan made to a minor which is made void by statute,[7] the guarantors of a loan where the fact of the minority is known to all parties, cannot be liable on the guarantee.[8]

Liability of surety collateral not necessarily conditional

The liability of a surety is often spoken of as a liability to pay "if the principal does not." This does not mean that his liability is necessarily only conditionally enforceable[9] but merely that it is collateral. Being collateral the liability of a surety is in substance from the surety's point of view certainly contingent, because if the principal pays, the debt is satisfied, and the surety is free.[10] What is contemplated is that the principal shall pay.

---

[4] *Wauthier* v. *Wilson* (1912) 27 T.L.R.582, 28 T.L.R.238; *Cf. Maggs* v. *Ames* (1828) 4 Bing.470; *White* v. *Cuyler* (1795) 1 Esp.200. Also *Ex p. Chippendale* (1853) 4 De. G.M. & G.19; *Chambers* v. *Manchester and Milford Railway* (1864) 5 B.& S.588, 612; *Yorkshire Railway Wagon Co.* v. *Maclure* (1881) 19 Ch.D.478, 21 Ch.D.309; and *Garrard* v. *James* [1925] Ch.616.

[5] *McGregor* v. *Dover and Deal Railway Co.* (1852) 18 Q.B.618; on the question of corporate power to give guarantees see *Re Lee Behrens* [1932] Ch.46, *Introductions Ltd.* v. *National Provincial Bank Ltd.* [1966] 2 Q.B.656 and *Re Horsley & Weight Ltd.* (C.A. unreported: July 30, 1980). See further on the question of a company's powers to give guarantee *post*, Chap. 3, part 2 and Chap. 4, part 7.

[6] See *Garrard* v. *James*, [1925] Ch. 616, and also *Coutts & Co.* v. *Browne-Lecky* [1947] K.B.104, 111 where it was suggested that this type of case may be different in its consequences from voidness brought about by the express provisions of a statute. See also *Heald* v. *O'Connor* [1971] 1 W.L.R.497 and Chap. 4, part 7 and Chap. 6.

[7] Infants Relief Act 1874, ss.1 and 2; Betting and Loans (Infants) Act 1892, s.5. See also Steyn (1974) 90 L.Q.R. 246.

[8] *Coutts & Co.* v. *Browne-Lecky, supra,* following *Swan* v. *Bank of Scotland* (1836) 10 Bli. (N.S.) 927, H.L. where a bank was precluded by statute from recovering against a principal debtor because it had knowingly honoured unstamped drafts. *Wauthier* v. *Wilson, supra,* was not followed. But a contract to repay money lent to an infant will, it seems, be enforceable if on its proper construction it is a contract of indemnity. See *Harris* v. *Huntbach* (1757) 1 Burr. 373; *Duncomb* v. *Tickridge* (1648) Alleyn 44; *Yeoman Credit Ltd.* v. *Latter* [1961] 1 W.L.R. 828. *Cf. Western Credit Ltd.* v. *Alberry* [1964] 1 W.L.R. 945. In the 3rd edition of this work it was suggested that in some such cases the liability is here more accurately explicable as that of suretyship by estoppel. As to guarantees by minors, see further Chap. 4. There are interesting articles touching on guarantees by infants by Steyn, *op. cit.,* Else Mitchell (1947) 63 L.Q.R.355 and Cohn (1974) 10 M.L.R. 40.

[9] *Cf. Amott* v. *Holden* (1852) 18 Q.B.593, 607, 608; *White* v. *Corbett* (1859) 1 E. & E.692. And see *post*, p.108.

[10] *Ibid.* and see *Ex p. Whittaker* (1891) 63 L.T.727.

This may be so, although the undertaking of the surety is as absolute as that of the principal. To say, therefore, that a debtor is surety only does not necessarily imply more than that he has become bound as an additional party, and only as security for another, the principal debtor, who alone has enjoyed or is to enjoy the consideration,[11] and upon the terms, express or implied, of being indemnified by him. The rights which a surety can claim at the hands of a creditor depend not upon any term in the contract between them but upon an equity arising out of the knowledge of the creditor of the relation between the surety debtor and the principal debtor, which binds him to respect, subject to his own right to exact payment from either, the right of the surety to have the money found by the principal.[12]

Surety need not expressly contract as such

This being the basis of the rights of a surety, it follows that he need not be expressed to contract as surety, inasmuch as his admission to the rights of one will not vary or add to his written contract. A typical example is where a person gives another his promissory note to secure an advance to a third person.[13] Here the legal right of the creditor is to demand payment from the maker unconditionally according to the tenor of the note.[14] The equitable right of the maker is, without limiting that legal right of the creditor,[15] to have the creditor respect in his dealings with the principal the right of the maker to be indemnified by the principal. This is not contradicting or modifying the terms of the note. The unconditional promise to pay does not import that the maker gives up equities which introduce no conditions. Similarly an I.O.U. can be given as a guarantee.[16]

Rights of surety depend not on contract but on notice

In strictness perhaps, no-one under a liability *ex facie* absolute should be described as a surety, unless that liability was from the first, to the knowledge of the creditor at that time, only undertaken for the purpose of affording security for the payment

---

[11] See *per* Stuart V.–C., in *Wright* v. *Sandars* (1857) 3 Jur. (N.S.) 504, at p.507; *Re Keily* (1856) 6 Ir.Ch.R.394. In the latter case the question was whether a son, entitled in remainder, who had joined with his father, the tenant for life, in mortgaging the property, was in the position of a surety. It was held under the circumstances there existing that he was. Contrast *Huggard* v. *Representative Church Body* [1916] 1 I.R.1.

[12] See *Pooley* v. *Harradine* (1857) 7 E. & B.431; *Greenough* v. *McLelland* (1860) 2 E. & E.424; *Leicestershire Banking Co.* v. *Hawkins* (1900) 16 T.L.R.317.

[13] See cases cited in the previous footnote.

[14] For an attempt to impose conditions, see *Abrey* v. *Crux* (1869) L.R.5 C.P.37; and compare *Hitchings* v. *Northern Leather Co.* [1914] 3 K.B.903. See generally Chapter 13.

[15] See *Ewart* v. *Latta* (1865) 4 Macq.H.L.903.

[16] *R.* v. *Chambers* (1871) L.R.1 C.C.R.341.

of the principal debt.[17] It is however a logical development from the principle that the rights of a surety depend not upon contract but upon notice only that a person whose liability is *ex facie* that of a principal may acquire the equitable rights of a surety by notice to the creditor, even after such person has become liable,[18] that either at the time of his becoming liable or since[19] it was agreed between him and the other debtor that the latter should assume the whole interest in the consideration and the whole duty of discharging the liability.

This proposition itself was conclusively established by the decision of the House of Lords in *Rouse* v. *Bradford Banking Co.*[20] The doctrine at common law was (except in two decisions by Lord Ellenborough, which were later overruled) never extended beyond the case where the creditor, at the time of taking an instrument not under seal, actually agrees to regard as surety only one who by the instrument contracts in form as principal.[21] In equity though, the wider rule always prevailed that the creditor was constrained to regard the position of the surety not by contract but by notice only,[22] and that notice given after the contract has been entered into was sufficient.[23]

Furthermore, there was no difficulty, in equity, in applying this principle to instruments under seal[24]; and consequently an obligor in a bond by which he appeared to be principal could show that he became bound as surety only, and from the date of notice of that circumstance to the obligee, claim the rights of a surety.[25]

The decision in *Rouse* v. *Bradford Banking Co.* finally settled the question of whether a notification to the creditor, after the

---

[17] See *Duncan Fox & Co.* v. *North & South Wales Bank* (1880) 6 App. Cas.1 *per* Lord Selborne at p.11 where at least three different kinds of suretyship were listed.

[18] *Oriental Financial Corporation* v. *Overend, Gurney & Co.* (1871) L.R.7 Ch.142; 7 H.L.348; *Duncan Fox & Co.* v. *North & South Wales Bank, supra.*

[19] *Rouse* v. *Bradford Banking Co.* [1894] A.C. 586.

[20] *Supra.*

[21] *Manley* v. *Boycot* (1853) 2 E. & B.46 (decided just before the introduction of equitable pleas); following *Kerrison* v. *Cooke* (1813) 3 Campbell 362; *Fentum* v. *Pocock* (1813) 5 Taunt 192; *Price* v. *Edmunds* (1829) 10 B. & C.578; *Nichols* v. *Norris* (1831) 3 B. & Ad.41, note; *Harrison* v. *Courtauld* (1832) 3 B. & Ad.36; and overruling *Laxton* v. *Peat* (1809) 2 Camp.185 and *Collott* v. *Haigh* (1812) 3 Camp.281, the decisions of Lord Ellenborough referred to in the text. And see *Mutual Loan Fund* v. *Sudlow* (1858) 5 C.B. (N.S.) 449.

[22] *Bank of Ireland* v. *Beresford* (1818) 6 Dow.233; *ex p. Glendinning* (1819) 8 Buck.517; *Oakeley* v. *Pasheller* (1836) 4 C. & F.207; *Hollier* v. *Eyre* (1840) 9 C. & F.1; *Wythes* v. *Labouchere* (1859) 3 De G. & J.593; *Davies* v. *Stainbank* (1855) 6 De G.M. & G.679; *Pooley* v. *Harradine* (1857) 7 E. & B.431; *Greenough* v. *McLelland* (1860) 2 E. & E.424; *Wright* v. *Sandars* (1857) 3 Jur. (N.S.) 504; *Rayner* v. *Fussey* (1859) 28 L.J.Ex.132.

[23] *Oriental Financial Corporation* v. *Overend, Gurney & Co., supra,* but see *Ex p. Graham* (1854) 5 De G.M. & G.356.

[24] See *per* Lord Loughborough in *Rees* v. *Berrington* (1795) 2 Ves.540; 2 W. & T.L.C. Eq. (8th ed.), p.571 and compare *Davey* v. *Prendergrass* (1821) 5 B. & Ald 187.

[25] *Wythes* v. *Labouchere* (1859) 3 De G. & J.593, *Wright* v. *Sandars* (1857) 3 Jur. (N.S.) 504, and see *Wyke* v. *Rogers* (1852) 1 De G.M. & G.408; *Tucker* v. *Laing* (1856) 2 K. & J.745; *Oakeley* v. *Pasheller, supra; Hollier* v. *Eyre, supra.* For the same principles regarding accommodation bills of exchange see *infra,* pp.214 *et seq.*

contract, of the fact that one of a number of debtors had since the contract become, as between himself and the others, a surety only, would bind the creditor to respect his position as a surety, if it could not be made out that the creditor had consented to a modification of the original position, and actually agreed to regard him as surety.[26] On this principle it was held in that case that a partner retiring with the ordinary provision for indemnity had the rights of a surety as against a creditor of the old firm having notice of that provision, and that no assent of the creditor to the change of the relation between the parties was necessary.[27]

Cases analogous to suretyship

There lies, however, just beyond the borderline of suretyship a class of cases in which, without any contract between the debtors, there is a primary and secondary liability of two persons for one and the same debt, the debt being, as between the two, that of one of those persons only, and not equally of both; so that the other, if he should be compelled to pay it, would be entitled to reimbursement by the person by whom, as between the two, it ought to have been paid.[28] Such persons, when both have become liable to the creditor, and it is within his choice upon which to put the burden, do stand in a relation to one another which gives rise to an equity identical with one which exists between principal and surety—namely, that securities given by the primary debtor are attributable in the hands of the creditor to the satisfaction of the debt, and do not go back to that debtor or his general creditors.[29]

This relation is not, however, genuinely that of principal and surety.[29] Thus the drawer of a bill of exchange is not in the complete sense a surety for the acceptor,[30] although (on grounds independent of suretyship) he is discharged by time being given to the acceptor, and is only liable on his default, and although, after the bill has been dishonoured, he is entitled as against the acceptor to securities covering the bill given by the acceptor and in the hands of the holder,[31] and although, even if not the holder of the bill, he can recover over against the acceptor any sum paid by him in his exoneration.[32] But an accommodation party to a

---

[26] See *Swire* v. *Redman* (1876) 1 Q.B.D.536; *Lindley on Partnership* (14th ed., 1979) at p.369; *Rouse* v. *Bradford Banking Co.* [1894] A.C.586.

[27] *Rouse* v. *Bradford Banking Co., supra; Goldfarb* v. *Bartlett* [1920] 1 K.B.639. As to the liability of retired partners see also *Stevens* v. *Britten* [1954] 1 W.L.R.1340.

[28] See *Duncan Fox & Co.* v. *North & South Wales Bank* (1880) 6 App.Cas. 1 *per* Lord Selborne at p.11. Such parties are sometimes referred to as "quasi-sureties." See, *e.g. Halsbury's Laws of England* (4th ed.), Vol. 20, para. 108.

[29] *Ibid.*

[30] *Ibid; Ex p. Yonge* (1814) 3 Ves. & B.31, 40. See generally Chapter 13.

[31] *Duncan Fox & Co.* v. *North & South Wales Bank* (1860) 6 App.Cas.1.

[32] *Pownal* v. *Ferrand* (1827) 6 B. & C.439.

bill of exchange known to be such is a surety in every sense[33] inasmuch as his liability upon the bill was only undertaken to afford security for the debt of the party accommodated.

Again, the transferor of shares, who is liable by statute under certain circumstances to pay calls if the transferee does not,[34] the owner of goods which by the law of distress may become liable for the rent of the premises upon which they are,[35] a lessee liable upon the covenants in a lease assigned,[36] a mortgagor liable for the mortgage money after the sale of the equity of redemption,[37] can none of them be classed as sureties, although in each case the liability is a secondary one, and in each case the person secondarily liable has upon payment the right to be reimbursed[38] by the person primarily liable, founded upon the same principle as the right of a surety to sue the principal for the money paid by him.[39]

Suretyship by pledge or mortgage

A person may also become a surety by pledging, mortgaging or charging his property for the debt of another as by pledging his personal credit: in fact he may well become a surety in both ways at once[40]; and he will be entitled to the same remedies for his indemnity and to have the security released upon the same grounds in the one case as in the other.[41] Thus a wife charging her separate estate to raise money for her husband's use was

---

[33] *Post*, Chapter 13.

[34] Companies Act 1948, s.212 (1)(c); *Hudson's Case* (1871) L.R.12 Eq.1; *Helbert's Case* (1871) L.R.5.H.L.28; *Roberts* v. *Crowe* (1872) L.R.7 C.P.629.

[35] See *Exall* v. *Partridge* (1799) 8 Term. Rep.308.

[36] See *Re Russell, Russell* v. *Shoolbred* (1885) 29 Ch.D.254; *Baynton* v. *Morgan* (1888) 21 Q.B.D.101; 22 Q.B.D.74. The covenant of the lessee is not collateral to the liability of the assignee of the lease, to pay if he does not, but is a covenant that the lessee or his assignee shall pay: *per* Fry L.J. 22 Q.B.D. at p.81. In truth the liability of the lessee is not undertaken in contemplation of a principal liability to be contracted by an assignee of the lease towards the lessor. The liability of the assignee to the lessor upon the privity of the estate, is, as regards the lessee, an accident. And the position of a mortgagor who has assigned his equity remaining liable upon his covenant, is in this respect very like that of a lessee who has assigned. See also Chap. 14.

[37] The mortgagor has an implied right of indemnity against his assignee: *Waring* v. *Ward* (1802) 7 Ves.332, 337; *Bridgman* v. *Daw* (1891) 40 W.R.253. There is no privity of contract between the assignee and the mortgagee: see *Re Errington* [1894] 1 Q.B.11, 14. The mortgagee cannot sue the mortgagor upon his covenant, if by reason of anything that has passed between him and the transferee of the equity, he is precluded from reconveying. See *Palmer* v. *Hendrie* (1859) 27 Beav. 349; 28 Beav. 341; *Walker* v. *Jones* (1866) L.R.1. P.C.50; *Rudge* v. *Richens* (1873) L.R. 8 C.P.358; *Kinnaird* v. *Trollope* (1888) 39 Ch.D.636. But this does not depend upon the law of suretyship. See also *Ellis* v. *Dixon-Johnson* [1925] A.C. 489.

[38] For the distinction between a right of reimbursement and a right to indemnity or protection against being called upon to pay see *Johnston* v. *The Salvage Association* (1887) 19 Q.B.D.458 at 460.

[39] See *post*, pp. 134 *et seq.*

[40] *Bolton* v. *Salmon* [1891] 2 Ch.48; *Smith* v. *Wood* [1929] 1 Ch.14; *Re Conley* [1938] 2 All E.R.127 *per* Luxmoore J. at pp.137 *et seq.*

[41] *Re Keily* (1856) 6 Ir.Ch.R.394; *McNeale* v. *Reed* (1857) 7 Ir.Ch. R.251; *Hodgson* v. *Hodgson* (1837) 2 Keen 704; *Ex p. Ford* (1885) 16 Q.B.D.305; *Bolton* v. *Salmon, supra*; *Rouse* v. *Bradford Banking Co.* [1894] A.C.586. He has, moreover, what a surety by covenant has not—a charge from the date of his mortgage on property of the principal mortgaged by the same instrument for the same debt: *Gee* v. *Liddell* [1913] 2 Ch.62. But see *Kennedy* v. *Campbell* [1899] 1 I.R.59.

under the old system of family property law in England regarded as entitled to have her property exonerated out of her husband's estate.[42]

Suretyship and insurance

The subject-matter of a contract by way of suretyship is always a debt either already incurred or intended to be incurred by the principal to the person taking the guarantee, or which, though not already incurred or intended to be incurred, may result in the future from some default or miscarriage of the principal in a relation already existing or intended to be entered into between himself and that person. The province of guarantee is therefore narrower than that of insurance by which indemnity may be secured against losses by the acts or omissions of strangers, considered as perils analogous to the risk of accident, and without regard to any legal responsibility of the persons guilty of them. The domain of insurance, however, is not restricted to the class of losses which cannot be provided against by taking sureties. The risk of default by a debtor can be insured against as effectually[43] as the debt can be guaranteed. But the two securities are not identical either in the form of the obligation imposed or in respect of the basis upon which the parties are taken to contract. A surety becomes bound, it may be, unconditionally and without previous notice or demand, to pay the debt or make good the default which the principal is or shall be liable to pay or make good, and the surety must see he does it.[44] An insurer only engages to pay the loss, measured in a certain way, upon the happening of a defined contingency,[45] against the happening of which, however, he is not considered capable of exercising an influence. An insurer is entitled to a disclosure of all facts material to the risk within the knowledge of the assured. But a surety can only complain of positive deception, by representations expressed or implied.[46] When a

---

[42] *Hudson* v. *Carmichael* (1854) Kay.613; *Dixon* v. *Steel* |1901| 2 Ch.602; *Paget* v. *Paget* |1898| 1 Ch.471; *Hall* v. *Hall* |1911| 1 Ch.487; *Quaere* how far this principle may apply in modern social conditions where property is put into the joint names of a husband and wife. See *Re Berry* |1978| 2 N.Z.L.R.373 and *Re Woodstock* (1980) C.L.Y. 148.

[43] *Dane* v. *Mortgage Insurance Corporation* |1894| 1 Q.B.54; *Finlay* v. *Mexican Investment Corporation* |1897| 1 Q.B.517.

[44] See *post*, Chap. 4, section 10.

[45] See *Dane* v. *Mortgage Insurance Corporation, supra; cf. Mortgage Insurance Corporation* v. *Pound* (1894), 64 L.J. Q.B.394.

[46] See *post*, p.20. *Seaton* v. *Heath* |1899| 1 Q.B.782 reversed without reference to this point *sub. nom. Seaton* v. *Bernard* |1900| A.C.135; *Workington Harbour, etc.* v. *Trade Indemnity Co.* (1933) 47 Ll.L.R.305; 49 Ll.L.R.430 (C.A.), where this passage was cited with approval by Greer L.J. at 443. The decision was reversed on another point, |1937| A.C.1, the House of Lords expressly not deciding the question whether in contracts of guarantee there is a duty to disclose similar to that in contracts of insurance. See also *Westcott* v. *J.H. Jenner Ltd.* |1962| 1 Lloyd's Rep.307 where a contract by sub-contractors to indemnify the contractors against all employers and third party risks was held to cover claims resulting from the contractor's own negligence; the substance and not the form of the transaction was held to be decisive.

principal debtor procures a third party to become bound for his, the principal's, debt by an instrument in form a policy of insurance, the result appears to be, as in the parallel case where the third party is bound by a promissory note or a bond,[47] that as to such matters as concealment[48] and equitable rights generally,[49] the third person is in the position of a surety, but the document remains a policy of insurance as far as concerns the form and extent of the obligation undertaken.[50]

---

[47] *Ante,* p.3.

[48] See *Seaton* v. *Heath, supra.* The result of this case seems to be that the test for this purpose is whether the instrument was obtained by the principal or the creditor.

[49] *Re Denton* [1904] 2 Ch.178 *Cf. Parr's Bank* v. *Albert Mines Syndicate* (1900) 5 Com. Cas.116.

[50] This appears to be the explanation of the dicta in *Shaw* v. *Rogers* [1911] 1 Ch.138, see also *Re Law Guarantee, Liverpool Mortgage Insurance Co.'s Case* [1914] 2 Ch.617; *American Surety Co.* v. *Wrightson* (1910) 103 L.T.663.

CHAPTER 2

CONSIDERATION

Consideration necessary

Like every other contract, a guarantee if not under seal must have a consideration to support it. It need hardly be added that the fact of its being in writing according to the Statute of Frauds does not dispense with the necessity[1]; nor that if the consideration totally fails a guarantee cannot be enforced.[2]

Where debt has been already incurred

In accordance with the well-known principle that an executed consideration will not support a promise,[3] a guarantee not under seal for a debt already incurred will not be valid unless there be some further consideration moving from the creditor.[4]

Where debt to be guaranteed has not yet been incurred

Where the guarantee is to secure a further debt or sums which may be due by virtue of a relation not yet entered into between a creditor and the debtor, the granting of the credit or entering into the relation will always be sufficient consideration. Such a consideration is either (i) entire, as where a lease is granted or an employment conferred, in consideration of which a third person guarantees the performance of the duties of the lessee or employee; or (ii) fragmentary, supplied from time to time, and therefore divisible, as where a guarantee is given for a running account in respect of money to be advanced or goods to be supplied.[5] The distinction is important upon the question of the right of a guarantor to bring his guarantee to an end.[6]

[1] *Barrell* v. *Trussell* (1811) 4 Taunt.117; *Sheffield* v. *Lord Castleton* (1700) 2 Vern.399; *Pillans* v. *Van Mierop* (1765), 3 Burr.1664; *Saunders* v. *Wakefield* (1821) 4 B. & Ald.395; *Ex parte Gardom* (1808) 15 Ves.286; *Boyd* v. *Moyle* (1846) 2 C.B.644; *French* v. *French* (1841) 2 Man. & G.644. And see *Rann* v. *Hughes* (1778) 7 Term Rep.350, note. See also *Performance Systems* v. *Pezim* [1971] 5 W.W.R. 433.
[2] See *Cooper* v. *Joel* (1859) 27 Beav.313; *Latter* v. *White* (1870) L.R. 5 Q.B. 622; 5.H.L. 578; *Walton* v. *Cook* (1888) 40 Ch. D.325; *Re Barber, ex p. Agra Bank* (1870) L.R.9 Eq.725; *Rolt* v. *Cozens* (1856) 18 C.B.673.
[3] For a recent example see *Astley Ind. Trust* v. *Grimston Electric Tools* (1965) 109 S.J.149.
[4] *French* v. *French* (1841) 2 Man. & G.644; *Forth* v. *Stanton* (1669) Saund.210; *Jones* v. *Ashburnham* (1804) 3 East 455, 463 and see *Wigan* v. *English and Scottish Law Life Assurance Association* [1909] 1 Ch.291, 297 holding that the mere existence of an antecedent debt cannot be valuable consideration for the giving of a security by a debtor; *Currie* v. *Misa* (1875) L.R.10 Ex.153 affirmed on other grounds *sub nom. Misa* v. *Currie* (1876) 1 App. Cas 554 H.L.
[5] *Lloyds* v. *Harper* (1880) 16 Ch. D.290 at p.319. See *post* pp. 60, 61.
[6] *Ibid.*

9

Consideration for guaranteeing existing debt

The consideration for a guarantee of an existing debt is commonly either a forbearance on the part of the creditor to press for the debt, or the allowance of a further credit or advance. But it may also be a payment by or on behalf of the creditor to the guarantor, or any other legal consideration moving from the creditor to the principal or the guarantor. A consideration moving merely from the principal to the surety will not suffice.[7]

Forbearance

Where the consideration for a guarantee is forbearance, it was a long debated question as to whether the time of forbearance should be defined, or whether any forbearance or forbearance for a reasonable time would be sufficient.[8]

The modern decisions in reversing the previous rule[8] seem now to have made it clear in the first place that it is not necessary that there should have been a binding contract by the creditor with the guarantor to forbear, inasmuch as if the promise of the guarantor is to pay if the creditor at his request will forbear, and the creditor does forbear and so accepts the offer, the guarantor is bound.[9]

Upon the question how far the time of forbearance must be specified the cases fall into two classes. The first is where, though the time of forbearance is not directly specified, the promise of the guarantor names a time at or before which he will pay, and the creditor has forborne until that time.[10] In these cases it is settled that the promise is enforceable upon the ground that the transaction amounts at least to an offer by the guarantor that if the creditor forbears till that time he will pay then; and the forbearance is an acceptance of that offer. Here the question whether a reasonable time for the forbearance is to be implied does not arise, the construction of such a contract being that the forbearance is to be till the date when the surety is to pay.[11]

The second class is where the time for payment is also

---

[7] *White* v. *Cuyler* (1795) 6 Term. Rep. 1176; *Dutchman* v. *Tooth* (1839) 5 Bing N.C.577.

[8] See 3rd edition of this work for fuller historical discussion. The old rule was laid down in *Phillips* v. *Sackford* (1595) Cro. Eliz. 455.

[9] *Oldershaw* v. *King* (1853) 2 H. & N.517; *Wynne* v. *Hughes* (1873) 21 W.R. 628; *Miles* v. *New Zealand Alford Estate Co.* (1886) 32 Ch.D.266; *Crears* v. *Hunter* (1887) 19 Q.B.D.341.

[10] *Payne* v. *Wilson* (1827) 7 B. & C.423; *Rolt* v. *Cozens* (1856) 18 C.B.673; *Wynne* v. *Hughes, supra.* And see *Coe* v. *Duffield* (1822) 7 Moore 252.

[11] *Rolt* v. *Cozens* (1856) 18 C.B.673. Cf. *Harris* v. *Venables* (1872) L.R.7 Exch.235.

undefined.[12] Notwithstanding a decision to the contrary never formerly overruled,[13] it is submitted that in this case also the promise is enforceable, if the creditor has forborne for such a time as judging from the circumstances and presumable intentions of the parties at the date of the promise a court may find to have been a reasonable time. There need not be any obligation to forbear nor any express request.[14]

In *Payne* v. *Wilson*[15] the declaration alleged that in consideration that the plaintiff would consent to stay proceedings upon a *cognovit*,[16] the defendant promised to pay "on the first April then next," and there was an averment that the plaintiff "did suspend all further proceedings." This was held good after verdict upon the ground that it must be taken that proceedings had been suspended either for a time required by law or for a definite or reasonable time.

Following some uncertainty[17] it was finally decided that the mere fact of forbearance *per se* will not constitute consideration for a surety becoming liable for payment of the debt by the debtor: there must be in addition either an undertaking to forbear or an actual forbearance at the surety's express or implied request.[18]

Forbearance by agreeing to accept a composition

The measure of forbearance contemplated by the guarantee, whatever it is, must of course be accorded. In *Latter* v. *White*,[19] creditors of a debtor agreed to accept a composition secured by a surety to whom the estate was to be made over. One of the creditors afterwards refused to execute the deed, alleging that he was not bound by it, and upon that issue recovered judgment

---

[12] *Semple* v. *Pink* (1847) 1 Exch.74; *Oldershaw* v. *King* (1853) 2 H. & N.517; *Miles* v. *New Zealand Alford Estates Co.* (1886) 32 Ch.D.266; *Crears* v. *Hunter* (1887) 19 Q.B.D.341. For a modern illustration of undertaking to forbear see *Board* v. *Hoey* (1948) 65 T.L.R. 43, applying *Rolt* v. *Cozens, supra.*

[13] *Semple* v. *Pink, supra.*

[14] *Crears* v. *Hunter, supra;* see also *Alliance Bank* v. *Broom* (1864) 2 Dr. and Sm.289; *Fullerton* v. *Prov. Bank of Ireland* |1903| AC.309, 313, 315.

[15] *Supra* at footnote 10.

[16] A formal written admission. Repealed by Administration of Justice Act 1956. Mrs. Bardell gave Dodson and Fogg a cognovit in respect of their costs in the action of *Bardell* v. *Pickwick* and ended up being taken in execution for those costs to Fleet Prison.

[17] For a detailed study of the older cases see the 3rd edition of this work, pp.15–17.

[18] It would now appear that an agreement to forbear for an indefinite period will provide consideration, at least where a reasonable time can be inferred or where the surety has benefited from the forbearance. In *Barber* v. *Mackrell* (1892) 40 W.R.618; 41 W.R.341, the renewal of bills was held sufficient consideration, though the period for which the bills were to run had not been specified.

[19] (1870) L.R. 8 Q.B.622; (1871) L.R. 6 Q.B.474; 5 H.L.572.

for his debt against the principal. It was held in the Exchequer Chamber, reversing the decision of the Queen's Bench, that the surety was released, on the ground of failure of the consideration, from the demand of that creditor, even though the judgment was useless to the creditor by reason of the subsequent bankruptcy of the debtor, and even though the surety had under the deed received all the property of the debtor.

Where, in consideration that the creditor would take effectively a composition of 50 per cent. on a certain debt, a surety guaranteed the payment of that amount, it was held that the consideration was not performed by the creditor agreeing to take such a composition in instalments, with a proviso that on default of paying any instalment or the commission of an act of bankruptcy the whole original debt should become due.[20] But a guarantee for a composition is held to contemplate that the creditor, if the composition as guaranteed is not paid, shall be remitted to his former rights, and in such case the surety is not released from his liability to pay the composition.[21] Where a composition deed contained a clause to the effect that it should be void if the debtor were adjudicated bankrupt, this was construed as against the sureties for the composition to mean voidable at the election of the creditors.[22]

In *Ex p. Powell*,[23] a creditor, with the assent of a surety by whom the debt was guaranteed, agreed to accept in satisfaction a reduced amount payable by instalments, for which notes were given, the surety becoming liable for the instalments; default being made in one of the instalments, it was held that the surety remained liable (upon the construction of that particular arrangement) only for the composition, and that the original guarantee did not revive.

Under the former section 126 of the Bankruptcy Act 1869, it was held that a surety for a composition was not released by the debtor being made bankrupt at the suit of the creditors outside the composition, as the composition was not thereby put an end to; although upon default in payment of the composition the compounding creditors might prove in the bankruptcy for the whole of their original debts.[24] Now under section 16 (16) of the Bankruptcy Act 1914 re-enacting section 18 (11) of the Bankruptcy Act 1883, if default is made in payment of any instalment due in pursuance of a composition or scheme under the Act, the court may annul the scheme and adjudge the debtor bankrupt:

[20] *Clarke* v. *Green* (1849) 3 Exch.619.
[21] *Glegg* v. *Gilbey* (1876) 2 Q.B.D. 6, 209; *Ex p. Gilbey* (1878) 8 Ch. D.248.
[22] *Hughes* v. *Palmer* (1865) 19 C.B. (N.S.) 393.
[23] (1836) 2 M. & A.533.
[24] *Glegg* v. *Gilbey* (1876) 2 Q.B.D.6; *Ex p. Gilbey* (1878) 8 Ch.D.248.

this will effect the total discharge of the surety from any liability in respect of the scheme.[25]

A surety for a composition to which a number of creditors are parties would not, it seems, be released if one creditor proceeded against the debtor contrary to the agreement. But in such a case he would probably be entitled to have the action stayed, at any rate if upon paying the composition he was to have the right to recover the debts for himself.[26] Similarly a surety for a composition has a right to have given up securities taken by one creditor for a preferential payment by the debtor.[27] Where there was no composition, but the creditors agreed to take payment by instalments, and one creditor carried in his debt at half its real value and took a security for the rest, a surety for the instalments obtained a decree for cancelling the security so taken.[28]

Total forbearance

If the consideration is the total forbearance by the creditor, he can recover from the guarantor upon showing that he has forborne to the date of the writ; for he is not bound, it is said, to wait all his life.[29] Whether in such a case, he could be required to wait a reasonable time before suing the guarantor will turn upon the terms of the particular bargain.[30] There would seem to be nothing to prevent a man undertaking to pay immediately himself in consideration of the creditor forbearing for good to sue the debtor. So forbearance until after a certain day will support a promise to pay on or before that day.[31]

Withdrawal of a legal process

When the consideration is a definite act, such as the withdrawal of a legal process, this will be sufficient of itself,

---

[25] *Walton* v. *Cook* (1888) 40 Ch.D.325. For a general discussion see Williams and Muir Hunter, *Law of Bankruptcy* (19th ed. 1979) at pp.95, 837. In *Cole* v. *Lynn* [1942] 1 K.B.142 there was a deed of arrangement whereby creditors covenanted not to sue the debtor without prejudice to their remedies against the surety who was held entitled to an indemnity against the debtor in respect of payment made.

[26] See *Anstey* v. *Marden* (1804) 1 B. & P.N.R.124.

[27] *Middleton* v. *Lord Onslow* (1721) 1 P.W. 768; *cf. Walton* v. *Cook, supra.* See also *Re Stock* (1896) 3 Mans. 324.

[28] *Cecil* v. *Plaistow* (1793) 2 Anstr. 202.

[29] *Mapes* v. *Sidney* (1624) Cro. Jac.683. See also *Therne* v. *Fuller, ibid.* 306; *Edwards* v. *Roberts* (1675) 2 Mod.24.

[30] *Mapes* v. *Sidney, supra; Clarke* v. *Green* (1849) 3 Exch.619.

[31] *Waters* v. *Glassop* (1704) 1 Ld. Raym.357.

even though a new process may be launched immediately.[32] In such a case the guarantee may be enforced even though such new process is launched,[32] at any rate if such new process has not the effect of disabling the principal debtor.[32] And though the promise of the guarantor is only to pay at some future date, it will not be implied that the creditor was to wait until that date.[32] Such a term is, however, implied where the consideration is not a definite act, but forbearance merely.[33] As to what constitutes a withdrawal of a legal process, it is sufficient if leave is obtained not to proceed with it,[34] or even if notice is given to the person against whom it is issued that he need not attend, and it will not be proceeded with.[35]

Surrender of invalid guarantee

In *Haigh* v. *Brooks*[36] the opinion was expressed by the Exchequer Chamber that the delivery up of a guarantee which does not comply with the Statute of Frauds, of the mere paper in fact, may be a good consideration for a new guarantee; but the decision itself was that the surrendered guarantee did comply with the Statute.

Further credit

Further advances or credit, or supply of goods or services on the part of the creditor, if and when granted, will support a guarantee covering not only the further advances, etc., but also the liability existing at the date of the guarantee, even though there might be no obligation to grant any such further advances.[37] But unless there is, or is to be,[38] a binding

---

[32] *Harris* v. *Venables* (1872) L.R.7 Ex.235 questioning *Ross* v. *Moss* (1597) Cro. Eliz. 560, *contra*. In *Harris* v. *Venables, supra*, it was held that the withdrawal of a winding up petition constituted sufficient consideration to support a promise to pay costs of and relating to the petition. *Cf. Clarke and Walker* v. *Thew* (1967) 116 C.L.R. 465 (service of notice under Australian equivalent of s.223 of the Companies Act 1948 held not to be consideration where there was an undertaking not to "take proceedings").

[33] *Rolt* v. *Cozens* (1856) 18 C.B.673.

[34] *Harris* v. *Venables* (1872) L.R. 7 Ex.235.

[35] *Alhusen* v. *Prest* (1851) 6 Exch.720.

[36] (1839) 10 A. & E.309.

[37] *Russell* v. *Moseley* (1822) 3 B. & B. 211; *Kennaway* v. *Treleavan* (1839 5 M. & W. 498; *Mayhew* v. *Crickett* (1818) 2 Swanst. 185; *Johnston* v. *Nicholls* (1845) 1 C.B. 251; *White* v. *Woodward* (1848) 5 C.B.810; *Oldershaw* v. *King* (1857) 2 H. & N. 399, 517; *Harris* v. *Venables* (1872) L.R. 7 Ex.235. For the difficulties arising in such cases prior to the 1856 Act, see 3rd edition of this work at p.21, footnote (c). Forbearance or the granting of extended time for payment at the request of the surety may be implied from the taking of security: *Clegg* v. *Bromley* [1912] 3 K.B.491. See also *Leask* v. *Scott Bros.* (1877) 2 Q.B.D.376. This will usually be avoided by such phrases as "opening or continuing an account" or "continuing advance." Note also *Provincial Bank of Ireland* v. *Donnell* [1934] N.I.33. Similar principles apply in the case of equitable mortgages of debts to secure existing loans. See, *e.g. Gorringe* v. *Irwell India* (1886) 34 Ch.D.128. For a case where the creditor knew of surety's belief that future advances would be made, but no advances were made, see *Bank of Montreal* v. *Sperling Hotel Co. Ltd.* (1973) 36 D.L.R. (3d) 130.

[38] See *King* v. *Cole* (1848) 2 Exch.628; *Bell* v. *Welch* (1850) 9 C.B.154.

agreement to supply certain further goods or make certain further advances, a guarantee for the existing liability will not attach unless the further supply or advance is granted within the meaning of the parties—that is to say, if no amount is named,[39] a real and bona fide further supply or advance.[40] And the mere use of a phrase such as "in consideration of your agreeing to supply," etc., when the amount to be supplied is not specified, but is left to the discretion of the creditor, does not imply either that the creditor has contemporaneously undertaken any liability to supply or that he is to undertake such liability. Such a guarantee will therefore only attach if and when a further supply is granted, as if it had run "in consideration of your supplying," etc.[41] If a guarantee is in consideration of an advance or supply "to the extent" of a sum named, it is a question of construction whether the guarantee is not to attach until that amount has been supplied or advanced, or whether that amount is merely the maximum for which the surety will be liable.[42]

Guarantees in consideration of present agreement

It may be, however, that the meaning is that the guarantee is to attach when some definite binding agreement for the advance or the like is made by the creditor; as where it ran "in consideration of your having by indenture agreed."[43] Similarly where, in consideration of the creditor "agreeing" to take a composition from his debtor, a surety undertook to guarantee the composition.[44] In such cases the specified agreement must be made; but the guarantee attaches without waiting for it to be performed.[45] Where an agreement recited the delivery of certain securities and proceeded "in consideration of the money so secured to be paid to us aforesaid, we hereby indemnify you" against certain other liabilities, it was held that the deposit of the securities was the consideration, and not the payment of the money secured.[46]

---

[39] See *White* v. *Woodward* (1848) 5 C.B.810, 818; *Broom* v. *Batchelor* (1856) 1 H. & N.255, 264; *Morrell* v. *Cowan* (1877) 6 Ch.D.166, 170; 7 Ch.D.151.

[40] *Westhead* v. *Sproson* (1861) 6 H. & N.728; *Morrell* v. *Cowan, supra; Provincial Bank of Ireland* v. *Donnell* [1934] N.I.33.

[41] *Westhead* v. *Sproson, supra; Morrell* v. *Cowan, supra.* But see *White* v. *Woodward* (1848) 5 C.B.810 where however the goods had been supplied; see *per* Martin B. in *Broom* v. *Batchelor* (1856) 1 H. & N.255 at 265. *Cf.* also *Payne* v. *Wilson* (1827) 7 B. & C.423; *Thornton* v. *Jenyns* (1840) I M. & Gr.166; *Dally* v. *Poolly* (1844) 6 Q.B.494. As to promissory notes given for existing debts and further advances, see *Mayhew* v. *Crickett* (1818) 2 Swanst.185; *Re Boys, ex p. Hop Planters Co.* (1870) L.R.10 Eq.467.

[42] *Dimmock* v. *Sturla* (1845) 14 M. & W.758 *Cf. Hill* v. *Nuttall* (1864) 17 C.B. (N.S.) 262.

[43] *King* v. *Cole* (1848) 2 Exch.628.

[44] *Clarke* v. *Green* (1849) 3 Exch.619.

[45] If afterwards repudiated, the surety will be released see *ante,* p.11.

[46] *Ikin* v. *Brook* (1830) 1 B. & Ad.124.

When consideration may be proved by parol evidence

In guarantees given before the Mercantile Law Amendment Act 1856,[47] the consideration had to appear in or by necessary implication from the note or memorandum required by section 4 of the Statute of Frauds, which otherwise was not sufficient.[48] The Act of 1856 removed this necessity and made it possible to have an enforceable guarantee in which there was no statement of the consideration in any note or memorandum in writing. Where, however, the contract itself is reduced to writing, and a consideration stated, the admission of parol evidence is governed by the ordinary law as to the construction of documents; and the 1856 Act has no bearing.[48] Where therefore a consideration is stated in the contract which is in law no consideration, and the terms of the contract do not show that there was in fact some other good consideration,[49] or where the contract states or shows that there was no consideration, oral evidence cannot be admitted to prove, in contradiction of the contract, that in fact there was a good consideration. Anything referred to in a contract may be identified by parol evidence within the limits of the description in the contract, though not so as to contradict that description. The evidence, however, must not that of conversations tending to show what the intention of the parties was apart from the words used in the contract,[50] but must be directed to show what state of circumstances the parties either knew then to exist or contemplated as about to come into existence, so as to establish in what sense the words were used by showing what the situation of the parties was at the time.[51]

Words capable of denoting either a past or a future consideration

In accordance with these principles, where words are used which may denote either a past or a future consideration, parol evidence of the circumstances may be admitted in order to show that a future consideration must have been referred to. Therefore in *Butcher* v. *Steuart*,[52] where the phrase was "in consideration of your having released," etc., and in *Goldshede* v. *Swan*,[53] where it was "in consideration of your having advanced," etc., it

---

[47] 19 & 20 Vict. c.97, s.3. See Appendix 2.
[48] *Wain* v. *Warlters* (1804) 5 East 10; *Saunders* v. *Wakefield* (1821) 4 B. & Ald.595.
[49] See, *e.g. Oldershaw* v. *King* (1857) 2 H. & N.517.
[50] See *Laurie* v. *Scholefield* (1869) L.R. 4 C.P.622, 626. But note general inadmissibility of extrinsic evidence of parties' intentions and negotiations. See *Prenn* v. *Simmonds* |1971| 1 W.L.R.1381, 1385 and 1390 and *Moschi* v. *Lep Air Services Ltd.* |1973| A.C. 331, 354.
[51] See Lord Campbell C.J. in *Bainbridge* v. *Wade* (1850) 16 Q.B.89 at 98. And see *Macdonald* v. *Longbottom* (1860) I.E. & E.977 at 983; *Heffield* v. *Meadows* (1869) L.R. 4 C.P.595, 600; *Grahame* v. *Grahame* (1887) 19 L.R. Ir 249.
[52] (1843) 11 M. & W.857.
[53] (1847) 1 Exch.154. And see *King* v. *Cole* (1848) 2 Exch.628.

being proved that the only release and advance respectively were not before but in pursuance of the guarantees, the plaintiffs recovered.[54]

The same rule was followed in *Steele* v. *Hoe*.[55] There the promise was "in consideration of your having resigned the office of Deacon," etc. "The expression," said Patteson, J., delivering the judgment of the court,[56] "that a promise is founded upon a consideration conveys the notion that the consideration precedes the promise in the mind of the party making the promise; he promises because the consideration exists, and this form of expression is shown by the authorities to have been frequently used when the consideration and the promise are concurrent. Each side of a contract is consideration or promise according to the party speaking, and, if each party were to put into writing his own promise, each side of the contract would in turn appear to have preceded the other, though both have formed one agreement: the plaintiff might write 'you having guaranteed, I resign'; the defendant 'you having resigned, I guarantee.' "[57]

Construction ut res magis valeat quam pereat

In some of the older cases it did not appear that there was any past advance, supply, or other dealing which could answer the description of the consideration. But even if there is an existing liability to which the description could apply, it seems established that, at any rate where the circumstances show that a future liability was also in contemplation, reference may be taken to be to the latter, an illustration of the operation of the maxim *ut res magis valeat quam pereat*.[58]

Where the consideration for a guarantee is expressed to be that the person to whom it is given "has agreed" or "has consented" to do something, the meaning has usually been taken to be that the future act, and not any past or contemporaneous binding agreement, is the consideration.[59]

[54] See also *Haigh* v. *Brooks* (1839) 10 Ad. & E.I.309.

[55] (1849) 14 Q.B.431.

[56] *Ibid.* at page 445.

[57] See for further examples, *Bainbridge* v. *Wade, supra; Hoad* v. *Grace* (1861) 7 H. & N.494. And see also *Bastow* v. *Bennett* (1812) 3 Camp.220.

[58] See *Steele* v. *Hoe* (1849) 14 Q.B.431; *Broom* v. *Batchelor* (1856) 1 H. & N.255; *Hoad* v. *Grace, supra; Wood* v. *Priestner* (1866) L.R.2 Ex 66, 282. Bramwell B. protested in the three last-named cases against the application of this principle where the language was in its primary sense past and there existed facts to which it could refer. Illustrations of the principle can be found in *Allnutt* v. *Ashenden* (1843) 5 M. & Gr. 392; *Edwards* v. *Jevons* (1849) 8 C.B.436; *Colbourn* v. *Dawson* (1851) 10 C.B.765; *Broom* v. *Batchelor* (1856) 1 H. & N.255; *Grahame* v. *Grahame* (1887) 19 L.R. Ir.249; *Wood* v. *Priestner* (1866) L.R.2 Ex.66, 282; *Mocket* v. *Ames* (1871) 23 L.T.729. See also *Chalmers* v. *Victors* (1868) 18 L.T.481. Cf. *Brunning* v. *Oldham Bros.* (1896) 75 L.T.602.

[59] *Payne* v. *Wilson* (1827) 7 B. & C.423; *Thornton* v. *Jenyns* (1840) 1 M. & Gr. 166; *Dally* v. *Poolly* (1844) 6 Q.B.494; *Tanner* v. *Moore* (1846) 9 Q.B.1; *Westhead* v. *Sproson* (1861) 6 H. & N.728; *Morrell* v. *Cowan* (1877) 6 Ch.D.166, 7 Ch.D.151. But see *White* v. *Woodward* (1848) 5 C.B.810, explained by Martin B. in *Broom* v. *Batchelor* (1856) 1 H. & N.255 at 264.

Consideration executed on the faith of a guarantee to be given

Where the only circumstance to which the words expressing the consideration can refer was past at the date of the guarantee, it would still be open to the plaintiff to prove that the guarantee was agreed to be given before the consideration was executed, and was only reduced into writing afterwards.[60]

Where advances were made to one of the makers of a promissory note upon the representation that the defendant would also sign it, and afterwards the defendant did sign it, he was held liable as having adopted the promise.[61]

Illegal consideration

A guarantee cannot be supported by an illegal consideration. It may also constitute a fraudulent preference where one creditor is preferred, by dint of the transaction, to the general body of creditors at the instance of an insolvent individual or company.[62]

---

[60] *Mumford* v. *Gething* (1859) 7 C.B. (N.S.) 305.

[61] *Dodge* v. *Pringle* (1860) 29 L.J. Ex.115.

[62] *Coles* v. *Strick* (1850) 15 Q.B.2; *Wood* v. *Barker* (1865) L.R. 1 Eq.139; for an example of where the guaranteed debt itself was illegal and thus irrecoverable even from the surety, see *Lougher* v. *Molyneux* |1916| 1 K.B.718. For a discussion of *ultra vires* loans and loans to minors see Chaps. 4 and 6. *Cf. Re O'Shea, ex p. Lancaster* |1911| 2 K.B.981 (guarantee of overdraft by principal debtor used to pay back debts held enforceable). A guarantee for an illegal consideration cannot be enforced and may be ordered to be delivered up and cancelled. *Jackman* v. *Mitchell* (1807) 13 Ves.581. See also *Coleman* v. *Waller* (1829) 31 Y. & J.212; *McKewan* v. *Sanderson* (1875) L.R.20 Eq.65.

CHAPTER 3

STATUTE OF FRAUDS

1. *To What Contracts it Applies*

By Section 4 of the Statute of Frauds[1]

"No action shall be brought whereby to charge the defendant upon any special promise to answer for the debt, default, or miscarriage of another person . . . unless the agreement upon which such action shall be brought, or some memorandum or note thereof, shall be in writing and signed by the party to be charged therewith or some other person thereunto by him lawfully authorised."

This enactment does not, except by requiring a writing as evidence of the promises to which it applies, in any way affect the common rules governing the validity of such promises. It does not dispense with the necessity for a consideration to support a promise not under seal, or make valid any contract not valid at common law.[2] Its only effect is to make unenforceable contracts, coming within its terms, which would have been valid at common law.[2] If the contract is within its terms, it does not matter what the consideration was.[3] Further, the doctrine of part performance is not applicable to contracts of guarantee.[4] A guarantee, though given abroad, cannot be sued upon in England unless it fulfils the requirements of the Statute.[5]

The Statute only says that no action shall be brought whereby to charge, etc. Therefore, if a solicitor in an action gave an undertaking to pay the claim, the old Common Law Courts enforced it against him summarily notwithstanding the Statute.[6] And each division of the High Court would no doubt do the same by virtue of its summary jurisdiction over its officers.

---

[1] For fuller treatment of this topic see Williams, *Section 4 of the Statute of Frauds* (Cambridge, 1932) and generally *Chitty on Contracts* (24th ed.), Vol. I, at pp.110 *et seq.* For questions relating to effect of the Statute of Frauds on the question of bills of exchange see Chapter 13.

[2] *Barrell* v. *Trussell* (1811) 4 Taunt. 117; *Rann* v. *Hughes* (1778) 7 Term.Rep. 350, note.

[3] See the notes to *Forth* v. *Stanton* (1669) 1 Williams' Saund. 211 e(l); *Fitzgerald* v. *Dressler* (1859) 7 C.B. (N.S.) 374, 392; *Sutton* v. *Grey* [1894] 1 Q.B. 285, 288. For an illustration of how a contract within the Statute can only be raised as a defence when recovery is sought of money or property passing under that contract, see *Brady* v. *Lewis* [1951] 3 D.L.R. 845.

[4] *Maddison* v. *Alderson* (1883) 8 App. Cas. 467 at 490.

[5] *Leroux* v. *Brown* (1852) 12 C.B. 801. For questions of conflict of laws see *post*, Chap. 4, part 1.

[6] *Evans* v. *Duncombe* (1831) 1 C. & J. 372; *Re Greaves, ibid.* 374, note; *Re A Solicitor* (1900) 45 S.J. 104.

Similarly money paid under a promise unenforceable by reason of the Statute cannot be recovered back.[7]

It has been held in a number of cases that the Statute will be an answer to any action which has the effect of charging the defendant upon a promise which by the Statute is unenforceable, even though the action is not on the promise.[8] None of such cases, however, affect the only clause of the Statute material to the subject of this work; nor is it easy to see how a defendant could be charged on a promise to answer for the debt of another, unless directly by an action on the promise. The cases referred to are therefore not discussed here.

Since before the Mercantile Law Amendment Act 1856,[9] it was necessary that the consideration for the promise should appear by the writing,[10] many of the older cases, in which now the writing would be sufficient, had to be discussed on the footing that there was no sufficient writing, and that the plaintiff could only succeed by showing that the Statute did not apply. In appreciating these cases, this change in the law must be borne in mind.

Forms of liability, in the nature of suretyship, without express guarantee

The effect of the clause now under consideration upon the law of principal and surety is, speaking generally, to require that every guarantee shall be evidenced by a writing fulfilling the conditions prescribed by the Statute. It must be remembered, however, that liabilities can exist to which some, at any rate, of the incidents of suretyship attach, which nevertheless do not come within this clause; as, for instance, the liability of a retired partner[11] or of a *del credere* agent.[12]

Where a sum of money is due from one person to another upon a judgment no writing under the Statute is necessary to show that it was agreed that it should stand as security for the debt of another, notwithstanding that facts have occurred which without such agreement would have put an end to the liability upon it.[13]

---

[7] *Sweet* v. *Lee* (1841) 3 M. & Gr. 452. And see *Shaw* v. *Woodcock* (1827) 7 B. & C.73. For the case of executors or administrators retaining debts in respect of oral guarantees and the commission thereby of a *devastavit*, see *Re Rownson* (1885) 29 Ch.D. 358; *Re Midgley* [1893] 3 Ch. 222.

[8] *Carrington* v. *Roots* (1837) 2 M. & W. 248; *Sykes* v. *Dixon* (1839) 9 A. & E. 693; *Felthouse* v. *Bindley* (1862) 11 C.B. (N.S.) 869.

[9] 19 and 20 Vict. c. 97, s.3. See Appendix 2.

[10] *Wain* v. *Warlters* (1804) 5 East. 10, *Saunders* v. *Wakefield* (1821) 4 B. & Ald. 595.

[11] See *Rouse* v. *Bradford Banking Co.* [1894] A.C. 586, *ante* p.4. See generally *Lindley on Partnership* (14th ed., 1979), pp.109, 337 *et seq.*

[12] See *post*, p.32. See generally Bowstead, *Agency* (14th ed., 1976) pp.11, 14–15.

[13] *Macrory* v. *Scott* (1880) 5 Exch. 907.

Former restriction of Statute to promises to pay existing debts, etc.

It was said at one time to have been laid down that the Statute did not apply to promises to answer future debts of another[14] but this distinction is now clearly not law.[15] The rule has long been settled that the question is whether the promise is original or collateral, it being within the Statute only if it is collateral.[16] It cannot, however, be collateral unless another is, or is to be, also liable.[16]

Promise must be collateral

When the promise is to be answerable for demands which may thereafter accrue to the promisee by reason of dealings with another, the question is whether the promisor intervenes to procure credit for the third person who is himself also to be liable to the promisee, or whether his own credit only is pledged to secure the consideration of the third person, to whom credit is not given.[17] In *Birkmyr* v. *Darnell*,[18] according to some reporters,[19] the phrases "I will be your paymaster," "I will see you paid," are instanced as creating an original and not a collateral undertaking. But whatever the form of words used, it is a question of fact to be ascertained from the transaction as a whole[20] and all its circumstances, as to whom credit was given.[21] And the words, "I will see you paid," have been held, under the circumstances of individual cases, to effect a collateral liability only.[22]

In *Birkmyr* v. *Darnell*[23] the promise was to answer for the safe return of a horse lent to another and it was held within the

[14] See *Mowbray* v. *Cunningham* cited (1774) 2 Term Rep. 81; 1 Cowper 228; *Peckham* v. *Faria* (1781) 3 Doug. K.B. 13.

[15] *Peckham* v. *Faria, supra; Matson* v. *Wharam* (1787) 2 Term Rep. 80; *Anderson* v. *Hayman* (1789) 1 H.Bl. 120.

[16] *Birkmyr* v. *Darnell* (1704) 2 Lord Raym. 1085, 6 Mod 248; 1 Salk, 27; 1 Sm. L.C. (12th ed.) 335; *Read* v. *Nash* (1751) 1 Wils. 305; *Hargreaves* v. *Parsons* (1844) 13 M. & W. 561. And see the notes to *Forth* v. *Stanton* (1669) 1 Williams' Saund. 211 e(l).

[17] *Watkins* v. *Perkins* (1697) 1 Lord Raym. 224; *Birkmyr* v. *Darnell, supra.*

[18] *Supra.*

[19] Not in 2 Lord Raym. 1085.

[20] *Simpson* v. *Penton* (1834) 2 C. & M. 430.

[21] *Keate* v. *Temple* (1797) 1 B. & P. 158; *Croft* v. *Smallwood* (1793) 1 Esp. 121; *Simpson* v. *Penton, supra; Beard* v. *Hardy* (1901) 17 T.L.R. 633. In *Tomlinson* v. *Gill* (1756) Ambl. 330, Lord Hardwicke called the distinction in *Birkmyr* v. *Darnell* "a slight and cobweb distinction." See also *Guild* v. *Conrad* [1894] 2 Q.B. 885 at 895 *per* Lopes L.J.

[22] *Matson* v. *Wharam* (1787) 2 Term Rep.80; *Anderson* v. *Hayman* (1789) 1 H. Bl.121; *Barber* v. *Fox* (1816) 1 Stark 270; *Keate* v. *Temple, supra; Bateman* v. *Phillips* (1812) 15 East. 272; *Thompson* v. *Bond* (1807) 1 Camp. 4; *Rains* v. *Storry* (1827) 3 C. & P. 130; *Walker* v. *Taylor* (1834) 6 C. & P. 752; *Clancy* v. *Piggott* (1835) 2 A. & E. 473; *contra, Austen* v. *Baker* (1698) 12 Mod. 250; *Mountstephen* v. *Lakeman* (1871) L.R. 5 Q.B. 613. These cases also show that in order to bring a case within the Statute there is no requirement that the principal debtor's liability precede the surety's undertaking to be answerable. See also *Jones* v. *Cooper* (1774) 1 Cowp. 227.

[23] (1704) 2 Lord Raym.1085. See Williams, *op. cit* at p.5, who points out that the principle of *Birkmyr* v. *Darnell* is repeatedly accepted in the later cases, *i.e.* that the only contracts included under the present head of the Statute are those of a guarantor.

Statute, the bailment having been to that other. If the bailment had been to the defendant it would not have been within the Statute even though in tort a direct liability to the owner might have been afterwards incurred by a third person in whose hands the horse had been placed by the bailee.[24] Similarly in cases where the promise is to pay for goods to be supplied or services to be rendered to another, the question is who is to be the purchaser or employer. If it is the promisor, the promise is not within the Statute, though the consideration is exclusively for the use of the other,[25] and whether or not there is any further consideration for the promise.[26] Even where two promised jointly to pay for goods which it was known to the seller were for the use of one only, the Statute was held not to apply, though the seller knew that there was no partnership nor community of interest between the two, and that the second joined only to procure credit for the first.[27]

Prima facie rule as to whom primarily liable

Prima facie, it is taken that the person for whom the goods or services are ordered is intended to be liable, although another may give the order. Thus where a creditor of a landlord promised to pay a man who went into possession upon a distress by the landlord, the Statute was considered applicable.[28] Similarly where a friend of a debtor who had been arrested promised a solicitor to pay his charges if he would continue to act for the debtor, it was held that the debtor must have been intended to be liable, though the object was that through the solicitor he should take the benefit of the bankruptcy laws.[29] But where an execution creditor employed a solicitor to move for a new trial in an action against a sheriff arising out of the execution, the execution creditor, and not the sheriff, was treated as primarily liable.[30] In *Austen* v. *Baker*[31] Holt C.J. said that when such questions arose on the supply of goods, he always required the tradesman to produce his books to show he had not debited the person for whom they were ordered. Where it cannot be said that the goods were for any individual, as where the order was for a

---

[24] See the report in 2 Lord Raym. 1085.

[25] See *Edge* v. *Frost* (1824) 4 D. & R. 243.

[26] See the notes to *Forth* v. *Stanton* (1669) 1 Williams' Saund.211 e(l); *Fitzgerald* v. *Dressler* (1859) 7 C.B. (N.S.) 374, 379, 392; *Sutton* v. *Grey* [1894] 1 Q.B. 285, 288.

[27] *Hampson* v. *Merriott* Lancaster Spring Assizes 1806 *per* Chambre J., reported in Fell on Mercantile Guarantees (2nd ed., 1820) at pp.27, 28, where some doubt is expressed as to the correctness of the decision.

[28] *Colman* v. *Eyles* (1817) 2 Stark. 62.

[29] *Barber* v. *Fox* (1816) 1 Stark 270.

[30] *Noel* v. *Hart* (1837) 8 C. & P. 230.

[31] (1698) 12 Mod. 250.

cup intended to be presented to the winner of a race, if one person is debited it requires very clear evidence to show that any other person who may have promised to pay is primarily and not merely collaterally liable.[32]

A person requesting a consideration for himself may have actual or ostensible authority to make another exclusively liable for it.[33] Conversely, a person requesting a consideration for another may, though he pledges his own credit, also purport to pledge primarily the credit of the other. If in such cases the meaning is that the first-named is to make good the payment for which the other is assumed to be liable, this is a collateral promise. It will not become an original promise if it turns out that the other is not liable, but will become void.[34]

Promise to pay whether another is liable or not

When the purport of a promise is to secure the promisee, not against the failure of the person named to meet what is assumed to be a liability upon him, but against the possibility that the intended transaction may not impose any valid liability upon that person at all, the promise is an original promise and not within the Statute. Thus, in *Mountstephen* v. *Lakeman*,[35] where a contractor was asked by the chairman of a local board to do certain work to sewers vested in the board, and hesitated for want of a formal order, whereupon the chairman said, "You do the work, and I will see you paid," the promise was held original and not within the Statute. It was pointed out by Lord Selborne in the House of Lords that to construe it as a promise to pay, if the board became liable, would defeat the very intention of the parties, which was that the contractor should be protected against the chance of the board not becoming liable.[36]

It is clear from this decision that the Statute does not apply where, though it is contemplated that the person who is to enjoy the consideration may become liable, the promise is intended to hold good whether he becomes liable or not.[37] On this principle a promise for something to be supplied to one who is known to be an infant is not within the Statute, unless perhaps where the things supplied are assumed on both sides to be necessaries.[38]

---

[32] See *Storr* v. *Scott* (1833) 6 C. & P. 241.

[33] *Darnell* v. *Tratt* (1825) 2 C. & P. 82; *Smith* v. *Rudhall* (1862) 3 F. & F. 143.

[34] *Mountstephen* v. *Lakeman* (1871) L.R. 5 Q.B. 613; 7 Q.B. 196; 7 H.L.17. See *per* Willes J. (1871) L.R. 7 Q.B. at p.202.

[35] *Supra.* The House of Lords affirmed the judgment of the Court of Exchequer Chamber which had reversed the Court of Queen's Bench.

[36] (1874) L.R. 7 H.L. at 25.

[37] (1871) L.R. 7 Q.B. at p.203 *per* Willes J.

[38] *Harris* v. *Huntbach* (1757) 1 Burr. 373. And see *Duncomb* v. *Tickridge* (1648) Aleyn 94. Note the discussion in Chap. 4, part 7, *i.e.* guarantees of infants' contracts.

In such cases as *Mountstephen* v. *Lakeman,* if the person enjoying the consideration should afterwards ratify the transaction and become liable, it is submitted that the promise would not be brought *ex post facto* within the Statute. This seems justified by the language of Willes J.,[39] in the Exchequer Chamber, and by that of Lord Cairns in the House of Lords. "Against that primary liability," said Lord Cairns, "the defendant might afterwards have sheltered himself by obtaining from the board the consent to make a formal order and acting upon and paying under that formal order."[40]

On a similar principle, where the object of a promise is to prevent the prosecution of a disputed claim against another, the promise being absolute to pay a certain amount without regard to the validity of the claim, the Statute does not apply. It was apparently so held very early in the history of the Statute in *Stephens* v. *Squire.*[41] In that case the promise which was held not within the Statute was to pay the promisee £10 and his costs, if he would not further prosecute an action against a solicitor and two others for appearing for him without warrant. But the promisor himself appears to have been the solicitor. The point arose clearly, however, in *Read* v. *Nash,*[42] where the record in an action for assault was withdrawn in consideration of a promise by a third person to pay a lump sum, and the Statute was held not to apply. This decision is questioned in the notes[43] to *Forth* v. *Stanton,*[43] as indistinguishable from the cases where the promise is in consideration of forbearing to sue, which cases are within the Statute.[44] But in *Bird* v. *Gammon,*[45] *Read* v. *Nash*[42] was treated as proceeding on the ground that the intention was that the claim, (which was not admitted) should not be prosecuted. In *Kirkham* v. *Marter,*[46] which is said in the notes to *Forth* v. *Stanton* to overrule *Read* v. *Nash,* the promise was in consideration of forbearance to sue one who had killed the plaintiff's horse; and the Statute was held to apply. There seems to have been no dispute as to the liability. The promise

---

[39] (1871) L.R. 7 Q.B. at 203. And see the reasoning on *Birkmyr* v. *Darnell* as reported in 2 Lord Raym. 1085.

[40] (1874) L.R. 7 H.L. at 23. It might be a question on any given transaction whether the original promisor was to remain liable after the other had accepted the liability. As to promises to procure another to pay see *post,* p.27.

[41] (1696) 3 Mod. 205.

[42] (1751) 1 Wils. 305. *Cf. Roe* v. *Haugh* (1703) 1 Salk. 29; 3 Salk. 14.

[43] (1669) Willams Saund. 211 e(l), *i.e.* notes to Saunders' Reports 1871 edition, p.232.

[44] *Fish* v. *Hutchinson* (1759) 2 Wils. 94; *Kirkham* v. *Marter* (1819) 2 B. & Ald. 613: *Cole* v. *Dyer* (1831) 1 C. & J. 461.

[45] (1837) 3 Bing. N.C. 883. And see *Williams* v. *Leper* (1766) 3 Burr. 1886; *Tomlinson* v. *Gill* (1756) Ambl. 330; *Fish* v. *Hutchinson* (1759) 2 Wils. 94.

[46] (1819) 2 B. & Ald. 613. This case also established that the Statute applied to guarantees of liability arising *ex delicto* as well as to those arising *ex contractu, i.e.* liability for tort was to be included in the term "miscarriage." For the meaning of "default," apparently referable to any future liability whether contractual or not, see *Re Young and Harston's Contract* (1885) 31 Ch. D. 168.

was simply to pay the value of the horse, which was to be ascertained. There was nothing to suggest that the wrongdoer was to be discharged, and *Read* v. *Nash* was distinguished as proceeding on the compromise of a doubtful claim.[47]

If a claim is preferred against several, and one promises to pay a sum by way of compromise of the whole matter, the Statute does not apply, though it could have been shown that the others were liable.[48]

The principal must remain liable notwithstanding the promise

Where the promise has relation to a claim already incurred by the third person, it is not collateral, so as to be within the Statute, unless the third person is also to remain liable after the promise becomes binding. If it is agreed between all parties that a sale be transferred to the account of a third party and the original buyer released, the Statute will not apply.[49] But a promise to pay a debt transferred from another's account to that of the promisor may be shown to be a guarantee from circumstances indicating that the original debtor was not treated as released.[50] And a promise by an original debtor, if the creditor will transfer the debt to the account of another, to pay it if that other does not, is within the Statute.[51] But no writing is required to make a new partner in a firm liable to an existing creditor, the joint liability of the partners being substituted for that of the original debtor.[52]

No writing is required where the promise is to pay if the crditor will release the debtor by deed.[53] And this is so even where the promise is that, after his release, the debtor shall pay, if this only means that the promisor will get him to pay by his hand, and not that the debtor is to renew his liability to the promisee.[54] If the promise is that, if the creditor will release his present claim and take from the debtor a new liability (*e.g.* take a bill or note) the promisor will see he fulfils that liability, this would clearly be within the Statute.[55]

---

[47] This distinction is discussed and criticised by Williams, *op. cit.*, on the ground that such an objection would apply to any guarantee where the third party's liability had not first been ascertained by the judgment of a court of law.

[48] *Orrell* v. *Coppock* (1856) 26 L.J. Ch. 269.

[49] *Browning* v. *Stallard* (1814) 5 Taunt. 480. And see *Taylor* v. *Hilary* (1835) 1 C.M. & R. 741; *Goodman* v. *Chase* (1818) 1 B. & Ald. 297; *Butcher* v. *Steuart* (1843) 11 M. & W. 857; *Scarf* v. *Jardine* (1882) 7 App.Cas. 345.

[50] *French* v. *French* (1841) 2 M. & Gr. 644.

[51] *Brunton* v. *Dullens* (1859) 1 F. & F. 450.

[52] *Re Lendon, Ex p. Lane* (1846) De Gex 300.

[53] See *Emmett* v. *Dewhurst* (1851) 3 Mac. & G. 587.

[54] *Lane* v. *Burghart* (1841) 1 Q.B. 933.

[55] *Maggs* v. *Ames* (1828) 4 Bing. 470; *Emmett* v. *Dewhurst* (1851) 3 Mac. & G. 587.

Novation

If A is owed money by B, and B is owed money by C, and all three agree that C shall owe the money to A and B be released, the promise of C is not within the Statute.[56] In such a case A could at common law recover from C.[57] But unless B was discharged by the new arrangement, such an action would not lie.[58] However, upon a promise by C to pay A out of money then being or thereafter to be in C's hands for B, an action would lie and would not be within the Statute, even though B is not discharged.[59] Apart from such cases are those where a debtor assigns equitably to his creditor a debt owing to him. In this case the assignee could recover at law only in the name of and upon the promise of the assignor, and no question upon the Statute could arise in such an action. And though now since the Judicature Acts the assignee can sue the debtor directly, the Statute of Frauds has clearly no application. It is the defendant's own debt, not that of another, that is sued for.[60]

A promise to pay the debt of another is within the Statute though the promisee undertakes with the promisor not to sue the debtor. For this affords no defence to the debtor, who thus remains liable after the promise.[61] Thus a promise to pay a sum in satisfaction of a debt is within the Statute if the debtor remains liable till the payment.[62] If there is a general arrangement by which a third person takes over the property of a debtor and promises the creditors to pay in his stead, the promise of such third person is not within the Statute, inasmuch as such an arrangement itself, without a formal release of the debtor, prevents an action being brought by any creditor being party to the arrangement.[63]

Agreement to purchase debt

An executory agreement to purchase a debt seems not to be within the Statute. This at least seems to have been the opinion of the Court of Common Pleas in *Anstey* v. *Marden*,[64] where,

---

[56] *Lucy* v. *McNeile* (1824) 4 D. & R.7: *Hodgson* v. *Anderson* (1825) 3 B. & C. 842.

[57] *Israel* v. *Douglas* (1789) 1 H. Bl. 239; *Tatlock* v. *Harris* (1789) 3 Term.Rep. 174; *Hodgson* v. *Anderson, supra*; *Wilson* v. *Coupland* (1821) 5 B. & Ald. 228; *Lucy* v. *McNeile, supra*.

[58] *Wharton* v. *Walker* (1825) 4 B. & C. 163; *Fairlie* v. *Denton* (1828) 8 B. & C. 395.

[59] *Dixon* v. *Hatfield* (1825) 2 Bing. 439; *Andrews* v. *Smith* (1835) 2 C.M. & R. 627; *Sweeting* v. *Asplin* (1840) 7 M. & W. 165; *Walker* v. *Rostron* (1842) 9 M.& W. 411. But *cf. Parkins* v. *Moravia* (1824) 1 C. & P. 376.

[60] *Hodgson* v. *Anderson* (1825) 3 B. & C. 842; *Commercial Bank of Tasmania* v. *Jones* [1893] A.C. 313; *Re Lendon, Ex p. Lane*, (1846) De G. 300. See also *Wilson* v. *Coupland* (1821) 5 B. & Ald. 228.

[61] *Rothery* v. *Curry* (T.21 Geo. 2) cited in Buller's N.P. 281; *Lee* v. *Bashpole* (M.1 W. & M.), *ibid. King* v. *Wilson, ibid;* 2 Stra. 873.

[62] *Case* v. *Barber* (1681) T. Raym. 450; *Chater* v. *Beckett* (1797) 7 Term.Rep. 201; *Tomlinson* v. *Gell* (1837) 6 A. & E. 564 at 569.

[63] *Bird* v. *Gammon* (1837) 3 Bing. N.C. 883; and *cf. Anstey* v. *Marden* (1804) 1 B. & P.N.R. 124.

[64] *Supra*.

however, the transaction was not so much an executory agreement for the sale of the debt as a present transfer of the debt in consideration of a promise to pay the price, the arrangement being a general one among creditors, which *ipso facto* puts an end to the right of every creditor party to it to sue on his own behalf.[65] In *Mallet* v. *Bateman*,[66] it was held in the Common Pleas and in the Exchequer Chamber, that a promise, in consideration that the promisee would supply goods to a third party and draw bills upon the buyer for the price, to take over the bills from the seller, indorsed without recourse to him, or indorsed with a collateral indemnity to him against his liability as indorser, was within the Statute, the transaction being in substance a guarantee of the intended debt. Some of the judges seem to have suggested that a promise to purchase a debt is always within the Statute.[67] But these dicta ought perhaps to be confined to cases like that then before the court, where the substantial object in view is to secure that the money owing should be paid from one source or another to the creditor. They do not seem to apply where the object is not that the debt should be paid to the creditor, but, on the contrary, that the purchaser should collect it for himself, the creditor receiving from him a price for parting with his right.

When a promise is to pay a sum which is not shown to be the debt of another, the Statute does not apply. Thus, where it was in consideration of forbearance to sell under a bill of sale which appeared to be absolute and was not shown to be security for any debt, the Statute did not apply.[68] However, a promise to pay the debt of a deceased person is within the Statute, apparently even though no personal legal representative has been constituted.[69]

Promises to pay debt not owed to the promisee

It follows from the principle that the Statute only applies where the other person is or is to be also liable that it does not apply to a promise to make good the debt of another not owed to the promisee. This may have been the reasoning of Lord Hardwicke in *Tomlinson* v. *Gill*,[70] where he decided that the Statute did not apply to a promise to an intending administratrix that if she would admit the promisor to join in the administration he would pay the creditors in full. And in *Howes*

---

[65] See *per* Sir J. Mansfield C.J., 1 B. & P.N.R. at 131.

[66] (1865) 16 C.B. (N.S.) 530; L.R. 1 C.P. 163 (Exch. Ch).

[67] See *per* Blackburn J., L.R. 1 C.P. at p.169, and *per* Pollock C.B. at p.170.

[68] *Barrell* v. *Trussel* (1811) 4 Taunt. 117.

[69] *Lexington* v. *Clarke* (1689) 2 Vent. 223. But *cf. Tomlinson* v. *Gill* (1756) Ambl. 330.

[70] *Supra* and see also *Lexington* v. *Clarke, supra.*

v. *Martin*,[71] it was held that a promise to indemnify against the demand of another was not within the Statute. The rule was, however, finally settled in *Eastwood* v. *Kenyon*,[72] where the promise was made to the debtor; and it has been adhered to ever since.[73]

On the same principle, a guarantee given by one person party to a contract to another person to whom he transferred the benefit of the contract, that the contractor would carry it out, was held enforceable though not in writing, on the ground that there was no privity between the contractor and the transferee, and that the so-called guarantee operated only as a contract to procure another to do such and such a thing.[74] Such contracts, if the person who is to be procured to do or to abstain from doing the thing in question, neither is, nor is to be, under any obligation in that behalf to the promisee, are not within the Statute. Thus, a promise that a debtor should not leave the country,[75] and even a promise that another should pay, provided that credit was not stipulated to be given to that other[76] are not within the Statute. So too a promise to procure another to give a guarantee.[77] Similarly a promise by a third person to a county court bailiff, about to arrest a debtor for contempt in not paying under an order, that he will pay himself or surrender the debtor by a given date, is not within the Statute.[78] And even a promise by one partner to make good to the firm the debt of a debtor of the firm has been held not within the Statute on the ground that the true effect of the transaction was not a promise to his partners and himself to pay the debt, but a promise to his partners (who could not alone sue the debtor) to indemnify them against individual loss if the firm debt should turn out bad.[79]

Indemnities

A promise is not the less within the Statute because it is called an indemnity, if the effect of it is to indemnify at the expense of a stranger a creditor against the default of his debtor.[80] The word "indemnity" is, however, often employed in cases such as those just examined where the Statute does not apply, *viz.* where one

---

[71] (1794) 1 Esp. 162.

[72] (1840) 11 A. & E. 438. And see *Harburg India Rubber Co.* v. *Martin* [1902] 1 K.B. 778, 784.

[73] See *Hargreaves* v. *Parsons* (1844) 13 M. & W. 881; *Reader* v. *Kingham* (1862) 13 C.B. (N.S.) 344; *Re Hoyle* [1893] 1 Ch. 84.

[74] *Hargreaves* v. *Parsons* (1844) 13 M. & W. 561.

[75] *Elkins* v. *Heart* (1731) Fitzg. 202.

[76] *Gordon* v. *Martin* (1731) Fitz. 302; *Lane* v. *Burghart* (1841) 1 Q.B. 933. And see *Mountstephen* v. *Lakeman* (1871) L.R. 5 Q.B. 613; 7 Q.B. 196; 7 H.L. 17.

[77] *Bushell* v. *Beavan* (1834) 1 Bing. N.C. 103.

[78] *Reader* v. *Kingham* (1862) 13 C.B. (N.S.) 34. See also *Love's Case* (1706) 1 Salk. 28.

[79] *Re Hoyle* [1893] 1 Ch. 84.

[80] *Mallet* v. *Bateman* (1865) 16 C.B. (N.S.) 530.

co-adventurer undertakes to relieve another from all loss,[81] or where a person engages to protect another from demands by a third person.[82]

There has been some conflict of authority upon the question whether a promise to indemnify against loss by becoming a surety is within the Statute.[83] In *Thomas* v. *Cook*,[84] it was held that a promise by one surety to indemnify another was not within the Statute: and in Ireland it has been held that a surety could successfully rely upon such a verbal promise, at any rate for the purpose of resisting contribution.[85] In *Green* v. *Cresswell*[86] it was held, apparently questioning *Thomas* v. *Cook*, that a promise to indemnify against becoming bail in civil proceedings was within the Statute, because there was an obligation on the debtor towards his bail to keep him harmless. In *Batson* v. *King*[87] a drawer of a bill who had received a verbal indemnity from the acceptor and a subsequent indorser, who were both found to be the principals in the transaction, recovered against that indorser the money he had been compelled to pay without any writing to show the promise to indemnify. In this case the defendant was himself principal, and Martin B., with whom the court concurred, expressly reserved the case of a surety who was promised by a stranger indemnity against default by the principal. In *Cripps* v. *Hartnoll*[88] it was held in the Exchequer Chamber, reversing the decision of the Queen's Bench, that a promise by a stranger to indemnify bail in a criminal proceeding need not be in writing, there being no obligation on the prisoner towards the bail.[89] And *Green* v. *Cresswell* was distinguished as relating to bail in a civil proceeding. In *Wildes* v. *Dudlow*,[90] however, Malins V.-C. treated *Green* v. *Cresswell* as overruled, and decided that a promise by a stranger to indemnify a person who joined as surety in a promissory note given by a third person was not within the Statute, this being the point left open in *Batson* v. *King*. *Wildes* v. *Dudlow* was followed by Chitty J., in *Re Bolton*,[91] and was approved with *Thomas* v. *Cook* and *Re Bolton*

---

[81] See *Re Hoyle* [1893] 1 Ch. 84; *Sutton* v. *Grey* [1894] 1 Q.B. 295. And see *post*, pp. 30, 31.

[82] *Adams* v. *Dansey* (1830) 6 Bing. 506; *Guild* v. *Conrad* [1894] 2 Q.B. 885. But see *Winckworth* v. *Mills* (1796) 2 Esp. 484.

[83] The history of the principle that the guaranteed obligation need not be owed to the person to whom the guarantee is given as is reflected in this paragraph is treated in detail in Williams *op. cit.*

[84] (1828) 8 B. & C.728.

[85] *Rae* v. *Rae* (1857) 6 Ir. Ch. R. 490.

[86] (1837) 10 A. & E. 453. The Restatement, Security § 96 (1941) endorses the view in *Green* v. *Cresswell* but is only adopted by a minority of States in the U.S.A.

[87] (1859) 4 H. & N. 739.

[88] (1863) 4 B. & S. 414.

[89] *Cf. Herman* v. *Jeuchner* (1885) 15 Q.B.D. 561.

[90] (1874) L.R. 19 Eq. 198.

[91] [1892] W.N. 163, 8 T.L.R. 668.

by the Court of Appeal in *Guild* v. *Conrad.*[92] In that case the plaintiffs had accepted without assets bills drawn on them by a firm abroad, upon the verbal undertaking of the defendant to find the money to enable the plaintiffs to meet these acceptances, there being no expectation that the drawers would be able to pay. It was held that the Statute did not apply.

Contract to give a guarantee

A contract to give a guarantee is as much within the Statute as a guarantee.[93] But a contract to procure another to give a guarantee is not.[94] If, however, the guarantee contracted for would be unenforceable by reason of the Statute, the damages would be nominal.[94]

Where promisor is also liable independently of the promise

The Statute does not apply where the person promising is, independently of the promise, under a liability personally or by his property for the debt to which the promise relates.[95] So a promise by a member of a firm to be separately liable for a debt of the firm need not apparently be in writing.[96] On the same principle, where a sub-purchaser, in consideration of the original vendor delivering to him the property, on which he had a lien for the purchase-money payable by his immediate purchaser, promised to pay that money, the Statute did not apply, inasmuch as the promisor was, subject to that lien, entitled to that property.[97]

Promise in consideration of the relinquishment of a lien

It has been held, moreover, in a number of cases, that if a creditor gives up to a third person, though not a purchaser, property upon which he has a lien for debt, in consideration of a promise by a third person to pay the debt, that promise is not within the Statute.[98] If the promise by the third person is merely

---

[92] |1894| 2 Q.B. 885.

[93] *Mallet* v. *Bateman* (1865) 16 C.B. (N.S.) 530; L.R.1 C.P. 163. But see *Jarmain* v. *Algar* (1826) 2 C. & P. 249.

[94] *Bushell* v.*Beavan* (1834) 1 Bing. N.C.103.

[95] See notes to *Forth* v. *Stanton* (1669) 1 Williams Saund. 211 e(l).

[96] *Ex p. Harding* (1879) 12 Ch. D. 557, 566.

[97] *Fitzgerald* v. *Dressler* (1859) 7 C.B. (N.S.) 274. And compare *Williams* v. *Leper* (1766) 3 Burr. 1886; *Castling* v. *Aubert* (1802) 2 East. 325; *Huggard* v. *Representative Church Body* |1916| 1 I.R.1.

[98] *Williams* v. *Leper, supra; Castling* v. *Aubert, supra; Houlditch* v. *Milne* (1800)3 Esp. 86; *Edwards* v. *Kelly* (1817) 6 M. & S. 204; *Thomas* v. *Williams* (1830) 10 B. & C. 604; *Bampton* v. *Paulin* (1827) 4 Bing. 264; *Walker* v. *Taylor* (1834) 6 C. & P. 752; *Gregory* v. *Williams* (1817) 3 Mer. 582. Williams, *op. cit.* at p.19 in discussing these cases, states it is clear they do not require evidence that the fund or property which is disencumbered, produced more or was more valuable than the debt constituting the encumbrance.

to realise the property and pay the debt out of the proceeds, its only effect is to secure the due administration of a fund.[99] Similarly, a promise to pay merely out of the moneys of the debtor which shall come to the hands of the promisor is not in any case within the Statute. Thus, where an employer[1] of a contractor, or an agent of such employer,[2] promises to a sub-contractor to pay him out of moneys, not his own, but which he shall have in his hands for the contractor, the Statute does not apply. So a promise by the drawee of a cheque to the payee to pay the amount out of a balance to the credit of the drawer, if the payee would discount it for the drawer, was held good to the extent of such balance without writing.[3] Some of the cases where the Statute has been held inapplicable to a promise by a person to whom property subject to a lien is surrendered, and where the claim does not extend beyond money actually realised, may be supported on this principle.[4] It is established, however, that the exemption goes further than this, and takes the promise out of the Statute, though the goods have not produced, or cannot produce, the amount to which the lien extended.

The principle is that the object of the transaction was not merely to secure the debt by the interposition of the promise of a stranger, but to secure an arrangement in which the promisor was independently interested.[5] A person who is or who intends to become interested in property upon which there is a charge, and on obtaining possession promises to pay the same, intervenes not as a stranger guaranteeing a debt, but as a person interested bargaining for the disincumbrance of his own interest.[6]

The explanation is consistent with two limitations to which the rule is undoubtedly subject. These are (i) that the promisor cannot without writing go beyond the amount charged upon the goods; (ii) that the goods must be surrendered to the promisor and not to the debtor. The first was laid down in *Thomas* v.

---

[99] *Macrory* v. *Scott* (1850) 5 Exch. 907.

[1] *Dixon* v. *Hatfield* (1825) 2 Bing. 439; *cf. Griffith* v. *Young* (1810) 12 East 513 at 514.

[2] *Andrews* v. *Smith* (1835) 2 C.M. & R. 627; *Sweeting* v. *Asplin* (1840) 7 M. & W. 165 (see the distinction *per* Parke B., at pp. 170, 171); *Walker* v. *Rostron* (1842) 9 M & W. 411. Cf. *Morley* v. *Boothby* (1825) 3 Bing. 107, but see *Parkins* v. *Moravia* (1824) 1 C. & P. 376.

[3] *Ardern* v. *Rowney* (1805) 5 Esp. 254.

[4] *Williams* v. *Leper* (1766) 3 Burr. 1886, 2 Wils 308 (see *per* Aston J.); *Castling* v. *Aubert* (1802) 2 East 325.

[5] A money payment merely to induce one who is otherwise a stranger to guarantee a debt does not make him independently interested within the meaning of this rule; see *Couturier* v. *Hastie* (1856) 8 Exch. 40 at 55; *Tomlinson* v. *Gell* (1837) 6 A. & E. 564 at p.571.

[6] *Sutton* v. *Grey* [1894] 1 Q.B. 285. See also *Harburg India Rubber Comb. Co.* v. *Marten* [1902] 1 K.B. 778; *Davys* v. *Buswell* [1913] 2 K.B. 47. (No distinction appears to exist between legal as distinct from equitable rights *per* Joyce J. at 58); *Fitzgerald* v. *Dressler* (1859) 7 C.B. (N.S.) 374; *Huggard* v. *Representative Church Body* [1916] 1 I.R.1. For a more detailed discussion of the earlier cases, see the first edition of this book.

Williams,[7] where, upon goods under distress being surrendered to a broker for sale, the broker promised to pay not only the rent then in arrear, but also that which would fall due next quarter day; and it was held that the Statute applied. But in such cases, to the extent of the amount charged on the goods, the promise can be enforced and the excess rejected.[8] The second limitation above-mentioned seems involved in *Rounce* v. *Woodyard*[9] and the Irish case of *Fennell* v. *Mulcahy.*[10] In both those cases it was held that a promise by a third party to pay rent distrained for, if the landlord withdrew and allowed the tenant to resume the goods, was within the Statute, notwithstanding a dictum attributed to Lord Eldon in *Houlditch* v. *Milne,*[11] to the effect that the Statute never applied where the plaintiff gave up a lien. That dictum as reported was questioned in the notes to *Forth* v. *Stanton.*[12] It is not clear to whom the property was given, or whether the owner, who was apparently abroad, had ever been looked to by the plaintiff, whose claim and lien was for work done to the property.

Promises in consideration of a lien not being asserted

Further, the case is not taken out of the Statute, where the promise is not in consideration of the surrender of a lien, but in consideration of a lien not being asserted, without regard to the question whether it existed or not.[13]

Promises by a person independently interested in the transaction

It is on the same principle that a *del credere* agent is not within the Statute.[14] That was decided in *Couturier* v. *Hastie,*[15] where it was held, following an American decision, that the responsibility of the agent was regarded, not as a collateral undertaking, but as an incident of the agency. In *Wickham* v. *Wickham,*[16] Wood V.-C. seems to have treated the decision as

---

[7] (1830) 10 B. & C. 664.

[8] *Wood* v. *Benson* (1831) 2 C. & J. 94, where *Lexington* v. *Clarke* (1689) 2 Vent. 223, *Chater* v. *Beckett* (1797) 7 Term Rep. 201 and *Thomas* v. *Williams* (1870) 10 B. & C. 667 (where the contrary appeared to be decided), were explained on the ground that in those cases there was no count applicable to a severed portion of the claim. See too *Head* v. *Baldrey* (1837) 6 A. & E. 459; *Lord Falmouth* v. *Thomas* (1832) 1 C. & M. 89 at 101 *per* Bayley J.

[9] (1846) 8 L.T. (o.s.) 186.

[10] (1845) 8 Ir. L.R. 434.

[11] (1800) 3 Esp. 86.

[12] (1669) 1 Williams Saund. 211 e(l).

[13] *Gull* v. *Lindsay* (1849) 4 Exch. 45.

[14] *Harburg India Rubber Comb. Co.* v. *Marten* [1902] 1 K.B. 778.

[15] (1852) 8 Exch. 40. The decision appears to be based to a large extent on the American case of *Wolff* v. *Koppel* 5 Hill N.Y. Rep. 458 (1843). See also Restatement, Security § 98 (1941).

[16] (1855) 2 K. & J. 478.

proceeding on the ground that the agent was primarily liable.[17] But in *Fleet* v. *Murton*,[18] Blackburn J. applies the decision in *Couturier* v. *Hastie* to an agent liable by custom to make good the engagements of those with whom he deals, and excludes his engagement from the operation of the Statute, as "merely regulating the terms of the employment." And in *Sutton* v. *Grey*,[19] where a person who was to receive from a stockbroker half of the commission payable by clients whom he should introduce, undertook also to pay half the loss which might be incurred by their default, the Court of Appeal, in deciding that the Statute did not apply, laid down the doctrine, as deducible from *Couturier* v. *Hastie*,[20] and *Fitzgerald* v. *Dressler*,[21] that the Statute only applies where a promisor is, but for his promise, totally unconnected with the transaction. And this distinction was treated as the dividing line between a guarantee and an indemnity.

Where the defendant became agent to the plaintiff on the terms that his first six months' salary should be applied to the liquidation of the former agent's account, it was held, in an action by the employer for money in the hands of the agent on the balance of accounts, that the latter could not claim such six months' salary.[22] There was no promise to answer for the debt, but only in effect to serve the six months for nothing.[22]

A promise to pay a sum in compromise of the liability of another is not within the Statute, if the promisor is also alleged to be liable to the same claim, even though in truth he could have resisted the claim successfully.[23] And a promise to honour a bill to be drawn upon the promisor for the account of a third person is not within the Statute, at any rate if the facts are consistent with the supposition that the party undertaking undertakes because he has, or expects to have, goods of the third person in his hands.[24]

Guarantee amounting to a representation

In *Pasley* v. *Freeman*[25] it was established that an action would lie for a fraudulent misrepresentation by word of mouth only of

[17] *Ibid* at 486. The agent is certainly not primarily liable: *Gabriel* v. *Churchill and Sim* [1914] 3 K.B. 1272.

[18] (1871) L.R. 7 Q.B. 126 at 133.

[19] [1894] 1 Q.B. 285.

[20] (1852) 8 Exch. 40.

[21] (1859) 7 C.B. (N.S.) 374. But the mere fact that the promisor is financially interested in the principal's business, and even that he is the holder of a floating charge on the principal's assets, does not make him interested in the transaction for the purposes of this rule: *Harburg India Rubber Comb. Co.* v. *Marten* [1902] 1 K.B. 778: *Davys* v. *Bushell* [1913] 2 K.B. 47.

[22] *Walker* v. *Hill* (1860) 5 H. & N. 419.

[23] *Orrell* v. *Coppock* (1856) L.J. Ch. 269.

[24] *Pillans* v. *Van Mierop* (1765) 3 Burr. 1664 at pp. 1666, 1667.

[25] (1789) 3 Term Rep. 51.

the credit or solvency of another. This opened the door to evasion of section 4 of the Statute of Frauds; for many transactions, intended to operate as verbal guarantees, might also support a claim of this kind. By the Statute of Frauds Amendment Act 1828,[26] s.6, this was put an end to, it being there enacted that no representations of that kind should be actionable unless in writing. This branch of the law is, however, not properly within the scope of this work.[27]

2. *What Note or Memorandum is sufficient*

If a defendant by his pleading admits an enforceable contract, he cannot take the objection that there is no sufficient memorandum to satisfy the Statute of Frauds.[28] So where he pleads tender and payment into court.[29] But if, though he admit the fact of a parol agreement, he at the same time pleads the Statute, the objection is open to him.[30]

Memorandum made after action

The memorandum must, moreover, be in existence when the action is commenced.[28] Therefore an affidavit in the cause admitting the facts will not do.[29] It has been said, however, that it could be made available by discontinuing the action and commencing another.[30] This dictum was followed in *Farr, Smith* v. *Messers*,[31] where a paragraph in a defence put in before the plaintiffs, who ultimately succeeded, had been joined, was held to be a good memorandum under section 4 of the Sale of Goods Act 1893. In *Rondeau* v. *Wyatt*,[32] however, the Court of Common Pleas held that an answer in Chancery admitting the facts, but taking the objection there was no memorandum, was not available in an action subsequently commenced.

---

[26] Lord Tenterden's Act. 9 Geo. 4, c.14. See Appendix 2.

[27] Section 6 has been held applicable to fraudulent representations only. *Banbury* v. *Bank of Montreal* [1918] A.C. 626; *Anderson and Sons Ltd.* v. *Rhodes* [1967] 2 All E.R. 850. See generally Clerk and Lindsell, *Torts* (14th ed., 1975), paras. 1649 *et seq.*

[28] *Lucas* v. *Dixon* (1889) 22 Q.B.D. 357 *per* Bowen L.J. at 361. The written memorandum need not be contemporaneous with the actual contract and will usually be a memorandum of an already completed contract. See *Parker* v. *Clark* [1960] 1 W.L.R. 286, 295 *per* Devlin J., where reliance was placed on a written offer subsequently accepted.

[29] *Middleton* v. *Brewer* (1790) 1 Peake 20; *Spurrier* v. *Fitzgerald* (1801) 6 Ves. 548. *Semble* where the original written evidence of a guarantee is lost, oral evidence of its having existed is admissible. *Barrass* v. *Reed, The Times* March 28, 1898; *Grays Gas Co.* v. *Bromley Gas Co., The Times* March 23, 1901, C.A.

[30] *Lucas* v. *Dixon* (1889) 22 Q.B.D. 357 *per* Fry L.J. at 363.

[31] [1928] 1 K.B. 397. See *supra, Grindell* v. *Bass* [1920] 2 Ch. 48. s. 4 of the 1893 Act was later repealed.

[32] (1792) 2 H. Bl. 63.

Statement of consideration

Section 4 of the Statute requires that the *agreement*, or some note or memorandum thereof should be in writing. This was held to require that not only the promise but the consideration should be in writing.[33] But now by section 3 of the Mercantile Law Amendment Act 1856,[34]

> "no special promise made by any person after the passing of this Act to answer for the debt, default or miscarriage of another person, being in writing and signed by the party to be charged therewith or some other person by him thereunto lawfully authorised, shall be deemed invalid to support an action, suit or other proceeding to charge the person by whom such promise shall have been made, by reason only that the consideration of such promise does not appear in writing or by necessary inference from a written document."[35]

In *Wynne* v. *Hughes*,[36] the question was raised but not decided, whether, where an executor personally guarantees the debt of his testator, in order to get delay, the Mercantile Law Amendment Act applies: the terms of that section follow the very words of clause 2 of section 4 of the Statute, whereas there is a separate clause requiring any special promise by an executor to be in writing. Bramwell B. appeared to favour the doubt.

Limits of the ambit of the 1856 Act

It has always been held, even before the Mercantile Law Amendment Act 1856, that where it sufficiently appeared on the writing that the liability to be guaranteed was a prospective one, a consideration—namely, the permitting of that liability to

---

[33] *Wain* v. *Warlters* (1804) 5 East 10; *Saunders* v. *Wakefield* (1821) 4 B. & Ald. 595. It was otherwise under s.17. *Egerton* v. *Mathews* (1805) 6 East 307.

[34] 19 and 20 Vict. c.97.

[35] This statute only applies to "special promises being in writing," whereas the Statute of Frauds allows not only agreements in writing, but agreements of which there is a note or memorandum in writing. It has never been suggested, however, that the Mercantile Law Amendment Act 1856, does not cover the whole ground covered by the Statute of Frauds, or that where there is not a promise in writing, but only a memorandum of an oral promise (*e.g.* in a letter to a third person), the consideration must still appear. The words "promise being in writing" seem to have included promises evidenced by a note or memorandum.

[36] (1873) 21 W.R. 628.

be incurred—was sufficiently stated.[37] Where, however, the liability, though itself sufficiently defined (as where it was described as such and such a bill or account), appeared to be already existent, and the writing did not state any consideration, such as forbearance, the plaintiff failed.[38] It is this difficulty that the Mercantile Law Amendment Act removed; so that if a good consideration exists in fact for a guarantee of an existing debt, it may be proved by parol according to the ordinary law applicable to a contract partly oral.

Parol evidence not admissible to explain the promise

There must in every guarantee be sufficient statement in writing of the liability which a guarantee is to cover. Before the 1856 Act the question whether there was such a sufficient statement was generally involved in the discussion whether there was such sufficient statement of the consideration.[39] The explanation is obvious. In nearly every case the consideration for a guarantee is either the forbearing a present liability or the permitting a new one to be incurred, and the promise is to make good the liability so to be forborne or incurred. A statement of the consideration, therefore, reveals the liability guaranteed, and so serves also to measure the promise. Accordingly decisions upon the sufficiency, as disclosing the consideration, of a statement of the liability guaranteed, are also decisions upon its sufficiency, as disclosing the scope of the promise, and cover the whole question of the sufficiency of the writing. Such decisions still contain the law. Although since the 1856 Act the consideration need not be in writing, the promise must still be so. And parol evidence of the consideration cannot be used to bring in what is wanted in the written statement of the promise.[40]

Parol evidence to identify matters referred to in memorandum

Anything referred to in the guarantee can and must be identified by parol evidence. Therefore where payment is to be

---

[37] *Stadt (or Stapp)* v. *Lill* (1808) 1 Camp. 242, 9 East 348; *Morris* v. *Stacey* (1816) Holt N.P. 153; *Ex p. Gardom* (1808) 15 Ves. 286; *Boehm* v. *Campbell* (1820) 3 Moore 15; *Russell* v. *Moseley* (1822) 3 B. & B. 211; *Lysaght* v. *Walker* (1831) 5 Bligh (N.S.) 1; *Pace* v. *Marsh* (1823) 1 Bing. 216; *Newbury* v. *Armstrong* (1829) 6 Bing. 201; *Combe* v. *Woolf* (1832) 8 Bing. 156; *Kennaway* v. *Treleavan* (1839) 5 M. & W. 498; *Jarvis* v. *Wilkins* (1841) 7 M. & W. 410; *Emmott* v. *Kearns* (1839) 5 Bing. N.C. 559; *Johnston* v. *Nicholls* (1845) 1 C.B. 251; *Chapman* v. *Sutton* (1846) 2 C.B. 634.

[38] *Wain* v. *Warlters* (1804) 5 East 10; *Saunders* v. *Wakefield* (1821) 4 B. & Ald. 595; *Jenkins* v. *Reynolds* (1821) 8 B. & B. 14; *Morley* v. *Boothby* (1825) 3 Bing. 107; *Cole* v. *Dyer* (1831) 1 C. & J. 461; *Wood* v. *Benson* (1831) 2 C. & J. 94; *James* v. *Williams* (1834) 5 B. & Ad. 1109; *Bentham* v. *Cooper* (1839) 5 M. & W. 621; *Price* v. *Richardson* (1846) 15 M. & W. 539; *Clancy* v. *Piggott* (1835) 2 A. & E. 473; *Hawes* v. *Armstrong* (1835) 1 Bing. N.C. 761; *Raikes* v. *Todd* (1838) 8 A. & E. 846; *Allnutt* v. *Ashenden* (1843) 5 M. & Gr. 392.

[39] *Bateman* v. *Phillips* (1812) 15 East. 272; *Shortrede* v. *Cheek* (1834) 1 A. & E. 57. And see *Holmes* v. *Mitchell* (1859) 7 C.B. (N.S.) 361.

[40] *Holmes* v. *Mitchell, supra.*

made out of a particular fund, the fund may be identified by parol evidence, provided it answers to the description.[41] Where the guarantee refers to a liability existing at the date of the guarantee, it may be identified by parol evidence; as where the promise was to pay "the promissory note," it was identified by parol.[42] Where the only description of the debt was that involved in the phrase in a letter, "I trust you will give D.W. indulgence till next week when I will see you paid," it was held that the plaintiff might show what debt D.W. was owing him at that date, and also that the person to whom the letter was addressed was the plaintiff's agent, and that the debt referred to was a debt owing to the plaintiff and not to the addressee of the letter.[43]

Parol evidence of principal liability not yet existing

Where, however, the liability guaranteed is a future liability, it must appear in the writing what the liability is to be which the guarantee is to cover. Otherwise there might arise a conflict of parol testimony as to the limit of a guarantee—in other words, as to the extent of the promise.[44] Thus where the guarantee was to cover "the mortgage," no mortgage then being in existence, it was held that the action could not succeed.[44]

Writing to identify person to whom guarantee given

The word "guarantee" need not appear in the memorandum, and indeed no particular form of words is necessary.[45] The person to whom the guarantee is given must appear from the written document or documents evidencing the guarantee,[46] or from a written answer accepting a guarantee offered.[47] But this does not prevent it being shown that the addressee of the guarantee was an agent only; in which case the principal can sue upon it.[48]

---

[41] See *Brown* v. *Fletcher* (1876) 35 L.T.165.

[42] *Shortrede* v. *Cheek* (1834) 1 A. & E. 57.

[43] *Bateman* v. *Phillips* (1812) 15 East. 272.

[44] *Holmes* v. *Mitchell* (1859) 7 C.B. (N.S.) 361 *per* Cockburn C.J. at 368. See also *Sheers* v. *Thimbleby* (1897) 76 L.T. 709. In *Fleetwood Corp.* v. *Imperial Investments Corp. Ltd.* [1965] 51 D.L.R. (2d.) 654, it was held to be a sufficient memorandum when a guarantor signed a sales order at the bottom having written "to be paid Jan. 19,1960" at the top.

[45] *Welford* v. *Beazeley* (1747) 3 Atk. 503. See also *Seaton* v. *Heath* [1899] 1 Q.B. 782 at 792; *Re Denton's Estate* [1904] 2 Ch. 178 at 188; *Reynolds* v. *Wheeler* (1861) 10 C.B. (N.S.) 561. As to the evidence of intention see, *e.g. Dane* v. *Mortgage Insurance Corp.* [1894] 1 Q.B. 54.

[46] *Williams* v. *Lake* (1863) 2 E. & E. 349; *Williams* v. *Byrnes* (1863) 1 Moo. P.C. (N.S.) 154. *Cf. Glover* v. *Halkett* (1857) 2 H. & N. 487; *Brettel* v. *Williams* (1849) 4 Exch. 623; *Vanderbergh* v. *Spooner* (1866) L.R. 1 Exch. 316; *Gibson* v. *Holland* (1865) L.R. 1 C.P.1. But see *Walton* v. *Dodson* (1827) 3 C. & P. 162 1.

[47] *Williams* v. *Byrnes, supra* at p.198. *Re Agra and Masterman's Bank* (1867) L.R. 2 Ch. App.391.

[48] *Bateman* v. *Phillips* (1812) 15 East 272; *Gibson* v. *Holland* (1865) L.R. 1 C.P.1. *Cf. Walton* v. *Dodson, supra; Garrett* v. *Handley* (1825) 4 B. & C. 664.

Alteration of document

Where the agreement has been altered, parol evidence is admissible to show what the state of the document was when it became an agreement and the parties meant their signatures to apply to it. Thus in *Stewart* v. *Eddowes*,[49] where the document was altered after one party had signed, but before the other had done so, and then as so altered was signed by the latter, and agreed to by the former, becoming then for the first time a binding contract, there was held to be a sufficient memorandum. The reasoning in that case seems to indicate that, if an alteration were interpolated by consent after the document became an agreement, a recognition of the previous signature would not suffice. However, in *Bluck* v. *Gompertz*,[50] where an error in a guarantee was corrected, after it had been delivered to the plaintiff and after he had performed the consideration, by an endorsement, written on the face of it by the guarantor, but not signed by him, the Court of Exchequer held that the Statute had been complied with.

Memorandum may consist of several documents

The note or memorandum may consist of several documents,[51] provided that the document signed by the guarantor refers to the other document or documents requisite to complete the memorandum, as the connection cannot be supplied by oral evidence.[52] If, however, the document contains the reference, the paper referred to can be identified by parol[53]; and the covering envelope may be looked at to supply the name and addressee of a letter of guarantee.[54] It is immaterial whether the guarantor ever saw the other document to which the paper signed by him refers.[55]

Memorandum need not be of contract itself

The memorandum need not contain or form part of the contract itself, nor need it be addressed to the person to whom

[49] (1874) L.R. 9 C.P. 311.

[50] (1852) 7 Exch. 862.

[51] *Coe* v. *Duffield* (1822) 7 Moo. 252; *Macrory* v. *Scott* (1850) 5 Exch. 907; *Brettel* v. *Williams* (1849) 4 Exch. 623; *Williams* v. *Byrnes* (1863) 1 Moo. P.C. (N.S.) at 198; *Sheers* v. *Thimbleby* (1899) 76 L.T. 709. *Cf. Timmins* v. *Moreland Street Property Co. Ltd.* [1958] 1 Ch. 110.

[52] *Boydell* v. *Drummond* (1809) 11 East 142.

[53] *Oliver* v. *Hunting* (1890) 44 Ch. D. 205; *Macrory* v. *Scott, supra.*

[54] *Freeman* v. *Freeman* (1891) 7 T.L.R. 431. It is permissible to identify by parol evidence a document actually referred to in another document so as to connect them, or to show that a reference in the document which may be to another is so in fact. *Long* v. *Millar* (1879) 4 C.P.D. 450; *Ridgway* v. *Wharton* (1857) 6 H.L.C. 238. For examples of where the written evidence consists of correspondence see *Bristol, Cardiff and Swansea Aerated Bread Co.* v. *Maggs* (1890) 44 Ch. D. 616; *Hussey* v. *Horne Payne* (1879) 4 App. Cas. 311.

[55] *Macrory* v. *Scott* (1850) 5 Exch. 907.

the guarantee is given. All that is required is that there should be evidence of the guarantee under the hand of the guarantor. Therefore even a recital of a guarantee in the will of the guarantor is sufficient.[56]

Signature

The signature may be by a printing of the name,[57] if done with authority,[58] or by initials,[59] or, in the case of an illiterate (who, if he so executes, must be taken to be such), by a mark.[60] It need not be at the foot or end of the memorandum, provided it governs and authenticates the whole.[61]

A memorandum may be signed by an agent, and it is well settled that such agent need not be authorised in writing; verbal authority,[62] or subsequent verbal ratification,[63] is sufficient. Two parties may be represented by a common agent who signs for both, as, in the case of sales within the Statute, an auctioneer.[64] But one party cannot be agent to sign for the other.[65] The agent of one party may also be agent of the other to sign the memorandum, if in fact authorised by him to put his name to it as a binding memorandum.[66] But a mere note, by way of record of the promise, written by the clerk of the promisee in the presence of the guarantor, is not sufficient.[67]

Guarantee by a partner

A partner has no implied authority to bind his firm by guarantee, unless the giving of guarantees is necessary to the

---

[56] *Re Hoyle* [1893] 1 Ch. 84.

[57] *Saunderson* v. *Jackson* (1800) 2 B. & P. 238.

[58] *Schneider* v. *Norris* (1814) 2 M. & S. 286. See also *Leeman* v. *Stocks* [1951] Ch. 94.

[59] *Re Blewitt* (1879) L.R. 5 P.D. 116. The signatures may be printed or pencilled. *Geary* v. *Physic* (1826) 5 B. & C. 234.

[60] *Baker* v. *Dening* (1838) 8 A. & E. 94. Or even *semble* by signed instructions for a telephone or telegraphic message. *Godwin* v. *Francis* (1870) L.R. 5 C.P. 295.

[61] See *Caton* v. *Caton* (1865–7) L.R. 2 H.L.127; *Durrell* v. *Evans* (1862) 1 H. & C. 174. On the question of the intention with which the memorandum is signed as not being decisive, see *Wallace* v. *Roe* [1903] 1 I.R.32; *Welford* v. *Beazely* (1747) 3 Atk. 503. *Cf. Gobbell* v. *Archer* (1855) 2 A. & E. 800. One surety signing where several are the subject of the guarantee is bound *per Norton* v. *Powell* (1842) 4 M. & G. 42.

[62] *Emmerson* v. *Heelis* (1809) 2 Taunt. 38.

[63] *Maclean* v. *Dunn* (1828) 4 Bing. 722.

[64] Where though the agent expressly signs as principal he remains liable as such, no doubt in an action on the guarantee oral evidence would establish the existence of an undisclosed principal. See *Higgins* v. *Senior* (1841) 8 M. & W. 834; *Basma* v. *Weekes* [1950] A.C. 441.

[65] *Wright* v. *Dannah* (1809) 2 Camp. 203; *Farebrother* v. *Simmons* (1822) 5 B. & Ald.333; *Sharman* v. *Brandt* (1871) L.R.6 Q.B. 720. But a party can be a signatory in such a manner that his signature would be sufficient to deal both with his personal capacity as guarantor and with a representative capacity, *e.g.* a director. See, *e.g., Young* v. *Schuler* (1883) 11 Q.B.D. 651; *VSH Ltd.* v. *BKS Air Transport Ltd.* [1964] 1 Lloyd's Rep. 460.

[66] See *Durrell* v. *Evans* (1862) 1 H. & C. 174, 187, 191; *Peirce* v. *Corf* (1874) L.R. 9 Q.B. 210, 215; *Caton* v. *Caton* (1867) L.R. 2 H.L. 127.

[67] *Dixon* v. *Broomfield* (1814) 2 Chit. 205.

conduct of the business.[68] It is not enough that the guarantee was given incidentally to further objects within the scope of the partnership,[68] as that it was given by merchants for merchants,[69] by contractors for sub-contractors,[70] or by solicitors for a client.[71] It is necessary to show that it has been usual, to the knowledge of the partners, to give such guarantees.[72] And the same rule holds with regard to the manager of a company.[73] If authority to give guarantees, express or implied, exists, or if the giving of it has been ratified, sufficient signature by one partner is sufficient within the Statute of Frauds.[74]

Guarantees by company

Provided they have authority so to do, the directors of a company can bind it by signing a guarantee thereby satisfying the requirements of the Statute of Frauds.[75] If the giving of guarantees is fairly within the scope of the company's business, then presumably a general power of management vested in any directors would be sufficient authority for this purpose.[76] General principles of agency in such cases will apply so that directors will need to ensure that the guarantee is framed so as to avoid any question of their own liability.[77]

The memorandum of association to a company may provide a limited power to give a guarantee or the power may be unrestricted. Where a power is contained in an independent objects clause, it would appear that a company might give guarantees for any purpose whatever,[78] otherwise the exercise of the power must be in furtherance of the main purposes of the

---

[68] *Brettel* v. *Williams* (1849) 4 Exch. 623. But *cf. ex p. Gardom* (1808) 15 Ves. 286; *Hope* v. *Cust* (1774) cited 1 East at 53. See also Partnership Act 1890, s.5. The giving of guarantees will be outside the normal business of an average partnership, in which case all partners should be required to sign a guarantee by a firm.

[69] *Duncan* v. *Lowndes* (1813) 3 Camp. 478.

[70] *Brettel* v. *Williams* (1849) 4 Exch. 623.

[71] *Hasleham* v. *Young* (1844) 5 Q.B. 833. See *Mayfield* v. *Sankey* (1890) 6 T.L.R. 185.

[72] *Duncan* v. *Lowndes* (1813) 3 Camp. 478. *Crawford* v. *Stirling* (1802) 4 Esp. 207.

[73] *Simpson's Claim* (1887) 36 Ch. D. 532.

[74] *Duncan* v. *Lowndes, supra. Sandilands* v. *Marsh* (1819) 2 B. & Ald. 673.

[75] *Re Eva Life Ass. Soc.* [1866] W.N. 309. See also *Colman* v. *Eastern Counties Ry Co.* (1846) 10 Beav. 1; *Reading* v. *Plymouth Grinding Co.* (1843) 2 Exch. 711; *Simpson's Claim* (1887) 36 Ch. D. 532. Note *Jay* v. *Gainsford* (October 4, 1977, C.A., Transcript No. 362B of 1977) illustrating how a note or memorandum satsifying the Statute of Frauds can be effected by a company in respect of the liabilities as guarantors of its individual directors.

[76] See *Re West of England Bank, ex p. Booker* (1880) 14 Ch. D. 317. *Cf. Small* v. *Smith* (1884) 10 App. Cas. 119. For cases on the question of vires, a question properly outside the scope of this work, see cases noted at p.2, Chap. 4 (part 7) and Chap. 6.

[77] See *Re Dover and Deal Ry.* (1854) 4 De G. M. & G. 411; *Chapleo* v. *Brunswick Permanent Building Society* (1881) 6 Q.B.D. 696. *Cf. Chapman* v. *Smethurst* [1909] 1 K.B. 927; *Ward and T. Avery Ltd.* v. *Charlesworth* (1914) 31 T.L.R. 52.

[78] *Cf. Cotman* v. *Brougham* [1918] A.C.514.

company.[79] A company may not gratuitously dispose of its assets[80]; and accordingly it is unlikely that it could gratuitously give a guarantee. There must be some benefit to the company; the fact that the guarantee is for the benefit of a parent company may not be sufficient.[81]

---

[79] *Re German Date Coffee Co.* (1882) 20 Ch. D. 169; *Stephens v. Mysore Reefs (Kangundy) Mining Co. Ltd.* [1902] 1 Ch. 745; *Re Jon Beaufort (London) Ltd.* [1953] 1 Ch. 131. See however *Bell Houses Ltd.* v. *City Wall Properties Ltd.* [1966] 2 Q.B.656.

[80] *Parke* v. *Daily News Ltd.* [1962] Ch. 927.

[81] In the absence of a general power in the memorandum it would be *ultra vires* a company to guarantee debts of a company promoted by it. See *Re Queen Anne and Garden Mansions Co.* (1894) 1 Mans. 460.

CHAPTER 4

CONSTRUCTION AND EFFECT OF GUARANTEES

1. General Rules

It was said by Bayley B. in *Nicholson* v. *Paget*[1] that guarantees were to be construed favourably to the guarantor. This dictum, which was contrary to the ruling in earlier cases,[2] has since been disapproved, and it is now settled that guarantees are not to be construed more strictly than other contracts.[3]

Intention to assume liability

It does not follow that a letter requesting a person to deliver goods to a third party, and stating that payment will be promptly made, amounts to a guarantee. It may appear from the terms of the document and the surrounding circumstances that a mere favour was requested and no liability intended to be undertaken.[4] But where an actual order is given, the person ordering must be liable either as principal or as guarantor.[5] Where a person guaranteed the "performance" of a contract which provided for the supply of goods, the terms of settlement being expressed by the clause "month's account and bill at 5 months," it was held that the guarantee was that the bills should be paid, not merely that they should be given.[6]

---

[1] (1832) 1 C. & M. at p. 52.

[2] *Merle* v. *Wells* (1840) 2 Camp. 413; *Mason* v. *Pritchard* (1810) 2 Camp. 436; *Bastow* v. *Bennett* (1812) 3 Camp. 220.

[3] *Mayer* v. *Isaac* (1840) 6 M. & W. 605; *Hargreave* v. *Smee* (1829) 6 Bing. 244; *Edwards* v. *Jevons* (1849) 8 C.B. 436; 440; *Wood* v. *Priestner* (1866) L.R. 2 Ex. 66, 282; *Heffield* v. *Meadows* (1869) L.R. 4 C.P. 595; *Nottingham Hide, Skin, etc., Co.* v. *Bottrill* (1873) L.R. 8 C.P. 694. See also *Eshelby* v. *Federated European Bank* |1932| 1 K.B. at 266. Although the *contra proferentem* rule seems not to apply, sureties are favoured in the manner in which guarantees are construed to the extent that the surety can demand from the creditor strict compliance of any terms imposed by the conditions of the suretyship, see, *e.g. Wheatley* v. *Bastow* (1855) 7 De G. M. & G. 261, at 279 per Turner L.J. and cases cited at note 2, *supra*. However, it has also been said, without apparent reference to previous authority that in the event of ambiguity, the *contra proferentem* rule does apply, see *Eastern Counties Building Society* v. *Russell* |1947| 2 All E.R. 734, at 736 and 739 cited in *Barclays Bank Ltd.* v. *Thienel* (1977) 247 E.G. 385. In *National Bank of New Zealand Ltd.* v. *West* |1977| 1 N.Z.L.R. 29 at 34, the principle was applied by Casey J. in holding that if a bank wished to include in a guarantee the principal's liability as surety, it should say so in clear terms. See also *Swan* v. *Bank of Scotland* (1836) 10 Bl. (N.S.) 627 H.L.

[4] *Bank of Montreal* v. *Munster Bank* (1876) 11 Ir. C.L. 47. See also *Faber* v. *Earl of Lathom* (1897) 77 L.T. 162, 169.

[5] *Langdale* v. *Parry* (1823) 2 D. & R. 337.

[6] *Haymen* v. *Gover* (1872) 25 L.T. 903.

Construction with reference to surrounding circumstances and recitals

Guarantees are to be construed with reference to the surrounding circumstances and the relative positions of the parties at the time.[7] The condition, expressed in general terms, of a bond given by a surety will be restricted in construction by a recital qualifying the nature or duration of the principal engagement.[8] Upon a similar principle a promise in general terms contained in a letter or other inartificial document may be cut down by the words in which the request or the consideration is expressed.[9] A guarantee for the price of work "done and to be done" was held to be limited to the work included in an estimate shown to the guarantor before he became liable, and not to include extra work ordered afterwards.[10]

Guarantee by estoppel

The principle that where the words of a guarantee are clear, the court will give effect to their natural and ordinary meaning was reaffirmed by Robert Goff J. in *Amalgamated Investment & Property Co. Ltd. (In liquidation)* v. *Texas Commerce International Bank Ltd.*[11] On the facts of that case, where a principal debtor had represented to the creditor, a bank, that a guarantee covered a loan made by a different though connected bank, and the original creditor was thereby influenced in continuing to rely on the guarantee for the purpose of securing a second loan, it was held unconscionable for the debtor to take advantage of such an error and the latter was estopped from asserting the invalidity of the guarantee. It appeared not to affect the estoppel that (a) it gave effect to an otherwise gratuitous promise made by the debtor, and (b) the guarantee was not of itself legally binding.[11]

---

[7] *Horlor* v. *Carpenter* (1857) 3 C.B. (N.S.) 172, 180; *Montefiore* v. *Lloyd* (1863) 15 C.B. (N.S.) 203; *Wood* v. *Priestner* (1866) L.R. 2 Ex. 66, 282; *Heffield* v. *Meadows* (1869) L.R. 4 C.P. 595; *Laurie* v. *Scholefield* (1869) L.R. 4 C.P. 622; *Burgess* v. *Eve* (1872) L.R. 13 Eq. 450; *Coles* v. *Pack* (1869) L.R. 5 C.P. 65; *Leathley* v. *Spyer* (1870) L.R. 5 C.P. 595; *Nottingham Hide, Skin, etc. Co.* v. *Bottrill* (1873) L.R. 8 C.P 694; *Morrell* v. *Cowan* (1877) 6 Ch.D. 166, 7 Ch.D. 151. And see *Carr* v. *Montefiore* (1864) 5 B. & S. 408; *Grahame* v. *Grahame* (1887) 19 L.R. Ir. 249. In *Hyundai Shipbuilding & Heavy Industries Co. Ltd.* v. *Pournaras* [1978] 2 Lloyd's Rep. 502 at 506, Roskill L.J. said that the guarantee should be construed as a whole against "the factual matrix of the background."

[8] *Lord Arlington* v. *Merricke* (1672) 2 Williams' Saund. 411 a: *Horton* v. *Day* cited *ibid.* at 414; *African Co.* v. *Mason* cited in *Stibbs* v. *Clough* (1733) 1 Str. 227; *Barker* v. *Parker* (1786) 1 T.R. 287; *Pearsall* v. *Summersett* (1812) 4 Taunt. 593; *Liverpool W.W. Co.* v. *Atkinson* (1805) 6 East. 507; *Webb* v. *James* (1840) 7 M. & W. 279; *Napier* v. *Bruce* (1842) 8 C. & F. 470; *Chapman* v. *Beckinton* (1842) 3 Q.B. 703; *Re Medewe's Trusts* (1859) 26 Beav. 588. The conditions of fidelity bonds are often explained in the recital. See the above cases and also *London Assurance Co.* v. *Bold* (1844) 6 Q.B. 514; *Danby* v. *Coutts & Co.* (1885) 29 Ch.D. 500.

[9] See *Smith* v. *Brandram* (1841) 2 M. & Gr. 244; *Morrell* v. *Cowan* (1877) 6 Ch.D. 166, 7 Ch.D. 151.

[10] *Plastic Decoration Co.* v. *Massey-Mainwaring* (1895) 11 T.L.R. 205. *Cf. Mann, Taylor & Co.* v. *Royal Bank of Canada* (1935) 40 Com. Cas. 267.

[11] [1981] 2 W.L.R. 554; [1981] 1 All. E.R. 923 at 929 affirmed *The Times*, August 1, 1981, C.A.

Estoppel by recital

A surety is not estopped by a recital in a guarantee if it was included as the statement of the creditor and not of the surety.[12]

If the obligation is expressly carried beyond the recital, it must have effect.[13] The question is in every case whether it can be collected from the recital that the intention of the parties requires that the condition should be qualified.[14] Where a bond recited that the obligees, bankers, had agreed to make advances not exceeding a certain amount, it was held that the condition, which was for the repayment of such advances, could not be read as making the security conditional on the amount not being exceeded, though, of course, it was limited to that amount.[14] And where the recital is only explanatory of the motive of the principal in requesting credit, the condition must not be read as applying only to the transactions referred to as part of such explanation[15]; as where it was recited that advances were required by C to continue the business of a late firm, but the operative words of guarantee included all C's debts to the obligee in respect of his trade and commerce.[16] But if the bond recites duties to be performed by the principal under a certain agreement referred to, and then is conditioned for his discharge of all his duties under that agreement, the engagement of the surety is nevertheless restricted to the duties recited,[17] at any rate where the surety has no notice of the whole terms of the agreement.[17]

Guarantees for officers

A guarantee for the performance of the duties of an office created by law, or owed to an officer or body created by law, must be construed with reference to the duration, incidents and character of the office according to the then law.[18] So a bond for the payment over of moneys collected for commissioners of sewers was held applicable to moneys collected under a commission which had expired before the date of the bond, the court taking notice of the fact that the commissioners to whom the bond was given were entitled to receive the moneys

---

[12] See *Greer* v. *Kettle* [1938] A.C. 156; *Anglo-Canadia Bank Ltd.* v. *London & Provincial Marine Co. Ltd.* (1904) 20 T.L.R. 665.

[13] *Sansom* v. *Bell* (1809) 2 Camp. 39; *Bank of British N. America* v. *Cuvillier* (1861) 4 L.T. 159; *Saunders* v. *Taylor* (1829) 9 B. & C. 35; *Dumbell* v. *Isle of Man Ry.* (1880) 42 L.T. 945.

[14] *Parker* v. *Wise* (1817) 6 M. & S. 239, 247; *Australian Joint Stock Bank* v. *Bailey* [1899] A.C. 396.

[15] *Bank of British N. America* v. *Cuvillier* (1861) 4 L.T. 159.

[16] *Ibid.* And see *Dumbell* v. *Isle of Man Ry.* (1880) 42 L.T. 745.

[17] *Napier* v. *Bruce* (1842) 8 C. & F. 470. And see *Pemberton* v. *Oakes* (1827) 4 Russ. 154; *Chapman* v. *Beckinton* (1842) 3 Q.B. 703.

[18] See *McGahey* v. *Alston* (1836) 1 M. & W. 386. Fidelity bonds, not having principal debtors, are not within the Statute of Frauds.

outstanding when they took office.[19] On the other hand, the duration of the guarantee will prima facie be confined to the period for which the office is by law held, and will not cover the officer if re-elected[20]; nor, speaking generally, will it cover the officer when his duties or position have been changed by law, even in respect of matters not specially mentioned in the guarantee.[21]

Guarantees for performance of contractual duties

A guarantee for the performance of duties resting merely on contract must be construed in favour of the creditor with reference to the actual terms of that contract, being one which comes within the general scope of the guarantee, although not specifically agreed to by the surety.[22] Also in favour of the surety it must be taken to embody all the essential terms of that contract, material to his risk, though not specifically contracted for by the surety[23]—that is to say, all the terms that may affect, not merely that do affect, his position.[24]

The canons of construction applicable to guarantees and the rules governing the reference to surrounding circumstances and the admission of parol evidence for that purpose, deal, of course, only with those documents which on the face of them are guarantees.[25] Where a promissory note or common money bond has been given to secure the existing or future debt of another, the terms on which it was given, and the debt it was to cover, are matters entirely for parol evidence.[26] It is not here a question of the construction of a written promise, but merely of the debt to which it refers.

Conflict of laws

Where a guarantee is given in one country to secure obligations contracted or to be contracted, and also to be fulfilled

---

[19] *Saunders* v. *Taylor* (1829) 9 B. & C. 35.

[20] See *post*, p. 57.

[21] See part 8 of this chapter.

[22] *Simpson* v. *Manley* (1831) 2 C. & J. 12; *Coombe* v. *Woolf* (1832) 8 Bing. 156; *Howell* v. *Jones* (1834) 1 C.M. & R. 97, 107; *Grahame* v. *Grahame* (1887) 19 L.R. Ir. 249.

[23] *Holme* v. *Brunskill* (1878) 3 Q.B.D. 499, 505; *Croydon Gas Co.* v. *Dickinson* (1876) 2 C.P.D. 46; *Sanderson* v. *Aston* (1873) L.R. 8 Ex. 73.

[24] *Holme* v. *Brunskill, supra.* See *post*, p. 86.

[25] For an interesting example of the evidence required to convert an indemnity ("deficiency agreement" by a vendor of commercial premises to make up underpayment of rent by tenants) into a guarantee, see *Royal Trust Co.* v. *Pacific Petroleum Ltd.* (1967) 63 D.L.R. (2d.) 255, citing the last edition of this work.

[26] *Ex p. Brook* (1815) 2 Rose 334; *Henniker* v. *Wigg* (1843) 4 Q.B. 792; *Hartland* v. *Jukes* (1863) 1 H. & C. 667; *Macrory* v. *Scott* (1850) 5 Exch. 907; *Re Boys* (1870) L.R. 10 Eq. 467.

in another,[27] a double question upon the conflict of laws arises—*viz.* (i) by what law is the guarantee itself to have effect; (ii) by what law is it to be determined whether the principal obligation has been fulfilled. The first question must be answered in accordance with the rule applicable to any contract of whatever kind upon which such a point arises—namely, that that law must be applied with reference to which the parties appear to have contracted.[28] Where a letter was written from England to a bank in Scotland guaranteeing the future obligations and engagements towards a bank of merchants in Scotland, the court was inclined to think that English law applied.[29] And in another case where a letter was written from England guaranteeing to a Scottish firm the "intromissions" of their agent in Scotland, the case was determined according to English law without any question as to its applicability being raised.[30]

The question remains by what law it is to be decided whether the principal obligation has been fulfilled, in cases where the contract of guarantee is governed by a different law from that which, as between a creditor and a principal at all events, governs the principal obligation. The parties to such a guarantee would prima facie contemplate fulfilment of the principal obligation as between the parties to it—that is to say, according to the law with reference to which the principal obligation was entered into. Authority indicates that the guarantee would have effect in that sense.

In *Allen* v. *Kemble*,[31] it was held in the Privy Council, and the decision was approved, as applicable to cases of principal and surety, by the Court of Queen's Bench in *Rouquette* v. *Overmann*,[32] that a foreign drawer of a bill accepted in England could, in accordance with the foreign law, rely as against the holder in England, upon a set off available to the acceptor, which by the foreign, but not by English, law, amounted to an extinction of the debt by the acceptor. But the ground of that decision as appears from the judgment in *Rouquette* v. *Overmann*[32] was not that the foreign guarantor had a right to have it decided, conformably with the foreign law, that the

---

[27] As to the conflict of laws where the question is between co-sureties as to contribution, see *American Surety Co.* v. *Wrightson* (1910) 103 L.T. 663, where at 665 it is suggested that the *lex fori* should determine questions of contribution. The basis of this suggestion is questioned in Dicey and Morris, *The Conflict of Laws* (10th ed., 1980) at p. 1199.

[28] Often called the proper law of the contract. See generally Dicey and Morris, *op. cit.* at pp. 747 *et seq.*

[29] *Ex p. Littlejohn* (1843) 3 M. D. & De G. 182 *per* Knight-Bruce V.C.

[30] *Stewart* v. *McKean* (1855) 10 Exch. 675. And see *Allen* v. *Kemble* (1848) 6 Moo. P.C. 314 as explained in *Rouquette* v. *Overmann* (1875) L.R. 10 Q.B. 525 at 540, 541.

[31] (1843) 6 Moo. P.C. 314.

[32] (1875) L.R. 10 Q.B. 525, 540.

principal debt had been paid within the meaning of the guarantee, but that he had the right which the foreign law gave *him* as surety to take the benefit of a cross-claim by the principal against the creditor.[33] And it was laid down with reference to the liability of the drawer in England of a bill in France to the person to whom he endorsed it in England that, the drawer being surety to the indorsee for the performance of the contract of the acceptor, "his liability was to be measured by that of the acceptor whose surety he was, and, as the obligations of the acceptor were to be determined by the *lex loci* of performance, so also must be those of the surety."[34] The decision was that a moratorium, enacted by the French Government, of which the acceptor had the benefit, entitled the holder, as between himself and the drawer, to postpone presentment until it had expired.[35] The effect of the decision seems to be that the question whether the principal has performed his obligation, and also the question whether and at what moment there was a complete default by the principal (where the liability of the guarantor only arises upon such default), must be determined by the law governing that obligation.

Surety liable on joint contract

The legal incidents of a joint contract are not modified by the circumstance that one of the joint debtors is a surety.[36] If therefore either dies, the remedy of the creditor survives against the other only, whether principal[37] or surety.[38] It formerly followed that if judgment was recovered against either upon the joint contract the creditor could not afterwards sue the other.[39] But in England this rule has been abolished and under section 3 of the Civil Liability (Contribution) Act 1978 judgment

---

[33] See *per* Cockburn, C.J., in *Rouquette* v. *Overmann, supra.*

[34] *Ibid.* at p. 537.

[35] *Ibid.* at p. 537. A moratorium can be relied on by the debtor if the relevant legislation is enacted according to the proper law of the contract. See *National Bank of Greece and Athens S.A.* v. *Metliss* [1958] A.C. 809; *Adams* v. *National Bank of Greece S.A.* [1961] A.C. 255 and generally Dicey & Morris, *op. cit.* at p. 821.

[36] But the principal debtor will not necessarily be a party to the surety's contract to be answerable to the creditor. See *Bain* v. *Cooper* (1841) 1 Dowl. (N.S.) 11, 14 *per* Parke B.

[37] *Rawstone* v. *Parr* (1827) 3 Russ 424, 539; *Jones* v. *Beach* (1851) 2 De G. M. & C. 886; *Other* v. *Iveson* (1855) 3 Drew. 177; *Strong* v. *Foster* (1855) 17 C.B. 201. See also *General Produce Co.* v. *United Bank Ltd.* [1979] 2 Lloyd's Rep. 255 for an illustration of a plaintiff's liability starting as that of a guarantor and continuing, after release of the principal debtor's liability, as that of a principal debtor. *Cf.* approach in *Khan* v. *United Bank Ltd.* (May 22, 1981, C.A. Transcript No. 237 of 1981). Both these cases dealt with so-called letters of lien, construed as ordinary guarantees and held binding on the guarantor, even though on the facts the principal debtor had been deprived of its title to the principal debt and was therefore no longer indebted to the creditor. In the latter case, the Court of Appeal emphasised the commercial reality of the transaction.

[38] *Richardson* v. *Horton* (1843) 6 Beav. 185.

[39] See *King* v. *Hoare* (1844) 13 M. & W. 494 But *cf. Wegg-Prosser* v. *Evans* [1894] 2 Q.B. 101, [1895] 1 Q.B. 108.

recovered against any person liable in respect of any debt shall
not be a bar to an action against any other person jointly liable
with him in the same debt. Where surety and principal are not
bound by a joint contract, recovery of judgment against one
party is no bar to an action against the other.[40]

2. *Retrospective or Prospective*

The first question upon the promise in a guarantee is whether it
covers a past or future debt. If an existing debt is recited, mere
general words will not extend the obligation to future debts,[41]
but express mention of them will, of course, do so.[42] If future
debts only are recited, mere general words will not make the
guarantee also retrospective.[43]

When words used are ambiguous

The principles of construction applicable, where the difficulty
arises from the use of words of doubtful tense, have already been
discussed, and all the cases dealt with in the chapter on
Consideration, and it is sufficient here to refer to that chapter.[44]
Of course a future credit may be the consideration for a
guarantee exclusively for a past debt and not including the
future debt.[45] But where continuing credit, resulting in a fresh
debt, is the consideration, the guarantee prima facie covers the
future debt.[46] If in such a case it is intended that a past debt
should also be included, that must be clearly expressed.[47]
   Where a bond was given, conditioned for payment over to
commissioners of sewers of moneys already received, or to be
thereafter received, by a collector on their account, reciting the
appointment by the then commissioners, under which the
collector would be entrusted to receive various moneys, it was
held that this security was applicable to moneys received under
a commission which had expired before the date of the bond, the
court observing that the commissioners were entitled to the
balances due to their predecessors.[48]

---

[40] *Bermondsey* v. *Ramsey* (1871) L.R. 6 C.P. 247, 252.
[41] *Pearsall* v. *Summersett* (1812) 4 Taunt 593. And see *ante*, p. 44.
[42] *Sansom* v. *Bell* (1809) 2 Camp. 39.
[43] *Morrell* v. *Cowan* (1877) 6 Ch.D. 166, 7 Ch.D. 151 But see *Wilson* v. *Craven* (1841) 8 M. & W. 584.
And *cf. Napier* v. *Bruce* (1842) 8 C. & F. 470.
[44] See also *Woolley* v. *Jennings* (1826) 5 B. & C. 165.
[45] See *ante*, p. 14.
[46] *Mayer* v. *Isaac* (1840) 6 M. & W. 605; *Wood* v. *Priestner* (1866) L.R. 2 Ex. 66, 282.
[47] *Morrell* v. *Cowan* (1877) 6 Ch.D. 166; 7 Ch.D. 151. *Cf. Brunning* v. *Odhams Bros.* (1896) 13
T.L.R. 65. But see *Wilson* v. *Craven* (1841) 8 M. & W. 584 and *cf. Napier* v. *Bruce* (1842) 8 C. & F. 470.
[48] *Saunders* v. *Taylor* (1829) 9 B. & C. 35.

In *Morrell* v. *Cowan*,[49] the guarantee was: "in consideration of you' having at my request agreed to supply and furnish goods to M. M. Cowan, I hereby guarantee to you the sum of £500. This guarantee is to continue in force for a period of six years and no longer." At the date of the guarantee there was money owing to the principal for goods already supplied in consequence of which further supply had been refused. The Court of Appeal, reversing Fry J., held that the guarantee was prospective only. In *Glyn* v. *Hertel*[50] the guarantee was "I will be answerable to the extent of £5,000 for the use of the House of S. & Co." It was treated throughout the case as being prospective only.[51]

A guarantee under seal, given by a father to a banking company in consideration of their discounting a note for £2,000 given by him to his son, and of the sum of 5s., by which the father undertook liability for all money due or to become due from the son to the company on any account whatsoever, was held to cover not only the £2,000 but also a large sum then already due to the bank, as well as further advances beyond the £2,000.[52]

In *Chalmers* v. *Victors*[53] a promise "to be responsible for liabilities incurred by A.B. to the extent of £50," the fact being that A.B. was then indebted to the extent of £41 was construed as a guarantee of a future indebtedness which, with the existing debt, should make up £50.[54]

In *Re Medewe's Trust*,[55] a deed recited that there was a considerable balance due on three banking accounts, and that "the bank having required security for the balance due on the said several banking accounts," M. had agreed to charge his estate with the payment of the balance of all the said several accounts limited to £3,000. The deed then charged M.'s estate with the three several sums of money which should or might be found due on the balance of the said several accounts, not exceeding £3,000. It was held to apply to the existing balances only, and the charge was extinguished by the satisfaction under the rules in *Clayton's Case*[56] of the existing debit items.

Where a bond conditioned for the payment of money with interest from the date of the bond is executed by a surety, this prima facie applies only to a present debt. It might be given as security for a future advance or for an ultimate balance, but if so

---

[49] (1877) 6 Ch.D. 166; 7 Ch.D. 151.
[50] (1818) 2 Moore 134.
[51] See *ibid.* at p. 151, *per* Dallas, C.J.
[52] *Burgess* v. *Eve* (1872) L.R. 13 Eq. 450.
[53] (1868) 18 L.T. 481.
[54] (1864) 33 L.J. Q.B. 209.
[55] (1859) 26 Beav. 588.
[56] See *post*, p. 97.

it must be proved that the surety has so agreed.[57] It is not enough in the case of such a bond to prove that the principal delivered it to the creditor as such.[58]

A guarantee for the price of goods to be supplied covers goods contracted for before the guarantee if not delivered till after.[58] It has been held in Ireland that sureties for a Clerk to an Urban District Council were liable for sums embezzled before the date of their bond, although the bond was only for the future good behaviour of the clerk, inasmuch as his failure to account for moneys so embezzled took place after the date of the bond.[59]

The Hyundai Shipbuilding Cases

In *Hyundai Shipbuilding & Heavy Industries Company Limited* v. *Pournaras*[60] and *Hyundai Heavy Industries Company Limited* v. *Papadopoulos*,[61] the Court of Appeal and House of Lords respectively had to consider identical guarantees of instalments due from shipbuilders who had entered into shipbuilding contracts. On the wording employed, the guarantors guaranteed "the payment in accordance with the terms of the contract of all sums due or to become due by the buyer to you under the contract." In the first case there were instalments accrued due when there was a repudiation which was accepted by the builder and the contract was terminated. The Court of Appeal, construing the guarantee as a whole against "the factual matrix of the background"[62] held that the true meaning of the guarantee was that if the buyer did not pay the instalments accrued due, the guarantor would.[63] This liability resulted on the true construction of the guarantee[64] despite the termination of the main contract.[65]

---

[57] *Walker* v. *Hardman* (1837) 4 C. & F. 258.
[58] *Simmons* v. *Keating* (1818) 2 Stark 426.
[59] *Tullamore Urban District Council* v. *Robins* (1913) 48 I.L.T. 160.
[60] [1978] 2 Lloyds Rep. 502.
[61] [1979] 1 Lloyds Rep. 130, C.A. and [1980] 1 W.L.R. 1129, H.L.
[62] At p. 504. The commercial background was that there were "too many ships chasing too few cargoes so that those who had in more optimistic days entered into shipbuilding contracts were trying to escape from them, as were their guarantors." The purchasers were "one-ship Liberian companies" not thought to have substantial assets.
[63] Relying on passages from the speeches of Lords Reid and Diplock in *Moschi* v. *Lep Air Services Ltd.* [1973] A.C. 331 at 344 and 380 as to which see further p. 91. In that case the liability of the guarantor was to ensure that the principal debtor made certain instalment payments at a weekly rate.
[64] Another ground of the decision involving the guarantor's right to enjoy a right of set-off otherwise enuring to the benefit of the principal debtor is dealt with below at p. 103.
[65] This decision is probably to be limited to the special background involved. *Cf.* the result in *Moschi* v. *Lep Air Services Ltd.*, *supra.*, where it was held that after the main contract had been terminated as a result of a repudiatory breach, the guarantor's obligation continued, but was transmuted by operation of law into an obligation to compensate the creditor by way of damages for his loss.

In *Hyundai Heavy Industries Company Limited* v. *Papadopoulos*,[66] there were two factual differences from the *Pournaras* case: first, in this case, the builder had invoked a contractual provision entitling him to retain any instalments paid, but which provision did not in terms deal with any rights to any instalments accrued due prior to cancellation under the provision and, secondly, the action against the guarantor in the *Papadopoulos* case was instituted before repudiation, whereas in the *Pournaras* decision, proceedings had apparently been issued after termination. The House of Lords followed the decision in the Pournaras case holding that the cancellation of the contract had not deprived the builders of their accrued rights to payments as against the guarantors.[67]

3. *Specific or Continuing*

General Rule

A guarantee for a future debt may either be restricted to a debt of that amount to be incurred once and for all, or it may be continuing.[68] The construction will turn upon the wording of the individual contract, the principle being that the guarantee is continuing, unless either it appears that only dealings to the extent of the limit, which are then to cease, are contemplated, or the guarantor distinctly limits his undertaking to a definite transaction or to the first items of the credit amounting to the total named.[69]

Continuing guarantees: examples

The following have been held to be continuing guarantees, but of course in each case the circumstances under which the document was given influenced the construction put upon it:

> "I consider myself bound to you for any debt my brother may contract for his business as a jeweller, not exceeding £100, after this date."[70]

---

[66] [1980] 1 W.L.R. 1129.

[67] *Ibid.* at pp. 1137F–1137H, 1142H–1143A, 1144B, 1144C, 1153A and 1153B.

[68] The term "revolving credit" is sometimes used of bankers' commercial credits. Such credits are not contracts of guarantee. But it would seem that the term "revolving" as applied to such credits has the same meaning as "continuing" applied to a guarantee. See generally Gutteridge and Megrah, *The Law of Bankers' Commercial Credits* (6th ed., 1979) at p. 14.

[69] See *per* Alderson B. in *Mayer* v. *Isaac* (1840) 6 M. & W. 605 at 612 questioning the dictum of Bayley B. in *Nicholson* v. *Paget* (1832) 1 C. & M. at 52. See also *Merle* v. *Wells* (1910) 2 Camp. 413; *Mason* v. *Pritchard* (1810) 2 Camp. 436; *Bastow* v. *Bennett* (1812) 3 Camp. 220; *Woolley* v. *Jennings* (1826) 5 C.B. 165; *Edwards* v. *Jevons* (1849) 8 C.B. 436, 440. See also *Ulster Bank Ltd.* v. *Lambe* [1966] N.I. 161 and *Re an Arranging Debtor* [1971] N.I. 96, for the related question of whether a surety is liable for the whole or part of the debt guaranteed, dealt with *post* at p. 67.

[70] *Merle* v. *Wells* (1910) 2 Camp. 413.

"I hereby promise to be responsible to T.M. for any goods he hath or may supply my brother W.P. to the amount of £100."[71]

"I undertake to be answerable to the extent of £300 for any tallow or soap supplied by B to F and B, provided they shall neglect to pay in due time."[72]

"My son, G.C.D., is desirous of commencing business in your line and wants the usual credit for four or six months. If you think well to supply him I will be answerable for the amount of £100."[73]

"I agree to guarantee the payment of goods to be delivered to S. according to the custom of their trading with you in the sum of £200."[74]

"Whereas W.C. is indebted to you in a sum of money and may have occasion to make further purchases from you, as an inducement to you to sell him such goods and continue your dealings with him I hereby undertake to guarantee you in the sum of £100, payable to you on default on the part of W.C. for two months."[75]

"In consideration of your supplying A.L.V. with china and earthenware, I hereby guarantee the payment of any bills you may draw upon him on account thereof to the amount of £200."[76]

"In consideration of your extending the credit already given to T.H., and agreeing to draw upon him at 3 months from first of the following month for all goods purchased up to the 20th of the preceding month, I hereby at your request guarantee the payment and agree to pay you any sum that shall be due and owing to you upon his account for goods supplied."[77]

---

[71] *Mason* v. *Pritchard* (1810) 2 Camp. 436, *Cf. Weston* v. *Empire Assurance Corporation* (1868) 19 L.T. 305.
[72] *Bastow* v. *Bennett* (1812) 3 Camp. 220. See also *Grahame* v. *Grahame* (1887) 19 L.R. Ir. 249.
[73] *Dry* v. *Davy* (1839) 10 A. & E. 30.
[74] *Hargreave* v. *Smee* (1829) 6 Bing. 244.
[75] *Allan* v. *Kenning* (1833) 9 Bing. 618.
[76] *Mayer* v. *Isaac* (1840) 6 M. & W. 605.
[77] *Hitchcock* v. *Humfrey* (1843) 5 M. & Gr. 559.

"In consideration of your agreeing to supply goods to F.K. at 2 months' credit, we agree to guarantee his present or any future debt with you to the amount of £60."[78]

"In consideration of the credit given by the H.G. Co. to J.P. for coal supplied by them to him, I hereby hold myself responsible as a guarantee to them for the sum of £100, and in default of his payment of any accounts due I bind myself by this note to pay to the H.G. Co. whatever may be owing to an amount not exceeding the sum of £100."[79]

"I, T.M. will be answerable for £50 sterling that W.Y., butcher, may buy of J.H." [It appeared from the surrounding circumstances that a continued supply of stock by the plaintiff, a dealer, to the principal, a butcher, was contemplated.][80]

"In consideration of the Union Bank agreeing to advance and advancing to R. & Co. any sum or sums of money they may require during the next 18 months, not exceeding in the whole £1,000, we guarantee the payment of any such sum as may be owing to the said bank at the expiration of the said period of 18 months and hereby undertake to pay the same on demand in the event of R. & Co. making default in the payment of the same."[81]

In reply to a request for a guarantee for the price of particular goods to be supplied by the Plaintiffs to D., the Defendants wrote giving such guarantee and adding:

" . . . having every confidence in him, he has but to call upon us for a cheque and have it with pleasure for any account he may have with you." The Plaintiffs afterwards supplied still further goods to D. It was held that they were also covered by the guarantee.[82]

"We request you to accept the drafts of W.P.L. in your London House at 60 days' sight to the extent of £1,000 and we undertake to provide you with funds to meet such acceptances before maturity."[83]

---

[78] *Makin* v. *Wright* (1845) 6 Q.B. 917.
[79] *Wood* v. *Priestner* (1866) L.R. 2 Ex. 66, 282.
[80] *Heffield* v. *Matthews* (1869) L.R. 4 C.P. 595.
[81] *Laurie* v. *Scholefield* (1869) L.R. 4 C.P. 622.
[82] *Nottingham Hide, Skin, etc. Co.* v. *Bottrill* (1873) L.R. 8 C.P. 694. See also *Burgess* v. *Eve* (1872) L.R. 13 Eq. 450.
[83] *Browning* v. *Baldwin* (1879) 40 L.T. 248. See also *Simpson* v. *Manley* (1831) 2 C. & J. 12; *Australian Joint Stock Bank* v. *Bailey* [1899] A.C. 396.

Non-continuing guarantees: examples

The following have been held not to be continuing guarantees:

"You may let L. have coals to £50 for which I will be answerable at any time."[84]

"I.V., hereby engages to be responsible for liabilities incurred by M. & V. to the extent of £50 to A. & Co."[85]

"I engage to guarantee payment of A.M. to the extent of £60 at quarterly account, bill two months, for goods to be purchased by him of W. & D. M."[86]

"I hereby agree to be answerable to K. for the amount of five sacks of flour to be delivered to W.T. payable in one month."[87]

"I hereby agree to be answerable for the payment of £50 from T.L., in case T.L. does not pay for the gin, etc., which he receives from you and I will pay the amount."[88]

"You having agreed to advance to Messrs. H. S. & Co. a sum not exceeding £5,000 on deposit of their lease ... and policies ... we hereby undertake and agree to guarantee, and indemnify you to the extent of £800 each, or to the extent of a sixth part of any deficiency of the said advance that may remain due to you after the sale of the said lease; this undertaking being given on the understanding that the said lease shall be sold and the purchase money realised before we are severally called upon for the deficiency (if any) and that this guarantee shall last for a period not exceeding two years from this date."[89]

Where amount is limited

A limitation of the amount risked by the surety, whatever its form, does not prevent a guarantee being continuing so as to cover to the extent named the balance ultimately due from the debtor. Where, however, the limiting words are meant to define a particular transaction contemplated, a guarantee is not

[84] *Bovill* v. *Turner* (1815) 2 Chit. 205.
[85] *Chalmers* v. *Victors* (1868) 18 L.T. 481.
[86] *Melville* v. *Hayden* (1820) 3 B. & Ald. 593.
[87] *Kay* v. *Groves* (1829) 6 Bing. 276.
[88] *Nicholson* v. *Paget* (1832) 1 C. & M. 48. But see *Mayer* v. *Isaac* (1840) 6 M. & W. 605.
[89] *City Discount Co.* v. *McLean* (1874) L.R. 9 C.P. 692.

continuing. For instance, a bond reciting a general agreement by the obligees, as bankers, to discount bills and pay and advance money for the principal, and conditioned for the payment of the sums for the time being due, with a limit in amount, is a continuing guarantee.[90] But where, though the condition was general, the recital referred only to an agreement to advance a definite amount, the security was held not to be continuing.[91]

Promissory notes and bonds

Where a promissory note is given by a surety the presumption is that it is given to secure a definite advance or an existing debt, and it lies upon the creditor to show that it was intended by the surety to stand as security for the ultimate balance on a running account.[92] Where the document itself suggests the contrary, the material thing to show is not that the principal delivered it to the creditor as such security, but that the surety gave it as such.[93] The same applies where the document itself indicates that an existing debt is contemplated, as where a bond was conditioned for payment of a sum with interest from the date of the bond,[94] or that a definite advance is intended, as where a note was payable, not on demand, but on a future day.[95] The case of *Pease* v. *Hirst*,[96] where a promissory note payable on demand with interest was treated as a continuing security, is not inconsistent with this principle. It was taken there that the intention in fact was that it should be so. Moreover, in that case, even had it not been a continuing security, the result would have been the same, as the advance covered by the note was kept outstanding on the accounts notwithstanding subsequent credits.[97] Where the sureties in a bond after the date at which, if not a continuing security, the bond would have been satisfied by payments in account, wrote letters treating the bond as still available to cover the creditor, the court treated this as showing that it was always intended as a continuing security.[98] In any case, a collateral memorandum between the parties defining the

---

[90] *Batson* v. *Spearman* (1838) 9 A. & E. 298. And see *Williams* v. *Rawlinson* (1825) 3 Bing. 71; *Parker* v. *Wise* (1817) 6 M. & S. 239; *Seller* v. *Jones* (1846) 16 M. & W. 112; *Gee* v. *Pack* (1863) 33 L.J. Q.B. 49; *Gordon* v. *Rae* (1858) 8 E. & B. 1065; *Henniker* v. *Wigg* (1843) 4 Q.B. 792; *Laurie* v. *Scholefield* (1869) L.R. 4 C.P. 622.

[91] *Kirby* v. *Duke of Marlborough* (1813) 2 M. & S. 18 see *ante*, p. 43.

[92] *Re Boys* (1870) L.R. 10 Eq. 467. See *Ex p. Brook* (1815) 2 Rose 334; *Walker* v. *Hardman* (1837) 4 C. & F. 258. *Cf. Ex p. Whitworth* (1841) 2 M. D. & De G. 164.

[93] *Walker* v. *Hardman* (1837) 4 C. & F. 258.

[94] *Ibid.*

[95] *Re Boys* (1870) L.R. 10 Eq. 467.

[96] (1829) 10 B. & C. 122.

[97] See too *Ex p. Whitworth* (1841) 2 M.D. & De G. 164.

[98] *Henniker* v. *Wegg* (1843) 4 Q.B. 792.

object of a promissory note, and what it was given to cover, will have effect given to it.[99]

In *Woolley* v. *Jennings*,[1] a warrant of attorney given by the debtors themselves, with the following defeasance[2]: "The within warrant of attorney is given to secure the payment of the sum of £4,000 with lawful interest thereon," was held a continuing security on the ground that there was nothing expressed to the contrary. This, however, was not the case of a surety at all, and the debtors who gave the warrant of attorney were, when they gave it, dealing upon a current account with the persons to whom it was given and to this account it was obviously applicable.

4. *Limitations in Time*

A continuing guarantee may either be subject to a limit of time within which the liabilities which are to be covered by it must be contracted, and at the end of which it will expire *ipso facto* without any express revocation[3]; or it may be unlimited in that respect, in which case it will cover all liabilities falling within its scope, until put an end to, where that is possible, by revocation.[4]

Limitation introduced by recital

The condition of a bond given by a surety in general terms will be restricted in construction by a recital qualifying the duration of the engagement of the principal. Thus in *Lord Arlington* v. *Merricke*,[5] a surety bond reciting an employment of the principal for six months was conditioned for his due accounting during all the time he should be employed. The surety was held not liable for default after the six months. Similarly, where a bond was given to one of two partners to secure him against default by the other, the partnership, as was recited, being for five years, it was conceded that the bond only covered defaults in respect of matters occurring during those five years, though the partner-

---

[99] *Hartland* v. *Jukes* (1863) 1 H. & C. 667.

[1] (1826) 5 B. & C. 165.

[2] A collateral and contemporaneous deed containing certain conditions on the performance of which the appropriate bond, etc., is undone.

[3] What is here referred to is a maximum limit of time, which may not prevent the security being revoked before that limit is reached. There may also be a limit of time named as a maximum within which it shall not be revoked. This subject is discussed *post*, p. 63. For a case dealing with the construction of a guarantee of present and future performance see *Newman Industries Ltd.* v. *Indo-British Securities Ltd.* [1956] 2 Lloyd's Rep. 279, *per* Sellers J. and [1957] Lloyd's Rep. 219, C.A.

[4] See *post*, p. 59.

[5] (1672) 2 Williams' Saund. 411a. See also *Horton* v. *Day*, cited *ibid.* at p. 414; *African Co.* v. *Mason*, cited (1733) 1 Str. p. 227; *Liverpool W.W. Co.* v. *Atkinson* (1805) 6 East. 507; *Sansom* v. *Bell* (1809) 2 Camp. 39; *Webb* v. *James* (1840) 7 M. & W. 279; *Bamford* v. *Iles* (1849) 3 Exch. 380; *N.W. Ry.* v. *Whinray* (1854) 10 Exch. 77 *Cf. ante*, p. 43.

ship was afterwards to continue.[6] But a provision that on the death of a surety another is to be found will generally be read to be merely for the protection of the creditor, and the estate of the deceased surety (if otherwise liable) will not be discharged by a new surety becoming bound in pursuance of such a provision.[7]

In *Coles* v. *Pack*,[8] the guarantee was worded as follows:

> "I do hereby, in consideration of your forbearing to take immediate steps for recovery of the said sum (outstanding debts to the amount of £2,205. 3s. 9d., covered by a guarantee of the defendant), guarantee the payment of and agree to become responsible for any sum of money for the time being due from D.F. to you whether in addition to the said sum of £2,205. 3s. 9d. or not."

This was held unlimited as to time as well as in amount, and not confined to the time during which the sum involved was outstanding on the former guarantee.

Guarantees for officers appointed for fixed periods

A guarantee in general terms for the faithful discharge of duties of an office which by law is annual, or under an appointment made in fact for a year only, does not extend beyond the year,[9] although the legal period of the office[10] or the time for which the appointment has actually been made[11] is not recited; and the mere assent of a surety to a reappointment does not renew his liability.[12]

If, though the appointment is annual only, there are words in the bond expressly extending the surety's engagement to future years, they must, naturally, have effect,[13] as where the guarantee was for money to be received upon any reappointment to the office.[14] But mere general words such as, "at all times hereafter during the continuation of such his employment",[15] or a

---

[6] *Small* v. *Currie* (1854) 2 Drew. 102.

[7] *Re Ennis* [1893] 3 Ch. 238.

[8] (1869) L.R. 5 C.P. 65.

[9] *Wardens of St. Saviour's, Southwark* v. *Bostock* (1806) 2 B. & P.N.R. 175; *Hassell* v. *Long* (1814) 2 M. & S. 363; *Curling* v. *Chalklen* (1815) 3 M. & S. 502; *Peppin* v. *Cooper* (1819) 2 B. & Ald. 431; *Leadley* v. *Evans* (1824) 2 Bing. 32; *Bamford* v. *Iles* (1849) 3 Exch. 380; *Kitson* v. *Julian* (1854) 4 E. & B. 854.

[10] *Wardens of St. Saviour's Southwark* v. *Bostock, supra; Hassell* v. *Long, supra.*

[11] *Kitson* v. *Julian* (1854) 4 E. & B. 854; *Bamford* v. *Iles* (1849) 3 Exch. 380; *Mayor of Birmingham* v. *Wright* (1851) 16 Q.B. 623.

[12] *Kitson* v. *Julian, supra.*

[13] *Augero* v. *Keen* (1836) 1 M. & W. 390: *Mayor of Berwick on Tweed* v. *Oswald* (1856) 1 E. & B. 295; *Mayor of Dartmouth* v. *Silly* (1857) 7 E. & B. 9.

[14] *Ibid.*

[15] *Liverpool W.W. Co.* v. *Atkinson* (1805) 6 East 507; *Peppin* v. *Cooper* (1879) 2 B. & Ald. 431; *Bamford* v. *Iles* (1849) 3 Exch. 380; *Kitson* v. *Julian* (1854) 4 E. & B. 854.

reference to the "successors" of the obligees,[16] or to "rates or taxes which might thereafter be imposed" which the officer would have to collect,[17] or to future statutes which might govern his duties,[18] being all capable of being read as provisions for contingencies which might happen within the year, do not, if the office is annual, continue the liability of a surety beyond the year.

Guarantees for officers in other cases

If the office is not annual, but is held from year to year until determined, the guarantee covers it until that event happens[19]; and this notwithstanding the fact that the superior officer who is secured by the bond is an annual officer.[20] The same applies with sureties for a tenant from year to year.[21] A mere reduction of salary corresponding to a reduction of duties, or a reduction of rent in consideration of the surrender of a small portion of the premises, do not of themselves constitute a determination of the office or tenancy and a reappointment or reletting, so as to prevent, on that ground, the guarantee continuing applicable.[22] But such a change might discharge the surety, as being a variation of the principal obligation capable of prejudicing him.[23]

Guarantees of tenancy

Where there is a surety for a tenant, and the tenancy is determined by a notice to quit, which is afterwards withdrawn, the surety is not liable in respect of the obligations of the tenant after the date for which the notice to quit was given, it being, after that date, a new tenancy.[24] But if the tenancy is brought to a close at the date on which the notice to quit would in fact have brought it to a close, if that had not been withdrawn, though it

---

[16] *Leadley* v. *Evans* (1824) 2 Bing. 32.

[17] *Warden of St. Saviour's Southwark* v. *Bostock* (1806) 2 B. & P.N.R. 175; *Hassell* v. *Long* (1814) 2 M. & S. 363; *Peppin* v. *Cooper* (1819) 2 B. & Ald. 431.

[18] *Mayor of Cambridge* v. *Dennis* (1858) E. B. & E. 660.

[19] *Frank* v. *Edwards* (1852) 8 Exch. 214.

[20] *McGahey* v. *Alston* (1836) 1 M. & W. 386; *Frank* v. *Edwards, supra.*

[21] *Holme* v. *Brunskill* (1878) 3 Q.B.D. 495, 504.

[22] *Frank* v. *Edwards* (1852) 8 Exch. 214; *Holme* v. *Brumskill, supra.*

[23] This happened in *Holme* v. *Brunskill, supra.* In *Frank* v. *Edwards, supra* the condition of the bond could alone be looked at; so this point could not arise.

[24] *Giddens* v. *Dodd* (1856) 3 Drew 485; *Tayleur* v. *Wildin* (1868) L.R. 3 Ex. 303. So where the guarantee was for the fidelity of the holder of an office who resigned and was reappointed at a larger salary: *Toames* v. *Foley* [1910] 2 I.R. 277. The effect of waiving a notice to quit served on a yearly tenant is to create a fresh tenancy: *Freeman* v. *Evans* [1922] 1 Ch. 36. The surety of rent of a business tenancy is not liable for rent accruing due for the period in which the tenancy is statutorily extended: *Junction Estates Ltd.* v. *Cope* (1974) 27 P. & C.R. 482. See also Chapter 14.

purported to be given for an earlier date, the surety is bound to the end of the tenancy.[25]

Guarantees to cover bills

Where a guarantee "to continue in force for a year" is given to secure repayment of moneys which may become payable by the acceptor of bills, or to cover other similar future contingent liabilities, the question will arise whether the limit of time applies to the maturity of the liability or to the transaction out of which it grows. It was decided in *Hollond* v. *Teed*,[26] upon such a guarantee that bills accepted payable before the date when it would have in the ordinary course expired were covered, although the guarantee was subsequently determined by the death of the guarantor before the maturity of the bills. It was expressly pointed out, however, that this did not decide what the effect would be if bills payable at a future date were accepted on the day preceding the contemplated expiry of the guarantee.

Guarantees expiring on a certain date to cover bank overdrafts

In the case of a guarantee of a bank overdraft where the guarantee was expressed to expire on a certain date, it was held that the liability under the guarantee nevertheless continued but was limited to the sum due as at the date on which the guarantee expired.[27]

Revocation of guarantees not under seal

A continuing guarantee not under seal for future advances or supplies, in consideration of the granting of such advances or supplies, as it does not become binding until the person to whom it is given acts upon it, may be revoked before it is acted upon.[28] And even if it has been acted upon, it may, if it contain no stipulation to the contrary, be revoked as to further transactions.[29] The reason for this as given by the Court of Common Pleas in *Offord* v. *Davies*,[30] is that each advance is a

---

[25] *Holme* v. *Brunskill* (1878) 3 Q.B.D. 495.

[26] (1848) 7 Hare. 50.

[27] See *Westminster Bank Ltd.* v. *Sassoon* (*The Times*, November 27, 1926) and Vol. V, *Legal Decisions affecting Bankers* (1955 ed.) at p. 19 where the Court of Appeal upheld the decision of Rowlatt J. reported in *The Times*, June 8, 1925. Note *Wright* v. *New Zealand Farmers Co-operative Association of Canterbury* [1939] A.C. 439 where a guarantee for goods supplied was held to constitute a liability by the surety for the balance due from time to time up to the termination of the guarantee.

[28] *Offord* v. *Davies* (1862) 12 C.B. (N.S.) 748.

[29] *Ibid.* And see *Coulthart* v. *Clementson* (1879) 5 Q.B.D. 42, 46; *Beckett* v. *Addyman* (1882) 9 Q.B.D. 783, 791; *Lloyds* v. *Harper* (1880) 16 Ch.D. 290, 314, 318, 320.

[30] (1862) 12 C.B. (N.S.) 748.

separate transaction, the view apparently being that the guarantee is divisible as to each advance, and ripens as to each advance into an irrevocable promise or guarantee only when the advance is made.[31] It has been held, too, that the acceptor of bills for the accommodation of another, who endorses them over, may reclaim the bills in the hands of the indorsee, if at the time they fall due there is nothing owing to him from the party accommodated.[32] But if not so reclaimed they will stand, if originally intended as a continuing security, as cover for subsequent advances.[32]

Where, however, a continuing guarantee for the price of future advances or supplies is under seal, this reasoning cannot apply. And it seems that at common law no right to determine a future operation of security exists in such cases.[33] In *Hough* v. *Warr*[34] it was suggested before Abbot C.J., that after receipt of notice of revocation the advances could not be considered as in fact made upon the guarantee. It was intimated, however, that the only relief was in equity, though the decision proceeded on the ground that at any rate the point ought to have been specially pleaded. It ought to be noted that in that case, as in other cases referred to above,[34a] the guarantee was not for divisible advances or the like, but for the performance of the duties of an employment, to which special considerations apply[35]: but, apart from this, it is hard to see on principle how any bond or specialty guarantee could at common law be got rid of by a mere notice from the obligor.[36]

Principle in equity

But whatever may have been the common law rule, there seems no reason to doubt that in equity a guarantor in a continuing guarantee under seal for future indebtedness can, where the consideration is "fragmentary, supplied from time to time, and therefore divisible,"[37] prohibit by notice the further use of the guarantee.

In *Burgess* v. *Eve*,[38] Malins V.-C., speaking of a guarantee under seal to a bank for future advances, said that he had no

---

[31] See *per* Bowen J. in *Coulthart* v. *Clementson* (1879) 5 Q.B.D., at 46; *Lloyd's* v. *Harper* (1880) 16 Ch.D. 290, 314, 318, 320.
[32] *Atwood* v. *Crowdie* (1816) 1 Stark 483. See *Sturtevant* v. *Ford* (1842) 4 M. & Gr., at p. 106, note.
[33] *Hassell* v. *Long* (1814) 2 M. & S. 363 at 370; *Calvert* v. *Gordon* (1828) 7 B. & C. 809; 3 M. & Ry. 124; *cf.* the report of this case in 7 L.J. (o.s.) K.B. at 77; *Hough* v. *Warr* (1824) 1 C. & P. 151.
[34] *Supra.*
[34a] See note 33, *supra.*
[35] See *post*, p. 62.
[36] See, too, *Burgess* v. *Eve* (1872) L.R. 13 Eq. 450, 460.
[37] *Per* Lush L.J. in *Lloyd's* v. *Harper* (1880) 16 Ch.D. at 319; *Re Crace* [1902] 1 Ch. 733 at 738.
[38] (1872) L.R. 13 Eq. 450, 460.

doubt that, if the guarantor found the customer untrustworthy, he was entitled, on payment of what had been advanced up to date, to get the guarantee back, and that advances made after notice not to advance more would in equity, upon the principle of *Hopkinson* v. *Rolt*,[39] not be chargeable upon the security. In *Beckett* v. *Addyman*,[40] where the guarantee was by bond, the court clearly thought that its continuance as a future security might be interrupted by notice to the creditor. In *Coulthart* v. *Clementson*,[41] and *Lloyd's* v. *Harper*,[42] though the instruments before the court in those cases were not under seal, the right to determine a guarantee is affirmed in general terms without anything to suggest that guarantees under seal were excluded. "It may be considered equitable and right," said James L.J., in the latter case, "that where a man is not under any obligation to make further advances or to sell further goods, a person who has guaranteed repayment of such advances, or payment of the price of the goods, may say, 'Do not sell any further goods or make any further advances. I give you warning that you are not to rely on my guarantee for any further advances which you make, or any further goods you sell.' That might be in many cases a very equitable view. It might perhaps be hardly equitable for a banker or merchant to go on making advances after receiving a distinct notice from a guarantor that he would not further be liable."

It is submitted that this reasoning applies to all guarantees, whether under seal or not, where the dealings between the principals, which may give rise to the liability guaranteed, can be at once put an end to; and that the right to determine is not subject to the rather vague limitation suggested in *Burgess* v. *Eve* that the principal must have been "found untrustworthy." Such limitation is only necessary in cases where, unless the principal has been "found untrustworthy," the creditor is bound to continue to trust him, and a continuing relation, created on the strength of the guarantee, would be left uncovered by the determination, as a continuing security, of the guarantee.[43]

[39] (1861) 9 H.L.C. 514.
[40] (1882) 9 Q.B.D. at 791.
[41] (1879) 5 Q.B.D. at 46.
[42] (1880) 16 Ch.D. 290.
[43] See *Lloyd's* v. *Harper* (1880) 16 Ch.D. at pp. 305, 306. The previous edition of this work commented that the phrase "revocation of the guarantee" is apt to cause some confusion. The right of the surety is not so much to revoke the security (which, if it is a deed, is hardly intelligible) as to call upon the creditor not to give, and upon the principal not to take, further advances upon it. The principle depends, perhaps, upon the relation between the principal and the surety. The surety has the right to call upon the principal to pay off debts that have been incurred upon the guarantee and it seems only just, seeing that there is no consideration (in such cases as those above considered) between the principal and the surety, that the surety should be able to call upon the principal not to incur further debts. The creditor, being notified of this, and having no right on his part to insist on further advances being accepted by the principal suffers no wrong in not being allowed to collude with the principal further to charge the surety.

No revocation where consideration moves once for all

The right to revoke a guarantee by notice forthwith does not, however, exist where the consideration moves to the principal once for all; as where he was elected to a member of Lloyd's, which membership he was entitled to retain until he did some act which under the rules deprived him of his right to retain it,[44] or where he obtains a lease[45] or an office or employment which cannot be arbitrarily determined.[46]

A guarantee of the rent of a cottage held on a weekly tenancy has, however, been held to be revocable.[47]

Where principal has committed default

Where the principal has committed any defaults or breaches of duty, whether amounting to dishonesty or not, under such circumstances that the employer might have dismissed him, the surety is regarded in equity as entitled to call on the employer to dismiss him, even though the guarantee be under seal.[48] Upon the discovery of misconduct, the whole foundation for the continuation of the contract as regards the surety fails,[49] and the master, who knows that the surety anticipated good conduct, has no just claim to continue the employment at the risk of the surety in the altered circumstances against his will.

Whether surety can require principal liability to be determined by notice

It is an open question whether, if there is no misconduct, the guarantee must go on for an indefinite period or whether the guarantor may not, to obtain his release, take advantage of provisions in the contract itself, performance of which is guaranteed, for its determination by the parties to it. It seems extraordinary that a surety for rent upon a tenancy from year to year should continue bound, and perhaps his estate after death,[50] during the joint lives of the landlord and tenant (which, if they are both corporations, might be for ever), because neither party will give notice to determine the tenancy; or that a surety for a servant must wait for and take the risk of alleging actual

---

[44] *Lloyd's* v. *Harper* (1880) 16 Ch.D. 290.
[45] *Ibid.* at p. 319.
[46] *Burgess* v. *Eve* (1872) L.R. 13 Eq. 450. As to offices held during pleasure see *Reilly* v. *Dodge* 131 N.Y. 153, 29 N.E. 1011 (1892) discussed in Simpson, *Suretyship* (West 1950) at p. 56.
[47] *Wingfield* v. *de St. Croix* (1919) 35 T.L.R. 432.
[48] *Shepherd* v. *Beecher* (1725) 2 P.W. 288; *Burgess* v. *Eve* (1872) L.R. 13 Eq. 450; *Phillips* v. *Foxall* (1872) L.R. 7 Q.B. 666; *Sanderson* v. *Aston* (1873) L.R. 8 Ex. 73.
[49] *Philips* v. *Foxall, supra.*
[50] See *Lloyd's* v. *Harper* (1880) 13 Ch.D. 290. *Cf. post*, p. 64.

misconduct, and cannot take the more moderate course of asking that notice be given to determine the service.

This, however, seems to have been the view of Joyce J., in *Re Crace*, though the judgment on this point was *obiter*.[51]

What is sufficient notice of revocation

Notice determining the continuance of a guarantee need not by law be in writing, but it is frequently stipulated in guarantees that it must be so; and so it may be specified that the writing shall fulfil certain conditions, as that it must be addressed to such and such person (especially if the creditor is a firm or company), or be signed by the surety, etc.[52] Further, it is often stipulated that the guarantee shall continue until a given period after notice of revocation shall have been given.[53] In such cases the right of revocation, at any rate where the guarantee has been once acted upon, must be limited in accordance with the stipulation.[54] A guarantee not under seal, which has not been acted upon can be revoked independently of any stipulation to that effect. This is because the transaction has never progressed beyond the stage of a proposal and there is no consideration binding upon the proposed guarantor.[55]

Right of revocation may be limited by express stipulation

It may, again, be stipulated that a guarantee shall continue for a fixed period; or for a fixed period and, in default of a stipulated notice to determine it, a further fixed period; or for a series of fixed periods until determination by such notice or by such event as may be stipulated.[56] And such stipulation, where the guarantee is given in consideration of a reward payable to the guarantor, may be relied upon by the guarantor to enable him, if the guarantee has not been determined as stipulated, to recover his fee from the party liable to pay it.[56] But if it is

---

[51] [1902] 1 Ch. 733, following *Gordon* v. *Calvert* (1828) 2 Sim. 253. See also *Burgess* v. *Eve* (1872) L.R. 13 Eq. 450, 459, 460; *Hassell* v. *Long* (1814) 2 M. & S. 363 at 370; *Calvert* v. *Gordon* (1828) 7 B. & C. 809 and 3 M. & Ry. 124. But *cf.* report in 7 L.J. (o.s.) K.B. 77; *Hough* v. *Warr* (1824) 1 C. & P. 151. In the United Kingdom in considering this point in the case of a contract of employment, one must bear in mind the relevant legislation. See Employment Protection (Consolidation) Act 1978, as amended by the Employment Act 1980.

[52] *Harris* v. *Fawcett* (1872) L.R. 15 Eq. 311; *Coulthart* v. *Clementson* (1879) 5 Q.B.D. 42.

[53] *Ibid.*

[54] *Ibid.* and see *Bradbury* v. *Morgan* (1862) 1 H. & C. 249.

[55] See *Offord* v. *Davies* (1862) 12 C.B. (N.S.) 748. *Cf. ante*, p. 59.

[56] See *Solvency Mutual Guarantee Co.* v. *Froane* (1861) 7 H. & N. 5; *Solvency Mutual Guarantee Co.* v. *Freeman, ibid.* at p. 17. In *Egbert* v. *National Crown Bank* [1918] A.C. 903 the Privy Council held on the construction of the guarantee in that case that it was irrevocable except by notice given by all the guarantors, and that a notice given by one of them was inoperative. This decision is of importance in the context of revocation in the case of a guarantee by several guarantors. See the following section in the text.

intended that the guarantee should, in default of this agreed notice, run on indefinitely, from period to period, that intention should be clearly expressed. Where it was a condition that, from the expiration of the original term, the guarantee should "be treated as a renewed contract of the like nature and conditions," unless either party should give two months' notice of an intention not to renew, it was held that only one renewal, and not renewal from time to time, was meant.[57]

The ordinary phrase in a continuing guarantee to the effect that the guarantor guarantees for such and such a period repayment of advances, etc., made to the principal, does not import that the guarantee is necessarily to continue for that period, but only that it will *ipso facto* cease to be available for advances after that date. Consequently, in such a case the right to revoke before that period is not excluded by such language.[58]

Revocation in case of guarantee by several guarantors

Where a guarantee was entered into by several guarantors and provided that it should be continuing "until the undersigned or the executor of the undersigned shall have given the bank notice in writing to make no further advances," it was held that notice by only one executor was ineffective.[58a]

Death of guarantor

As to the effect of the death of the guarantor by way of revocation of a guarantee, several difficult questions have arisen. In the case of a guarantee not under seal (whether continuing or limited to an isolated transaction) for further advances or supplies, where the making of such advances is the only consideration for the guarantee, and when there is no obligation to make them, the question will arise as to what is the result of the death of the guarantor before any advances are made. The guarantee at the moment of the death would seem to amount to an offer only, there being as yet no consideration to make it binding.[59] If, as has been assumed to follow from the decisions on questions of agency, an offer is revoked by the death of the maker *ipso facto*, though no notice of it reach the person to whom it was made before he accepts it by performance, it might

---

[57] *Solvency Mutual Guarantee Co.* v. *Froane, supra.*

[58] *Offord* v. *Davies* (1862) 12 C.B. (N.S.) 748.

[58a] See note 56, *supra.*

[59] See *Offord* v. *Davies, supra; Coulthart* v. *Clementson* (1879) 5 Q.B.D., 42, 46; *Beckett* v. *Addyman* (1882) 9 Q.B.D. 783, 791; *Lloyd's* v. *Harper* (1880) 16 Ch.D. 290. It seems that the offer should be taken as intended to remain open notwithstanding the death, if unknown to the recipient of the offer. See *Chitty on Contracts* (24th ed., 1977), Vol. I at para. 47.

be said that in the case of such a guarantee the creditor would not be covered if he made the advances after, though without notice of, the death of the guarantor. However, in *Bradbury* v. *Morgan*,[60] there is a dictum directly to the contrary. "If the guarantee," said Bramwell B., "had been in these terms, 'I request you to deliver to A tomorrow morning goods to the value of £50, and in consideration of your doing so I will repay you', and before the morning the guarantor died, but the goods were duly delivered, I can see no reason why the personal representative of the guarantor should not be liable." In that case the guarantee had been acted upon, and the question was only as to the effect of the death of the guarantor as to further advances made subsequently. In such circumstances, at any rate, it is now settled that the death of the guarantor does not put an end to the continuance of the security, unless it comes to the knowledge of the creditor.[61]

Where, however, it does come to his knowledge, it was held by Bowen J., in *Coulthart* v. *Clementson*,[62] that the right to continue advances upon the security ceases unless the guarantee contains a provision for special notice not confined to the case where the guarantor is still alive. The principle followed by Bowen J., was that notice of the death of a surety, and that he left a will, is notice of the creation of new interests in the property liable to be applied in satisfaction of the guarantee, which cannot be assumed to be compatible with the continuance of the security, and that the guarantee must, therefore, be taken to have been determined, unless the will has provided for its continuance. This reasoning, however, as pointed out in the Irish case of *Re Whelan*,[63] must apply *a fortiori* to an intestacy. The question of the effect of notice of the death of a surety in a continuing guarantee was treated as an open one in by the Court of Appeal in *Beckett* v. *Addyman*[64] and *Re Sherry*.[65] The reasoning of Bowen J. in *Coulthart* v. *Clementson*[66] has been disapproved by Romer J. and Joyce J.[67] but was acted upon by the Vice-Chancellor in Ireland in *Re Whelan*.[68]

Where the guarantee contains a stipulation that it shall be

[60] (1862) 1 H. & C. 249 at 255, 256.
[61] *Bradbury* v. *Morgan, supra; Harris* v. *Fawcett* (1873) L.R. 15 Eq. 311; *Coulthart* v. *Clementson* (1879) 5 Q.B.D. 42.
[62] *Supra.*
[63] [1897] 1 I.R. 575.
[64] (1882) 9 Q.B.D. at 792.
[65] (1884) 25 Ch.D. at 703, 705.
[66] (1879) 5 Q.B.D. 42.
[67] *Re Silvester* [1895] 1 Ch. 573 at 577 (where, however, there was a special provision for notice applicable after the death of the surety); *Re Crace* [1902] 1 Ch. 733 (where there was no such special provision).
[68] See note 63, *supra.*

withdrawn only upon a certain notice from the guarantor, but the terms of such stipulations show that it can refer only to a notice given by the guarantor during his life, as where it has to be under his hand, the effect of notice of death of the guarantor is held not to be subject in its operation to revoke the guarantee to the terms of the stipulation as to the length of the notice which the guarantor himself would have been required to give; and the revocation may therefore be immediate.[69] This is so even in cases where the stipulation as to the length of notice might be read as binding the executor, and the notice is to be taken as given at once if the principal is to the knowledge of the creditor the executor, and under a duty to the estate to terminate the guarantee.[70] But where there is merely notice of the death and of the existence of a will, it is not to be assumed that it would be a breach of trust to omit to give the special notice required, without which the guarantee by the terms of it runs on.[71]

Revocation by notice of the death of the guarantor, however, can only take place where the guarantee is such as, apart from special stipulation, might have been required by the guarantor himself at any moment.[72]

Death of surety only jointly bound

Where the surety is only bound jointly with his principal, or with another surety,[73] and not severally also, his whole liability both for existing and future debts of the principal comes to an end with his death, and the survivor or survivors become alone liable both at law and in equity unless it can be shown that the security was made joint by mistake, and was intended to be joint and several.[74] But the death of one joint and several surety in a continuing guarantee for advances to be made does not, even when notified to the creditor, prevent the surviving surety remaining liable for further advances.[75] Nor does the death of one guarantor have such effect even if the guarantee was joint only, and not joint and several.[76]

---

[69] *Coulthart* v. *Clementson* (1879) 5 Q.B.D. 42.

[70] See *Harris* v. *Fawcett* (1873) L.R. 8 Ch. App. 866.

[71] *Re Silvester* | 1895| 1 Ch. 573.

[72] This appears to follow from *Re Crace* |1902| 1 Ch. 733.

[73] See *Pratt's Trustees* v. *Pratt* |1936| 3 All E.R. 901 on whether an equitable charge can be created between co-sureties.

[74] *Rawstone* v. *Parr* (1827) 3 Russ. 424, 539; *Jones* v. *Beach* (1852) 2 De G.M. & G. 886; *Other* v. *Iveson* (1855) 3 Drewr. 177.

[75] *Beckett* v. *Addyman* (1882) 9 Q.B.D. 783.

[76] *Ashby* v. *Day* (1885) 33 W.R. 631. This point was not dealt with in the Court of Appeal (1886) 34 W.R. 312 but see 54 L.T. 410.

The death of the principal debtor before he has committed default, discharges the surety, at least in circumstances where the obligation of the principal ceases upon death.[77]

Lunacy of guarantor

Lunacy of a guarantor operates as a revocation from the date of notice to the creditor.[78]

Bankruptcy of guarantor

It seems that the bankruptcy of a surety would not operate as the revocation of a guarantee.[79] But under the Bankruptcy Act 1914, the guarantee would not be put an end to by the discharge of a bankrupt guarantor.[80]

5. *Limitation in Amount*

Two forms of limitation

Besides a possible limit as to time, a guarantee may be subject to a limit upon the amount for which the surety may be liable. This may be effected either by restricting the application of his promise to a certain amount only of the debt or of the ultimate balance, or by naming a sum as the maximum which he shall pay, although the whole debt or ultimate balance is guaranteed.[81]

This distinction is highly material where the principal is bankrupt and the question is whether the surety is liable to the full extent of his guarantee for the balance remaining after deducting the dividends paid by the estate of the principal on the whole debt, or only for the amount of his guarantee less the dividends attributable to a part of the debt equal to that amount.[82] In whichever form the limit upon the surety's risk is imposed, its functions are confined to limiting the actual amount payable by the surety, and words introduced with that object will not prima facie be read as meaning that the guarantee shall be exhausted when the creditor has once made advances totalling the amount guaranteed, in other words, the guarantee

---

[77] *Sparrow* v. *Sowgate* (1621) W.Jo. 29.
[78] *Bradford Old Bank* v. *Sutcliffe* [1918] 2 K.B. 833.
[79] *Boyd* v. *Robins* (1859) 5 C.B. (N.S.) 59.
[80] Bankruptcy Act 1914, s. 28(4).
[81] See *Ellis* v. *Emmanuel* (1876) 1 Ex. D. 157; *Ulster Bank Ltd.* v. *Lambe* [1966] N.I. 161; *Re An Arranging Debtor* [1971] N.I. 96. *Ellis* v. *Emmanuel* was applied and discussed in *Forster Dry Cleaning Co. Ltd.* v. *Davidson* (1963) 187 E.G. 519 *per* Plowman J.
[82] *Ibid.* See *post*, p. 99.

is not continuing,[83] or that it is made a condition that the sum owing by the principal shall not exceed that sum, so that the surety is not liable, if it does.[84]

Where a bond was given to a banker conditioned for the repayment of advances with interest and charges, with a proviso that the principal moneys to be recovered on the bond should not exceed £250, it was held by a majority of the Court of Queen's Bench that not more than £250 and interest on that amount should be recovered, and that the obligor was not liable for interest on the balance of the advances.[85] Where two persons by one instrument guaranteed "the sum of £400, in the proportion of £200 each," it was held that each was liable for a separate £200, but neither liable for more."[86]

Limitation introduced by recital

A limitation of the amount guaranteed may be introduced by the recital,[87] or, in a more informal document, by the terms of the request by the surety for the credit or advance to the principal, in consideration of which he promises,[88] even though the subsequent promise itself may be in general words. So where a surety wrote, "I beg that you will continue to advance the sum of £2 per week to Mr. B., and I hereby engage to repay you all moneys you may advance to him in addition to the £24 which you have already let him have at my request to this date" he was held liable only for the £2 per week and the £24 and not for other advances which had been made since the letter.[88]

6. When the Liability of the Surety Attaches

Guarantees for future advances or credit

A guarantee for which the consideration is a future advance, supply, or other credit, the forbearance of any existing liability, or the withdrawal of any existing process, is not binding until the creditor acts upon it,[89] and performs the consideration. The surety will become liable as soon as the consideration is performed without notice from the creditor of its performance.[89]

---

[83] See the continuing guarantees set out *ante* pp. 51–53.
[84] See *post*, p. 81.
[85] *Meek* v. *Wallis* (1872) 27 L.T. 650.
[86] *Fell* v. *Goslin* (1852) 7 Exch. 185.
[87] *Ibid.* And see *ante*, p. 000.
[88] *Smith* v. *Brandram* (1841) 2 M. & Gr. 244.
[89] *Offord* v. *Davies* (1862) 12 C.B. (N.S.) 748; *Westhead* v. *Sproson* (1861) 6 M. & N. 728; *Morrell* v. *Cowan* (1877) 6 Ch.D. 166, 7 Ch.D. 151.

Notice of the performance of an act upon which a liability is to arise need only be given where such act is unknown to anyone save the creditor, as where liability is to arise on his election to do or refrain from doing something.[90] Where the act is to give credit, discontinue proceedings, or even intimate that proceedings will be discontinued, no notice of performance need be given to the guarantor.

Acceptance of offer of guarantee

This is, however, true only of concluded guarantees. Where a letter is addressed by one person to another the true effect of which is only to offer a guarantee, the offer must be accepted, or notice given that the document is about to be treated as a concluded guarantee.[91] Where a guarantee is offered, and references named for approval, the person to whom it is addressed must give notice that he has approved,[92] or, if he waives the references, must give notice that he waives them.[93]

7. Parties

Guarantees enforceable by trustees on behalf of others

A bond or guarantee, whether under seal,[94] or not, may be given to a trustee on behalf of third persons to secure the performance of obligations to those persons, as, for instance, obligations to be incurred towards a shifting body like an unincorporated association,[95] or towards unknown persons,[96] or intending shareholders in a company,[97] or the persons to whom, whether members or not, the person guaranteed should be under liability in respect of business done at Lloyd's.[98] In such cases the obligee is bound to enforce the security for the protection of those concerned, and can recover for them the full damages which they have incurred.[98] So the holders of a guarantee given

---

[90] *Alhusen* v. *Prest* (1851) 6 Exch. 720.

[91] *Melver* v. *Richardson* (1813) 1 M. & S. 557; *Symmons* v. *Want* (1818) 2 Stark. 371; *Mozley* v. *Tinkler* (1835) 1 C.M. & R. 692; *Morten* v. *Marshall* (1863) 2 M. & C. 309; *Bank of Montreal* v. *Munster Bank* (1876) 11 Ir. R.C.L. 47; *cf. Sorby* v. *Gordon* (1874) 30 L.T. 528; *Gaunt* v. *Hill* (1815) 1 Stark 10; *Pope* v. *Andrews* (1840) 9 C. & P. 564; *Nash* v. *Spencer* (1896) 13 T.L.R. 78.

[92] *Mozley* v. *Tinkler, supra; Marten* v. *Marshall, supra.*

[93] *Morten* v. *Marshall* (1863) 2 H. & C. 305.

[94] See *Lloyds* v. *Harper* (1880) 16 Ch.D. 290.

[95] *Metcalf* v. *Bruin* (1810) 12 East 400. *Cf. McGahey* v. *Alston* (1836) 1 M. & W. 386; *Worth* v. *Newton* (1854) 10 Exch. 247.

[96] *Lamb* v. *Vice* (1840) 6 M. & W. 467; *Stansfield* v. *Hellawell* (1852) 7 Ex. 373.

[97] *Hallet* v. *Taylor* (1921) 6 Ll. L.R. 416.

[98] *Lloyd's* v. *Harper* (1880) 16 Ch.D. 290. *Cf. Leathley* v. *Spyer* (1870) L.R. 5 C.P. 595. But see *Cosford* v. *Poor Law, etc., Association* (1910) 103 L.T. 463 at 465 *per* Phillimore J.

to them jointly can recover the amount of the default by the principal for the benefit of those among them whom it may concern, although no joint damage can be shown[99]; and one partner can sue alone on behalf of his firm upon a guarantee for a debt owing to the firm given to him alone.[1] This principle applies even when the obligee is not, strictly speaking, in a position of a trustee, provided that it appears from the instrument creating or evidencing the obligation that it was the intention of the parties to that instrument to protect the persons who have actually suffered the damage. It need not appear that the person so intended to be protected had any right to the protection or even was informed of it at the time. Thus, in the Irish case of *Kenney* v. *Employers' Liability Insurance Corporation*[2] the mortgagees of an estate appointed a receiver under their statutory power and took a bond from the defendants conditions for the due discharge by the receiver of his duties as such. The receiver made default, but the mortgagees by selling the estate were paid their demand in full. It was held by the Irish Court of Appeal that the mortgagees could recover under the bond the amount of the default for the benefit of the mortgagor, notwithstanding that they were under no duty to the mortgagor to take the bond at all, or having taken it, to put it in suit on his behalf. With this case may usefully be contrasted *Re British Power, etc., Co.*[3] There a receiver and manager in a debenture holders' action properly incurred and was held to be entitled to be indemnified by the estate against trade liabilities for £900, but was deficient in his cash account by £400 which he could not pay, and it was held that trade creditors had no rights against the receiver's sureties, inasmuch as their bond was given to secure the estate and the estate had suffered no loss.[4]

Guarantees of minors' debts

In the case of guarantees of minors' debts it has now been decided in *Coutts & Co.* v. *Browne-Lecky*[5] that once a guarantee, as distinct from an indemnity is found to exist, no liability will attach to the guarantor for what is in essence no debt at all.[6]

---

[99] *Pugh* v. *Stringfield* (1858) 4 C.B. (N.S.) 364.

[1] *Agacio* v. *Forbes* (1861) 14 Moo. P.C. 160.

[2] [1901] 1 I.R. 301; *cf. Robertson* v. *Wait* (1853) 8 Exch. 299.

[3] [1910] 2 Ch. 470; *cf. Re Barned's Banking Co., ex p. Stephens* (1868) L.R. 3 Ch. 753; *Sheers* v. *Thimbleby* (1897) 76 L.T. 709.

[4] The judgment is directed to the point that the trade creditors had only the rights of the receiver against the estate, but this was only material on the basis that the sureties were not liable except for loss to the estate, and as going to show that there had been no such loss.

[5] [1947] K.B. 104.

[6] See E. J. Cohn (1947) 10 M.L.R. 40.

Stadium Finance Co. Ltd. v. *Helm*[7] although in the result endorsing this view, appears to have involved a concession that the particular guarantee of a minor's void debt was unenforceable.[8] One resolution of this problem may be to treat such a guarantee as enforceable if the guarantor knew the debtor was a minor,[9] in which case his promise is in effect the assumption of primary liability, *i.e.* an indemnity.

Persons who may sue although not named in guarantee

Generally speaking, the person to sue on a guarantee must be the person named therein as party[10] but a guarantee given to an agent, as representing his principal, for a debt due to his principal,[11] or given to a partner for his firm[12] may be issed upon by the principal or the firm, as the case may be. The benefit of a guarantee is usually assignable.[13]

Moreover, a letter of credit, written in order to be shown, promising to honour bills to be drawn upon the writer, particulars of which were to be endorsed upon the letter, constitutes an offer which will make the writer liable to persons who act upon it.[14] Where the defendant, upon the occasion of a run upon a bank, undertook, by a notice addressed to the inhabitants of the neighbourhood, to be accountable for the payment of the notes of the bank "so far as £30,000 would extend," it was held he could not be sued by an individual holder who had taken some of the notes after notice of the undertaking.[15] The discounters of bills accepted for the accommodation of the drawers cannot enforce a guarantee or indemnity, of which they had notice, given by third parties to the acceptors to protect them against liability.[16]

---

[7] (1965) 109 S.J. 44.

[8] *Per* Steyn, "The Co-Extensiveness Principle" (1974) 90 L.Q.R. 246 at 253.

[9] Steyn, at *op cit.* p. 253. See also Furmston (1961) 24 M.L.R. 644 who points out that the problem is now less important in practice than formerly and that in any event the appropriate documents ought to be drafted as indemnities to invoke the rule applied in *Yeoman Credit Ltd.* v. *Latter* [1961] 1 W.L.R. 828 whereby the indemnifier of an infant's contract will be bound.

[10] But see *Alcoy, etc.* v. *Greenhill* (1897) 76 L.T. 542. *Cf. Brandt* v. *Dunlop* [1905] A.C. 454 at p. 462.

[11] *Bateman* v. *Phillips* (1812) 15 East 272.

[12] *Walton* v. *Dodson* (1827) 3 C. & P. 162; *Garrett* v. *Handley* (1825) 4 B. & C. 664.

[13] See *Wheatley* v. *Bastow* (1855) 7 De G.M. & G. at 279; *Re Barrington* (1804) 2 Sch. & L. 112; *Re Hallett & Co.* [1894] 2 Q.B. 256; *British Union* v. *Rawson* [1916] 2 Ch. 476; *Bradford Old Bank* v. *Sutcliffe* [1918] 2 K.B. 837. *Cf. Sheers* v. *Thimbleby* (1897) 76 L.T. 709 *per* Chitty L.J. In *Sacher Investments Pty. Ltd.* v. *Forma Stereo Consultants Pty. Ltd.* [1976] 1 N.S.W.L.R. 5 the fact that the guarantors of rent under a lease had covenanted with the lessor "its successors and assigns" did not *per se* allow them to sue upon the guarantee in the absence of an assignment however informal.

[14] *Re Agra and Masterman's Bank* (1870) L.R. 2 Ch. App. 391 *Cf. Autocar, etc., Insurance* v. *London J.C. and M. Bank* (1924) 19 Ll. L. R. 292. See generally Gutteridge and Megrah, *The Law of Bankers' Commercial Credits* (6th ed., 1979), Chap. 5.

[15] *Phillips* v. *Bateman* (1872) 16 East. 356.

[16] *Re Barned's Banking Co., ex p. Stephens* (1868) L.R. 3 Ch. App. 753.

Limited to transactions between the principals named: Partnership Act 1890, s. 18

Unless a contrary intention appears, a guarantee to or for a given person or number of persons will prima facie not cover debts incurred to or by such person or persons and others, or to or by some only of those persons,[17] nor to the executors of the original obligee,[18] even if a time was named for the continuance of the guarantee, and the debt was incurred within that time.[19] This rule in the case of guarantees given to or for firms, (with regard to which the question has mainly arisen) is now declared by section 18 of the Partnership Act 1890[20] which is as follows:

> "A continuing guaranty . . . given either by a firm or to a third person in respect of the transactions of a firm is, in the absence of agreement to the contrary, revoked as to future transactions by any change in the constitution of the firm to which, or of a firm in respect of the transactions of which, the guaranty . . . was given."

Examples

The difficulty, both before the statute and since, has been to determine whether an intention that the guarantee shall continue sufficiently appears. Where a bond was given to trustees for an unincorporated association the changes in the membership of which were proved to number from 50 to 100 in a year, conditioned for the due accounting of a clerk "during his continuance in the service of the said company, to the said company or to such persons as the court of directors thereof for the time being should appoint . . . and for the indemnity of the said company and the directors and all the members thereof," it was held that the security continued notwithstanding changes in the members of the company.[21] There is no difficulty in providing by proper words that the security should continue notwithstanding a change in the persons intended to be secured.[22] The point is that the surety may rely on the discretion

---

[17] *Wright* v. *Russell* (1774) 3 Wils. 530; *Myers* v. *Edge* (1797) 7 T.R. 254; *Bellairs* v. *Ebsworth* (1811) 3 Camp. 53; *Strange* v. *Lee* (1803) 3 East 484; *Dance* v. *Girdler* (1804) 1 B. & P. N.R. 34; *Weston* v. *Barton* (1812) 4 Taunt. 673; *Simson* v. *Cooke* (1824) 1 Bing. 452; *Dry* v. *Davy* (1839) 10 A. & E. 30; *Bank of Scotland* v. *Christie* (1841) 8 C. & F. 214; *Spiers* v. *Houston* (1829) 4 Bligh (N.S.) 515; *Chapman* v. *Beckinton* (1842) 3 Q.B. 703; *Hollond* v. *Teed* (1848) 7 Hare 50; *Montefiore* v. *Lloyd* (1863) 15 C.B. (N.S.) 203; *London Assurance Co.* v. *Bold* (1844) 6 Q.B. 614; *Mills* v. *Alderbury Union* (1849) 3 Exch. 50; *Backhouse* v. *Hall* (1865) 6 B. & S. 50.
[18] *Barker* v. *Parker* (1786) 1 T.R. 287.
[19] *Pemberton* v. *Oakes* (1827) 4 Russ. 154; *Chapman* v. *Beckinton* (1842) 3 Q.B. 703; *Hollond* v. *Teed* (1848) 7 Hars 50.
[20] Replacing s. 4 of the Mercantile Law Amendment Act 1856.
[21] *Metcalf* v. *Bruin* (1810) 12 East 400.
[22] See *Strange* v. *Lee* (1807) 3 East. 484.

of a particular obligee or principal to prevent any loss occurring.[23]

Knowledge of intended changes in firms

The mere fact that a surety for an intended agent knows that the agent is about to take a partner does not make him responsible for the default of the firm, unless the circumstances show that the surety contemplated that the firm was to have the agency[24] and where the surety is bound for an agent who has an existing partner, knowledge of that fact by the surety only makes clearer his intention to limit his liability to the acts of the agent personally.[25] So where a surety became bound for money to be received by a treasurer to guardians, and the guardians paid their money into an account of their own with a bank in which the treasurer was a partner, drawing cheques on that account for their payments, it was held that the surety was not responsible; and he recovered back a payment which he had made to the guardians in ignorance of the facts.[26]

But surrounding circumstances may show that the guarantee was intended to cover debts incurred by the principal named and his partner. Thus, in *Leathley* v. *Spyer*,[27] a guarantee given to the committee of Lloyd's to secure the debts which a proposed member might incur, had been revoked, and then afterwards renewed after the sureties had learned that the principal had taken a partner. By the rules of Lloyd's only one partner in a firm could be a member; but by means of a "substitute's ticket" another partner could deal for him. It was held that the guarantee as renewed covered the debts of the firm, whether resulting from dealings of the partner named in the guarantee or those of the other partner acting for him.[28]

Intention to cover credit to be given after change in firm to be clearly expressed

Similar to the principle declared by the Partnership Act 1890, it has often been held that a guarantee is not extended to transactions entered into after a change in the creditors merely by the use of words which can be read as providing for the case of

---

[23] See *Myers* v. *Edge* (1797) 7 T.R. 254, 255; *per* Mansfield C.J., in *Weston* v. *Barton* (1812) 4 Taunt. at pp. 681, 682; *Backhouse* v. *Hall* (1865) 6 B. & S. 507 at 519; *Strange* v. *Lee* (1807) 3 East. 484, 490.
[24] *Bellairs* v. *Ebsworth* (1811) 3 Camp. 53; *London Assurance Co.* v. *Bold* (1844) 6 Q.B. 514; *Montefiore* v. *Lloyd* (1863) 15 C.B. (N.S.) 203.
[25] *Mills* v. *Alderbury Union* (1849) 3 Exch. 590; *London Assurance Co.* v. *Bold, supra.*
[26] *Mills* v. *Alderbury Union, supra.* And see *Lacey* v. *Hill* (1872) L.R. 8 Ch. App. 441.
[27] (1870) L.R. 5 C.P. 595.
[28] See also *Bank of British North America* v. *Cuvillier* (1861) 4 L.T. 159.

debts being incurred towards some of the obligees on behalf of all, or of defaults being committed towards the new body arising out of transactions with the old.

A bond given to five persons, bankers, to secure repayment to the five, their executors or administrators, of certain advances to be made by them "or any of them," was held not to cover advances made by four of them after the death of one, the words "or any of them" being read as merely providing for the case of an advance made by some on behalf of the five.[29] The same applied where the condition was for repayment to the obligees, or "either of them," of all moneys advanced "at their banking house."[30] And where the bond was for advances to meet bills drawn by S.C. and T.C. (who were described in the bond as partners), "or either of them, or any other person authorised by them or either of them," it was held not to cover advances to meet bills drawn after the death of one of them.[31] Similarly, where the bond, reciting that E.P. had taken J.H. into his employment as "clerk to the said E.P.," was conditioned for due accounting by J.H. to "the said E.P., his executors or administrators," it was held that these words did not extend the obligation to moneys received by the clerk after the death of the obligee and as the servant of the executors, but only to money in his hands at the date of the death.[32]

When the bond recited a co-partnership for a term of years between three persons, of whom one was to be acting partner, and was conditioned for the honesty of the acting partner "during such time as he shall continue the acting partner in the said trade or business of the said co-partnership," it was held that defaults after the death of one partner were not covered, although the time from which the partnership had been entered into had not expired, and the partnership deed contained provisions for the transmission of the share of a deceased partner and a continuance of the business.[33] Where a guarantee to a firm was expressly framed to cover debts which might be incurred to the survivors of the surviving partners, it was held that it did not apply after the death of one partner, where under his will and pursuant to the articles his representatives assumed his share in the business and intervened in every way as partners.[34]

Where a bond, given for a firm of three, was expressed to cover

[29] *Weston* v. *Barton* (1812) 4 Taunt. 673.
[30] *Strange* v. *Lee* (1803) 3 East 484.
[31] *Simson* v. *Cooke* (1824) 1 Bing. 452.
[32] *Barker* v. *Parker* (1786) 1 Term Rep. 287.
[33] *Chapman* v. *Beckinton* (1842) 3 Q.B. 703.
[34] *Pemberton* v. *Oakes* (1827) 4 Russ. 154.

also the defaults of the survivors or survivor of them, and of any future partners of them or either of them, it was held that defaults after the retirement of one of the original partners were not covered.[35]

In *Backhouse* v. *Hall*,[36] decided after the Mercantile Law Amendment Act 1856, but before the Partnership Act, the guarantee was for advances to be made to "the firm of G. W. & W. J. Hall, shipbuilders." The business so described was really, as both plaintiff and defendant knew, carried on by S. Hall, E. Hall, and G. E. Moore. It was held that the mere use of the firm name in the guarantee did not show an intention that it should continue after a change in the then partners. But where a bond was conditioned for indemnifying certain plaintiffs against costs awarded to "the defendants," it was held that costs awarded to one defendant, the other having died, were covered by the words of the condition.[37] Where a guarantee was to extend to all the engagements of C to the obligee "in trade and commerce," it was held in the Privy Council that it covered debts incurred after C had taken in a partner.[38] Where a bond was given to the governors of an unincorporated society for due accounting by the collector of the society, to the governors or their successors, it was held that defaults after the society had been incorporated were not covered.[39]

Form of instrument intended to operate notwithstanding changes in firm

Where it is intended that a bond or guarantee should continue to enure for the benefit of a firm, notwithstanding changes in its composition, this should not perhaps, as a point of form, be specified in that part of the instrument which describes the obligees or addressees of the guarantee, for these cannot be a shifting body.[40] There is no objection to the persons to whom the debts secured shall be payable being a shifting body, and being so described in the condition of a bond or in the body of a guarantee; and the original obligees, or the survivor or his representatives, will be trustees to enforce the bond or guaran-

[35] *University of Cambridge* v. *Baldwin* (1839) 5 M. & W. 580.
[36] (1865) 6 B. & S. 507.
[37] *Kipling* v. *Turner* (1821) 5 B. & Ald. 261.
[38] *Bank of British North America* v. *Cuvillier* (1861) 4 L.T. 159. The principal, who had previously carried on business with two others of whom one had died and the other was absent, apparently obtained the guarantee in order to carry on the business. It seems to have been contemplated that he would or might have partners. Their Lordships considered that the decisions upon changes in the construction of a firm had no bearing on the question in that case.
[39] *Dance* v. *Girdler* (1804) 1 B. & P.N.R. 34.
[40] *Dance* v. *Girdler, supra.* A bond given to a firm by a firm name could be sued upon by those who were the members at the date of the bond; *Moller* v. *Lambert* (1810) 2 Camp. 548.

tee for the creditors for the time being.[41] A promissory note payable to order and deposited with a firm to secure a debt may, of course, as a negotiable instrument, be enforced directly by the indorsees for the time being[42]; but, if not endorsed, it should be sued upon by the original payees or the survivors of them.[42] And it will be inferred that such a note given to a firm, upon the face of which the maker does not appear to be merely a surety, is intended to continue as security notwithstanding any changes in the firm.[42]

Amalgamation of companies

Where a bond was given to a railway company to secure the payment over of moneys to be received by a booking clerk at a station jointly used by that and two other railway companies for the three railways, the surety was held bound for defaults after the company to which the bond had been given had been by statute amalgamated with one of the others under the name of the latter, the statute likewise transferring the rights of action.[43] So, where two railway companies were amalgamated by statute, which enacted that the new company should be entitled to enforce all the bonds, etc., belonging to the old, and should take over its staff, it was held that a surety for a clerk to one of the old companies was bound for defaults after the amalgamation, notwithstanding the increase of business.[44]

Principal's appointment to new office

Where a bond was given to overseers to secure the faithful execution of his office by an assistant overseer, who was bound to accept for all moneys received by him, not to the overseers, but to the person or persons duly authorised to receive the same when required by the overseers or vestry, and the assistant overseer was appointed an overseer by the justices, it was held that such appointment did not affect the liability of the surety, first, because the possibility that he might use his position to prevent the accounts being called for by the overseers was too remote; and, secondly, because the change was made not by the obligees but by the justices.[45]

---

[41] See *ante*, p. 69. The object of the parties is commonly attained by inserting a clause to the effect that the guarantee shall subsist notwithstanding changes in the parties secured. This in point of law operates on the theory explained in the text.

[42] *Pease* v. *Hirst* (1829) 10 B. & C. 122.

[43] *L.B. & S.C. Ry.* v. *Goodwin* (1849) 3 Exch. 320.

[44] *Eastern Union Ry.* v. *Cochrane* (1853) 9 Exch. 197 *Cf. Wilson* v. *Craven* (1841) 8 M. & W. 584.

[45] *Worth* v. *Newton* (1854) 10 Exch. 247.

8. *What Principal Liability is Covered*

General rule

A guarantee will only extend to a liability precisely answering the description contained in the guarantee.[46] The onus is upon the creditor to show that the surety consented to any alteration.[47] But the surety can afterwards ratify his liability, though the principal contract has been varied or only partly performed.[48] "It must always be recollected," said Lord Westbury in *Blest* v. *Brown,*[49]

> "in what manner a surety becomes bound. You bind him to the letter of his engagement. Beyond the proper interpretation of that engagement you have no hold upon him. He receives no benefit and no consideration. He is bound therefore, merely according to the proper meaning and effect of the written engagement that he entered into. If that written engagement be altered in a single line, no matter whether it be altered for his benefit, no matter whether the alteration be innocently made, he has a right to say, 'the contract is no longer that for which I engaged to be surety: you have put an end to the contract that I guaranteed, and my obligation, therefore, is at an end.' "

Immaterial variations

With regard to any alterations "for the benefit" of the surety, a surety is not discharged by a change which is not contrary to any express stipulation and could only operate for his benefit.[50] If the creditor releases a portion of the principal debt, the surety remains liable for the remainder.[51] This applies where the change is in respect to a matter not reasonably capable of being considered by the surety, either from its bearing on the risk or in any other way, as of any importance whatever; as where a bond was given for the good conduct of an engineer to be employed in

[46] Often referred to as the principle of co-extensiveness. See Else Mitchell, "Is a Surety's Liability Co-extensive with that of the Principal?" (1941) 63 L.Q.R. 355, and Steyn, "Guarantees, the Co-Extensiveness Principle" (1974) 90 L.Q.R. 246; see generally Chapter 8 of this work; *Compania Sudamericana de Fletes S.A.* v. *African Continental Bank* [1973] 1 Lloyd's Rep. 21 (guarantee whereby party's obligation under charterparty containing arbitration clause fulfilled); British Columbia Law Reform Commission, Report on Suretyship (1979) Ch. IX.

[47] *General Steam Navigation Co.* v. *Holt* (1858) 6 C.B. (N.S.) 530.

[48] *Ex p. Ashwell* (1832) 2 Deac. & Ch. 281; *Mayhew* v. *Crickett* (1818) 2 Swanst. 185.

[49] (1862) 4 De G. F. & J. 367, 376. And see *Straton* v. *Rastall* (1788) 2 T.R. 366, 370; *Bacon* v. *Chesney* (1816) 1 Stark. 192.

[50] *General Steam Navigation Co.* v. *Rolt* (1858) 6 C.B. (N.S.) 550 at 575; *Holme* v. *Brunskill* (1878) 8 Q.B.D. 495 at 507.

[51] See *Hollier* v. *Eyre* (1840) 9 C. & F. 1 at 57. *Holme* v. *Brunskill* (1878) 3 Q.B.D. 495 at 507. *Cf. Egbert* v. *National Crown Bank* [1918] A.C. 903.

India "at a salary to commence from his embarkation at Southampton," and his employers sent him overland, it was held that the surety was bound.[52] But any change, either contrary to express stipulation or such as cannot plainly be seen without enquiry to be insubstantial or necessarily beneficial to the surety,[53] will discharge him whether in fact prejudiced or not.[54] Where a surety gave a bond to secure an obligee being indemnified according to a deed providing for a partnership for five years between the obligee and the principal, and the partnership was not wound up at the end of the five years, but was continued, the surety was held to have been discharged.[55]

Change in office, duties of which are guaranteed

A guarantee given for the due performance of the duties of an office created by the law applies only so long as it remains the same office, though its tenure or duties are not recited in the guarantee,[56] unless the guarantee is so expressed as to cover the office after the alteration.[57] It was held in *Bartlett* v. *Att.-Gen.*,[58] that a guarantee for a collector of customs did not extend to a new duty, afterwards imposed by statute, which the collector was by a new deputation appointed to collect. A surety for a county court bailiff was held not liable after the duties of the office had been largely extended by legislation, even for defaults in the performance of duties which existed at the date of the bond.[59]

A mere reduction in the salary of an officer whose office is created by law, accompanied by a reduction of the duties performance of which is guaranteed, the office itself remaining the same, will not put an end to a guarantee in which the salary

---

[52] *Evans* v. *Earle* (1854) 10 Exch. 1.

[53] *Holme* v. *Brunskill* (1878) 3 Q.B.D. 495 (where it was held that this was a question to be decided by the court, as distinct from being left to the jury); *Whitcher* v. *Hall* (1826) 5 B. & C. 269. The rule has often been applied. See *e.g. Adelaide Motors Ltd.* v. *Byrne* (1963) 49 M.P.R. 197; *Bell* v. *National Forest Products Ltd.* (1964) 45 D.L.R. (2d.) 249; *Nelson Fisheries Ltd.* v. *Boese* |1975| 2 N.Z.L.R. 233. Note however that the acceptance by the creditor of wrongful repudiation by the debtor is not such a change or variation. *Moschi* v. *Lep Air Services Ltd.* |1973| A.C. 331.

[54] See *Blest* v. *Brown* (1862) 4 De G.F. & J. at 376; *General Steam Navigation Co.* v. *Rolt* (1858) 6 C.B. (N.S.) at 575; *Holme* v. *Brunskill* (1878) 3 Q.B.D. at 507. In *Burnes* v. *Trade Credits Ltd.* |1981| 2 All E.R. 122, the Privy Council held that an increase in the rate of interest from 9 per cent. to 16 per cent. was not a liability which was contemplated by the guarantee. It was also held that it could not be said to constitute the granting to the principal debtor of "any other indulgence or consideration" such as to dispense with the guarantors' consent.

[55] *Small* v. *Currie* (1854) 5 De G.M. & G. 741.

[56] *Oswald* v. *Mayor of Berwick-upon-Tweed* (1856) H.L.C. 856, 866; *Pybus* v. *Gibb* (1866) 6 E. & B. 902. And see *Wardens of St. Saviour's, Southwark* v. *Bostock* (1806) B. & P.(N.S.) 175; *Hassell* v. *Long* (1814) 2 M. & S. 363; *Wembley U.D.C.* v. *Local Government, etc., Association* (1901) 17 T.L.R. 516.

[57] *Oswald* v. *Mayor of Berwick-upon-Tweed, supra*; but *cf. R.* v. *Herron* |1903| 2 I.R. 474.

[58] (1709) Parker 277. *Cf. Skillett* v. *Fletcher* (1867) L.R. 1 C.P. 217, *post*, p. 82.

[59] *Pybus* v. *Gibb* (1866) 6 E. & B. 902. See also *Malling Union* v. *Graham* (1870) L.R. 5 C.P. 201; *Holland* v. *Lea* (1854) 9 Exch. 430; *N.W. Ry.* v. *Whinray* (1854) 10 Exch. 77.

is not referred to.[60] Where a bond was given for a collector of rates for a parish generally, the surety was not liberated because the class of rates assigned to that collector to collect had been changed.[61]

Defaults must be in the performance of the duties guaranteed

Sureties for an officer will only be responsible for defaults in the duties of the office.[62] Sureties for the due accounting by a collector of rates or taxes are not liable for moneys which have been collected illegally as such rates or taxes.[63] It will always be a question upon the construction of the contract, whether the money in the hands of the collector has been collected, even though not quite regularly, in such a way as was contemplated by the surety[64] and if so, unless perhaps where the collection has been quite illegal, and the employers of the collector could not enforce payment over by him to them,[65] the sureties would be liable. Where a banker's clerk was sent eleven miles in the country to fetch money from a customer and lost the money, it was held that the guarantor for the clerk was responsible, though it was not customary for bankers to send a clerk to fetch money as mentioned.[66]

Principal liabilities unconnected with offices

Where the guarantee is for the performance of duties other than those of an office, the principal liability must answer to the guarantee in character, in extent, and in respect of the circumstances out of which it arises. Thus a guarantee for the price of goods to be sold will not cover the amount of bills on third persons, transferred without endorsement in exchange for goods supplied, there being a distinction between payment for goods by bill and transferring bills by way of discounting.[67] A surety on a replevin bond (the condition of which is that the tenant shall prosecute his action for the taking of the distress, and, if unsuccessful, return the things distrained) cannot be made liable for the amount of rent found due to the landlord by

---

[60] *Frank* v. *Edwards* (1852) 8 Exch. 214. But see *Holme* v. *Brunskill* (1878) 3 Q.B.D. 495.
[61] *Portsea Island Union* v. *Whillier* (1860) 2 E. & E. 755.
[62] Even where the holder of the office by statute holds another office besides that guaranteed: *Cosford* v. *Poor Law, etc., Association* (1892) 103 L.T. 463.
[63] *Nares* v. *Rowles* (1811) 14 East. 510; *Weiss* v. *James* (1840) 7 M. & W. 279, 287; *Kepp* v. *Wiggett* (1850) 10 C.B. 35; *Re Walker* [1907] 2 Ch. 120 (moneys received by a receiver in lunacy after the death of the lunatic).
[64] *Mayor of Durham* v. *Fowler* (1889) 22 Q.B.D. 394, 415.
[65] See *Nares* v. *Rowles* (1811) 14 East 510.
[66] *Melville* v. *Doidge* (1848) 6 C.B. 450.
[67] *Evans* v. *Whyle* (1829) 5 Bing. 485.

an arbitrator to whom the action had been referred by a judge's order expressing that the bond should stand as security for the award.[68] Where a surety gave a bond conditioned for payment of bills of exchange, if returned from abroad protested for non-payment, he was held not liable where they had been returned protested for non-acceptance, under circumstances where they might have been protested for non-payment.[69]

Extent of the principal liability

With regard to the extent of the principal contract, in *Whitcher* v. *Hall*,[70] a leading case on this point, where the surety guaranteed rent payable for the milking of 30 cows, and the lessor by agreement with the lessee let him have 32 for a short time and 28 for another short time, which was found to make no difference to the profits, the surety was held not liable, it being a contract for 30, neither more nor less. Where an Act of Parliament authorised the abandonment of part of a railway undertaking, deviations in the route, and an increase of capital, it was held, in a question between the vendor and purchaser of lands which had belonged to a surety in a bond given to the Crown, conditioned for the completion of the undertaking as originally authorised, that the surety (and consequently the land) was discharged.[71] Similarly, a surety for the payment of instalments under a hire purchase agreement was held not liable after the lessor had seized the goods for default in paying such instalments, since by such seizure the agreement and the principal's liability to pay the instalments thereunder were determined.[72]

A guarantee for payment of a bill of £500 will apparently only cover a bill for that amount exactly.[73] But where the contract was, "I hereby guarantee the payment by F. of two bills you intend to renew for him, one for £1,048. 10s. 5d. and the other for £462. 6s. 6d., due respectively on the 28th instant and 4th proximo," it was held by the Court of Appeal, reversing North J., that the guarantee was substantially for the debt and covered two bills drawn in place of the old bills for £1,025. 6s. 11d. and

---

[68] *Archer* v. *Hall* (1828) 4 Bing. 464, following *Bowmaker* v. *Moore* (1816) 3 Price 214; (1819) 7 Price 223.

[69] *Campbell* v. *French* (1795) 6 Term Rep. 200; reversing the decision in C.P. 2 H. Bl. 163.

[70] (1826) 5 B. & C. 269 But *cf. Hoole Urban Council* v. *Fidelity and Deposit Corporation* [1916] 2 K.B. 568.

[71] *Finch* v. *Jukes* [1877] W.N. at 211.

[72] *Hewison* v. *Ricketts* (1894) 63 L.J.Q.B. 711. *Cf. Astley Ind. Trust* v. *Grimston Electric Tools Ltd.* (1965) 109 S.J. 149.

[73] *Philips* v. *Astling* (1809) 2 Taunt. 206.

£485. 10s. 0d. respectively though they also differed from the former bills in parties and in length of currency.[74]

Guarantees for limited amounts

A guarantee for a debt of a certain amount will cover that amount though more is incurred, unless this is contrary to express stipulation. If there is a guarantee for "£500, say a bill," and a bill for more is given, it seems it would be a question of degree whether the excess would prevent the accommodation given up to £500 answering the description.[75]

A guarantee for advances "not exceeding" a certain sum is construed as merely limiting the liability of the surety to that amount, and not, unless it clearly appears to be the intention, as making the liability conditional upon the debtor's liability being limited to that sum.[76] And this construction has been adopted, even where grammatically the limit seems imposed, not upon the liability, but upon the advance.[77] A bond to brewers conditioned to be void if the principal, a publican, from time to time should pay the obligees for all ale, etc., which he should from time to time have had from them, to an amount not exceeding £50, before he should have a fresh supply, was held to cover the debt of the publican, although a fresh supply was granted in spite of there being already an outstanding indebtedness of £50.[78]

Permitting principal to incur other liabilities

Permitting the principal to incur other liabilities to the creditor beyond and separable from the liability guaranteed does not affect the guarantee as to the last-named liability. Thus

---

[74] *Barber v. Mackrell* (1892) 67 L.T. 108.

[75] See *Philips v. Astling* (1809) 2 Taunt. 206. *Cf.* the point argued but not decided in *Pickles v. Thornton* (1875) 33 L.T. 658.

[76] See *Ex p. Rushforth* (1805) 10 Ves. 409; *Paley v. Field* (1806) 12 Ves. 435; *Parker v. Wise* (1817) 6 M. & S. 239; *Seller v. Jones* (1846) 16 M. & W. 112; *Gee v. Pack* (1863) 33 L.J.Q.B. 49; *Backhouse v. Hall* (1865) 6 B. & S. 507; *Gordon v. Rae* (1858) 8 E. & B. 1065; *Laurie v. Scholefield* (1869) L.R. 4 C.P. 622.

[77] *Laurie v. Scholefield, supra.* As pointed out by the South Australian Law Reform Committee Report on Suretyship (39th Report, 1976), para. 3, as the law now stands, a surety may restrict his liability under the contract of suretyship to a certain fixed amount but the creditor can still lend up to any amount and thereby bring into existence other debts which will compete with that of the surety forcing the principal debtor into bankruptcy to produce a liability on the surety quite unintended by him: see, *e.g. Total Oil Products (Austr.) Pty. Ltd. v. Robinson* (1970) 1 N.S.W.L.R. 701. The typical bank guarantee therefore will not make the guarantor's liability conditional upon the principal debtor's liability remaining beneath that sum. See *Queensland National Bank Ltd. v. Queensland Trustees Ltd.* (1899) 9 Q.L.J. 282. The Report therefore suggests that when a creditor advances money to the debtor beyond the limit of liability so imposed and accepted by the creditor without first obtaining the consent of the surety, the latter's liability should be diminished to the extent of those further advances.

[78] *Seller v. Jones* (1846) 16 M. & W. 112.

an office does not cease to be within a guarantee merely because the officer is allowed to contract other liabilities towards his employers, unless this is contrary to stipulation or amounts to the substitution of a new office for that which the surety had in view.[79] In *Bonar* v. *Macdonald*,[80] where a bond was given for the good conduct of a bank official, who joined in the bond and undertook not to become connected with any trade, and afterwards without communication with the surety the official received a rise of salary and became liable for one-quarter of losses on discounts, it was held in the House of Lords, that the bond could not be enforced, even to make good defaults in the course of the original duties of the official, on the ground that there had been an essential change in the principal obligation. Following this decision, it was held in *Pybus* v. *Gibb*[81] that a surety for a county court high bailiff was not liable after the duties had been largely extended by legislation, even for defaults in the performance of duties which existed at the date of the bond. The ground of the decision was that the office was no longer the office mentioned in the bond. Coleridge J., however, seems to suggest that the mere fact that the person to whom a guarantee is given putting collateral liabilities upon the person for whom the guarantee is given operates as a discharge of the surety, because his risks are thereby increased.[82] The dictum, if it means this, was however disapproved in *Skillett* v. *Fletcher*[83] where *Bonar* v. *Macdonald*,[84] is explained as turning on the stipulation that there should be no collateral liabilities,[85] and where *Pybus* v. *Gibb* is supported on the ground that the office which the parties had in view had been changed.

In *Skillett* v. *Fletcher*[86] the bond was for the due performance of his duties by a collector of poor rates and of sewers rates, and was to remain valid if either office was held separately, the breach assigned being default in both capacities. It was held no defence that by Act of Parliament a main drainage rate had been created, of which he had also been appointed collector, and that the sewers rate, though not changed in nature, had been increased by further charges upon it.[87] Similarly, a guarantee

---

[79] *Cf.* in addition to the cases cited on this point, *Eyre* v. *Everett* (1826) 2 Russ. 381.
[80] (1850) 3 H.L.C. 226.
[81] (1856) 6 E. & B. 902.
[82] *Ibid.* at 914.
[83] (1867) L.R. 1 C.P. 217.
[84] (1850) 3 H.L.C. 226.
[85] From Lord Cottenham's speech, which was adopted by the House, this stipulation appears to have been in wider terms than appears from the statement at the commencement of the report.
[86] See note 83, *supra.*
[87] See also *Worth* v. *Newton* (1854) 10 Exch. 247. *Cf. Bartlett* v. *Att.-Gen.* (1709) Parker 277, *ante,* p. 78.

for the faithful service of a clerk will not be put an end to by a mere extension of the business of his employer.[88]

The transaction out of which the liability guaranteed is to spring

The question whether a given liability is covered by a given guarantee must not be considered merely with reference to the extent and incidents of the liability itself, which is imposed upon the principal. It is also necessary that the transaction as a whole out of which it springs should be such as was contemplated by the surety. A very strong instance of this is *Blest* v. *Brown*.[89] In that case the defendant had given a bond, reciting that M. had entered into a contract with the Government for the supply of a certain quantity of bread, and had applied to the obligees to supply him with flour "to enable him to carry out such contract," which the obligees had agreed to do, and conditioned for the payment of the price of "the flour so supplied as aforesaid." It turned out that the flour, which was supplied in good faith to the order of the contractor, did not comply with the requirements of the Government contract. The surety was held not liable, because the vendor was by the terms of the bond bound to know (whether in fact he did or did not know) what those requirements were.[90] But where the defendant guaranteed to the plaintiffs, a firm in New York, acceptance and payment of any bills, to be drawn on him on his account by his agent in Charlestown, which the plaintiffs should discount, it was held that the plaintiffs were justified in discounting any bill drawn by the agent on the defendant, and represented by the agent to be on the defendant's account, and could recover against the defendant in respect of every such bill, whether in fact drawn on his account or not.[91]

In *Squire* v. *Whitton*,[92] a lady executed a bond (in blank and therefore invalid as a bond) conditioned to secure a "loan." The real transaction, however, was that the obligee permitted the so-called borrower to realise for his own use funds of a trust under which the obligee and his wife (who concurred in the arrangement) were beneficiaries. The Court of Chancery and the House of Lords refused to give effect to the imperfect bond in order to cover such a transaction. And where a promissory note

---

[88] See *L.B. & S.C. Ry.* v. *Goodwin* (1849) 3 Exch. 320, 321. And *cf. Eastern Union Ry.* v. *Cochrane* (1853) 9 Exch. 197.

[89] (1862) 4 De G. F. & J. 367. See also *Vavaseur Trust Co. Ltd.* v. *Ashmore* (1976) (unreported, C.A.), discussed below, note 95.

[90] If the Government had waived the inferiority, the surety might have been liable. See *Oastler* v. *Pound* (1863) 7 L.T. 852, *post*, p. 85.

[91] *Ogden* v. *Aspinall* (1826) 7 D. & R. 637.

[92] (1848) 1 H.L.C. 333.

was given by a lady to secure the floating balance on a bank account, and the bank, after so treating it for three years, upon the eve of the marriage of the lady, in order to make the note "a tangible security" and without apparently consulting the principal, placed £500 to his credit so as to "have it on the passbook before the marriage," Lord Langdale said he would, had it been necessary, have held the surety discharged upon the ground that this was not carrying out the transaction agreed upon.[93]

Where a surety joined in a deed, whereby the principal covenanted to repay to A. all that A. might pay to B., the deed reciting that A. was under a liability to B., the surety was held not to be bound upon it turning out that A. was not in fact liable to B.[94]

The principal must enjoy the full benefit stipulated for

It is essential that the principal should get the full benefit to procure which the surety intervened; otherwise the surety will not be bound.[95] Thus where the debt guaranteed was to be incurred in consideration of the conveyance of property subject to specified incumbrances, and there was another incumbrance unknown to the surety and forgotten by the creditor, the surety was relieved.[96]

Where in consideration that the plaintiffs would give up to W.Y. certain goods upon which they had a lien, and would take his acceptance for £140, the defendant guaranteed due payment of such acceptance, it was held that the plaintiffs could not recover anything, if they only gave up the goods on receiving acceptances for £145.[97] Where a surety guaranteed payment by a building owner of £1,500 in four equal instalments for repairs and decorations to be executed by a builder "subject to the said works being duly executed in accordance with this agreement" and the owner did not pay the first instalment, but it was found that at the date of the writ it was necessary to spend £80 in order

---

[93] *Archer* v. *Hudson* (1844) 7 Beav. 551, affirmed (1846) 15 L.J. Ch. App. 211.

[94] *Lake* v. *Brutton* (1856) 18 Beav. 34.

[95] This passage and some cases cited below, *e.g. Bacon* v. *Chesney* (1816) 1 Stark. 192 and *Blest* v. *Brown* (1862) 4 De C. F. & J. 367 were referred to and discussed in *Vavaseur Trust Co. Ltd.* v. *Ashmore* (April 2, 1976, Court of Appeal, Transcript No. 157 of 1976). *Blest* v. *Brown* was described as a case of "embodied terms," since the guarantee referred to the Government contract but without setting out its terms. In *Vavaseur* the Court of Appeal found, for the purposes of upsetting an order for summary judgment, that it was reasonably arguable that there was an implied term in a guarantee that certain principal fixed term contracts of loan would be adhered to, where there had been a breach of such contracts by the creditor with the principal debtor. See also *Royal Bank of Canada* v. *Salvatori* (1928) 3 W.W.R. 501 P.C.

[96] *Willis* v. *Willis* (1850) 17 Sim. 218. See also *Vavaseur Trust Co. Ltd.* v. *Ashmore* (1976) (unreported, C.A.) discussed in previous note.

[97] *Pickles* v. *Thornton* (1875) 33 L.T. 658.

to complete the work in accordance with the agreement, the surety was held not liable.[98]

Where the guarantee was in consideration of a bank "lending" the principal the sum of £1,000 for seven days from the date of the guarantee, and the bank, without placing £1,000 to his credit, merely honoured cheques upon his current account, which did not create an overdraft of £1,000 within the seven days, it was held that the surety was not liable.[99] Where again a surety joined in a promissory note "for value received by a draft at three months' date," and the creditor advanced cash, the surety was held not liable, though no demand was made upon him until after the three months.[1] On the other hand, a guarantee for "advances" to be made by a bank has been held to include sums placed to the credit of the principal in respect of bills and notes discounted.[2]

Where the defendant gave a continuing guarantee for the price of goods to be supplied, and after goods had been supplied the purchasers being in difficulties called their creditors together, who agreed to continue to supply goods against cash which was to be applied to the existing debts until they were satisfied, it was held that the guarantee did not cover the price of the goods supplied by the plaintiffs, on these terms.[3] So in *Pidcock v. Bishop*,[4] where a surety guaranteed payment for iron to be supplied to the principal, but it had been secretly arranged that 10s. per ton was to be added to the price of each consignment, and was to go in liquidation of an old debt, a verdict for the plaintiff creditor was set aside and a nonsuit entered.

Where a guarantee was given for the price of goods to be supplied to a Government contractor, and the goods were not supplied in time, but the Government waived the consequent delay and the contractor accepted the goods, the surety was held bound for the full price of the goods, though it was alleged that a specially high price had been given by the contractor, owing to the short time allowed for the supply.[5]

Where, in compliance with an order giving conditional leave to defend, two sureties became bound for the amount which

---

[98] *Eshelby* v. *Federated European Bank* [1932] 1 K.B. 254, 423.
[99] *Burton* v. *Gray* (1873) L.R. 8 Ch. App. 932.
[1] *Bacon* v. *Chesney* (1816) 1 Stark. 192; *Bosner* v. *Cox* (1841) 6 Beav. 110.
[2] *Grahame* v. *Grahame* (1887) 19 L.R. Ir. 249. In *Burnes* v. *Trade Credits Ltd.* [1981] 2 All E.R. 122 P.C., it was held that the word "advance" normally implies the furnishing of money for a specified purpose. Therefore the term "further advances" did not cover an extension of the period for repayment of the original principal sum.
[3] *Bastow* v. *Bennett* (1812) 3 Camp. 220.
[4] (1825) 3 B. & C. 605.
[5] *Oastler* v. *Pound* (1863) 7 L.T. 852.

should be recovered from the defendants in the action, and upon the bankruptcy of one of the sureties an order was made, without notice to the other surety, that further security should be found, or in default the judgment should be entered for the plaintiff, and no further security being found judgment was entered without a trial, it was held that the other surety was discharged.[6] Similarly, where judgment was entered by consent for an amount to be paid by instalments.[7]

Variation of terms of principal liability not set forth in guarantee

Where the terms of the principal contract are not set forth in the bond or guarantee of a surety, the rule is laid down in *Holme v. Brunskill*[8] that a material variation in that contract will discharge the surety—a material variation meaning for this purpose any variation which cannot be seen without inquiry to be insubstantial, or one that cannot be otherwise than beneficial to the surety.[8] If this is not self-evident, no inquiry as to the materiality of the variation will be entered on.[9] It is not necessary that the variation should result from an agreement between the creditor and the principal: it is enough if the principal's liability is altered by the exercise of a right by the creditor, such as the forfeiture of shares for non-payment of calls.[9]

In *Calvert v. London Dock Co*,[10] a bond had been given for the performance of the "promises and agreements" in a contract for

---

[6] *Luning* v. *Milton* (1890) 7 T.L.R. 12.

[7] *Tatum* v. *Evans* (1885) 54 L.T. 336.

[8] (1878) 3 Q.B.D. at 505. And see *per* Cockburn, L.J. in *General Steam Navigation Co.* v. *Rolt* (1858) 6 C.B. (N.S.) at 575; and see *Re Darwen and Peace* [1927] 1 Ch. 176, 183, 184 noted in (1927) 163 L.T. 424 and said by Megaw L.J. in *Lep Air Services Ltd.* v. *Rolloswin* [1971] 3 All E.R. 45 to depend on the special terms of the guarantee there involved. See also *Vavaseur Trust Co. Ltd.* v. *Ashmore* (1976) (unreported, C.A.) discussed *supra* at note 95. Most guarantees will make provision for variation of the terms of the principal contract without effecting a discharge of the surety. See Appendix 1. But for a recent illustration of such a clause proving to be ineffective in a particular case, see *Dowling* v. *Ditanda* (1975) 236 E.G. 485. *Holme* v. *Brunskill* was applied in *National Bank of Nigeria Ltd.* v. *Awolesi* [1965] 2 Lloyd's Rep. 389 where a bank guaranteed an "existing" bank account which the Privy Council found on its true construction to contemplate the account as it existed at the date of the guarantee. Consequently by permitting the opening of a second account, the bank allowed a substantial variation of the terms of the principal contract to occur without the guarantor's consent, thereby discharging him. In *National Bank of New Zealand Ltd.* v. *West* [1977] 1 N.Z.L.R. 31 at 33, Casey J. held that a guarantee of all moneys which a bank was "at liberty to charge or debit to the account" of the principal debtor was not wide enough to impose liability for the debtor's own further guarantee of a third party's indebtedness. The learned judge applied Lord Hodson's dictum at p. 315 in *Awolesi* that the way in which the consideration for a guarantee is expressed is not conclusive but may be relevant in construing the terms of the contract itself.

[9] *Re Darwen and Pearce Ltd.*, *supra*. *Stiff* v. *Eastbourne Local Board* (1868) 19 L.T. 408, (1869) 20 L.T. 339. See also *per* Cockburn L.J. in *General Steam Navigation Co.* v. *Rolt* (1858) 6 C.B. (N.S.) at 575.

[10] (1838) 2 Keen 638.

works "which on the part of the contractor were or ought to be performed, according to the true intent and meaning of the contract." The contractee advanced to the principal the retention money provided for by the contract, and the obligor was held discharged in equity, though at law it had been held that he was liable for nominal damages, the condition of the bond not having been performed.[11]

In *Sanderson* v. *Aston*,[12] the guarantee was for the good conduct of a servant, and the plea material for the present purpose alleged that the engagement of the latter had been altered by being made terminable on three months' instead of one month's notice. The term as to notice had not been made part of the surety's contract. The court held that the surety was not discharged, the change being neither a breach of any condition in the guarantee nor material.[13] The latter finding seems to have meant that the engagement of the surety would remain, notwithstanding the alteration, terminable by one month's notice to the servant, so that the alteration could produce no effect on the surety's position.[14] If, however, it was meant (as the language held by Pollock B. seems to imply) that the surety is not discharged if, though the change was capable of operating disadvantageously on the surety's position, the court are of opinion that he is not injured in fact, such a doctrine was disapproved in *Holme* v. *Brunskill*,[15] and is not to be regarded as law.

In *Holme* v. *Brunskill*[15] the guarantee was to secure the redelivery of a flock of sheep, let with a farm called Riggindale. The landlord afterwards accepted a surrender of one field and made a small reduction in rent. The jury found that the variation was not material. In the Court of Appeal it was held that, though the tenancy was not a new one, but still the tenancy which had subsisted when the bond was given, nevertheless the surety was discharged on the ground that the alteration was not one which could be said, without inquiry, to be incapable of prejudicing the surety, and that the question of its materiality could not in effect be litigated. Brett L.J., however, dissented from this judgment, holding that the change, when not violating a specific condition of the surety's contract must be proved to be material.

---

[11] *Warne* v. *Calvert* (1837) 7 A. & E. 143.
[12] (1873) L.R. 8 Ex. 73.
[13] *Cf.*, however, *Nicholson* v. *Burt* (1882) 10 R. 121 (Sc.).
[14] See *per* Pigot B. (1873) L.R. 8 Ex. at 78. This is not the only point, however. The surety might think a servant with a less secure tenure would be more scrupulous in performing his duty.
[15] (1878) 3 Q.B.D. 495.

Application of rule where guarantee is for liability under future transactions not precisely specified

The application of the rule in *Holme* v. *Brunskill*,[15] presents no difficulty, where, as in that case, in *Calvert* v. *London Dock Co.*,[16] and in *Sanderson* v. *Aston*,[17] the guarantee, though in general terms, was given with reference to a principal contract then already negotiated, of the existence of which (though not perhaps of its exact terms), the surety was aware.[18] It would also apply, it is submitted, to cases where the creditor alters in any material particular liabilities already incurred by the principal debtor, and covered by an antecedent general guarantee, even though the alteration would leave the liability such as, if incurred in that form in the first instance, would have been covered by the guarantee.[19]

However, where a guarantee is given in general terms to cover the liabilities which are to result from a future course of dealing generically specified in the guarantee, the creditor can vary the course of dealing under which successive liabilities arise, so long as the course of dealing continues to be of the character coming within the scope of the guarantee, and no change is made in the terms of any liability after it is actually incurred and the guarantee is attached to it.[20] If a course of dealing other than that subsequently adopted had been arranged between the principals at the date of the guarantee, this will not cause the surety to be discharged by the alteration, unless at the time of the giving of the guarantee the surety knew that some arrangement existed, so that the liabilities to arise

[16] (1838) 2 Keen, 638.   [17] (1873) L.R. 8 Ex. 73.

[18] But see *Nicholson* v. *Burt* (1882) 10 R. 121 (Sc.).

[19] The authorities are indistinct on this point. It is established that the surety is discharged if the creditor interferes with the "principal obligation, performance of which is guaranteed." See *Ward* v. *National Bank of New Zealand* (1883) 8 A.C. 755, 763; *Taylor* v. *Bank of New South Wales* (1886) 11 A.C. 596, 603. But this might be taken to refer only to a principal obligation existing or provisionally arranged before the guarantee is entered into, which might be said to be specifically guaranteed, and the terms of which, so far as they can affect the surety, might be considered as incorporated in the guarantee. See *Vavaseur Trust Co. Ltd.* v. *Ashmore* (1976) (unreported, C.A.) discussed *supra* at p. 84. Guarantees to cover transactions entirely in the future, and which permit to the creditor some latitude as to the exact terms on which those transactions shall be arranged, might be treated as standing on a somewhat different footing: it is submitted, however, that the moment the principal comes under any liability to the creditor to which the guarantee attaches, the surety acquires an interest in every term of that liability and that the creditor has no authority to modify it even though he would in the first instance have been within his rights if he had taken it in another form. So much, at any rate, seems warranted by the principle upon which a surety has a vested interest in all collateral securities which the creditor may have taken for the debt, even though he was under no obligation to obtain them, and even though the surety is ignorant of their having been taken, and has not intervened to pay the debt and claim the benefit of them (see *post*, p. 145). In such cases the surety is entitled to relief by way of compensation for the actual loss suffered by him, if such securities are interfered with by the creditor; and the question raised in the text seems to be reduced to this, whether the surety under the circumstances there stated is entitled to any relief beyond such damage as can show himself to have suffered by the alteration. It is submitted that he cannot be compensated in that way when it is the principal obligation itself, and not a mere collateral advantage, that has been interfered with.

[20] *Stewart* v. *McKean* (1855) 16 Exch. 675. And see the following Scottish cases, *Ellice* v. *Finlayson* (1832) 10 S. 345; *Stewart* v. *Brown* (1871) 9 R. 763; *Nicolson* v. *Burt* (1882) 10 R. 121.

out of such arrangement, whatever it might be (and no other), were really the subject matter of the guarantee.[20]

In *Stewart* v. *McKean*,[21] a guarantee was given simply for W.M.'s "intromissions as agent," intromission being a Scottish term signifying dealings by an agent with stock and cash, for which he is accountable. At the time when the guarantee was given a course of dealing had been arranged by which the agent was to account monthly; but the surety was unaware that any arrangement had been made at the date of the guarantee, and knew nothing and never asked about the manner in which the principal was to account, nor the nature of his employment. At first the agent accounted monthly, then every six months, but afterwards it was arranged that he should give promissory notes at four months, which often largely exceeded the amount for which he had to account, and the employers discounted the notes, and when they became due, furnished the agent with cash to the extent by which the amount for which he was then accountable fell short of the amount of the note. The result that the agent accounted monthly instead of ever six months; and, on the other hand, the employers obtained accommodation from him, for which they paid him commission. It was held by the majority of the Court of Exchequer that, the mode of accounting being left open by the surety, he was liable. Pollock C.B. dissented, on the ground that the position of the principal was not such as could have been contemplated by the surety when he guaranteed his intromissions "as agent."

In *Egbert* v. *National Crown Bank*,[22] the guarantee was for further advances, and the creditor and the principal agreed on a higher rate of interest than the creditor could legally charge. It was held by the Privy Council that the agreement as to interest was merely invalid and that therefore the surety was liable for interest at the rate properly chargeable by the creditor against the principal.

Variation of one of several distinct obligations guaranteed

Where the guarantee extends to several distinct debts, duties or obligations, a variation in the nature of one of them not capable of affecting the position of the surety with respect to the other or others will not discharge him as to that other or

---

[21] *Supra.* See *per* Parke B. at 690.
[22] [1918] A.C. 903. See also *Nelson Fisheries Ltd.* v. *Boese* [1975] 2 N.Z.L.R. 233 where it was stated that there must be a variation to effect a discharge, not simply a "waiver" or "default" under the terms of the guarantee.

others.[23] However, a binding agreement to give time to pay instalments in arrears under a hire purchase agreement will discharge a surety not only in respect of those instalments, but from any other further liability in respect of the whole contract.[24]

Assent of surety to variation

A surety will not be discharged by a variation to which the creditor (on whom the onus lies) can show he assented,[25] or which is provided for in the guarantee.[26] This, however, must be an assent to a transaction between the creditor and the principal which the surety knows to be a variation of the contract; he is not put upon inquiry as to every transaction he hears of so as to ascertain whether it is a variation of the contract.[27] Thus a surety for a contractor was released by the advance of the retention money, notwithstanding that he knew of payments which had been made (though he did not know they represented advances in variation of the contract), and notwithstanding that some of the money had come into his own pocket, to be paid over to him by the contractor in respect of independent accounts pending between them.[28] Where the surety takes any active part in the transaction constituting the variation, he is clearly not discharged; as where solicitors, who were sureties, prepared documents referable to the variation.[29] Similarly, if the surety permits the creditor to think he has assented.[30] However, mere knowledge by the surety of an intended variation, against which he does not protest, is not the equivalent of assent, nor is the surety bound to warn the creditor against carrying it out.[31] And guarantors of instalments to be paid on shares will be dis-

---

[23] *Bingham* v. *Corbitt* (1864) 34 L.J.Q.B. 37; *Skillett* v. *Fletcher* (1867) L.R. 1 C.P. 217; 2 C.P. 469; *Harrison* v. *Seymour* (1866) L.R. 1 C.P. 518; *Croydon Gas Co. Dickinson* (1876) 1 C.P.D. 707, 2 C.P.D. 46, where the surety had joined in a bond for £1,000 and the creditor subsequently agreed with the debtor that the debt should only be £500 which was held not to discharge the surety from liability for the greater amount. As pointed out by the South Australian Law Reform Committee Report on Suretyship (39th Report, 1976) at para. 6, since the surety was guaranteeing whatever the debtor's liability was, it should have been limited to the lesser amount. In *W. R. Simmons Ltd.* v. *Meek* |1939| 2 All E.R. 645 Oliver J., in applying *Croydon Gas Co.* v. *Dickinson*, discusses the concept of a "severable" guarantee, *i.e.* whenever a surety is liable for two separate liabilities, a subsequent variation as to one will not affect his liability for the other. See also *Davies* v. *Stainbank* (1855) 6 De G.M. & G. 679, 689. *Cf. Eyre* v. *Bartrop* (1818) 3 Madd. 221; *Polak* v. *Everett* (1876) 1 Q.B.D. 669. *Midland Motor Showrooms* v. *Newman* |1929| 2 K.B. 256.

[24] *Midland Motor Showrooms* v. *Newman, supra; cf. W.R. Simmons Ltd.* v. *Meek, supra.*

[25] *General Steam Navigation Co.* v. *Rolt* (1858) 6 C.B. (N.S.) 550.

[26] *British Motor Trust Co.* v. *Hyams* (1934) 50 T.L.R. 230.

[27] *General Steam Navigation Co.* v. *Rolt* (1852) 6 C.B. (N.S.) 550.

[28] *Ibid. Cf. Enright* v. *Falvey* (1879) 4 L.R. Ir. 397.

[29] *Woodcock* v. *Oxford and Worcester Ry.* (1853) 1 Drew 521.

[30] See *Hollier* v. *Eyre* (1840) 9 C. & F. at p. 52.

[31] *Polak* v. *Everett* (1876) 1 Q.B.D. 669, 673.

charged if the company, on non-payment of a call, exercises its right under the original contract for the shares to forfeit them.[32]

Assent by surety without fresh consideration

A surety is not discharged by a variation to which he assents afterwards, even though there may be no fresh consideration for the assent.[33] However, it is apprehended that assent, whether previous or subsequent to a variation, only renders the surety liable for the contract as varied, where it remains a contract within the general purview of the original guarantee,[34] and the assent can operate as the waiver of something in the nature of a condition, or of an equitable claim to the cancellation of a security whose express terms cover the contract as varied.[35] If a new contract is to be secured, there must be a new guarantee.[36]

Breach of principal contract by principal debtor

The decision of the House of Lords in *Moschi* v. *Lep Air Services Ltd.*[37] makes it clear that a guarantor's position is not affected by a breach of the principal contract which leads to the termination of that contract by reason of an acceptance of the breach by the creditor. The House of Lords held that the nature of a guarantor's contractual promise was to ensure that the debtor performed his obligations under his contract with the creditor.[38] Consequently when the debtor failed to perform his obligations *vis-à-vis* the creditor the latter could recover damages from the guarantor by dint of such failure, the measure of damages being in theory the same. The obligation of both guarantor and debtor upon default by the latter was a secondary obligation to pay damages as distinct from the primary obligation under the main contract itself.[39] Much of the decision turns upon the actual wording of the guarantee involved, but some reliance was placed on *Chatterton* v. *Maclean*,[40] where it was assumed by Parker J.[41] that on a creditor's acceptance of the

---

[32] *Re Darwen and Pearce* [1927] 1 Ch. 176, 187.

[33] *Mayhew* v. *Crickett* (1818) 2 Swanst. 185; *Smith* v. *Winter* (1838) 4 M. & W. 454.

[34] *Trade Indemnity Co.* v. *Workington Harbour, etc.* [1937] A.C. 1 especially, *per* Lord Atkin.

[35] All releases come under one or other of these heads: *e.g. General Steam Navigation Co.* v. *Rolt* (1858) 6 C.B. (N.S.) 550 under the former; and *Hollier* v. *Eyre* (1840) 9 C. & F. 1, *Mayhew* v. *Crickett* (1818) 2 Swanst. 185 and *Smith* v. *Winter* (1838) 4 M. & W. 454 under the latter.

[36] See *Pybus* v. *Gibb* (1856) 6 E. & B. 902 at 911. *Cf. Kitson* v. *Julian* (1855) 4 F. & B. 854; *Leathley* v. *Spyer* (1870) L.R. 5 C.P. 595. The effect of the Statute of Frauds must also be borne in mind.

[37] [1973] A.C. 331.

[38] See below at p. 108.

[39] See, *e.g. per* Lord Reid at p. 345, *per* Lord Diplock at p. 350, and *per* Lord Simon at p. 352. *Cf.* the approach of Megaw L.J. in the Court of Appeal [1971] 3 All E.R. 45.

[40] [1951] 1 All E.R. 761. See *Moschi* v. *Lep Air Services Ltd., supra* at 357.

[41] *Supra* at 764, 765.

principal debtor's repudiation of the contract between them, the surety will not be released in respect of the indebtedness accrued due or future liabilities for damages.[42]

9. *With What Amount the Surety is Chargeable*

Amount owing by principal

The surety can only be made liable for the amount which the principal owes in respect of the debt secured.[43] Thus, if a promissory note is given to secure advances, it cannot be relied on to sue either party to it, whether principal or surety, for more than the amount actually advanced.[44] Similarly, if one person accepts or endorses a bill to secure the debt of another to the drawer or indorsee, the latter can only sue him for the amount of the debt.[45] Where a promissory note is given to secure a proportion of an advance to be made, and only part of that advance is given, his note will in equity be available to the creditor only to secure a similar proportion of the credit actually given, even though the amount owing be more than the *ex facie* amount of the note.[46]

Payment by the principal

The surety is, of course, not liable if the principal has paid the guaranteed debt, nor, if part has been paid, for more than the amount unpaid.[47] It would be beyond the scope of this work to examine the law as to what constitutes a valid payment, the question in each case being in no way affected by the circumstance that there is a surety for the debt.[48]

Where the condition of a surety's bond was that the treasurer of a union (a banker) should "honestly, diligently and faithfully perform and discharge the duties of his office," one such duty being to pay out of any money of the guardians in his hands all orders drawn upon him, and the treasurer paid an order with his own notes, which the plaintiffs accepted, and at the time of the banker stopping payment still held, the surety was held not

---

[42] *Cf. Hyundai Shipbuilding and Heavy Industries Ltd.* v. *Pournaras* [1978] 2 Lloyds Rep. 502 and *Hyundai Heavy Industries Co. Ltd.* v. *Papadopoulos* [1980] 1 W.L.R. 1129, H.L., both discussed above at p. 50.
[43] The so-called "principle of co-extensiveness" which reflects this rule is discussed *infra* at p. 77.
[44] *Hartland* v. *Jukes* (1863) 1 H. & C. 667.
[45] *Ex p. Reader* (1819) Buck 381.
[46] *Mayhew* v. *Crickett* (1818) 2 Swanst. 185.
[47] *Perry* v. *National Provincial Bank* [1910] 1 Ch. 464.
[48] See *City Discount Bank* v. *McLean* (1874) L.R. 9 C.P. at 698; *Guardians of Lichfield Union* v. *Greene* (1857) 1 H. & N. 884.

liable on the ground that the case came within the principle whereby a bank note, taken for a debt at the time of the transaction which gives rise to it, is taken at the peril of the taker[49]; and that the circumstance that the person paying was also the maker made no difference.[50] Even if a creditor takes a bank note for a pre-existing guaranteed debt, so that it would not, *prima facie*, according to the above rule be taken at his peril, still, if he neglects to present it, he makes it his own, and the liability of the surety is extinguished, even though the debtor be himself the maker of the note.[50] Similarly, if in the place of cash the creditor takes for his own convenience a draft payable at another place.[50] If a creditor takes a bill or note for the debt, not being by express understanding but by the operation of the rules just mentioned a satisfaction of the debt, a surety (apart from any effect which the transaction may have as a giving of time),[51] remains liable in the event of the bill being dishonoured, the giving of the bill being conditional payment only.[52] Where a bond was given to secure payment for goods to be supplied at the expiration of the usual period of credit, and the purchaser gave a bill which was dishonoured, whereupon the creditor gave him the money to take up the bill, calling it a "loan," it was held that in substance it was not a loan, but that the goods had never been paid for, and that the surety was liable.[53]

Payment by co-sureties

With regard to payments by co-sureties, a deposit of money by some of a number of sureties to a suspense account with a creditor, as security for payment by those sureties of the amount deposited, beyond which they are not to be liable, the remedies against other sureties being reserved, is not a payment in relief of another surety not a party to the arrangement.[54]

Payment by third parties

A payment by a third party not in the position of a co-surety under circumstances such that there is no discharge of the principal does not discharge the surety.[55]

[49] *Camidge* v. *Allenby* (1827) 6 B. & C. 373.
[50] *Guardians of Lichfield Union* v. *Greene* (1857) 1 H. & N. 884.
[51] See *post*, p. 165.
[52] See *Belshaw* v. *Bush* (1851) 11 C.B. 191; *Bottomley* v. *Nuttall* (1858) 5 C.B. (N.S.) 122; *Keay* v. *Fenwick* (1870) 1 C.P.D. 745.
[53] *Davey* v. *Phelps* (1841) 2 M. & Gr. 300.
[54] *Commercial Bank of Australia* v. *Official Assignee* [1893] A.C. 181.
[55] *Cf. Kenney* v. *Employers' Liability Assurance Corporation* [1901] 1 I.R. 3.

Repayment voidable as fraudulent preference

If a payment received by the creditor from the principal is afterwards, upon the bankruptcy of the principal, adjudged a fraudulent preference, and has to be restored to the estate by the creditor, the surety is liable for the amount[56] where the creditor was not a party to the fraudulent preference.[57] There has been no valid payment, and the creditor has not done anything to discharge the surety upon equitable grounds.[58] In such a case the decision as between a creditor and the trustee of the bankrupt's estate, though admissible in evidence as between the creditor and the surety, is not binding upon the surety, but the creditor must prove in the action against the latter that the payment was a fraudulent preference.[59]

Appropriation of payments

The question whether payments made by the principal debtor, not being dividends in his bankruptcy, are to be appropriated in discharge or reduction of the guaranteed or some other indebtedness, is one which, in the absence of special agreement between the creditor and the surety, must be determined as if it arose merely between the creditor and the principal debtor,[60] a surety having no right of his own to dictate either to the creditor or the debtor how payments made by the latter are to be appropriated.[61] The surety's ignorance of the other debt is immaterial.[61] Similarly, a surety for a collector or other accountable agent is liable, although the collector or agent has paid over the full amount that he received during the period covered by the guarantee, if the payment was appropriated to pre-existing arrears either by the act of the collector or agent or of the person who received it from him.[62]

---

[56] *Pritchard* v. *Hitchcock* (1843) 6 M. & Gr. 151; *Petty* v. *Cooke* (1871) L.R. 6 Q.B. 790.

[57] *Cf. Re Seymour* [1937] Ch. 668. Note that the Blagden Report on Bankruptcy in 1957 (Cmnd. 220) at paras. 121–125 citing *Re Lyon* [1935] 152 L.T. 201, suggested that fraudulent preference proceedings ought to be available against guarantors dependent on the establishment of the requisite intention to prefer on the part of the debtor. But see effect of ss. 92 and 115(4) of the Companies Act 1947.

[58] *Petty* v. *Cooke* (1871) L.R. 6 Q.B. 790.

[59] *Pritchard* v. *Hitchcock* (1843) Man. & G. 151. By the Bankruptcy Act 1914, s. 44, as amended by the Companies Act 1947, ss. 92 and 115, when a creditor is sued for the return of a fraudulent preference he can join the surety as a third party so that the latter will become bound by the decision.

[60] See *City Discount Co.* v. *McLean* (1874) L.R. 9 C.P. at 698; *Ex p. Whitworth* (1841) 2 M.D. & De G. 164, 169.

[61] *Kirby* v. *Duke of Marlborough* (1813) 2 M. & S.18; *Williams* v. *Rawlinson* (1813) 3 Bing. at 76; *Lysaght* v. *Walker* (1831) 5 Bligh (N.S.) 1; *Re Sherry* (1884) 25 Ch.D. 692.

[62] *Att-Gen. for Jamaica* v. *Manderson* (1848) 6 Moo. P.C. 239; *Gwynne* v. *Burrell* (1835) 6 Bing. N.C. 453; *L.B. & S.C. Ry.* v. *Goodwin* (1849) 3 Exch. 736. This passage in the last edition was approved by the Privy Council in *Fahey* v. *M. S. D. Spiers Ltd.* [1975] 1 N.Z.L.R. 240, where on the facts it was held not necessary in order to give business efficacy to a guarantee to imply a term that the guarantor would be entitled to the benefit of any payment which might be made by the principal debtor.

Separate accounts

The creditor may close the account guaranteed when the guarantee expires (as at the death of the guarantor), and open a new account without transferring to it the old debit; and the payments into the new account will not wipe off the old debt.[63] However, the creditor cannot, by dividing the account guaranteed during the currency of the guarantee, charge the surety with the debits and withhold from him the benefits of the credits; the two accounts should be looked at as one.[64]

A surety for a loan by a money club to a member cannot claim credit, as extinguishing the loan, for the monthly subscriptions paid by the principal, the loan and the subscriptions being distinct matters.[65]

Where a guarantee is given to a banker for a loan account, or advances by way of the acceptance of bills, the surety has no right to have any credit balance that may exist from time to time on a current account kept by the principal with the same banker applied in reduction of the account guaranteed.[66] A balance on current account existing at the moment when the guarantee terminates may be afterwards paid over by the banker to the principal without affecting his rights against the surety.[67] Similarly, even if separate accounts are not kept, where it is the intention of the parties that the advance shall remain at the disposal of the customer, so that he shall be at liberty to draw against the items credited to him.[68] Thus where £5,000 had been advanced by a discount company to a customer on a guarantee to last for two years, and in the same account there appeared as credits the amounts of accommodation bills given by him to the company, as well as trade bills discounted, the proceeds of which were handed to him, and debited in the account, it was held that the advance guaranteed was not wiped out though the guarantee was not a continuing one.[69] However where in consideration of an advance to the principal, for which the principal gave a series of promissory notes, a surety agreed, if the notes were not paid at the due dates, to give a mortgage to secure the amount, it was held that the mortgage was only to be given if there was not money in hand to meet the notes, and that, sufficient money coming in, the creditor could not appropriate it to other purposes.[70]

---

[63] *Re Sherry* (1884) 25 Ch.D. 692.
[64] *Ibid*. And see *Bechervaise* v. *Lewis* (1872) L.R. 7 C.P. 372; *Ex p. Hanson* (1806) 18 Ves. 232.
[65] *Wright* v. *Hickling* (1866) L.R. 2 C.P. 199.
[66] *Hollond* v. *Teed* (1848) 7 Hare 50; *York City and County Banking Co.* v. *Bainbridge* (1880) 43 L.T. 732; *Bradford Old Bank* v. *Sutcliffe* [1918] 2 K.B. 833.
[67] *Hollond* v. *Teed, supra.*
[68] *City Discount Co.* v. *McLean* (1874) L.R. 9 C.P. 692; *Browning* v. *Baldwin* (1879) 40 L.T. 248.
[69] *City Discount Co.* v. *McLean, supra.*
[70] *Kinnaird* v. *Webster* (1878) 10 Ch.D. 139, explained in *Browning* v. *Baldwin* (1879) 40 L.T. 248.

By whom payments are to be appropriated

The well-settled rule as to the appropriation of payments is that the debtor may at the time of the payment appropriate it to any subsisting debt he chooses. If he makes no appropriation, the creditor can either then or at any time afterwards,[71] appropriate the money as he pleases,[72] even to a debt statute-barred,[73] though not to a debt incurred during infancy[74]; and the payment will not be presumed to have been appropriated by the debtor to the more burdensome debt.[75] An appropriation by the creditor is not complete, and is therefore irrevocable until it is communicated to the debtor.[75] Appropriation by the debtor need not be expressed, if it is sufficiently shown by the circumstances. Thus where the debtor paid sums exactly tallying in amount with certain items, and obtained discount for prompt payment, which he was only entitled to if those items were discharged by those payments, it was held that he had appropriated the payment to those items.[76] Where new bills were given in exchange for dishonoured bills, it was held that they must be applied to the debt for which the old bills had been given, and could not be appropriated by the creditor to debts incurred since the old bills had been given.[77] Similarly, where an interview was held between an attorney employed by the agents of the creditor, the principal debtor, and the surety, at which the attorney pressed the principal debtor to make a payment and the surety also remonstrated with him for not paying, and the principal said he would pay something that afternoon, and on the following day did pay a large sum, it was held that it must be taken as appropriate to the debt guaranteed, and could not be applied to other debts which he owed the agents personally.[78]

The right of the creditor to appropriate payments made without appropriation by the debtor does not extend to sums

---

[71] *Simson* v. *Ingham* (1823) 2 B. & C. 65; *Mills* v. *Fowkes* (1839) 5 Bing. N.C. 455; *City Discount Co.* v. *McLean* (1874) L.R. 9 C.P. 692, 700.

[72] See *Goddard* v. *Cox* (1743) 2 Str. 1194; *Newmarch* v. *Clay* (1811) 14 East 229; *Plomer* v. *Long* (1816) 1 Stark. 153.

[73] *Mills* v. *Fowkes* (1839) 5 Bing. N.C. 455.

[74] *Keeping* v. *Broom* (1895) 11 T.L.R. 595.

[75] *Simson* v. *Ingham* (1827) 2 B. & C. 65. As pointed out by the South Australian Law Reform Committee Report on Suretyship (39th Report, 1976) at para. 4, where this passage is cited, it seems wrong that a creditor, with or without the principal debtor, should be able to appropriate payments without informing the surety. The Report suggests that legislation should impose an option on the creditor either to retain his power to appropriate payments as he pleases or to secure himself by obtaining a surety but not allow both. See further herein at p. 101 where *Blackstone Bank* v. *Hill* (1830) 10 Pick. 129 is discussed. The recommended solution is therefore to cause all payments by the debtor to operate to relieve the surety *pro tanto* of his obligation to the creditor in the absence of agreement to the contrary by the surety of the time of appropriation.

[76] *Marryatts* v. *White* (1817) 2 Stark. 101.

[77] *Newmarch* v. *Clay* (1811) 14 East 239.

[78] *Shaw* v. *Picton* (1825) 4 B. & C. 715 And see *Att.-Gen. for Jamaica* v. *Manderson* (1848) 6 Moo. P.C. 239.

which he has received from third persons for the debtor, without the knowledge of the debtor, and which the latter had therefore had no opportunity of appropriating.[79]

The rule in Clayton's Case

If, there being no appropriation by the debtor, the payments are credited by the creditor to a current account, and nothing points to a contrary intention, they will be taken, from the moment when that fact is communicated to the debtor,[80] to have been applied to the earliest items in the account then unpaid.[81] Interest is presumed to be paid before principal, unless by a course of dealing binding upon the parties it has been added to and become part of the principal.[82]

The general rule as to the presumed appropriation of payments is known as the rule in *Clayton's Case*.[83] It cannot operate where the question is which of two debts in different accounts is to be taken as paid, nor where there having been a current account, that account is closed, and a new account not covered by the guarantee is opened, to which payment is credited.[84] It applies only where a person who has the right to appropriate money received as he pleases appropriates it in the manner shown in his books.[85] In a word, it is no more than a rule for the interpretation prima facie of the creditor's conduct in carrying the payment to the credit of the same account as is debited with the sum guaranteed. It may be excluded by circumstances showing that no appropriation was intended by the manner of keeping the account; as where the amounts credited were intended to be at the disposal of the debtor to draw out again, or merely represented bills discounted, of which he took the

---

[79] *Walker* v. *Lacy* 1 M. & Gr. 34.

[80] *Simson* v. *Ingham* (1823) 2 B. & C. 65.

[81] *Devaynes* v. *Noble*, known as *Clayton's Case* (1816) 1 Mer. 572 *Brooke* v. *Enderby* (1820) 2 B. & B. 70; *Bodenham* v. *Purchas* (1816) 2 B. & Ald. 39; *Pemberton* v. *Oakes* (1827) 4 Russ. at p. 168; *Bank of Scotland* v. *Christie* (1841) 8 C. & F. 214; *Cory Brothers* v. *Owners of Turkish SS. Mecca* [1897] A.C. 286; *Deeley* v. *Lloyds Bank* [1912] A.C. 788; *Albermarle Supply Co.* v. *Hird* [1928] 1 K.B. 307. See also *Bank of Nova Scotia* v. *Neil* (1968) 69 D.L.R. (2d) 357. This last decision is criticised by the South Australian Law Reform Committee in its report on Suretyship (39th Report, 1976) on the broad ground that it allows the creditor to circumvent any limitation imposed under the guarantee simply by entering into a new agreement with the debtor leaving the surety's contract intact and without notifying the surety of what he is doing. In that case the guarantee was for $2,000. The creditor bank later entered into fresh agreements with the debtor unknown to the surety, amounting to $8,000. The bank in recovering the greater sum were held to remain entitled to recover the $2,000 from the surety. See also *Royal Bank of Canada* v. *Slack* (1958) 11 D.L.R. (2d) 737; *Dickson* v. *Royal Bank of Canada* (1976) 66 D.L.R. (3d) 242; *Hopkinson* v. *C.I.B.C.* [1977] 6 W.W.R. 490. The law in some American States appears to allow a more equitable allocation. See Stearns and Elder, *The Law of Suretyship*, Section 7.23 (5th ed., 1951). See also the British Columbia Law Reform Commission Report on Consumer Guarantees (1979).

[82] *Parr's Banking Co.* v. *Yates* [1898] 2 Q.B. 460.

[83] (1816) 1 Mer. 572.

[84] *Simson* v. *Ingham* (1823) 2 B. & C. 65; *Re Sherry* (1884) 25 Ch.D. 692.

[85] Per Lord Selborne in *Blackburn Building Society* v. *Cunliffe Brooks & Co.* (1882) 22 Ch.D. at 71.

proceeds in cash.[86] Of course as regards a surety the rule in *Clayton's Case*, even if applicable, does not help the surety the guarantee is a continuing one covering the ultimate balance on the account.[87] It helps the surety, if applicable, where the guarantee is only for a specific debt, which is carried by the creditor into a running account, or where a continuing guarantee has ceased to cover the further items in an account by reason of effluxion of time, revocation, death of parties or otherwise.[88] Furthermore, inasmuch as the creditor's right of appropriation does not arise, and consequently no rule interpreting his conduct comes into play, unless the debtor pays without himself making any appropriation, it does not signify how the payments are dealt with by the creditor, if there is evidence of appropriation by the debtor.[89]

Dividends in bankruptcy

With regard to dividends obtained by the creditor in the bankruptcy of the principal, these are considered as made rateably in respect of every part of the debt, and operate, if not otherwise agreed by the surety, in relief of the guarantor or guarantors rateably. The creditor, therefore, in suing the surety, must give credit for all dividends received from the bankrupt upon the amount for which he is suing the surety, unless the proper construction of the guarantee is that it covered the amount remaining due after payment of any such dividends.[90] Where a surety was bound for the payment of the principal debt by instalments, and, the principal debtor becoming bankrupt, the creditor received a dividend on the whole debt, it was held that this must be distributed over all the instalments, and that the surety could not have it applied in discharge of the next instalment that fell due.[91] However, dividends which are declared upon the amount of the debt and interest owing at the date of the bankruptcy may be applied as against the surety to interest accrued since the bankruptcy, though such is not the subject of proof against the bankrupt.[92]

---

[86] *City Discount Co.* v. *McLean* (1874) L.R. 9 C.P. 692; *Browning* v. *Baldwin* (1879) 40 L.T. 248. And see *Ex p. Whitworth* (1841) 2 M.D. & De G. 164.

[87] *Henniker* v. *Wigg* (1843) 4 Q.B. 792.

[88] See *Eyton* v. *Knight* (1838) 2 Jur. 8.

[89] *Marryatts* v. *White* (1817) 2 Stark. 101; *Lysaght* v. *Walker* (1831) 5 Bligh (N.S.) 1.

[90] *Ex p. Rushforth* (1805) 10 Ves. 409; *Paley* v. *Field* (1806) 12 Ves. 435; *Martin* v. *Brecknell* (1813) 2 M. & S. 39; *Raikes* v. *Todd* (1838) 8 A. & E. 846; *London Assurance Co.* v. *Buckle* (1820) 4 Moore 153; *Ellis* v. *Emmanuel* (1876) 1 Ex. D. 157. And see the cases cited *infra*, notes 93 and 94.

[91] *Martin* v. *Brecknell, supra.*

[92] *Bower* v. *Morris* (1841) Cr. & Ph. 351.

Guarantees for running accounts

If the amount for which the surety is liable is less than the total debt owing to the creditor by the principal, it becomes material to consider whether the surety is bound for the whole of that debt with a limitation of his liability, or whether he is bound only for a part of it equal to the amount for which he is liable. If the former is the case, he has no right to a dividend until the creditor has received 100 pence in the pound on the whole. If the latter, he is relieved to the extent of the proportion of the dividend attributable to that part of the debt which he has guaranteed, just as if the amount he has guaranteed were a separate distinct debt from the rest of the creditor's claim. The rule is that where the surety gives a continuing guarantee of limited amount to secure an indefinite liability, as, for instance, the amount of advances which may be made to the principal, the guarantee is prima facie[93] to be taken as extending only to a part of the ultimate amount of the debt equal to the amount of the guarantee, and the surety will be entitled to that proportion of the dividends, the principle being that the surety is a stranger to the excess, and that the creditor swells his demand beyond the sum guaranteed at his own risk. The principle is exemplified in a line of cases referred to and distinguished in *Ellis* v. *Emmanuel*.[94]

Such a principle does not apparently apply where the surety is not a stranger to the excess, but expressly guarantees (subject to the limit as to the amount he is actually to pay) the whole amount to become due from the principal,[95] even though that may be the ultimate balance on a running account.[95] And in such cases the creditor would, perhaps, be entitled to retain the dividends even without an express proviso to that effect.[95]

Guarantees for ascertained debt of larger amount

Where the guarantee is given in respect of a floating balance, it is clear from *Ellis* v. *Emmanuel*,[95a] that, where it is given in respect of an ascertained debt, the full amount of which is named as the subject of the guarantee, a limitation of the liability cast upon the surety will not be construed as preventing the guarantee applying to the whole debt, so that in such a case

---

[93] It is therefore usual in bank guarantees to insert a clause providing that the bank may prove for its own benefit and that the guarantee is to stand security for the ultimate balance. See, *e.g. Midland Banking Co.* v. *Chambers* (1869) L.R. 7 Eq. 149; *Re Sass* [1896] 2 Q.B. 12. See specimen guarantees set out in Appendix 1.

[94] (1876) 1 Ex. D. 157.

[95] *Re Rees* (1881) 17 Ch.D. 98; *Re Sass* [1896] 2 Q.B. 12.

[95a] (1876) 1 Ex. D. 157.

the surety has no right to dividends until 100 pence in the pound is paid on the whole debt. In that case, a number of sureties gave a joint and several bond for £14,000 conditioned to be void if the obligors or any or either of them should pay £7,000 and interest by certain instalments, with the proviso that the individual sureties should not be liable, whether by reason of a joint or several demand, for more than certain amounts in each case, making in all £7,000. Accordingly, the creditor was held entitled to recover from one of the sureties the full amount of his liability although a dividend of almost 50p in the £ had been received out of the estate of the principal. If, however, the sureties had engaged not jointly for the whole but severally for the amounts, together equalling the whole, for which they respectively became liable, it is probable that the true construction would have been that the engagement of each was confined to his proportionate part, and that each would have shared rateably in the dividends received by the creditor.[96]

Undertaking to pay a fixed proportion of unascertained loss

Where the plaintiffs were entitled to certain bills of lading to enable them to recoup themselves an amount which they had paid for the consignee, and the defendants, who were interested in one-half of the goods, promised in consideration of the sale of the goods being left in their hands "to bear one-half of whatever loss might appear on the transaction," it was held, the consignee having become bankrupt, that the defendants were liable to pay half the loss upon the sale, without any deduction in respect of dividends which had been received by the plaintiffs out of the estate of the consignee of the whole of such loss.[97]

Special proviso dealing with dividends

It is open to the surety, in a case where prima facie he would be entitled to a proportion of any dividend received out of the estate of the principal, expressly to make over this right to the creditor and permit him to receive all dividends until he has received 100 pence in the pound,[98] and a clause to this effect is commonly found. It is no objection to the creditor's right to prove for the full amount, after receiving payment from the surety, that the surety had a security upon the debtor's estate by means

---

[96] (1876) 1 Ex. D. at 162. And see *Pendlebury* v. *Walker* (1841) 4 Y. & C. Ex. 424; *Collins* v. *Prosser* (1823) 1 B. & C. 682. See also *Ex p. Brook* (1815) 2 Rose 334; *Mayhew* v. *Cricket* (1818) 2 Swanst. 185.

[97] *Liverpool Borough Bank* v. *Logan* (1860) 5 H. & N. 464.

[98] See, *e.g. Midland Banking Co.* v. *Chambers* (1869) L.R. 7 Eq. 179; *Re Rees* (1881) 17 Ch.D. 98; *Re Sass* [1876] 2 Q.B. 12. See specimen guarantees set out in Appendix 1.

of which he has paid the creditor the amount of the guarantee at the expense of the debtor.[99]

Proceeds of execution

In 1830 it was held by the Supreme Court of Massachusetts that when a creditor obtained one judgment in respect of several debts, some of which were and some were not covered by guarantee, the proceeds of an execution issued upon the judgment could not be appropriated by the creditor to the unguaranteed debts, but must be apportioned rateably to all the debts included in the judgment.[1]

Appropriation of payments as between several sureties

With regard to payments made by a debtor owing several debts and not appropriated by him, it has been seen that the general rule is that the creditor can appropriate them at his pleasure. But where a number of sureties guarantee the same debt, but in distinct portions, splitting it up amongst themselves for that purpose, the point arises whether payments by the principal reducing the debt below the total of all the guarantees put together must not be rateably applied in reducing the liability of each. In *Pendlebury* v. *Walker*,[2] the liability for the principal debt was by contract with each surety (each being bound in a separate instrument) to be distributed by means of the rateable apportionment of any payments by the principal among a specified number of named co-sureties; and in *Ellis* v. *Emmanuel*,[3] it seems to have been thought by Blackburn J., that even without such a stipulation the creditor would probably have been bound impliedly to apportion any payments by the principal among a number of sureties guaranteeing by the same instrument the same debt in distinct portions.[4]

In cases like *Pendlebury* v. *Walker*,[5] and the case put by Blackburn, J. in *Ellis* v. *Emmanuel*,[6] one result of the compulsory rateable appropriation of payments by the principal would be that no case would arise for contribution. It does not appear, however, to follow that conversely where there is no contribution payments by the principal must be apportioned. In *Coope* v. *Twynam*,[7] the principal was to give three separate bonds, in

---

[99] *Midland Banking Co.* v. *Chambers, supra. Cf. Re Melton* |1918| 1 Ch. 37; *Re Lennard* |1934| 1 Ch. 235.

[1] *Blackstone Bank* v. *Hill* 10 Pick. 129 (1830). See *infra*, p. 96.

[2] (1841) 4 Y. & C. Ex. 424.

[3] (1876) 1 Ex. D. 157.

[4] *Ibid.* at 162. *Cf.* the form of guarantee in *Fell* v. *Goslin* (1852) 7 Exch. 185.

[5] See note 2, *supra*.

[6] See note 3, *supra*.

[7] (1823) T. & R. 426.

each of which a separate surety was to join, each bond being for a third of the debt. Lord Elton held there would be no contribution, but there is nothing to show that he thought payments by the principal would be apportionable. He considered each bond "a separate transaction," and upon this footing it would seem that the principal could pay off any bond he chose, and that the surety may in another bond paying the whole of the sum secured by that bond would have no claim for contribution upon the surety in the bond paid off by the principal. If each bond had been security for every part of the principal debt, though involving the liability of only one-third of the amount of that debt, there would be no apportionment; but any surety paying more than his proportion of the deficiency would have had contribution.[8]

Payment by other sureties

Where a number of sureties engage severally by one instrument for a limited sum (or jointly or severally if there is a proviso limiting the effective liability of each by reason of either a joint or several demand,[9] the question arises whether they are liable for that sum each, so that the full amount can be recovered from each and all of them one after another, or whether, though severally liable, they all engage for the same sum, so that when once that sum is paid by any one of them all are relieved.[10] In *Collins* v. *Prosser*,[11] a bond for a number of sureties ran, so far as concerned three of them, as follows: "We are held firmly bound for £1,000 each, for which we bind ourselves and each of us for himself, for the whole and entire sum of £1,000 each." It was held that each surety was severally liable, and that a separate £1,000 was recoverable from each, that is to say £3,000 in all. In that case there was a total debt secured of £12,000, which amount, as appeared from the recital in the condition, was to be secured by the bond, each obligor being liable for the sum set against his name, and the construction adopted effected this object. In *Ellis* v. *Emmanuel*,[12] seven sureties were bound, and every two or more and each of them jointly and severally, in the penal sum of £14,000, conditioned for avoidance if the obligors or any or either of them should pay £7,000; and there was a proviso that

---

[8] *Coope* v. *Twynam, supra; Ellis* v. *Emmanuel* (1876) 1 Ex. D. 157; *Ellesmere Bravery Co.* v. *Cooper* [1896] 1 Q.B. 75.

[9] See the bond in *Ellis* v. *Emmanuel, supra.*, set out *infra.*

[10] See *Collins* v. *Prosser* (1823) 1 B. & C. 682 *per* Holroyd J. at 687, 688. See generally, Chapter 8, Part 3.

[11] *Supra.*

[12] (1876) 1 Ex. D. 157.

four of the sureties "shall not, nor shall either of them, be liable (whether by reason of a joint or several action or demand) for a sum or sums exceeding altogether in debt or damages £1,300." It was held that each of the four was liable for a separate £1,300 and that nothing paid by one of them reduced the liability of the others. This construction made the seven sureties between them responsible for the whole principal debt of £7,000; the other construction would have left some of the principal debt uncovered.

Similarly, where two persons by one instrument guaranteed "the sum of £400, in the proportion of £200 each," it was held that each was liable for a separate £200, but that neither was liable for more.[13]

In *Armstrong* v. *Cahill*,[14] a fidelity bond for four sureties ran, "we, A, B, C and D are hereby held and firmly bound in the sum of £50 each to E, his executors, administrators, and assigns, to which payment we hereby bind us and each of us, our and each of our heirs, executors and administrators, and every of them." There was nothing to show whether the total amount intended to be secured was £50 or £200. It was held by the Common Pleas Division in Ireland that each surety was liable for a separate sum of £50, and that the others were not discharged when one had paid £50.[15]

Where principal entitled to set-off

Where the principal is entitled to a set-off against the creditor's demand arising out of the same transaction as the debt guaranteed, and in fact reducing that debt, the surety is entitled to plead it in an action by the creditor against the surety alone.[16]

---

[13] *Fell* v. *Goslin* (1852) 7 Exch. 185.

[14] (1880) 6 L.R. Ir. 440.

[15] See also *R.* v. *O'Callaghan* (1838) 1 Ir. Eq. R. 439.

[16] See *Murphy* v. *Glass* (1869) L.R. 2 P.C. 408; *Bechervaise* v. *Lewis* (1872) L.R. 7 C.P. 372; See also *Gillespie* v. *Torrance* 25 N.Y. 30 (1862); *Newton* v. *Lee* 139 N.Y. 332 (1893) *Cf. Wilson* v. *Mitchell* [1939] 2 K.B. 869, where Finlay L.J. was of the view that a guarantor could not pray in aid a counterclaim for damages for breach of warranty against the creditor, and held that even if he was wrong in that view, it would not be available as a defence in an action between co-sureties without bringing in the debtor whose claim it was. The relevant passage in the previous edition of this work was commented upon by Roskill L.J. in *Hyundai Shipbuilding & Heavy Industries Co. Ltd.* v. *Pournaras* [1978] 2 Lloyd's Rep. 502 at 508 (see above p. 50) where on the special facts and placing considerable reliance on the commercial policy reasons involved, the Court of Appeal refused to allow guarantors to avail themselves of any right of set-off enuring to the benefit of the principal debtor. The House of Lords in the related case of *Hyundai* v. *Papadopoulos* [1980] 1 W.L.R. 1129 followed *Pournaras* on this point. Many of the cases cited in this section are subject to an exhaustive analysis by Isaacs J. in *Cellulose Products Pty. Ltd.* v. *Truda* (1970) 92 W.N. (N.S.W.) 561 where it was held that a surety cannot claim by way of set-off or cross-action, whether at common law or in equity, unliquidated damages resulting either from a breach of contract between the principal debtor and the creditor, or arising out of any other claim for unliquidated damages which the principal debtor may have against the creditor. This topic is discussed by Steyn, "The Co-Extensiveness Principle" (1974) 90 L.Q.R. 246 at pp. 261 *et seq.* See also a note on the *Cellulose* decision in (1970) 44 A.L.J. 562. *Semble* a surety cannot rely on a possible claim for rescission by the principal debtor: see *First National Bank of Chicago Ltd.* v. *Moorgate Properties Ltd.* (*The Times*, October 20, 1975, C.A.).

If the creditor is merely a trustee for other persons and is suing for their benefit and not his own, a set-off against the persons beneficially interested will be available to the surety, even though they are not before the court.[17]

In *Murphy* v. *Glass*,[18] it was held that a surety for the price of lands bought in a colony under a contract by which any dispute as to the matters connected with the sale was not to annul the sale, but be referred to arbitration, might plead in reduction of his liability an award of compensation to the purchaser in respect of a deficiency in the acreage of the lands on the grounds that such compensation was an abatement of the price. In *Bechervaise* v. *Lewis*,[19] a surety who had joined with the principal in a joint and several promissory note given for the price of the interest of the payee in certain debts to be transferred by him to the principal, but which the payee was to collect, was allowed to set off against the demand upon the note the amount of certain of those debts which had been collected by the payee and not paid over to the principal.[20]

But where the principal is not before the court, the mere existence of an independent cross-debt from the creditor to the principal is no defence to the surety.[21] In *Bowyear* v. *Pawson*,[22] where the defendant and one Wilson were co-sureties in a joint and several covenant, and the defendant, being sued for the whole amount due, pleaded an indebtedness of the plaintiff to Wilson in an amount exceeding the amount sued for, and claimed the benefit of the moiety of that indebtedness on the ground that as to a moiety he was entitled to be exonerated by his co-surety Wilson, it was held by Watkin, Williams and Mathew JJ., that no defence was disclosed, as it was not shown that "the defendant had any right to call upon Wilson to appropriate the debt due to him from the plaintiff to the exoneration of the defendant nor any contract with the plaintiff to accept a set-off of Wilson's debt as a discharge of the defendant." It has been held in America that a surety for the price of goods sold cannot set up a breach of warranty to the principal, even though the principal might have set it up in reduction of damages.[23]

---

[17] *Alcoy, etc.* v. *Greenhill* (1897) 76 L.T. 542. See also preceding note.

[18] (1869) L.R. 2 P.C. 408.

[19] (1872) L.R. 7 C.P. 372.

[20] See (1952) 96 S.J. 659 on the possible application of these two cases to the question of whether a tenant's surety can claim relief if the landlord has failed to discharge some obligation, *e.g.* to repair, as a result of which the tenant's ability to perform his own obligations becomes impossible.

[21] See *Wilson* v. *Mitchell* [1939] 2 K.B. 869 discussed *supra* at note 16.

[22] (1881) 6 Q.B.D. 540.

[23] *Gillespie* v. *Torrance* 25 N.Y. 306 (1862); *Newton* v. *Lee* N.Y. 332 (1893), both discussed at length by Isaacs J. in *Cellulose Products Pty. Ltd.* v. *Truda* (1970) 92 W.N. (N.S.W.) 561 at pp. 571 *et seq.*, as to which see above at note 16. But see next note.

Any other view than that adopted in *Bowyear* v. *Pawson* would lead to great difficulties. For example the principal might owe other debts than the debt guaranteed, for which, moreover, other sureties might be bound, and complete justice would not be done to all parties. Therefore in any case where a surety claims the benefit of a set-off or cross-claim available to the principal, and not operating directly to reduce the debt guaranteed, the principal ought at least to be made a party in order that the surety's right to the benefit of the set-off may be established against him, and that he may be bound by the set-off and precluded from afterwards requiring payment from the creditor.[24]

Set-off in foreign law

If a guarantee, though securing an English debt, falls to be construed by the law of a country where a debt is extinguished by set-off according to its law, and a surety is not liable for an amount to which the principal has a set-off, a set-off available in England available to the principal against the creditor which would have extinguished the debt by the foreign law affords a defence to the surety by virtue of that law.[25]

Set-off by principal

The principal debtor may of course set off whatever a creditor owes him against the demand of the creditor against him upon the debt guaranteed,[26] and this even though the principal and surety are jointly liable, the debt being really that of the principal alone, and the joint liability being a security only.[27] If the principal has done this the liability of the surety ought to be extinguished to the amount of the set-off,[28] otherwise the

---

[24] See *Murphy* v. *Glass* (1869) L.R. 2 P.C. 408; *Bowyear* v. *Pawson* (1881) 6 Q.B.D. 540. And *cf. Ex p. Hippins* (1826) 2 Gl. & J. 93; *Cheetham* v. *Crook* (1825) McCl. & Y. 307; *Gillespie* v. *Torrance, supra.* Isaacs J. in *Cellulose Products Pty. Ltd., supra,* at p. 587 approves the passage in the text. At 588 Isaacs J. concludes that when sued, the surety has the right to join the debtor as third party who can in turn join the plaintiff as fourth party, etc., all of which claims can then be determined at once. In the United States, despite the rules reflected in the cases discussed in the text, a guarantor may be allowed to assert his principal's cross-claim, in certain circumstances, *e.g.* if the latter is insolvent. See, *e.g. U.S. ex. rel. Johnson* v. *Morley Construction Co.* 98 F (2d) 781 (2nd circuit, 1938) at p. 789. See also Restatement, Security § 133 (1941). A leading Canadian authority is *Diebel* v. *Stratford Improvement Co.* (1917) 33 D.L.R. 296, where the Ontario Court of Appeal allowed the guarantor to set up a claim for breach of warranty available to the debtor. See the British Columbia Law Reform Commission Report on Consumer Guarantees (1979) Chapter IV, Section F in generally recommending such a right, but stopping short of requiring the guarantor to join his principal as a party to the proceedings.

[25] *Allen* v. *Kemble* (1848) 6 Moo P.C. 314, explained in *Rouquette* v. *Overman* (1875) L.R. 10 Q.B. 540. *Cf. ante,* pp. 45 *et seq.*

[26] *Ex p. Hanson* (1806) 12 Ves. 346; 18 Ves. 232; *Ex p. Hippins* (1826) 2 Gl. & J. 93; *Vulliamy* v. *Noble* (1817) 3 Mer. 593.

[27] *Ex p. Hanson, supra; Vulliamy* v. *Noble, supra.*

[28] *Per* Willes J. in *Owen* v. *Wilkinson* (1858) 5 C.B. (N.S.) 526.

principal would not be protected, as the surety if called upon to pay would come to him for indemnity.[29] On this ground, if the creditor sues the surety alone, and so gives the principal no opportunity of establishing his set-off, the principal may, it seems, in order to protect himself from the liability which judgment against the surety would indirectly bring upon him, go to the court himself and have the set-off declared, and, if the set-off is equal to the debt, have the guarantee or accommodation bill given up.[30]

Set-off by surety

If a surety, being severally liable, has money in the hands of the creditor, who becomes bankrupt, he is entitled before the trustee sues the principal to apply it in satisfaction of the debt.[31] Even after the trustee has sued the principal alone, the surety can still insist on such set-off, if the fact that the creditor had the money in hand has been concealed by the fraud of the creditor, so that the surety could not take advantage of this right before.[32] A surety jointly liable with the principal can at any time on learning the facts insist on the application to the extinction of the joint debt of the proceeds of securities belonging to himself severally, but pledged for the joint debt and wrongfully sold by the creditor before the debt became due, without the knowledge of the pledgor.[33]

A bank which has made advances to a customer abroad on the security of a guarantee given in England, is entitled, when recovering against the surety, to compare the sum owing abroad at the rate of exchange prevailing when the liability accrued and not that at the date of judgment.[34]

Interest

Whether sureties can be made liable for interest or costs recoverable from the principal is of course a question upon the construction of their engagement.[35] Where sureties had given a bond conditioned to be void if a receiver should "duly account for

---

[29] *Ex p. Hippins* (1896) 2 Gl. & J. 93.

[30] *Ex p. Hanson* (1806) 12 Ves. 346; *Ex p. Hippins, supra.*

[31] *Ex p. Stephens* (1805) 11 Ves. 24, as explained by Jessel M.R. in *Middleton* v. *Pollock* (1875) L.R. 20 Eq. 515, 519. See also the explanations in *Vulliamy* v. *Noble* (1817) 3 Mer. at p. 621; *Ex p. Hanson* (1806) 12 Ves. at 348; *Jones* v. *Mossop* (1844) 3 Hare at 573.

[32] *Vulliamy* v. *Noble, supra,* as explained by Jessel M.R. in *Middleton* v. *Pollock, supra,* at p. 521.

[33] See note 32.

[34] *Mann, Taylor & Co.* v. *Royal Bank of Canada* (1935) 40 Com. Cas. 267 at 280. Note generally effect of *Miliangos* v. *George Frank (Textiles) Ltd.* [1976] A.C. 443.

[35] As to penal interest payable by a defaulting trustee in bankruptcy see *Board of Trade* v. *Employers' Liability Association* [1910] 2 K.B. 649.

and pay what he should receive, as the Court had directed or should direct," Lord Eldon thought the penalty should in an ordinary case only be relieved against upon the terms of the money being accounted for with interest; but, under the special circumstances of that particular case, he did not act on that view.[36] A surety for the payment of a bill of exchange by the acceptor is liable for interest from the date it becomes due.[37] If the creditor obtains judgment against the principal for the debt, a surety for the payment of interest under the original contract is not liable for the interest carried by the judgment debt.[38] A surety for the payment of principal and interest is liable for interest though his liability for the principal may be barred by the statute of limitations.[39]

A guarantor of an advance by a banker to his customer was held not to be entitled to the repayment of tax on payments under his guarantee in respect of interest made without deduction of tax under section 36(1) of the Income Tax Act 1918.[40] In *Re Hawkins, deceased*[41] it was held that any sum that a guarantor paid in respect of interest due from the principal debtor ranked as payment of interest and not payment of a sum in lieu of interest, particularly where the guarantor had in terms guaranteed "the payment of interest."

Costs

Where a committee of a lunatic was ordered to pay over a balance in his hands and certain costs of proceedings against him, the sureties in a bond, of which the condition was that the committee should obey the Lord Chancellor's orders attaching or concerning the lunatic's estate, were ordered to pay the costs.[42] In Ireland it was held that a surety by recognisance for a tenant under the Court was liable for the costs of an attachment against the tenant, provided he was not made liable for more than the amount of the recognisance.[43] A surety for a receiver is chargeable (subject to the same limitation) with the costs of an

---

[36] *Dawson* v. *Raynes* (1826) 2 Russ. 466. A bond is here regarded as a security carrying interest beyond the date on which payment is due. See *Re Dixon* [1900] 2 Ch. 561.

[37] *Ackerman* v. *Ehrenspeger* (1846) 16 M. & W. 99.

[38] *Faber* v. *Earl of Lathom* (1897) L.T. 168.

[39] *Parr's Banking Co.* v. *Yates* [1898] 2 Q.B. 460; *Cf. Wright* v. *New Zealand Farmers' Co-operative Assn. of Canterbury Ltd.* [1939] A.C. 439 P.C. See further Chap. 10, *infra*.

[40] *Holder* v. *Commissioners of Inland Revenue* [1932] A.C. 624.

[41] [1972] Ch. 714 applying dicta of Lord Atkin in *Holder* v. *Commissioners of Inland Revenue*, *supra*. See also *Westminster Bank Executor and Trustee Co. (Channel Islands) Ltd.* v. *National Bank of Greece S.A.* [1970] 1 Q.B. 236. Interest will not, at least as between guarantor and creditor, forego its character simply because it is paid pursuant to an obligation imposed by a guarantee.

[42] *Re Lockey* (1845) 1 Ph. 509. But *cf. Hoole* v. *Fidelity and Deposit Co.* [1916] 1 K.B. 25 affirmed on different grounds [1916] 2 K.B. 568, distinguished in *The Rosarino* [1973] 1 Lloyds Rep. 21.

[43] *Keily* v. *Murphy* (1837) 1 Sau. & Sc. 479 approved in *Maunsell* v. *Egan* (1846) 9 Ir. Eq. R. 283.

attachment against the receiver being in default, and also of
removing him and appointing another.[44] The principle is that
the surety is answerable, to the extent of the penalty, for
whatever sum of money, whether principal, interest or costs, the
receiver has become liable for.[45] So a surety in a recognisance
conditioned that a receiver should duly account for all money
which he should receive "on account of the rents and the profits
of the real estate" of a testator, and duly pay the balance which
should from time to time be certified to be due from him, was
held liable for insurance moneys received by the receiver upon a
fire insurance effected by him, also for income paid to him under
orders of the court of funds in court designed to be reinvested in
real estate, and also for money paid to him under order of the
court to be spent on repairs.[45]

10. *When the Liability of the Surety becomes Enforceable*

General rule

The common expressions (accurate enough in their true sense)
that a surety "is only liable on default of the principal," or "only
promises to pay if he does not," must not be construed to convey
that there must, before the surety becomes liable, be any
demand and refusal between the parties of the principal
contract, or any final failure to pay on the part of the principal
debtor. When the subject-matter of the guarantee is conduct,
some breach of duty by the principal causing damage to the
holder of the guarantee must, of course, arise before there is
anything which the surety can be called upon to make good. But
as soon as a breach is committed of the duty performance of
which is guaranteed, or in the case of a debt that day of payment
arrives, the default of the principal is complete, and every surety
is, apart from any term to the contrary, immediately liable to
the full extent of his obligation, without being entitled to
require notice of the default.[46]

It is the surety's duty to see that the principal pays or
performs his duty, as the case may be.[47] This was the reason
given in the previous edition of this work for the rule that as

---

[44] *Maunsell* v. *Egan, supra; Re Graham* [1895] 1 Ch. 66.

[45] *Re Graham, supra.*

[46] A surety for the performance of a contract of indemnity could probably be sued *quia timet* as soon
as it was shown that damage was imminent but he could not be sued before: *Antrobus* v. *Davidson*
(1817) 3 Mer. 569. The last edition of this work took the view that the surety could not require
previous recourse against the principal or simultaneous recourse against co-securities. See now
discussion in Chapter 7.

[47] *Re Lockey* (1845) 1 Ph. 809; *Wright* v. *Simpson* (1802) 6 Ves. at 734. This passage in the text was
cited and approved in *Moschi* v. *Lep Air Services Ltd.* [1973] A.C. 337 *per* Lord Simon at 356.

soon as "the default of the principal is complete . . . every surety is, apart from special stipulation, immediately liable to the full extent of his obligation, without being entitled to require either notice of the default, or previous recourse against the principal, or simultaneous recourse against co-sureties."[48]

Surety contracting jointly with principal

A surety who contracts only jointly with the principal or with another surety is entitled by the general law of contract to have his co-contractor sued with him, a right formally enforced by a plea in abatement.[49] A promissory note beginning "I promise to pay," and signed by two persons, is the several note of each.[50] Where a number of sureties (say three) join in a guarantee each for a separate limited sum, this involves that the instrument imposes a several liability only on each; otherwise all might be sued three times over; and if only one was solvent, he might be compelled to pay three times the amount which *ex hypothesi* he has engaged for.[51] But the engagement might be joint in such a case if it provided that no surety shall be liable (whether by reason of a joint or several demand) for more than the amount limited in his case.[52]

Default by the principal

In the sense above[53] explained there must be a default by the principal before the surety can be made liable. Thus where the guarantee is that the principal will duly account for moneys coming into his hands it must be shown that money has been received by him.[54] In *Guardians of Belford Union* v. *Pattison*,[55] a surety for a treasurer was held liable for moneys due to his employers from their debtor with which the treasurer had debited himself in account with the debtor (who had supplied him with goods) in pursuance of a course of dealing between them the effect of which was that as between the two money had in substance passed, the employer having also treated the

[48] See *Ewart* v. *Latta* (1865) 4 Macq. 983. For a discussion of the rule and possible exceptions see *post*, pp. 132 *et seq.*

[49] Now see R.S.C. Order 15, r. 4. Note effect of Civil Liability (Contribution) Act 1978, as to which see Appendix 2.

[50] *March* v. *Ward* (1790) 1 Peake 177: *Clerk* v. *Blackstock* (1816) Holt 474.

[51] See *Collins* v. *Prosser* (1823) 1 B. & C. 682 *per* Bayley J. at 686.

[52] See, *e.g.* the bond in *Ellis* v. *Emmanuel* (1876) 1 Ex. D. 157, *i.e.* in previous sections of this sub-chapter.

[53] See also *Rickaby* v. *Lewis* (1905) 22 T.L.R. 130; *Eshelby* v. *Federated European Bank* [1932] 1 K.B. 254; (C.A.) 423.

[54] *Guardians of Belford Union* v. *Pattison* (1856) 11 Exch. 623; *Jephson* v. *Howkins* (1841) 2 M. & Gr. 366. Cf. *Harvell* v. *Foster* [1954] 2 Q.B. 367.

[55] *Supra*.

treasurer as paid by the debtor. In that case the treasurer had in effect been paid in goods which was owing to the employer. But it is suggested that it would not be open to an employer, generally speaking, to authorise his servant, instead of collecting the moneys due to the employer, to set them off against debts due by the servant, and then charge the surety for the servant, if the latter, perhaps having no money of his own, did not account to the employer for the amount of the sums set off. That would, in effect, be supplying the servant at the expense of the surety with money to pay his own debts to the debtors of his employer.[56]

Where a bond was conditioned that a collector should duly demand certain taxes, and duly enforce the law against those who should make default, the obligees were held entitled to recover on proof merely that less had been received than the proper amount, and that the collector had not returned a list of any defaulters, as was by law his duty, if there were any.[57] Similarly, a surety for an administrator is liable if the administrator has misapplied funds of the deceased, even though the time has not yet arrived for their distribution.[58]

Where the guarantee was that a poor law officer "should duly and faithfully discharge all and every the duties of his said office," it was held that the sureties were liable whether the breach of duty complained of was committed fraudulently or not.[59]

Where it is necessary to show that a loss has been sustained, it is not enough for the creditor merely to give evidence that the debtor has signed the deed of assignment for the benefit of his creditors.[60]

Surety for bill never presented

A surety for payment of a bill or note by the acceptor, is liable, though it is never presented, as it is his duty to see it is paid.[61] But where payment by the drawer or an indorser is guaranteed, the surety is discharged if the bill is not presented, or the drawer or indorser does not receive notice of dishonour, because then

---

[56] *Cf.* the cases as to payments to agents, *e.g. Stewart* v. *Aberdeen* (1838) 4 M. & W. 211; *Sweeting* v. *Pearce* (1861) 9 C.B. (N.S.) 534.

[57] *Loveland* v. *Knight* (1828) 3 C. & P. 106.

[58] *Archbishop of Canterbury* v. *Robertson* (1833) 1 C. & M. 690; *Dobbs* v. *Brain* (1898) 8 T.L.R. 630; *Harvell* v. *Foster* [1954] 2 Q.B. 367.

[59] *Bramley* v. *Guarantee Society* (1900) 64 J. P. 308.

[60] *Montague Stanley & Co.* v. *Solomons Ltd.* [1932] 2 K.B. 287.

[61] *Warrington* v. *Furbor* (1807) 8 East. 242; *Hitchcock* v. *Humfrey* (1843) 5 M. & Gr. 559; *Walton* v. *Mascoll* (1844) 13 M. & W. 452. It is said in these cases that the surety might be discharged if damnified.

the drawer or indorser is discharged.[62] But where the principal is liable without demand so is the surety.[63] The surety becomes liable to be sued when all the facts have occurred which show a default within the meaning of the guarantee, not when the fact of the default has been ascertained by litigation.[64]

Default involves a liability by the principal

There is no default by the principal, and the surety is, therefore, not liable, where the principal has a lawful excuse (not founded on the personal disability[65] or the statutes of limitation[66]) for the omission of which the creditor complains. Therefore where there was a guarantee for due accounting by a treasurer for moneys in his hands, and the treasurer was robbed by irresistible violence of such moneys specifically, the sureties were not liable.[67] Similarly, a mere mistake in book-keeping is not necessarily a breach of a bond for the good conduct of a clerk.[68] But where money was alleged by an employee to have been lost as he was travelling in his employer's service his surety was held liable.[69]

Refusal by creditor to accept performance

A surety is not liable when the creditor has refused to accept the performance of the duty guaranteed, as where a bond is given conditioned for service by an apprentice, and the master bids him go about his business.[70] The same applies if the apprentice leaves the service under a reasonable fear of ill-treatment.[71] However, where a banking company gave a letter of credit authorising a company to draw upon the bank, and it was stipulated that the company should forward goods the proceeds of which were to be applicable to the bills accepted by the bank, and the agents of the company guaranteed repayment to the bank of the amount to be due under the credit, it was held that they were not discharged although, owing to the bank stopping payment after it had accepted the bills, the principals declined to forward the goods. This was on the ground that the

---

[62] *Philips* v. *Astling* (1809) 2. Taunt. 206. And see *Hitchcock* v. *Humfrey, supra* at 564.
[63] See *Rede* v. *Farr.* (1817) 6 M. & S. 121.
[64] See *Colvin* v. *Buckle* (1844) 8 M. & W. 680.
[65] See *ante*, p. 2.
[66] See Chapter 10, *infra*.
[67] *Walker* v. *British Guarantee Association* (1852) 18 Q.B. 277.
[68] *Jephson* v. *Howkins* (1841) 2 M. & Gr. 366.
[69] *Melville* v. *Dridge* (1848) 6 C.B. 450.
[70] See *MacTaggart* v. *Watson* (1836) 3 C. & F. 525, 543.
[71] *Halliwell* v. *Counsell* (1878) 38 L.T. 176.

stoppage of the bank did not justify the principals in not forwarding the goods.[72]

Liability independent of default

The necessity of proof that the principal has failed to meet a valid claim does not, however, always exist. It is, of course, open to a party to agree to pay a sum in any event in order to put an end to a disputed claim against another. It is not necessary to show in such a case that the claim was valid.[73] But such agreements are not in reality guarantees, as the liability assumed is not collateral, but original.

Negligence of creditor

As it is the surety's duty to see the principal makes no default, he is liable notwithstanding any mere neglect by the creditor to safeguard his own interests.[74] Thus where the principal is a servant or agent, if the employer has omitted for long period to check and examine his accounts, the surety is not discharged.[75] Nor will neglect in the superintendence of a contract during the execution of works discharge a surety for the contractor.[76]

The surety guarantees the honesty of the person employed, and is not to be relieved because the employer fails to use all the means in his power to guard against the consequences of dishonesty.[77] And even where a bond is given under statute for securing the performance of the duties of an officer appointed under the statute, it is the duty of the surety to see that he does perform those duties and if any directions for securing that end are given by the statute to the superiors of the officer, those directions are for the additional security of the public only and neglect of them does not discharge the surety,[78] and this even though the persons guilty of that neglect are the obligees in the bond and plaintiffs in the action.[79] In Ireland it has been held

---

[72] *Ex p. Agra Bank* (1870) L.R. 9 Eq. 725.

[73] *Tempson* v. *Knowles* (1849) 7 C.B. 651. And see *Gull* v. *Lindsay* (1849) 4 Exch. 45.

[74] In *Bank of India* v. *Transcontinental Commodity Merchants Ltd., The Times*, October 22, 1981, Bingham J. held there was no duty on a creditor to avoid irregular dealings by the principal debtor which could prejudice both the creditor and the surety.

[75] *Trent Navigation Co.* v. *Harley* (1808) IO East. 34; *Black* v. *Ottoman Bank* (1862) 15 Moo. PC. 472; *Wilks* v. *Heeley* (1832) 1 C. & M. 249.

[76] *Mayor, etc., of Kingston-upon-Hull* v. *Harding* (1892) 2 Q.B. 494.

[77] *Black* v. *Ottoman Bank* (1862) 15 Moo. P.C. at 484.

[78] *Wilks* v. *Heeley* (1832) 1 C. & M 249; *Collins* v. *Gwynne* (1833) 9 Bing. 544; S.C. in error 2 Bing. N.C. 7; 6 Bing. N.C. 453 (H.L.); *MacTaggart* v. *Watson* (1836) 3 C. & F. 525; *Madden* v. *McMullen* (1860) 13 Ir. C.L.R. 305; *Guardians of Mansfield Union* v. *Wright* (1872) 9 Q.B.D. 683. See further *Donegal C.C.* v. *Life and Health Assurance Association* (1909) 2 I.R. 700; *Wicklow C.C.* v. *Hibernian Fire & General Ins. Co.* (1932) I.R. 58.

[79] See previous note. This proposition was doubted by Sir J. Hannen in *Guardians of Mansfield Union* v. *Wright* (1882) 9 Q.B.D. 683 where, however, *Collins* v. *Gwynne* was not cited. Jessel MR. in that case expressed a view in accordance with the principle stated in the text.

that the neglect or laches of a court officer will not discharge the surety.[80] Upon this ground not calling an officer to account according to a statute[81] and the omission to require him to bank moneys in his hands which the guarantors undertook he should bank[82] have been held not to discharge the sureties. However, actual connivance at the retention of moneys might discharge the surety,[83] as amounting to a receipt and a fresh credit to the principal.[84] And it might be that a statute directing a surety to be taken and that the principal be promptly called to account, should be so framed as to secure to the surety the benefit of that provision, and operate to discharge him if it was disobeyed.[85]

Express stipulations for diligence against the principal

A surety may, of course, by stipulation make it a condition precedent that active steps be taken by the creditor. Therefore, where the surety was not to be liable "but on failure of the creditor's utmost efforts and legal proceedings" to obtain the money from the principal, it was held that the meaning was that the surety was not liable unless these measures were taken promptly, and not that the surety was liable whenever they had been taken.[86] If the creditor, in taking a promissory note from principal and surety, agrees with the surety to call it in within three years, and does not, the surety is released.[87] However, a mere memorandum, "This note to be paid off within three years," does not bind the creditor to enforce it within that time. And where it was stipulated by a surety that the creditor should "see the principal make up his cash every month," the surety was not discharged in respect of the first month's embezzlements by neglect to carry this out, though he was discharged as to subsequent defalcations on the ground (it does not appear in the report) that he was then entitled to notice on order, if he wished it, to terminate the guarantee.[88]

Where it was stipulated that, before the surety was called on, the creditor "should avail himself to the utmost of any actual

[80] *Jephson* v. *Maunsell* (1847) 10 Ir. Eq. R. 38, 132.

[81] *Ibid.*

[82] *Creighton* v. *Rankin* (1840) 7 C. & F. 325.

[83] See *per* Lord Brougham in *MacTaggart* v. *Watson* (1836) 3 C. & F. at 543; *Dawson* v. *Lawes* (1854) Kay 280. See further *Dundee and Newcastle SS. Co. Ltd.* v. *National Guarantee & Suretyship Association Ltd.* (1881) 18 S.L.R. 685; *Bank of Scotland* v. *Morrison* (1911) S.C. 593.

[84] *Dawson* v. *Lawes, supra.*

[85] See *Bank of Ireland* v. *Beresford* (1878) 6 Dow. 233, 239. See also *Collins* v. *Gwynne* (1833) 9 Bing. 544. S.C. in error *sub. nom. Gwynne* v. *Burnell* (1835) 2 Bing. N.C. 7; 6 Bing N.C. 453 (H. & L.). See also *R.* v. *Fay* (1878) 4 L.R. Ir. 606.

[86] *Hall* v. *Hadley* (1835) 2 A. & E. 758. See also *Palmer* v. *Sheridan-Bickers, The Times*, July 20, 1910.

[87] *Lawrence* v. *Walmsley* (1862) 12 C.B. (N.S.) 799.

[88] *Mountague* v. *Tidcombe* (1705) 2 Vern. 519. See *Phillips* v. *Foxall* (1872) L.R. 7 Q.B. 666.

and bona fide security," it was held that this did not oblige him to bring an action upon a bill, given as such security, which was certain to be unproductive.[89] Where a guarantee was given to a mortgagee to cover any deficiency which might remain after the sale of the mortgaged property, it was held that this meant a completed sale, and that the guarantor could not be sued pending an action by the mortgagee upon a contract for sale, which was repudiated by the purchaser.[90]

Stipulation as to diligence to be expressed in guarantee

A stipulation that the creditor must exhaust any particular remedy against the principal before having recourse to the surety must be expressed in the guarantee. Thus oral evidence was held inadmissible to show that the indorsee of a bill of exchange drawn for the accommodation of the acceptor had taken the bill upon the terms of not calling upon the drawer until after certain securities to be deposited by the acceptor had been released.[91]

Notice of default

Upon the principle that it is the surety's duty to see that the principal performs the obligation guaranteed, the surety is not, apart from special stipulation, entitled to notice of the default.[92] Therefore, where the committee of a lunatic made default, and proceedings were taken and costs given against him, the surety for the committee was held liable for the costs (their undertaking extending to that), notwithstanding that they had received no notice of the default by reason of which costs were incurred.[93] "If they had no notice of it," said Lord Lyndhurst, "it was their own fault, for it was their duty to see that the committee duly passed his account."[93]

The right of the drawer or indorser of a bill to notice of dishonour is not an exception to this rule. Such a person is not by the law merchant liable at all until he has such notice.[94]

---

[89] *Musket* v. *Rogers* (1839) 8 Scott 51.

[90] *Moor* v. *Roberts* (1858) 3 C.B. (N.S.) 830.

[91] *Abrey* v. *Crux* (1869) L.R. 5 C.P. 37. See also *New London Credit Syndicate* v. *Neale* |1898| 2 Q.B. 487; *Hitchings* v. *Northern Leather Co.* |1914| 3 K.B. 907.

[92] *Nares* v. *Rowles* (1811) 14 East. 510; *Stothert* v. *Goodfellow* (1832) 1 N. & M. 202. See also Restatement, Security § 136 (1941): although American decisions have drawn a distinction between cases of specific debts and non-specific debts, this distinction is rejected by the Restatement. As to whether notice of default constituting "conclusive evidence" of liability under a guarantee is contrary to public policy see *Bache & Co. (London) Ltd.* v. *Banques Vernes* |1973| 2 Lloyds Rep. 437.

[93] *Re Lockey* (1845) 1 Ph. 509. See Heywood and Massey, *Court of Protection Practice* (10th ed., 1978) at p. 59.

[94] *Warrington* v. *Furbor* (1807) 8 East. 242, 245; *Black* v. *Ottoman Bank* (1862) 15 Moo. P.C. 472, 484; *Duncan Fox & Co.* v. *North and South Wales Bank* (1880) 6 A.C. 1, 13; *Carter* v. *White* (1883) 25 Ch.D. 666, 671.

However, a surety for payment of a bill or note by the acceptor, not being himself a party to the bill or having contracted to be treated as if he were, is not entitled to notice of dishonour; for it is his duty to see that it is paid.[95]

A surety may, of course, contract that the receipt of notice, either generally or within a certain time of the default, shall be a condition precedent of his liability.[96] But an omission by the creditor to give notice as contemplated does not necessarily discharge the surety.[97] Where there was a surety for the payment by instalments of a loan granted by a society to one of its members, and one of the rules stated that where a member was four weeks in arrears, the committee were to communicate with the sureties, it was held that non-communication was no breach of the engagement of the surety, and he was not discharged.[98] In *Gordon* v. *Rae,*[99] where a surety, before executing the bond, took a memorandum to the effect that he was to be informed if the account guaranteed exceeded £1,000 and was not reduced within a month, it was held that omission to do this did not discharge her.[1]

Demand upon the surety before action

A surety has not, unless his contract so provides, any right to require a demand to be made upon him before action. If a surety gives a bond conditioned to be void on the payment of a similar sum "on demand," or covenants or promises to pay the principal debt "on demand," a demand must be made upon him before he can be sued.[2] His obligation is to pay the collateral sum, and differs from a promise to pay on demand a present debt owing by the promisor.[3] In the latter case an action can be brought at once without any other demand than the writ.[4]

---

[95] *Warrington* v. *Furbor, supra; Swinyard* v. *Bowes* (1816) 5 M. & S. 62; *Hitchcock* v. *Humfrey* (1843) 5 M. & Cr. 559; *Walton* v. *Mascall* (1844) 13 M. & W. 452; *Carter* v. *White* (1883) 25 Ch.D. 666.

[96] *Gordon* v. *Rae* (1858) 8 E. & B. 1065. And see *Clarke* v. *Wilson* (1838) 3 M. & W. 208.

[97] *Gordon* v. *Rae, supra.* For a case where it did, see *Eshelby* v. *Federated European Bank* [1932] 1 K.B. 254, 423 (C.A.).

[98] *Price* v. *Kirkham* (1864) 3 H. & C. 437.

[99] (1858) 8 E. & B. 1065.

[1] See, too, *Cooper* v. *Evans* (1867) L.R. 4 Eq. 45.

[2] A surety has the right to have notice given to him in his capacity as a surety and not, *e.g.* as a director of the principal debtor. *Canadian Petrofina Ltd.* v. *Motormart Ltd.* (1969) 7 D.L.R. (3d) 330.

[3] *Re Brown's Estate, Brown* v. *Brown* [1893] 2 Ch. 300, following *Birks* v. *Trippet* (1666) 1 Williams' Saund. 32; *Bradford Old Bank* v. *Sutcliffe* [1918] 2 K.B. 833. In *Esso Petroleum Co. Ltd.* v. *Alstonbridge Properties Ltd.* [1975] 1 W.L.R. 1474, Walton J. held that where a demand was required by the guarantee and which demand of its own intrinsic nature changed the liability of the guarantors from one to pay instalments to one to pay the whole amount guaranteed at once, it was an essential ingredient of any cause of action to recover the lump sum. *Cf. General Produce Co.* v. *United Bank Ltd.* [1979] 2 Lloyds Rep. 255.

[4] *Ibid.* And see *Norton* v. *Ellam* (1837) 2 M. & W. 461; *Jackson* v. *Ogg* (1859) Johns. 397; *Re George* (1890) 44 Ch.D. 629.

If a surety joins with a principal in a promissory note payable on demand for money lent to the latter, the surety appearing on the face of the note as a principal, although known to have joined merely as surety, he can (notwithstanding the above rule) be sued without previous demand in the same way as the principal.[5] However, where a surety joined in such a note, and the payee gave a collateral memorandum that it was given to secure the banking account of the principal, the memorandum was treated as having the same effect as if it were a defeasance on the face of the note, and an action against the surety was held not maintainable until after demand made upon him.[6]

Where a surety joined in a lease to a third party and covenanted that the lessee should "at all times during the term pay the rent on the respective days" when it became due, and that in case the lessee should neglect to pay the rent for 40 days the defendant would pay it on demand, it was held that the earlier part of the covenant was qualified by the latter, and that the lessor could not sue the surety till after forty days' non-payment and demand made.[7] A guarantee for the repayment of money which was in fact secured by mortgage, though it was not so stated in the guarantee, was held to become enforceable so as to set time running under the Statute of Limitations without notice to pay off the mortgage or demand upon the surety; but apparently it would not be so if the debt had been guaranteed as a mortgage debt.[8]

Other express conditions

The guarantor can, of course, by stipulation, interpose any other condition precedent to his liability arising, as, for instance, that money shall be due from him to the principal on another account,[9] or that a certificate shall be given by a third party that the creditor has performed his part of the principal contract.[10] But where a building owner guaranteed the repayment of advances made to the builder "upon the completion" of the buildings "in accordance with the contract" between himself and the builder, it was held that he was liable when the buildings were, in fact, completed, though the builder could not have sued for want of a certificate of completion required by the contract.[11]

---

[5] *Ex p. Whitworth* (1841) 2 M.D. & De G. 158.

[6] *Hartland* v. *Jukes* (1863) 1 H. & C. 667.

[7] *Sicklemore* v. *Thistleton* (1817) 6 M. & S. 9.

[8] *Henton* v. *Paddison* (1893) 68 L.T. 405. See generally Chapter 10.

[9] *Hill* v. *Nuttall* (1864) 17 C.B. (N.S.) 262.

[10] See *Ex p. Ashwell* (1832) 2 Deac. & Ch. 281.

[11] *Lewis* v. *Hoare* (1881) 44 L.T. 66 *Cf. Eshelby* v. *Federated European Bank* [1932] 1 K.B. 254, 423 (C.A.).

Implied conditions precedent to surety's liability

Cases may also, of course, arise, where the creditor is unable to recover from the surety owing to non-fulfilment by him of a condition precedent being a necessary implication from the express terms of the contract between creditor and surety.[12]

Payment out of particular fund

Again, the promise may be only that the debt shall be paid out of a fund of the debtor, and this either absolutely,[13] provided the fund exists,[14] or contingently upon there being no prior charges.[15] And if the fund does not exist, the surety is not liable, provided, of course, there has been no fraud by him, and no express or implied warranty that it does.[15a] Thus, where three daughters agree to pay a debt of their mother "out of her estate at her decease," it was held that this was only a promise to pay out of what the mother might leave behind her available for the payment of her debts, and did not bind them to pay out of property of which the mother was tenant for life, with the remainder to the promisors, notwithstanding that it was shown that in fact (though the creditor did not appear to have notice of this) that the mother had no other property.[15a] Similarly, where a surety guaranteed payment of the price of bricks to be supplied to a Government contractor "when the amount of the contract is paid," and the contract was put an end to by the Government, owing to the default of the contractor (who was allowed for the work actually done, for which, however, he had been paid in advance by the consent of the plaintiff), the surety was held not liable for anything.[16]

Admission by a judgment against principal

Unless it is admissible (*e.g.* under the Civil Evidence Act 1972), an admission by the principal debtor is no evidence against the surety.[17] Nor is he bound by a judgment or award

---

[12] *Spencer* v. *Lotz* (1916) 32 T.L.R. 373; *Guy-Pell* v. *Foster* [1930] 2 Ch. 169.

[13] See *Stephens* v. *Pell* (1834) 2 C. & M. 710; *Brown* v. *Fletcher* (1876) 35 L.T. 165 *per* Bramwell B. *arguendo*; *Wilson* v. *Craven* (1841) 8 M. & W. 584.

[14] See *Brown* v. *Fletcher* (1876) 35 L.T. 165.

[15] See *Jupp* v. *Richardson* 26 L.J. Ex. 261.

[15a] See note 14, *supra*.

[16] *Hemming* v. *Trenery* (1835) 2 C.M. & R. 385.

[17] *Evans* v. *Beattie* (1803) 5 Esp. 26; *Re Kitchin* (1881) 17 Ch.D. 668. In *Bruns* v. *Colocotronis, The Vasso* [1979] 2 Lloyds Rep. 412, Robert Goff J. applied *Re Kitchin, supra*, in holding that words guaranteeing the due performance of all the obligations of the principal debtor did not *per se* mean that the surety was bound by an arbitration award between creditor and principal debtor. At 418 the learned Judge pointed out that to hold otherwise might result in the surety being bound by an award made in the absence of the principal debtor. Note also *Fisher* v. *P.G. Wellfair Ltd.* (1981) 125 S.J. 413.

against the principal.[18] This rule has, of course, no application to the admissibility of the accounts stated between the principal and creditor upon the question of appropriation of payments made by the principal. The effect of the accounts is in such cases the very issue to be tried.[19] But it has been held in Ireland that the books of a rate collector not deceased are evidence against his surety of the receipt of the money by the collector, at any rate where the surety bond was also conditioned for the correctness of the accounts.[20] However this may be, in an action against a surety for an officer or servant after the death of the principal, it is clear that evidence may be given of entries or ticks made by him in the books kept by him in the course of the duty the performance of which was guaranteed.[21] And even entries in a private book are admissible after his death on the ground that they were against interest,[22] a principle which, it seems, should also make receipts given by him to the debtors of his employers evidence against his sureties after his death.[23]

It is common,[24] however, to make express provision for the surety being concluded by the admission of the principal, or by the result of proceedings against him or by the certificate of a third person.[25] But if the debt itself is irrecoverable for illegality no such certificate will make the surety liable.[25]

Sureties for a liquidator, in the winding up of a company by or under the supervision of the court ought to be allowed to attend at their own expense the taking of the accounts, and if the liquidator is known, when the taking of the accounts commences, to be bankrupt or unlikely to be able to pay over the balance found due, the sureties should have notice of the fact in order to enable them to attend.[26] Where under such circumstances the accounts were taken without such notice, the surety was allowed to re-open them upon bringing into court the amount of the bond (in that case less than the balance due from the liquidator), with an undertaking to pay interest in respect of the delay, and paying the costs of the summons.[26]

---

[18] *Re Kitchin* (1881) 17 Ch.D. 668.
[19] This was the question in *Lysaght* v. *Walker* (1831) 5 Bligh (N.S.) 1. The headnote would suggest that the general admissibility of accounts stated by the principal was affirmed in that case. But see case cited in the next note.
[20] *Guardians of Abbeyleix Union* v. *Sutcliffe* (1890) 26 L.R. Ir. 332.
[21] *Goss* v. *Watlington* (1821) 3 B. & B. 132; *Whitnash* v. *George* (1828) 8 B. & C. 556.
[22] *Middleton* v. *Melton* (1829) 5 M. & Ry. 264.
[23] *Middleton* v. *Melton, supra* questioning the dicta to the contrary in *Goss* v. *Watlington* (1821) 3 B. & B. 132.
[24] *e.g.* in guarantees given to banks for advances, in bonds for liquidators, etc.
[25] See *Swan* v. *Bank of Scotland* (1836) 10 Bligh (N.S.) 627.
[26] *Re Birmingham Brewing, Malting and Distillery Co.* (1883) 31 W.R. 415.

Retainer

The executor of a creditor is entitled to retain the amount of the debt secured by the joint promissory note of the debtor and surety out of a legacy left by the creditor to the surety.[27]

The creditor is not entitled to call upon the executors of a deceased surety to impound a fund to answer future claims of a contingent character.[28] But the executor of an obligor in a money bond, whose liability on the face of the bond was that of a principal, though in fact he was surety only, was held entitled to keep in hand the amount against creditors of inferior degree, though the debt was not yet payable, and though another obligor who was really the principal might possibly pay.[29]

---

[27] *Coates* v. *Coates* (1864) 33 Beav. 249. See also *Re Melton* [1918] 1 Ch. 37.
[28] *King* v. *Malcott* (1852) 9 Hare 692. Cf. *Antrobus* v. *Davidson* (1817) 3 Mer. 569.
[29] *Atkinson* v. *Grey* (1853) 1 Sm. & G. 577.

CHAPTER 5

MISREPRESENTATION AND CONCEALMENT

General principles

A surety is not bound by his contract if it was induced by any misrepresentation by the creditor, whether fraudulently made or not, of any fact known to him and material to be known to the surety[1]; where the guarantee is voidable on this ground the surety may have the contract set aside and securities pledged thereunder returned.[2]

Circumstances changing before completion

If circumstances calculated to influence a proposed surety are represented by the creditor as existing, and they cease to exist before the guarantee is complete, that must be notified to the surety.[3] So, if it is represented that it is intended that part of the risk will be borne by the creditor himself or by any specified party,[4] a subsequent abandonment of that intention, if not communicated, will destroy the validity of the guarantee.[5]

State of accounts with principal

A guarantee will fail if the creditor misrepresents to the surety the state of accounts between the principal and himself.[6] But a surety proposing to guarantee a banking account should inquire whether there is any adverse balance already existing; he is not entitled to assume there is not.[7]

---

[1] *London General Omnibus Co.* v. *Holloway* [1912] 2 K.B. 72 at p.77; *Workington Harbour etc.* v. *Trade Indemnity Co.* (1934) 49 Ll. L.R. 305; 49 Ll.L.R. 430 (C.A.); 54 Ll. R.103 (H.L.); *Mackenzie* v. *Royal Bank of Canada* [1934] A.C.468; *Ben Line* v. *Henreux* (1935) 52 Ll.R. L.R. 27 at pp.31, 32. That the surety may have been induced to contract by the fraud of the principal is, of course, no defence, unless the creditor is a party to the fraud; *Spencer* v. *Handley* (1842) 4 M. & Gr.414; and *cf.* the cases as to duress, *post*, p.129.

[2] *Mackenzie* v. *Royal Bank of Canada* [1934] A.C. 1(P.C.) The fact that the bank had acted on the faith of the guarantee did not preclude relief. See also as to the form of relief: *Cooper* v. *Joel* (1859) 27 Beav. 313, (on appeal: (1859) 1 De G.F. & J.240). *Cf. Brooking* v. *Maudsley Son and Field* (1888) 38 Ch. D. 636.

[3] *Davies* v. *London and Provincial Marine Insurance Co.* (1878) 8 Ch. D.469; *Bank of Montreal* v. *Stuart* [1911] A.C.120; *Hawes* v. *Bishop* [1909] 2 K.B. 390.

[4] *Evans* v. *Brembridge* (1855) 2 K. & J.174; (1856) 8 De G.M. & G.100, where a sole surety was misled into thinking he was one of two sureties.

[5] See *Tail* v. *Baring* (1864) 4 Giff. 485; 4 De G.J. & S.318. Cp. *Hansard* v. *Lethbridge* (1892) 8 T.L.R. 346 (C.A.); *Ellesmere Brewery Co.* v. *Cooper* [1896] 1 Q.B.75.

[6] *Blest* v. *Brown* (1862) 3 Giff. 450; 4 De G.F. & J.367; *McKewan* v. *Thornton* (1861) 2 F. & F. 594.

[7] *Kirby* v. *Duke of Marlborough* (1813) 2 M. & S.18.

Misrepresentation as to extent of liability

In the case of a guarantor who was led to believe that he was simply guaranteeing a bank loan, but the guarantee in fact extended to "all debts and liabilities, direct or indirect" of the principal debtor, the bank was prevented from recovering in respect of "indirect" liabilities.[8]

Mispresentation by silence

Misrepresentation may, of course, be made by mere silence or concealment.[9] This may vitiate a security without it being wilful and intentional or made with a view to advantage to be gained by the creditor.[10] But a guarantee is not an insurance,[11] and there is no obligation on the creditor to disclose to the surety every circumstance within his knowledge material for the surety to know.[12]

The requirement in the earlier cases that the creditor disclose all known facts material to the risk was abandoned because "no creditor could rely upon a contract of guaranty, unless he communicated to the proposed sureties everything relating to his dealings with the principal. . . . "[13] This would be impracticable, and in some cases, *e.g.* where there is a banker/customer relationship between creditor and principal, also a breach of confidence.[14]

Despite earlier dicta to the contrary[15] it now seems settled that contracts of guarantee, as opposed to insurance contracts,[16]

---

[8] *Royal Bank of Canada* v. *Hall* (1961) 30 D.L.R. (2d) 138. The bank had taken assignments of other debts of the principal owed to other customers of the bank.

[9] As in *L.G.O.C.* v. *Holloway* [1912] 2 K.B.72. In *Shidiak* v. *Bank of West Africa* [1964] N.N.L.R. 96 the guarantor was held entitled to rescind because the bank manager taking the guarantee knew that the guarantor was mistaken as to the amount involved but failed to disclose the true position.

[10] *Railton* v. *Mathews* (1844) 1 B.C. and F.934: *Workington Harbour etc.* v. *Trade Indemnity Co.* (1934) 49 Ll.L. R.430, at pp.433, 444, 452, 453; 54 Ll.L. R.103; *Mackenzie* v. *Royal Bank of Canada* [1934] A.C. 468; *Ben Line* v. *Henreux* (1935) 52 Ll.L.Rep.27.

[11] See the judgment of Romer L.J. in *Seaton* v. *Heath* [1899] 1 Q.B. 782 at p.792. The decision of the C.A. was reversed on the facts [1910] A.C. 135.

[12] *Hamilton* v. *Watson* (1845) 12 C. & F.109; *North British Insurance Co.* v. *Lloyd* (1854) 10 Exch.523; *Wythes* v. *Labouchere* (1859) 3 De G. & J. 593, 609; *Pledge* v. *Buss* (1860) Johns.663; *Lee* v. *Jones* 14 C.B. (N.S.) 386; (1864) 17 C.B. (N.S.) 482; *Way* v. *Hearn* (1862) 13 C.B.292; *Davies* v. *London and Provincial Marine Insurance Co.* (1878) 8 Ch.D.469. *Lloyds Bank* v. *Harrison* (March 6, 1925) IV Legal Decisions Affecting Bankers 12 (C.A.).

[13] *Lee* v. *Jones* (1863) 17 C.B. (N.S.) 482 *per* Lord Blackburn at p.503.

[14] *Tournier* v. *National Provincial and Union Bank* [1924] 1 .K.B. 461.

[15] *Owen* v. *Homan* (1851) 3 Mac. & G. 378, 397 (Lord Truro), a case affirmed on other grounds by the House of Lords at 4 H.L.C. 997. Lord Truro's dictum was later disapproved; see *North British Insurance Co.* v. *Lloyd* (1854) 10 Exch. at p.532, (where it is pointed out that Lord Truro did not seem aware of *Hamilton* v. *Watson* (1845) 12 C. & F. 109); *Pledge* v. *Buss* (1860) Johns, 663; See also Sheridan, *Rights in Security* (1974), p.294. The dictum of Tudor Evans J. in *Wales* v. *Wadham* [1977] 1 W.L.R. at 214G referring to suretyship as an example of an *uberrimae fidei* contract appears to have been *per incuriam.*

[16] The courts will look at the essence of a contract to see whether they are for insurance or are guarantees and whether *uberrimae fidei* is required; *Seaton* v. *Heath* [1899] 1 Q.B. 782 at p.794.

are not *uberrimae fidei* and therefore non-disclosure, to avoid a guarantee, must amount to misrepresentation.

What matters must be disclosed

A creditor must reveal to the surety every fact which under the circumstances the surety would expect not to exist; for the omission to mention that such a fact does exist is an implied misrepresentation that it does.[17] But a banker taking a guarantee for an overdraft to a customer is not ordinarily bound to disclose to the intending surety the unsatisfactory character of a previous account of the customer or other matters generally affecting his financial credit,[18] because dissatisfaction with the customer's credit is the probable reason for requiring the guarantee.[19] In fact it has been held that the bank need not even disclose an existing overdraft unless specifically asked.[20] However, where the intending guarantor makes enquiries of the bank, he must be given a "true, honest and accurate answer" about any matters material to the giving of the guarantee.[20] If he is under a misapprehension which he communicates to the bank, the bank has a duty to correct it.[21]

A guarantee given to a bank to cover the deficiency in produce to be consigned to the bank against bills drawn was held good notwithstanding that the bank had been informed that there probably would be a deficiency and had not communicated it to the sureties.[22]

In *North British Insurance Co.* v. *Lloyd*[23] it was held that on

---

[17] *Hamilton* v. *Watson* (1845) 12 C. & F. 109, per Lord Campbell; *Lee* v. *Jones* (1864) 17 C.B. (N.S.) 482, 503, 504, *per* Blackburn J.; *Phillips* v. *Foxall* (1872) L.R.7 Q.B. 666. This obligation has been said to be subject to "a suitable opportunity to make the circumstances known"; *Franklin Bank* v. *Cooper* (1853) 36 Maine 179 at 196. The Law Reform Committee of South Australia in its 39th Report (1976) has proposed an obligation on a creditor to disclose to a proposed surety all matters material to the decision to enter the guarantee. A similar proposal has been made by the Law Reform Commission of British Columbia's Report on Guarantees of Consumer Debts (1979).

[18] *Hamilton* v. *Watson* (1845) 12 C. & F. 109, 119; *Wythes* v. *Labouchere* (1859) 3 D. & J. 593, 609; *National Provincial Bank* v. *Glanusk* [1913] 3 K.B.335; *Goodwin* v. *National Bank of Australasia* (1968) 117 C.L.R. 17, 42 A.J.L.R. 110. But see *Small* v. *Currie* (1854) 2 Drewr. 102, 118. Perhaps the extreme boundary of this rule was reached in *Cooper* v. *National Provincial Bank* [1946] K.B. 1 where the bank was held to be under no duty to disclose to the guarantor of a woman's account that her bankrupt husband was able to draw on the account, or that the account had been operated irregularly, *i.e.* the payment of properly issued cheques had been countermanded.

[19] See *Lee* v. *Jones* (1864) 17 C.B. (N.S.) 482. Alternatively, such matters can be dismissed as being "extrinsic" to the guarantee: *London General Omnibus Co. Ltd.* v. *Holloway* [1912] 2 K.B. 72 (C.A.) at p.87. A third explanation is that it can be expected that the customer has properly explained the general position to the surety: *per* Sargant L.J. in *Lloyds Bank* v. *Harrison* (March 6, 1925) IV Legal Decisions Affecting Bankers 12 at p.16. A fourth reason was suggested in the Scottish case of *Royal Bank of Scotland* v. *Greenshields* [1914] S.C. 259 *i.e.* that the bank is entitled to assume that the intending surety has made himself acquainted with the customer's financial position.

[20] *Westminster Bank Ltd.* v. *Cond* (1940) 46 Com. Cas. 60; *O'Brien* v. *The Australian and New Zealand Bank* (1971) 5 S.A.S.R. 347.

[21] *Royal Bank of Scotland* v. *Green Shields* [1914] S.C.259.

[22] *Welton* v. *Somes* (1888) 5 T.L.R.46; (1889) 5 T.L.R. 184 (C.A.).

[23] (1854) 10 Exch. 523.

taking a guarantee for a loan the creditor was not bound to disclose that the guarantee was taken because another surety was desirous of retiring. At the end of the judgment it is observed that a surety may retire for other reasons than distrust of the debtor's position. In *Roper* v. *Cox*[24] a landlord took a guarantee for a tenant without disclosing that the latter had in a previous tenancy to him been in default with his rent and was still indebted to him for it. This was held to be no defence without an allegation of fraud. In a building contract the employer need not usually reveal to the contractor or his surety the difficult nature of the site where under the contract this is a matter to be left to the skill and experience of the contractor.[25]

Existing indebtedness

But in some circumstances the fact of existing indebtedness may be a matter to be naturally assumed not to exist, and in such cases disclosure must be made. In *Lee* v. *Jones*[26] merchants obtained a guarantee for the payments over to them of the receipts of their agent, who sold for them upon a del credere commission and was recited in the guarantee to be employed on terms of settling with them at short intervals. In fact he was at the date of the guarantee in arrear with payment for coal sold. It was held that non-disclosure of these facts, was having regard to the recital, was evidence of fraud. "It depends," said Blackburn, J., in the Exchequer Chamber, "whether in such a transaction as that described in the agreement it might or might not naturally be expected that the matters might have allowed a balance of this extent to accumulate and might have allowed the amount to stand over unsettled for so long a time."[27]

Previous misconduct of a servant

So, too, where a guarantee is taken for good behaviour, the employer must disclose any previous misconduct of the principal in his office of which he is aware. For it is not naturally to be expected that, if he had misconducted himself to the employer's knowledge, he would be continued in the office.[28] And so where there is a continuing guarantee of this sort the creditor must

[24] (1882) 10 L.R. Ir.200.
[25] *Trade Indemnity Co.* v. *Workington Harbour and Dock Board.* [1937] A.C. 1 (H.L).
[26] (1861) 14 C.B. (N.S.) 386; (1864) 17 C.B. (N.S.) 482.
[27] (1864) 17 C.B. (N.S.) at p.505.
[28] *Smith* v. *Bank of Scotland* (1813) I Dow. 272, explained by Blackburn J. in *Lee* v. *Jones* (1864) 17 C.B. (N.S.) at p.504; *Phillips* v. *Foxall* (1872) L.R.7 Q.B. 666; *Sanderson* v . *Aston* (1873) L.R.8 Ex.73; *London and General Omnibus Co.* v. *Holloway* [1912] 2 K.B. 72. As to mere irregularities not amounting to misconduct, see *Durham Corporation* v. *Fowler* (1889) 22 Q.B.D. 394; *Caxton* v. *Drew* (1899) 68 L.J. Q.B.380.

communicate any misconduct for which the servant might be dismissed which he finds out during the employment, or he will lose the benefit of the guarantee in respect of future misconduct.[29] If the employer knows facts which give him reason to believe that there has been misconduct and he does not disclose them, the surety is discharged.[30] The disclosure of previous misconduct, which the employer must make if he is aware of it, must be sufficiently complete to enable the surety to judge whether he will assent to the servant being retained in office on his guarantee; and therefore it was held that notice of "defaults to a large amount" was not enough where there had been falsification of books and fabrication of entries.[31] It does not appear to have been decided whether an employer must disclose to a guarantor misconduct of the servant in other positions of which he is aware.[32]

The holder of a fidelity guarantee does not, by merely delaying to communicate a defalcation to the surety, lose his remedy against him for that defalcation, provided he does not actively conceal it from him, and the rights of the parties have not been altered.[33] A treatment of a defalcation in the books of the employer as a loan so as to prevent the other clerks knowing the fact does not discharge the surety either as a concealment from him or, if not so intended, by way of waiver or novation.[33] So a continuance of the employment or credit after a defalcation, and without communicating it, will not release the guarantor in respect of that defalcation.[34]

Principal defrauded by creditor

Where the debt guaranteed is the result of fraud practised upon the principal by the creditor, the surety may have the guarantee cancelled[35]; but he must make the principal a party in order that the whole transaction may be set aside.[35] Co-sureties are also necessary parties to an action by one surety to have the guarantee given up,[36] but not sureties for a distinct part of the same debt.[37]

---

[29] *Phillips* v. *Foxall* (1872) L.R. 7 Q.B.666; *Sanderson* v. *Aston* (1873) L.R. 8 Ex. 73; *Enright* v. *Falvey* (1879) 4 L.R. Ir 397.
[30] *Smith* v. *Bank of Scotland* (1813) 1 Dow. 272, *per* Lord Eldon.
[31] *Enright* v. *Falvey* (1879) 4 L.R.Ir 397.
[32] See, however, *Wythes* v. *Labouchere* (1859) 3 De G. & J. 593, 609.
[33] *Peel* v. *Tatlock* (1799) 1 B. & P.419.
[34] *Mountague* v. *Tidcombe* (1705) 2 Vern.519.
[35] *Allan* v. *Houlden* (1843) 6 Beav. 148.
[36] *Allan* v. *Houlden* (1843) 6 Beav. 148; *Ware* v. *Horwood* (1807) 14 Ves. 28, at p.34. But cp. *Coope* v. *Twynam* (1823) T. & R. 426.
[37] *Pendlebury* v. *Walker* (1841) 4 Y. & C. Ex. 424.

Secret arrangement as to application of advances

In *Hamilton* v. *Watson*[38] the surety guaranteed a cash credit. As expected, the cash was used to repay an existing debt to the creditor's bank. Non-disclosure of the expected use of the cash did not release the surety. However, had there been a contractual obligation so to use the advance the creditor would have been bound to disclose it as, "something between the creditor and the principal debtor which the surety would not naturally expect to take place."[39]

In *Stone* v. *Compton*[40] the mortgage securing the same sum as that covered by the guarantee was read over by the creditor's agent to the surety. It recited that the full sum was being advanced, whereas it had been agreed that part of it should be applied to an old debt which the morgage recited as paid. The Court of Common Pleas held that the creditor could not in law recover, though no intention to defraud was suggested.[41] However, there is no obligation to disclose to a surety an arrangement made by the debtor with another surety, to whom he is indebted, for the payment of part of that debt out of the money to be raised on the guarantee.[42]

Other secret arrangements

Any private arrangement modifying what from the terms of his guarantee the surety would take to be the transaction between the principal and the creditor must be communicated to the surety,[43] *e.g.* where a surety joined with the principal in a promissory note, but there was an understanding between the principal and the payee that the note should not be enforced for five years, and that interest at 10 per cent. should be payable, being secured by a distinct note of the principal.[43] Where a surety guarantees to one of a number of creditors repayment of an advance to be made by that creditor to enable the debtor to pay a composition_which the general body of creditors have agreed to accept, and the creditor making the advance secretly arranges for and takes payment of his own debt in full, the surety is entitled to be discharged.[44]

---

[38] (1845) 12 C. & F.109.
[39] (1845) 12 C. & F. at p.119. See, too, *Pendlebury* v. *Walker* (1841) 4 Y. & C. Ex.424; *Stone* v. *Compton* (1838) 5 Bing. N.C. 142; *Pidcombe* v. *Bishop* (1825) B. & C. 605; *Railton* v. *Mathews* (1844) 10 C. & F. 934 (H.L.) See also the Scottish cases of *Wallace's Factor* v. *M'Kissock* (1898) 25 R.642, *Sutherland* v. *W.M. Low Co. Ltd* (1901) 3 F.972.
[40] (1838) 5 Bing. N.C. 142.
[41] But see *Greenfield* v. *Edwards* (1865) 2 De G.J. & S.582.
[42] *Mackreth* v. *Walmsley* (1884) 51 L.T.19.
[43] See *Espey* v. *Lake* (1852) 10 Hare 260. Co. *Walker* v. *Hardman* (1837) 4 C. & F. 258.
[44] *Pendlebury* v. *Walker* (1841) 4 Y. & C. Ex.424.

Non-disclosure after suretyship entered into

There is no general duty to inform the surety of changes of circumstances or defaults by the principal debtor after suretyship has been entered into,[45] unless some specific provision is made.

---

[45] *National Provincial Bank* v. *Glanusk* [1913] 3 K.B. 335.

CHAPTER 6

ILLEGALITY AND UNDUE INFLUENCE[1]

Principal obligation illegal

A guarantee, like any other contract, may be void for illegality, which may effect either the debt itself guaranteed, or only the guarantee. If the debt itself is void for illegality, it cannot be recovered under the guarantee.[2] So guarantees have frequently been held void where given, for a secret preference by a bankrupt or compounding debtor.[3] A promise that a corporation shall do something beyond its legal powers is void.[4] On the other hand, a surety for the repayment of money borrowed by a company *ultra vires* is liable.[5] In *Heald* v. *O'Connor*,[6] Fisher J. suggested that the true distinction was not between guarantees of illegal and *ultra vires* contracts but whether the guarantor undertakes to pay only those sums which the principal debtor could lawfully be called on to pay or whether he undertakes to pay those sums which the debtor promised to pay whether or not the principal debtor could lawfully be called upon to do so.

Where a surety repaid a debt, which unknown to him or the principal was unenforceable (by reason of section 6 of the Moneylenders Act 1927), he was held entitled to recover from the principal.[7]

---

[1] See generally *Chitty on Contracts* (24th ed., 1977) Vol. 1, Chaps. 7 and 16; G. H. Treitel, *The Law of Contract* (Stevens, 5th ed., 1979), Chap. 11.

[2] *Swan* v. *Bank of Scotland* (1836) 10 Bligh (N.S.) 627. *Bentinck Ltd.* v. *Cromwell Engineering Co.* [1971] 1 Q.B. 324; *Heald* v. *O'Connor* [1971] 1 W.L.R. 497.

[3] *Jackman* v. *Mitchell* (1807) 13 Ves. 581; *Coleman* v. *Waller* (1829) 3 Y. & J.212; *McKewan* v. *Sanderson* (1875) L.R.20 Eq.65.

[4] *McGregor* v. *Dover and Deal Ry.* (1852) 18 Q.B.618 (Exch.Ch.)

[5] *Chambers* v. *Manchester and Milford Ry.* (1864) 5 B. & S. 588, 612; *Yorkshire Railway Wagon Co.* v. *Maclure* (1881) 19 Ch. D.478. *Garrard* v. *James* [1925] 1 Ch.616. In the U.S.A. the distinction is drawn between contracts merely beyond the powers of the corporation, *i.e.* a question of capacity, where the surety is liable: *Gates* v. *Tebbets* 83 Neb 573, 119 N.W. 1120 (1909); *Winn* v. *Sanford* 145 Mass. 302, 14 N.E.119 (1887); *Maledon* v. *Leflone* 62 Ark. 387, 35 S.W. 1102 (1896); *Mitchell* v. *Zurn* 221 S.W. 954 (1920) and where the principal contract requires the performance of *mala in se*, or *mala prohibita* where the surety is discharged; see *Swift* v. *Beers* 3 N.Y.70 (1849); *Basnight* v. *American Mfg. Co.* 174 N.C.206, 93 S.E. 734 (1917); *Edwards County* v. *Jennings* 89 Tex 618, 35 S.W. 1053 (1896); *Pendleton* v. *Greever* 80 Okl. 35, 193 P.885 (1920); *First National Bank* v. *Clark's Estate* 59 Colo. 455, 149 P.612 (1915).

[6] [1971] 1 W.L.R. 497 (s.54, Companies Act 1948: illegal assistance to company to purchase own shares). The point was expressly left open in *Argo Carribean Group* v. *Lewis* [1976] 2 Lloyd's Rep. 289. See Cohn [1947] 10 M.L.R. 40. It may be that the question of the validity of the guarantee should turn on whether the guarantor knows or believes the contract to be binding on the principal debtor: see Furmston (1961) 24 M.L.R. 644. See also Steyn (1974) 90 L.Q.R. 246, 253.

[7] *Re Chetwynd's Estate* [1938] Ch.13.

Illegal guarantee for legal debt

The guarantee may be illegal and void though the debt itself is enforceable, as where it is given in order to induce the creditor to conceal the existence of the debt, so as to deceive the Bankruptcy Court,[8] or is given to stifle a prosecution.[9]

Threat of prosecution

A mere promise not to institute a prosecution does not by itself make void for illegality a guarantee for which there is other consideration, *viz.* forbearing a civil suit.[10] But where there is an agreement to stifle a prosecution the guarantee is void, whether the alleged criminal was in fact guilty or not and whether the prosecution had been in fact stifled or not.[11]

There is a distinction in the inference to be drawn[12] between cases where a debtor gives a security for his own debt under apprehension of a prosecution and cases where, by a threat to prosecute a debtor, a guarantee or security is obtained from a third person under no independent liability.[13] In the former case the circumstance that the security was obtained by a threat of prosecution does not of itself show that there was an agreement not to prosecute, and thus does not necessarily vitiate the security.[14] But threats addressed to a third person to which he yields almost necessarily show that the guarantee was given on the terms of there being no prosecution.[15] In many cases there is no other consideration which can be suggested.[16]

Undue pressure

Where a security is obtained, by a threat of prosecution, from a father or other near relative of the suggested delinquent, it may also be invalid as extorted by undue influence or pressure.[17]

---

[8] *Coles* v. *Strick* (1850) 15 Q.B.2.

[9] *Cannon* v. *Rands* (1870) 23 L.T.817; 11 Cox C.C.631; *Seear* v. *Cohen* (1881) 45 L.T. 589; *Williams* v. *Bayley* (1866) L.R. 1 H.L.200; *Davies* v. *London and Provincial Marine Insurance Co.* (1878) 8 Ch. D.469; *Jones* v. *Merionethshire Building Society* [1891] 2 Ch. 587; [1892] 1 Ch.173; *Osborn* v. *Robbins* (1867) 36 N.Y.365.

[10] See *per* Bowen L.J. in *Jones* v. *Merionethshire Building Society* [1892] 1 Ch.173 at p.184.

[11] *Cannon* v. *Rands* (1870) 23 L.T.817; 11 Cox. C.C. 631; *Seear* v. *Cohen* (1881) 45 L.T. 589.

[12] See *per* Vaughan Williams J. in *Jones* v. *Merionethshire Building Society* [1891] 2 Ch. 587 at p.594.

[13] *Flower* v. *Sadler* (1882) 9 Q.B.D. 83; 10 Q.B.D.572, 576.

[14] *Flower* v. *Sadler* (1882). See the cases there cited and approved.

[15] *Jones* v. *Merionethshire Building Society* (1891) 2 Ch.587; (1892) 1 Ch.173; *Seear* v. *Cohen* (1881) 45 L.T.589.

[16] See *Williams* v. *Bayley* (1866) L.R.1 H.L. 200; *Flower* v. *Sadler* (1882) 9 Q.B.D.83; 10 Q.B.D.572; *cf. Rourke* v. *Mealy* (1878) 4 L.R.Ir.166; *Eldridge and Morris* v. *Taylor* [1931] 2 K.B.416; *Temperance Loan Fund* v. *Rose* [1932] 2 K.B. 522.

[17] *Williams* v. *Bayley* (1866) L.R. 1 H.L. 200; *Seear* v. *Cohen* (1881) 45 L.T. 589; *Jones* v. *Merionethshire Building Society* [1891] 2 Ch. 587; [1892] 1 Ch.173; *Kaufman* v. *Gerson* [1904] 1 K.B. 591.

Illegality alone will only enable the surety to resist, as defendant, a demand upon a guarantee. If he claims that money be repaid, or that a security be returned to him, he must show undue influence or pressure.[18] But in either case, if the surety has paid a fund to trustees to secure a debt, and the trustees still hold it, the Court will order it to be restored, as it cannot be left *in medio* for ever.[19]

The pressure, of course, must be pressure exerted by or with the privity of the creditor or his agent; what passes between the principal and the surety it is not the creditor's duty to inquire.[20]

Undue influence

A guarantee procured by undue influence to which the creditor is a party is voidable.[21] Where a wife seeks to set aside or avoid liability on a guarantee given by her for the indebtedness of her husband, or a company in which her husband is interested,[21a] the onus lies on her to prove that she entered into such a guarantee under the undue influence of her husband.[22] There is no presumption of undue influence in such a situation arising from the marital state.[23] In some cases it will be easy for the wife to discharge the onus and show her will was overborne by the stronger will of her husband.[24] It will be more difficult where the wife is "able generally to appreciate business conditions."[25] Where a wife suffers from a medically established infirmity and is pressured to sign, the court will set the guarantee aside.[26] Where parent/child relationships are concerned, the presumption of undue influence, tainting a guarantee which gives no benefit to the child guarantor, is not rebutted, simply by showing, for example that a daughter has reached the age of majority, married and has moved away from home.[26]

In *Lloyds Bank Ltd.* v. *Bundy*[27] an elderly farmer, a customer of the plaintiff bank, signed a guarantee and charge in respect of

---

[18] *Jones* v. *Merionethshire Building Society* [1892] 1 Ch.173. But *cf. Davies* v. *London Marine Insurance Co.* (1878) 8 Ch.D.469 at p.477.

[19] *Davies* v. *London and Provincial Marine Insurance Co.* (1878) 8 Ch.D.469 at p.477, *per* Fry J.

[20] *Talbot* v. *Von Boris* [1911] 1 K.B. 863; contrast *Turnbull* v. *Duval* [1902] A.C.429. This point appears to have been overlooked in *Howes* v. *Bishop* [1909] 2 K.B.390.

[21] *Mutual Finance Ltd.* v. *John Wetters and Sons Ltd.* [1937] 2 K.B.389.

[21a] *Lancashire Loans Co. Ltd.* v. *Black* [1934] 1 K.B.380 (C.A.)

[22] *Howes* v. *Bishop* [1909] 2 K.B.390; approving Cozens-Hardy J. in *Barron* v. *Willis* (1899) 2 Ch.578 at 585; *Talbot* v. *Von Boris* [1911] I.K.B.854.

[23] *Mackenzie* v. *Royal Bank of Canada* [1934] A.C.468 (P.C.). A wife is not within the class of "protected" persons where undue influence is assumed (*per* Lord Atkin).

[24] *Ibid. Quaere* whether this is still an appropriate view in the light of the changed social circumstances.

[25] *Bank of Montreal* v. *Stuart* [1911] A.C.120.

[26] *Lancashire Loans Co. Ltd.* v. *Black* [1934] 1 K.B. 380 (C.A.)

[27] [1975] Q.B. 326 (C.A.) See also in Canada, *Mackenzie* v. *Bank of Montreal* (1975) 55 D.L.R. (3d) 641 affd. (1977) 12 O.R. 719.

his only son's company's debt to the bank. The charge mortgaged the old farmer's home, his only asset. There had been no independent legal advice and the Court of Appeal set the guarantee and charge aside.

Lord Denning M.R. based his decision on a broad principle uniting cases where transactions have been set aside on the basis of an "inequality of bargaining power." In his view relief could be based on the facts that: (i) there was no independent advice; (ii) the contract transferred property for a consideration which was grossly inadequate; (iii) the old farmer's bargaining power was grievously impaired by reason of his own needs or desires, ignorance or infirmity, coupled with undue influences or pressures brought to bear on him by or for the benefit of the bank.

Cairns L.J., and Sir Eric Sachs, the other two members of the Court of Appeal, accepted that in the very unusual circumstances of the case there was a special relationship between the bank and the would-be surety, which imposed a special duty on the bank which in turn required that the old farmer should have been allowed to have independent advice.

The special circumstances in the *Bundy* case appear to involve: (i) the old farmer being a customer of the bank; (ii) the would-be guarantor's age and his limited means; (iii) his simplicity and trusting nature; (iv) his long-standing relationship with the bank and special trust in its manager; (v) the willingness of the old man to help his only son; (vi) the fact that the old man charged his only asset, his home; (vii) that the bank provided no cash for the company on the basis of the guarantee and the charge; (viii) that the charge was of no real benefit to any party save the bank.

There is also a particular danger in such cases where the creditor does not deal directly with the guarantor but, for example through the guarantor's husband. It has been held in Australia[28] that in such a situation if the wife does not understand the essential aspects of the transaction she will have a right to set it aside, unless she received adequate advice.[29]

---

[28] *Yerkey* v. *Jones* (1939) 63 C.L.R.649 (surety by mortgage of property).

[29] Advice from the creditor's lawyers was held sufficient in *Yerkey* v. *Jones* (above). The South Australia Law Reform Committee in their 39th Report (1976) have suggested that no guarantee over a certain sum should be valid unless there has been legal advice by a solicitor independent of those acting for any other party to the transaction.

CHAPTER 7

RIGHTS OF A SURETY

1. *General Principles*

The general principle here is the equity of the surety, subject to the paramount right of the creditor to be paid, to have the creditor's powers applied to produce an equitable result as between all persons liable.[1] The aim is to ensure that the person primarily liable should bear the whole burden in relief of others,[2] or if there is a deficiency that it should fall equally upon those with secondary liability.[3] These rights of a surety do not depend upon any contract involving the principal debtor or the sureties. Such rights depend upon equitable principles of readjusting the inequal placing of burdens upon persons or properties all equally liable at law[4]: " . . . if, as between several persons or properties all equally liable at law to the same demand, it would be equitable that the burden should fall in a certain way, the Court will so far as possible, having regard to the solvency of the different parties, see that if the burden is placed inequitably by the exercise of the legal right, its incidence should be afterwards readjusted." A surety against whom judgment has been obtained by the creditor for the full amount of the guarantee, even though he has paid nothing in respect of the guarantee, can sue his co-sureties to compel them to contribute towards the common liability.[5] Moreover, as soon as the surety becomes liable, he can sue the principal debtor for an order to pay the debt guaranteed so as to relieve the surety.[6]

---

[1] See *Dering* v. *Lord Winchelsea* (1787) 1 Cox 318; 2 B. & P. 270; 2 W, & T.L.C. Eq. (8th ed.) 539; *Stirling* v. *Forrester* (1821) 3 Bligh 575; *Craythorne* v. *Swinburne* (1807) 14 Ves. 160; *Duncan Fox & Co.* v. *North and South Wales Bank* (1880) 6 App.Cas. 1 Pennycuick J., in *Re Downer Enterprises Ltd.* [1974] 1 W.L.R.1460 considered on the basis of the *Duncan Fox* case that the rights of reimbursement and subrogation to rights and securities belonged not merely to sureties but to any person who paid a liability for which some other party was ultimately responsible. *Ibid.* 1468, 1469.

[2] *Anson* v. *Anson* [1953] 1 Q.B.636.

[3] See *Duncan, Fox & Co.* v. *North and South Wales Bank* (1880) 6 App.Cas. 1, *per* Lord Blackburn, at pp.19, 20.

[4] The quoted passage, from p.173 of the previous edition of this work, citing *Craythorne* v. *Swinburne* (1807) 14 Ves. 160, 165 was approved by the Court of Appeal in *Whitham* v. *Bullock* [1939] 2 K.B. 81.

[5] *Wolmershausen* v. *Gullick* [1883] 2 Ch. 514.

[6] *Ibid.* at p.528 (Wright J.)

2. *Surety's Equity against Creditor*

There is some authority for suggesting that a surety also has an equity against the creditor to prevent the creditor from bringing down the whole weight of the debt upon the surety. Wright J., in *Wolmershausen* v. *Gullick*[7] considered by way of *dictum* that a surety could in equity "be controlled and prevented from enforcing its legal right inequitably against one alone of the sureties." This in his view was the point of having the creditor joined as a party in *Dering* v. *Earl of Winchelsea.*[8] Lord Eldon in *Craythorne* v. *Swinburne*[9] commenting on *Dering* v. *Winchelsea*[8] accepted that case as deciding that " . . . the creditor, who can call upon all, shall not be at liberty to fix one with payment of the whole debt. . . . "

The previous edition of this work considered that in *Dering* v. *Winchelsea*[8] the creditor was only made a party in order to compel him to receive the money which the co-sureties were called upon to pay and in order to obtain a discharge for all parties, so that the surety's equity was primarily asserted against the co-sureties rather than against the creditor in order to control his remedies. The previous edition also considered that a surety could not resist the demand of the creditor pending resort to the principal or his estate, on the basis of Sir John Romilly's judgment in *Jackson* v. *Digby*[10] and the House of Lords decision in *Ewart* v. *Latta.*[11] In the latter case, which concerned Scottish law but where the same principle was said to apply in English law, it was said that a surety who had not paid could not compel the creditor to sue the principal debtor.[12] The underlying principle here is that a surety in default cannot dictate terms to the creditor. On that basis it would equally be the case that a surety could not compel the creditor to bring in co-sureties in an action against the surety.

Despite the considerable authority of the views examined in the previous edition of this work, it is felt that it is still arguable that a surety has an equity on the basis of *Wolmershausen* v. *Gullick*[13] and the authorities cited therein, including the views of Lord Eldon, to stay a creditor attempting unfairly to place the whole burden of the debt upon the surety, at least in special circumstances, *e.g.* where there is a solvent principal debtor, or solvent co-sureties who could easily be but are not joined in the

---

[7] [1893] 2 Ch. at p.522.
[8] (1787) 1 Cox 318; 2 B. & P.270.
[9] (1807) 14 Ves.160.
[10] (1854) 2 W.R.540.
[11] (1865) 4 Macq. H.L.983.
[12] (1865) 4 Macq. H.L. at p.989.
[13] [1893] 2 Ch. 514.

action, or a security which could easily be realised to pay the whole debt. That would be more consonant with the rights a surety possessed in late Roman law[14] and which passed into Scots and Continental legal systems. Lord Eldon himself changed his views on the matter: having appeared as counsel in *Dering* v. *Winchelsea* he was "much dissatisfied with the whole proceeding, and with the judgment," but subsequently was "convinced, that the decision was upon the right principles."[15]

Where the surety offers to pay the debt on condition that those remedies are made over to him, but the creditor refuses, the surety is entitled to pay the money into court and to bring an action for the assignment of the creditor's remedies.[16]

One situation in which the surety's equity has been held maintainable against the creditor is where the creditor has an opportunity to recover the debt from the principal debtor which will not be available to the surety. In *Cottin* v. *Blane*[17] it seems from the marginal note that the creditor was restrained from suing the surety, on the basis that the creditor but not the surety could have recovered the amount of the debt from another fund.[18] The principle appears to have been that the surety had an equity to compel the creditor to recover the debt from the alternative source. Relief was only granted upon the surety bringing the money into court, but this may have stemmed from possible doubts about the fund the creditor was to resort to.

Where the creditor is in possession of a fund belonging to the surety, the surety can insist on the creditor proceeding against the debtor or the debtor's fund in relief of the surety's fund.[19]

A rather special situation where the surety can exercise his equity against the creditor is where the creditor obtains payment from a surety under duress or oppression. In *Law* v. *East India Co*[20] the company compelled its servant, who was surety for another servant, to pay under duress. The company

---

[14] *Rights of Discussion*: see D.46. 1, 1.17, 1.51, s.3, and 1.62; Cod. 8.41.1.5 and 1.19; Nov. 4, c.l. *Rights of Division*: Cod. 8.41, 1.2 and 1.21; Nov. 99, c.l.; G.3, 121, 122. In the U.S.A., a surety will not be able to restrain a creditor unless there are special circumstances, *e.g.* where a security can be realised without prejudicing the creditor but a failure to realise it would result in unusual hardship to the surety: Restatement, Security § 131 (1941). The South Australia Law Reform Committee in its 39th Report (1976) suggested that a creditor should be compelled to realise securities before proceeding against the surety. In Quebec, the Civil Code Revision Office in its 1977 Report on the Quebec Civil Code suggested the repeal of the Right of Discussion contained in the Civil Code.

[15] *Craythorne* v. *Swinburne* (1807) 14 Ves. 160.

[16] *Goddard* v. *Whyte* (1860) 2 Giff. 449.

[17] (1795) 2 Anstr.544.

[18] The surety had guaranteed the performance of the charterers of an American vessel. The vessel was detained at Bordeaux under an embargo. The French National Convention resolved to compensate neutral owners. It seems that the surety was English and not a neutral whereas the creditor was a neutral and could claim compensation.

[19] See *ex p. Goodman* (1818) 3 Madd. 373. *Re Westzinthus* (1833) 5 B. & Ad. 817.

[20] (1799) 4 Ves.824.

was ordered to replace the amount pending the ascertainment of the parties' rights.

3. Surety's Remedies against Principal Debtor

General principles: right to indemnity

A surety who has paid the debt can recover against the principal debtor for money paid to his use.[21] This is based upon the common law action for money paid and is based upon an implied promise.[22] In equity, the surety has been given an order against the creditor for the assignment of the creditor's remedies against the principal debtor,[23] or has even been given a direct right of recoupment.[24]

Cases analogous to suretyship

By analogy to the rights of a surety, any person liable only secondarily who performs under compulsion of law an obligation for which another is primarily liable has a right of recoupment against the person primarily liable.[25] A common example is the position of an original lessee who has assigned the lease. If such an assignor is compelled to perform the convenants in the lease he can recover against the assignee, however remote, in possession of the land.[26] Similarly, a transferor of shares, if made contributory, can recover against the transferee.[27]

An analogous situation arises where the property of one person is lawfully seized for the debt of another,[28] *e.g.* in the case of distress for rent, where the right may be enforced against

---

[21] See *Morrice* v. *Redwyn* (1731) 2 Barnard 26; *Woffington* v. *Sparks* (1744) 2 Ves. Sen.569; *Taylor* v. *Mills* (1777) 2 Cowp.525; *Toussaint* v. *Martinnant* (1787) 2 Term Rep.100 at p.105.

[22] In *Re A Debtor* [1937] Ch.156 it was held that an implied contract arose at the time of the contract of suretyship. See also the discussion in *Anson* v. *Anson* [1953] 1 Q.B.636.

[23] See *Morgan* v. *Seymour* (1638) 1 Ch.R.120; *Greerside* v. *Benson* (1745) 3 Atk.248.

[24] Vin. Abr. Surety D.4. And see *Saunders* v. *Churchill ibid.* 2; *St. John* v. *Holford ibid.* 6; *Hungerford* v. *Hungerford ibid.* 7. In *Brook's Wharf* v. *Goodman Bros.* [1937] 1 K.B. 534 at p.543 Lord Wright stated that the court decided in the circumstances of the case what was just and reasonable with regard to the relationship between the parties. Alternatively, the direct recourse can be seen as equitable subrogation to the creditor's right to sue without express assignment; see *Brown Shipley & Co. Ltd.* v. *Amalgamated Investment (Europe) B.V.* [1979] 1 Lloyds Rep.488 and *Re Walters Deed of Guarantee* [1933] Ch.321 where a guarantor was subrogated to the rights of preference shareholders. (U.S.A., see *Re Dutcher* 213 F.908 (1914 D.C. Wash.) (subrogation of surety to preferential creditor's position), *Sanders* v. *Sanders* 49 Idaho 733, 291 P.1069, (1930) (surety subrogated to creditor's right to set aside fraudulent conveyance.)

[25] *Per* Willes J. in *Roberts* v. *Crowe* (1872) L.R. 7 C.P.629 at p.637. And see *Duncan Fox & Co.* v. *North and South Wales Bank* (1880) 6 App.Cas.1 at p.19.

[26] *Moule* v. *Garrett* (1872) L.R. 5 Ex. 132; 7 Ex. 101; *Walker* v. *Bartlett* (1856) 18.C.B.845.

[27] *Nevill's Case* (1870) L.R.: 6 Ch. App. 43; *Roberts* v. *Crowe* (1872) L.R.: 7 C.P. 629; *Killock* v. *Entover* (1882) L.R. 8 Q.B.458; 9 Q.B.241.

[28] *Exall* v. *Partridge* (1799) 8 Term Rep. 308; *Johnson* v. *Royal Mail Steam Packet Co.* (1867) L.R.: 3 C.P.38; *Edmunds* v. *Wallingford* (1885) 14 Q.B.D.811.

parties liable for rent even though they were not aware the property had been placed upon the premises, such as lessees who had assigned their interest.[29]

The right in question being based on equitable principles founded upon the right of the surety to the creditor's remedies, it is suggested that the surety's remedy is not dependent upon the "principal's" knowledge of the "guarantee" situation.[30] However, a surety has no right against a person who agrees to indemnify the principal debtor in respect of the debt.[31]

In the case of bills of exchange, an indorser who pays can sue the acceptor.[32] Although the parties may not be known to each other, the acceptor should contemplate the likelihood of indorsers.[33] In *Ex p. Bishop*[34] a bankrupt bill broker had deposited bills with the bank under a guarantee without indorsing them. The bank proved under the guarantee and were paid dividends. The bill broker's trustee in bankruptcy was held able to recover the sum paid by way of dividend from the acceptor. Cotton and James L.JJ. considered that an essential element of the decision was that the bill broker had authority, having regard to the usual course of dealing, from the parties to the bill to deal with it under a covering guarantee. Cotton L.J considered that mere compulsion to pay part of a bill of exchange will not necessarily entitle the person paying the bill to recover from the acceptor: the right to recovery arose only if the compulsion were undertaken at the request or implied request of the person primarily liable on the bill. In the case of an indorser, Cotton L.J considered that he was impliedly authorised by the acceptor to indorse the bill over. Thesiger L.J by contrast did not accept this view and even reserved his opinion as to whether a voluntary payment by a stranger of a debt did not "give him a right of action against the person who was liable to pay it," referring to the civil law and to the judgment of Willes J. in *Cook v. Lister*.[35]

Where a creditor sues the principal debtor for the benefit of the surety, the principal debtor may set off in equity any set-off available against the surety.[36]

---

[29] *Exall* v. *Partridge* (1799) 8 Term Rep.308.
[30] See *Powers* v. *Nash* 37 Maine 322 (1853).
[31] *Re Law Courts Chambers Co.* (1889) 61 L.T.669.
[32] See *Sleigh* v. *Sleigh* (1850) 5 Exch.514; *Ex p. Bishop* (1880) 15 Ch.D.400, 410.
[33] See *Ex p. Bishop* (1880) 15 Ch.D.400, 416; *Duncan Fox and Co.* v. *North and South Wales Bank* (1880) 6 App.Cas. at pp.13, 14 *per* Lord Selborne.
[34] (1880) 15 Ch.D.400.
[35] (1863) 13.C.B. (N.S.) 543, 594. There, Willes J. referred to the Civil Law rule that payment by a stranger in the name of the debtor might liberate the debtor from the demand; D.46. 3. 23, 53; J.3.29; G.3.168.
[36] *Thornton* v. *Maynard* (1875) L.R. 10 C.P.695.

Quia timet proceedings

As soon as a definite sum of money has become payable from the surety to the creditor, the surety has a right to have it paid by the principal. The surety can in equity obtain an order directing the principal to pay such sum to the creditor.[37] This remedy is available to the surety as long as the sum has become payable, even though no application has been made or is anticipated.[37] The surety's liability to the creditor for this purpose may be *qua* principal debtor rather than *qua* surety.[38]

By contrast, until there is an ascertained sum due and owing by the surety,[39] the surety in the absence of any special agreement[40] has no right to such relief. Nor can he call upon the principal debtor to make provision for the payment of the creditor or to bring the money into court.[41]

For the surety's relief to exist it must be shown that a debt is payable, not merely that a demand has been made by a creditor, and that thereafter the taking of accounts a debt may become due.[42]

It used to be the case that where a demand by the creditor was a condition precedent to the surety's liability, the surety would have no right against the principal before demand was made.[43] However, in *Thomas* v. *Nottingham Incorporated Football Club Ltd.*[44] Goff J. held that after the surety had given notice to the creditor of determination of the guarantee, he was entitled to call upon the principal debtor to pay. This was despite the fact that the surety was only liable on demand and no demand had been made. Goff J. thought it would be strange if the surety could not remove a cloud until it began to rain.

In the special situation of sureties to an administration bond,

---

[37] *Per* Lord Keeper North in *Ranelagh* v. *Hayes* (1683) 1 Vern. 189; *Bechervaise* v. *Lewis* (1872) L.R. 7 C.P. 372 at p.377; *Ex p. Snowdon* (1881) 17 Ch.D.44, 47; *Ferguson* v. *Lipson* (1874) L.R. 14 Eq.379; *Re Giles* |1896| 1 Ch. 956; *Ascherson* v. *Tredegar Dock Co.* |1909| 2 Ch. 401 (U.S.A. see: *Pavarini & Wyne Inc.* v. *Title Guarantee & Surety Co.* 36 App. D.C. 348 (1911); Canada, see *Double Diamond Bowling Supply Ltd.* v. *Eglington Bowling Ltd.* (1963) 39 D.L.R. (2d) 19). Once there is a debt there is no need for a "demand," a concept which is meaningless in this context, as opposed to a situation where a debt only accrues on demand *per* Scrutton L.J. in *Bradford Old Bank* v. *Sutcliffe* |1918| 2 K.B.833.

[38] In *Tate* v. *Crewdson* |1938| 1 Ch.869, a bank lent money to joint borrowers who agreed to be principals *vis-à-vis* the bank but surety/principal *inter se*. The surety was given an order that the other repay since the surety was himself immediately liable as principal as against the bank.

[39] *Re Ledgard* (1922) 66 S.J.404; *Morrison* v. *Barking Chemicals Co.* |1919| 2 Ch.325.

[40] *e.g.* a provision that the money shall be provided before it becomes payable to the creditor, as in *Toussaint* v. *Martinnant* (1787) 2 T.R.100.

[41] *Dale* v. *Lolley* (1808) Exch. Trin.T. referred to in a note to *Nisbet* v. *Smith* (1789) 2 Bro. C.C. at p.582. And see *Bellingham* v. *Freer* (1837) 1 Moo.P.C.333; *Coppin* v. *Gray* (1842) 1 Y. & C. Eq.205; *cf. Re Anderson-Berry* |1938| Ch.290.

[42] *Antrobus* v. *Davidson* (1817) 3 Mer.569; *Morrison* v. *Barking Chemicals Co.* |1919| 2 Ch.325.

[43] *Bradford* v. *Gammon* |1925| Ch.132.

[44] [1972] Ch.596, not following *Bradford* v. *Gammon* |1925| Ch.132 and applying *Ascherson* v. *Tredegar Dock and Wharf Co.* |1909| 2 Ch.401.

who had been told by the administrator that he intended to distribute the estate although he had been advised that there were liabilities still outstanding and not yet determined, the sureties were held entitled to bring a *quia timet* action restraining distribution and seeking administration by the court.[45] It is arguable that on analogous grounds relief should be given to a surety of a bankrupt person or company being wound up if the trustees or liquidator can be shown to be prejudicing the surety's position by, *e.g.* selling a security for the principal debt under value. However, the contrary is indicated by *Re Pratt*[46] where as between co-sureties it was agreed that one was primarily liable to the creditor. Both gave security to the creditor. Upon the bankruptcy of one it was held that the other had no right of action against the former's trustee in respect of a sale allegedly under value.

The special rules as to set-off in relation to bankruptcy and winding-up laid down by section 31 of the Bankruptcy Act 1914 have been interpreted so as to prevent a surety who has not paid from setting off his indemnity against a liquidator of the principal debtor.[47] This seems to be based on the rule against double proof: the creditor not having been paid could have proved in the principal debtor's estate, which estate would then have been subject to double proof. Moreover, a surety paying sums due to the creditor after the relevant date (the receiving order) of the principal's bankruptcy has been held to have no right of set-off against the trustee in bankruptcy of the principal.[48]

Wolmershausen v. *Gullick*[49] suggests that in any action by the surety to make the principal pay direct to the creditor, the creditor should be made a party. As to the form of relief granted to the surety, unless there is evidence before the court that the principal debtor clearly has the means to pay, the court may limit the surety to a declaration and liberty to apply.[50]

The surety of a company can now, contrary to the previous position under *Re Vron Colliery Co.*,[51] petition for winding up even before he has paid, on the basis of his being a contingent or prospective creditor within section 224(1) of the Companies Act

---

[45] *Re Anderson-Berry* [1928] Ch.290.
[46] *Pratt's Trustee in Bankruptcy* v. *Pratt* [1936] 3 All E.R. 901. See also the Irish case of *Hibernian Fire and General Insurance Co.* v. *Dorgan* [1941] I.R.514.
[47] *Re Fenton* [1931] 1 Ch.85.
[48] *Re Waite* [1956] 1 W.L.R. 1226. In *Re Hawkins* (unreported, Walton J., Feb. 2, 1978) it was explained that the *quia timet* rights of a surety who had not paid could not form the subject matter of a set-off.
[49] [1893] 2 Ch.514.
[50] *Watt* v. *Mortlock* [1964] 1 Ch.84 (Wilberforce J.) on a motion for judgment in default of appearance or defence.
[51] (1882) 20 Ch.D.442.

1948. The right to petition is based on the contingent or prospective right of indemnity. The *quia timet* right does not amount to a debt.[52]

Principal debtor covenants with surety to pay on given day

If the principal debtor covenants with the surety to pay the debt upon a given day, the surety without paying may recover the whole sum from the principal debtor when the day has passed.[53] The surety in turn would be obliged to apply the money in payment of the debt.[54] If the principal debtor had already paid the creditor, the surety's damages for breach of covenant may be reducible to a nominal sum.[55]

Surety has given note to extinguish principal debt but has not paid thereon

There is disagreement in the authorities as to whether a surety who has given his own promissory note in extinguishment of the principal debt can before paying sue the principal debtor for money paid. It was held that he could in *Barclay* v. *Gooch*[56] by Lord Kenyon. However, in *Maxwell* v. *Jameson*[57] following *Taylor* v. *Biggins*[58] an apparently contrary view was taken. Whilst in England the balance of authority suggests that the mere giving of a promissory note by a surety cannot found an action against the principal debtor for money paid, there is Irish authority for suggesting that the handing over of property can be the equivalent of payment in this regard.[59] Whatever the position in that regard in English law it is submitted that the value of such property can be recovered by suing the principal debtor for breach of the implied contract to indemnity.[59]

---

[52] *Re Mitchell* [1913] 1 Ch.201.
[53] *Carr* v. *Roberts* (1833) 5 B. & Ad. 78; *Loosemore* v. *Radford* (1842) 9 M. & W. 657; *Carpenter* v. *Park* 19 Cal.App. 2d 567, 66 P. 2d 224 (1937); *Gustafson* v. *Koehler* 177 Minn.115, 224 N.W. 699 (1929); *Re Allen* [1896] 2 Ch.345. And see *Toussaint* v. *Martinnant* (1787) 2 Term Rep.100; *Spark* v. *Heslop* (1859) 1 E. and E. 563; *Ashdown* v. *Ingamells* (1880) 5 Ex.D.280; *Re Perkins* [1898] 2 Ch.182. The whole sum of the debt is seen as the surety's quantum of loss in an action for breach of contract.
[54] *Loosemore* v. *Radford* (1842) 9 M. & W. 657 at p.658, *per* Parke B.; *cf. Re Richardson* [1911] 2 Q.B. 705.
[55] *Ibid. per* Alderson B.
[56] (1797) 2 Esp. 571, followed by the Court of Exchequer in Ireland in *McKenna* v. *Harnett* (1849) 13 Ir.L.R.206 and referred to without disapproval by Pollock C.B. in *Rodgers* v. *Maw* (1846) 15 M. & W. 444, 449.
[57] (1818) 2 B. & Ald.51.
[58] (1802) 3 East 169.
[59] *Fahey* v. *Frawley* (1890) 26 L.R. Ir.78; *Gore* v. *Gore* [1901] 2 I.R.269; *cf. Re Law Guarantee, Liverpool Mortgage Insurance Company's case* [1914] 2 Ch. 617; *British Dominions Insurance Co.* v. *Duder* [1915] 2 Q.B. 394; *Hope* v. *M'Gillivray* [1935] A.C.1.

Surety's right to prospective indemnity excluded by agreement

The surety's right to have the principal debtor pay off the creditor as soon as the debt becomes payable can be excluded by agreement or an exclusion may be implied from the nature of the liability guaranteed. For example the surety for a mortgage debt may be excluded from insisting upon the mortgagor paying the mortgage debt on the day named in the covenant, on the basis that the sense of the transaction involved the use of the land as a continuing security.[60] Likewise where the principal obligation is not of a nature to be extinguished before a determinate period.[61]

The right to prospective indemnity from the principal debtor does not extend to the situation where the surety holds an indemnity from a stranger. The surety cannot call upon the stranger to settle the creditor's claim unless the surety shows that he is about to be damnified.[62] The reason for the distinction is that the stranger is not, as the principal debtor is, the person in all events ultimately liable to pay. However, in the case of an indemnity from a stranger, if the surety has become liable but the stranger has not paid, the surety may sue *quia timet* to have the money provided by that person before actual damage to the surety.[63]

Interest

A surety is entitled as against the principal to charge interest upon the sums paid by him to the creditor.[64] This apparently applies even though the principal debt did not carry interest.[65] There is now statutory power in the Court in England to award in its discretion interest on debts and damages.[66]

The surety may recover from the principal debtor in full all interest paid to the creditor.[67] But where the principal debt carries high interest and the surety knows that the principal

---

[60] *Hungerford* v. *Hungerford* Gilb.Eq.Ca. at p.69.

[61] *Bellingham* v. *Freer* (1837) 1 Moo.P.C.333 (applying civil law).

[62] See *Antrobus* v. *Davidson* (1817) 3 Mer.569.

[63] *Wooldridge* v. *Norris* (1868) L.R.6 Eq.410. There the father of the principal debtor gave the surety a bond and when the surety was called on, the surety was held entitled as against the father's executors to an order that they raise and pay the sum demanded from the surety. See also *Re Anderson-Berry* [1928] Ch.290. It would seem that in such a case the surety would be under no obligation to apply the money to pay off the creditor: see *Re Law Guarantee, Liverpool Mortgage Insurance Company's Case* [1914] 2 Ch.617.

[64] *Petrie* v. *Duncombe* (1851) 20 L.J. Q.B. 242; *Hitchman* v. *Stewart* (1855) 3 Drew.271; *Ex p. Bishop* (1880) 15 Ch. D.400; *Re Watson* [1896] 1 Ch.925. This principle is part of the general law of indemnity. *Omnium Insurance Co* v. *United London and Scottish Insurance Co.* (1920) 36 T.L.R.386.

[65] See *Re Swan's Estate* (1869) Ir.R.Eq.209.

[66] See the Law Reform (Miscellaneous Provisions) Act 1934, s.3; Administration of Justice Act 1969, s.22.

[67] *Re Browne and Wingrove* [1891] 2 Q.B.574.

disputes his liability to indemnify, the surety should arguably pay the debt at once and stop the interest running: if he does not, his right to interest may be reduced.[68] However, it is submitted that since the principal debtor is in any event primarily liable he should as between himself and the surety have paid the debt and cannot complain that the surety has not done so.

Payments without suit

If there is no reasonable defence to the claim, the surety need not wait to be sued but may pay the creditor as soon as the debt becomes due and recover over against the principal debtor on the basis of money paid.[69] Equity certainly regarded the surety as able to pay the debt at maturity and sue the principal debtor in the name of the creditor.[70]

Costs

A surety can recover from the principal debtor all costs, including his own extra costs incurred in resisting the claim of the creditor.[71] This includes costs of a defence not expressly authorised by the principal debtor[72] unless there was clearly no defence.[73] Costs of execution by the creditor are not recoverable since the surety should have been paid on judgment.[74]

Compromise and notice to principal debtor

A surety may make a reasonable compromise of a doubtful claim, and recover the amount from the principal debtor, even though he compromised without notice to the principal debtor.[75] The effect of lack of notice is only to allow in evidence by the principal that the surety acted unreasonably or that the principal might have obtained better terms.[76] If notice is given

---

[68] See *Hawkins* v. *Maltby* (1868) L.R. 6 Eq.505,509.

[69] *Pitt* v. *Purssord* (1841) 8 M. & W. 538; *Broughton's Case* 5 Co.23(b).

[70] *Swire* v. *Redman* (1876) 1 Q.B.D.536, 541. In Canada it has been held that where the surety pays prior to the due date he cannot thereby accelerate his remedy against the principal, but has to wait until the due date to enforce his rights: *Drager* v. *Allison* [1959] S.C.R.661; 19 D.L.R. (2d) 431. Nevertheless, it was held in that case that where the principal committed an anticipatory repudiation of his obligations to the surety, the latter could obtain a declaration of his prospective rights.

[71] *Ex p. Marshall* (1751) 1 Atk.262; *Jones* v. *Brooke* (1812) 4 Taunt.464; *Stratton* v. *Mathews* (1848) 3 Exch.48; *Garrard* v. *Cottrell* (1847) 10 Q.B.679. Where recoverable, costs are recovered by the surety in respect of his defence against the creditor on a common fund basis: *Howard* v. *Lovegrove* (1870) L.R.6 Ex 43.

[72] *Smith* v. *Compton* (1832) B. & Ad.407; *Hornby* v. *Cardwell* (1881) 8 Q.B.D.329.

[73] *Roach* v. *Thompson* (1830) M. & M.487; *Beech* v. *Jones* (1848) 5 C.B.696.

[74] *Pierce* v. *Williams* (1854) 23 L.J.Ex 322.

[75] *Smith* v. *Compton* (1832) 3 B. & Ad. 407. Cf. *Webster* v. *Petre* (1879) 4 Ex D.127.

[76] *Smith* v. *Compton, supra.*

and the principal debtor ignores it, the surety is justified in taking any reasonable step towards testing or reducing the claim.[77]

Litigation for surety's benefit

The surety cannot claim the costs of litigation undertaken purely for his benefit, *e.g.* to show that he has been discharged as between himself and the creditor.[78] By contrast a surety for bail may recover the costs of arresting an absconding principal even though the arrest is for the surety's benefit.[79]

Surety's executors

Where the principal debtor is a legatee under the surety's will, the surety's executors are entitled to retain the amount of the surety's claim plus reasonable interest, even if the surety's action would have been statute-barred.[80] This applies even if the principal becomes bankrupt after the surety's death.[80] Similarly where the principal has executed a deed of assignment for the benefit of his creditors for payment according to the law of bankruptcy to which the creditor guaranteed has assented, the surety's executors can instead of proving in the creditor's place retain the amount of the debt out of the legacy payable to the principal.[81]

Death of principal debtor

A surety paying the debt even after the principal's death is entitled if the latter dies intestate to administration as a creditor.[82]

Release of principal debtor

Normally, the release of the principal debtor will release the surety, unless the creditor expressly stipulates the contrary. Where there is a reservation of remedies against the surety, the surety will also retain his right over against the principal debtor notwithstanding the "release," which is in such cases seen as a mere covenant not to sue.[83]

---

[77] *Hornby* v. *Cardwell* (1881) 8 Q.B.D.329.
[78] *Re International Contract Co., Hughes' Claim* (1872) L.R.13 Eq. at p.624 *per* Wickens V.-C. And see *South* v. *Bloxam* (1865) 2 H. & M.457.
[79] *Fisher* v. *Fallows* (1804) 5 Esp.171.
[80] *Re Watson* [1896] 1 Ch.925.
[81] *Re Whitehouse* (1887) 37 Ch.D.683.
[82] *Williams* v. *Jukes* (1864) 34 L.J.P. & M.60.
[83] *Kearsley* v. *Cole* (1846) 16 M. & W.128; *Cole* v. *Lynn* [1941] 1 K.B.142.

Surety given security by principal debtor

A creditor can derive no benefit from securities given by the principal debtor to the surety, except perhaps where he can show a direct interest by contract or under a trust or unless both principal and surety are bankrupt and the rule in *Ex p. Waring* is found applicable.[84] In *Ex p. Rushworth*[85] a security had been given to the surety on trust to apply the proceeds to pay off the creditor. Lord Eldon said that the creditor would have been entitled to call for its application accordingly. However, in *Wilding* v. *Richards*[86] where property was conveyed by the principal to the surety on trust to pay debts, it was held that the creditors, who had no notice of the conveyance, could not take advantage of it, but the surety could insist on retaining the property till the creditors were paid.

As between himself and co-sureties a surety must bring into account every security received by him from the principal.[87]

If a surety guarantees a composition, the deed may provide for the transfer of the principal debtor's estate to the surety.[88] Where the surety is also a creditor and may possibly get payment in full out of the balance of the estate this will not necessarily make the deed bad.[89] However, a creditor guaranteeing a composition cannot stipulate secretly for payment in full[90] or any other preference.[91]

No creditor can impeach an assignment to a surety for a composition so long as the composition stands[92] or if the surety has paid the sum guaranteed.[93] By contrast the assignment of property in consideration of the surety guaranteeing an existing debt is fraudulent and an act of bankruptcy.[94] However, an assignment to a surety who becomes bound in order to secure a fresh advance to enable the principal debtor to continue business is as valid as if it had been given to the creditor.[95]

---

[84] (1815) 19 Ves.345. It had been thought that the creditor was generally entitled to such security: *Maure* v. *Harrison* (1692) 1 Eq.Ca.Ab.93, and see *Wright* v. *Morley* (1805) 11 Ves.12 at p.22. However, this doctrine was not accepted by Lord Eldon in *Ex p. Waring* (1815) 19 Ves.345 and has been shown to rest on no authority: *Re Walker* [1892] 1 Ch.621. See also p. 200.

[85] (1805) 10 Ves.409, 421.

[86] (1845) 1 Coll.655.

[87] See *post*, p.160.

[88] *Bissel* v. *Jones* (1878) L.R. 4 Q.B.49; *Ex p. Nicholson* (1877) L.R. 5 Ch.332; *Latter* v. *White* (1870) L.R. 5 Q.B.622; 5 H.L.578.

[89] *Ex p. Nicholson* (1870) L.R. 5 Ch.332.

[90] *Wood* v. *Barker* (1865) L.R. 1 Eq.139.

[91] See *Caldwell* v. *Parker* (1869) 3 Ir.R. Eq.519.

[92] *Seymour* v. *Coulson* (1880) 5 Q.B.D.359.

[93] *Ex p. Burrell, Re Robinson* (1867) 1 Ch.D.537.

[94] *Ex p. Zwilchenbart* (1844) 3 M.D. & De.G.671; *Smith* v. *Cannan* (1853) 2 E. & B. 35; *Leake* v. *Young* (1856) 5 E. & B. 955. And see *Ex p. Defries, Re Myers* (1876) 35 L.T.392.

[95] *Ex p. Hawswell, Re Hemingway* (1883) 23 Ch.D.626. And see *Ex p. Defries, Re Myers, supra.*

Where a surety who has paid nothing has property made over to him by the principal debtor as a result of pressure by the surety to protect him from payments about to become due, the pressure may prevent the assignment being a fraudulent preference.[96]

In England fraudulent preferences are now governed by section 44 of the Bankruptcy Act 1914 as amended by section 115 of the Companies Act 1947 in the case of bankruptcy and sections 320 and 321 of the Companies Act 1948 in relation to winding up. A payment or security given by the principal to the lender will be recoverable if the dominant intention is to prefer the surety through the payment.[97] Where the principal debtor's trustee in bankruptcy claims to recover a payment by the principal to the creditor as a fraudulent preference, this will probably affect the surety and the surety should be joined as a party.[98]

Where the surety guarantees the loan of money for a specific purpose only and the debtor in default of such use returns the money to the lender on the eve of bankruptcy, such money would not have passed to the trustee in bankruptcy and cannot be recovered from the lender.[99]

Loss of surety's rights to counter-guarantor

In *Brown-Shipley and Co. Ltd.* v. *Amalgamated Investment (Europe) B.V.,*[1] the plaintiffs guaranteed a loan by a bank to the defendants, but took a counter-guarantee from the defendant's parent company. When the plaintiffs were forced to pay out on the guarantee, they made a demand on the counter-guarantee. The sum due under the counter-guarantee was met by a loan from the plaintiffs. The plaintiffs then sued the principal debtor upon the basis of subrogation to the creditor bank's rights. It was held that although the plaintiffs as sureties had become subrogated to those rights, the rights of subrogation themselves had been transferred by operation of law to the parent company upon payment under the counter-guarantee.

---

[96] *Thompson* v. *Freeman* (1786) 1 Term Rep. 155; *Crosby* v. *Crouch* (1809) 11 East 256.
[97] *Re Kushler* [1943] Ch.248 (C.A.); *cf. Re Lyons* (1935) 51 T.L.R.24.
[98] *Re Idenden* [1970] 1 W.L.R.1015. Under ss.92, 115 of the Companies Act 1947 a person who charged his property to secure the debt of a bankrupt or company being wound up has the same rights and liabilities as if they were sureties to the extent of the value of the property charged. In a claim for fraudulent preference, any surety can under the statutory provisions be brought in as a third party.
[99] *Edwards* v. *Glyn* (1859) 2 E. & E.29.
[1] [1979] 1 Lloyd's Rep.488.

Presumption of advancement

It seems that the entry by a husband into a guarantee for a wife's indebtedness is not to be seen as an advancement or gift to her.[2] Moreover, if a husband guarantor is compelled by the creditor to pay under his guarantee, this is not to be presumed to be a gift and the husband is entitled to repayment from the wife or her estate.[3]

Payment or undertaking of obligation by stranger not under liability

In *Owen* v. *Tate*[4] the defendants obtained a bank loan secured by a charge over another's property. At the request of that surety, the plaintiff deposited a sum with the bank and entered a guarantee of the defendants' debt. Despite the defendants' objections, the surety's property was released from charge. When the bank called in the defendants' debt, with the defendants' encouragement they applied the sum deposited by the plaintiff in payment. It was held that such a voluntary assumption of liability would not normally give a right to sue the principal debtor for an indemnity. Since the plaintiff had acted behind the backs of the defendants and against their wishes no reimbursement from them would be allowed.

Pre-trial attachment

In England there are limited rights available to the surety to try to prevent the principal debtor from fleeing the jurisdiction or transferring his assets abroad out of the surety's reach. To prevent the principal debtor from leaving, the surety would have to invoke the writ of *ne exeat regno* which in *Felton* v. *Callis*[5] was very severely limited to cases where the debtor's presence in the jurisdiction was essential to the prosecution of the case against him. Even then, there is required by analogy with section 6 of the Debtors Act 1869 that: (a) the action must be the equitable equivalent of one where the defendant was formerly liable to arrest at law; (b) there must be a good cause of action for at least £50; (c) there must be probable cause that the defendant will leave England unless arrested.

By contrast there is a wide and developing jurisdiction in

---

[2] *Re Salisbury-Jones* |1938| 2 All E.R.459.
[3] *Ibid.*
[4] |1976| Q.B. 402.
[5] |1969| 1 Q.B.200 (Megarry J.).

England to prevent, prior to judgment, the removal abroad of assets required to satisfy eventual judgment.[6] There must be a real risk of such removal, but once that is established, there is jurisdiction even if the defendant is not foreign or foreign-based.[7]

4. *Surety's Rights to Securities given by Principal Debtor to Creditor*

General principle

A surety paying off the debt is entitled to any securities given for the debt by the principal debtor to the creditor.[8] This right exists independently of contract and rests upon the surety's equity not to have the whole burden of the debt thrown upon him by the creditor's choice not to resort to other remedies available to him.[9]

The right being based on equity, the surety had a right to them although he did not know of their existence when he made himself liable,[10] or even if they did not exist at that time.[11]

The surety's right to securities is not affected by payments by strangers and a stranger making such payments need not be made a party to proceedings to gain the benefit of the security.[12]

Formerly, the surety's right after payment to the benefit of securities was only to such securities as were not *ipso facto* extinguished by the payment.[13]

[6] *Mareva Compania Naviera S.A.* v. *International Bulkcarriers S.A.* [1975] 2 Lloyd's Rep.509. (C.A.); *Third Chandris Shipping Corp.* v. *Unimarine S.A.* [1979] Q.B.645 (C.A.); *Chartered Bank* v. *Daklouche* [1980] 1 W.L.R. 107 (C.A.); *Barclay-Johnson* v. *Yuill* [1980] 1 W.L.R. 1259 (Megarry V.C.); *Allen* v. *Jambo Holdings Ltd.* [1980] 1 W.L.R. 1252 (C.A.); *Rahman* v. *Abu-Taha* [1980] 1 W.L.R. 1268 (C.A.).

[7] *Barclay-Johnson* v. *Yuill* [1980] 1 W.L.R. 1259 at 1265 D.

[8] *Morgan* v. *Seymour* (1638) 1 Ch.R.120; *Ex p. Crisp* (1744) 1 Atk. 133; *Geerside* v. *Benson* (1745) 3 Atk.248; *Mayhew* v. *Crickett* (1818) 2 Swanst. 185 at 191; *Goddard* v. *Whyte* (1860) 2 Giff.449, 452. This appears to include, in the case of a guarantor of a promissory note, a right to the assignment of the promissory note: *Armstrong* v. *Widmer* (1975) 65 D.L.R. (3rd) 345; (1976) W.W.R.734.

[9] See Sir S. Romilly's argument in *Craythorne* v. *Swinburne* (1807) 14 Ves. at p.162 approved by Lord Eldon; *per* Lord Eldon in *Aldrich* v. *Cooper* (1803) 8 Ves. at p.389; *Duncon Fox & Co.* v. *North and South Wales Bank* (1879) 6 App.Cas. 1 at p.12, 19; *Parsons* v. *Briddock* (1708) 2 Vern. 608; *Wright* v. *Morley* (1805) 11 Ves. at pp.22.23.

[10] *Mayhew* v. *Crickett* (1818) 2 Swanst.185 at p.191; *Newton* v. *Chorlton* (1853) 10 Hare 646 at p.651; *Pearl* v. *Deacon* (1857) 24 Beav.186; 1 De G. & J.461; *Coates* v. *Coates* (1864) 33 Beav.249; *Goddard* v. *Whyte* (1860) 2 Giff.449; *Duncan Fox & Co.* v. *North and South Wales Bank* (1879) 6 A.C. 1; *Leicestershire Banking Co. Ltd.* v. *Hawkins* (1900) 16 T.L.R. 317; *Re Jeffery's Policy* (1872) 20 W.R.857.

[11] *Scott* v. *Knox* (1838) 2 Jo.Ex.Ir.778.

[12] *Heyman* v. *Dubois* (1871) L.R.13 Eq.158; *Re Arcedeckne, Atkins* v. *Arcedeckne* (1883) 24 Ch.D.709.

[13] The authorities and reasoning for this rule are set out in the previous edition of this work at p.207–208. The reasoning behind the rule was not accepted by Roman Law: D.46.1.36. It was also rejected in the United States, even prior to 1856, where they preferred the Roman Law view as followed in English cases prior to the American Revolution; see, *e.g.* *Lumpkin* v. *Mills* (1848) 4 Ga.343.

Mercantile Law Amendment Act, 1856, s.5[14]

Under this section a surety who pays the debt is entitled to have assigned to him any judgment or security held by the creditor, whether or not the judgment or security is deemed at law to have been satisfied by the payment. The surety is further entitled to the creditor's remedies and upon a proper indemnity to use the creditor's name in any action or other proceeding in order to obtain an indemnity from the principal debtor. The section also gives such rights to co-debtors such as co-sureties.[15]

Under the section the surety is entitled to the benefit of a creditor's judgment without taking an assignment.[16] However, execution cannot be issued without leave.[17]

The surety can bring an action for specific performance of his statutory right to an assignment[18] or for damages.[18]

Co-debtors bound as principals vis-à-vis the creditor but as principal and surety inter se

This is Lord Selborne's third class of suretyship situations analysed in the House of Lords case of *Duncan Fox and Co.* v. *North and South Wales Bank.*[19] In this third class the co-debtor contracting as principal with the creditor, but who is in fact as between himself and the other debtor a surety, will upon giving notice to the creditor have the rights of a surety as against the creditor *inter alia* with regard to securities.[20]

It seems that the status or agreement between such co-debtors constituting them surety and principal respectively can arise by inference or implication as well as by express agreement.[21] Notice to the creditor can be given after the obligation is entered into and the principle applies even if the debtors contracted originally as principals inter se but later altered their positions, *e.g.* in the case of a retired partner.[22]

Conversely, where a surety stands *vis-à-vis* another surety in

---

[14] 19 & 20 Vict. c.97. The text is set out in Appendix 2.
[15] In this respect it recognises and enacts the position contained in the authorities: see Lord Blackburn in *Duncan Fox & Co.* v. *North and South Wales Bank* (1880) 6 App.Cas. 1 at p.19.
[16] *Re M'Myn* (1886) 33 Ch.D.575.
[17] R.S.C. Ord.46, r. 2(1)(*b*); *Dale* v. *Powell* (1911) 105 L.T. 291 at p.292. *Kayley* v. *Hothersall* [1925] 1 K.B.607.
[18] *Dale* v. *Powell* (1911) 105 L.T.291.
[19] (1880) 6 App.Cas.1 at pp.11 *et seq.*
[20] *Duncan Fox & Co.* v. *North and South Wales Bank* (1880) 6 App.Cas.1 at p.12 (Lord Selbourne).
[21] See *Re Marley* [1976] 1 W.L.R. 952 (D.C.)
[22] See *Rouse* v. *Bradford Banking Co.* [1894] A.C. 586.

the position of a person primarily liable, that other surety has a surety's right to the securities and remedies of the creditor.[23]

Surety's rights to securities given by persons other than the principal debtor

The surety's right to the creditor's securities extends to wherever it is needed to make the giver pay his due proportion in situations where there are equities requiring the burden of the debt to be placed in a particular way.[24] For example, the principle applies to securities given by co-sureties[25] or by a partner of the debtor.[26]

However, a surety is not entitled to the benefit of a wrongful pledge by the principal debtor to the creditor of the property of a third person on the contrary, that person will have the benefit of the guarantee to liberate his own property.[27]

Examples of particular securities

(i) Lien on shares: sureties for a receiver of a testator's estate were held to be entitled to be recouped out of the receiver's shares, upon his default and upon payment by the sureties.[28]

(ii) Insurance policy: a surety for premiums was held to have a right to be reimbursed out of the policy monies.[29]

(iii) Lease: a surety for the performance of covenants is entitled to recoupment out of the land in respect of any payments made by him on account of rent.[30]

(iv) Vendor's lien on goods: a surety for the price of goods is entitled upon paying the vendor to the unpaid vendor's lien.[31] A similar lien is available to a broker acting for an unnamed buyer who is by the custom of the trade personally liable for the principal's default.[31]

(v) Stoppage *in transitu*: a surety for the price of goods cannot stop them *in transitu* against the principal in his own

---

[23] *Parsons* v. *Briddock* (1708) 2 Vern.608 approved in *Wright* v. *Morley* (1805) 2 Ves. at pp.22, 23. In *Hodgson* v. *Shaw* (1834) 3 My. & K. at p.189 *Parsons* v. *Briddock* was treated as incorrectly decided by Lord Brougham and in *Armitage* v. *Baldwin* (1842) 5 Beav. 278 the opposite decision was reached on similar facts. However, the objection to the result in *Parsons* v. *Briddock* appears to have been based on there being no right to securities, etc., if the debt has been paid, a principle which was reversed by the Mercantile Law Amendment Act 1856 (19 and 20 Vict. c.97).

[24] See Lord Blackburn in *Duncan Fox & Co.* v. *North and South Wales Bank* (1880) 6 App.Cas.1 at p.19.

[25] See *Smith* v. *Wood* [1929] 1 Ch.14.

[26] *Goddard* v. *Whyte* (1860) 2 Giff. 449.

[27] *Ex p.Salting* (1883) 25 Ch.D.148.

[28] *Brandon* v. *Brandon* (1859) 3 De G. & J. 524. See also *Glossop* v. *Harrison* (1814) 3 V. & B.134.

[29] *Aylwin* v. *Witty* (1861) 30 L.J.Ch.860.

[30] *Lord Harberton* v. *Bennett* (1829) Beat 386.

[31] *Imperial Bank* v. *London and St. Katherine's Dock Co.* (1877) 5 Ch.D.195.

name[32] but can perhaps stop them in the name of the seller, who would in equity be bound to authorise or ratify such a stoppage.[33]

Surety's right to have securities in creditor's hands marshalled in surety's favour

Where the creditor has a security for a different debt which he can consolidate with that of the guaranteed debt, the surety would seem entitled to the benefit of this security.[34] However, a surety is not entitled to securities for a different debt or another part of the same debt.[35] Where a surety guaranteed the general account of a customer of a bank and the bank subsequently made separate specific advances against particular securities, it was held that the bank were entitled to and obliged to surrender them when those specific advances were repaid, and that the surety's liability was not affected by their so doing.[36] But where a creditor who is owed two debts, one guaranteed one not, takes a security for both, the surety is entitled as against the creditor to the benefit of a proportion of the security.[37]

Priority of surety over subsequent encumbrancers

The surety's right to the securities of the creditor is prior to that of later encumbrancers,[38] who are subject to the creditor's mortgage. This is on the basis that the surety stands in the place of the creditor he pays off and because the subsequent security is not lessened by the coming in.[39] Thus it does not seem material whether a subsequent encumbrancer had notice of the suretyship.[39]

Priority of surety over subsequent advances by creditor

After a period of uncertainty in the authorities,[40] it has been established that the surety's right on payment to be recouped

---

[32] *Siftken* v. *Wray* (1805) 6 East 371.

[33] See *Imperial Bank* case (*supra*).

[34] See *Praed* v. *Gardiner* (1788) 2 Cox 86, discussed in *Duncan Fox & Co.* v. *North and South Wales Bank* (1880) 6 App.Cas. at p.15; *Heyman* v. *Dubois* (1871) L.R.13 Eq.158. These cases also seem to show that a trustee in bankruptcy is bound by the equities upon which such marshalling is based.

[35] *Wade* v. *Coope* (1827) 2 Sim.155; *Wilkinson* v. *London and County Banking Co.* (1884) 1 T.L.R.63.

[36] *Wilkinson* v. *London and County Banking Co.* (1884) 1 T.L.R.63.

[37] *Perris* v. *Roberts* (1681) 1 Vern.34; *Coates* v. *Coates* (1864) 33 Beav.249; *Huggard* v. *Representative Church Body* (1916) 10 I.R. 1 at p.19.

[38] *Drew* v. *Lockett* (1863) 32 Beav.449; *Silk* v. *Eyre* (1875) 9 I.R.Eq.393; *Aylwin* v. *Witty* (1861) 30 L.J.Ch.860; *Dawson* v. *Bank of Whitehaven* (1877) 4 Ch.D.639.

[39] *Drew* v. *Lockett* (1863) 32 Beav.499 at 505, 506. The surety is subrogated to the creditor's position.

[40] The contrary proposition had been held in *Williams* v. *Owen* (1843) 13 Sim.597 followed in *Farebrother* v. *Wodehouse* (1856) 23 Beav.18;

out of the creditor's securities cannot be postponed merely by the creditor giving further advances on those securities.[41] The principle here is that the surety is entitled to have all the securities preserved for him which were taken at the time of the suretyship or subsequently and the surety's position cannot be affected by the creditor granting further advances on the same security.[42]

The situation may be different where the terms of the security give the debtor the option of calling for further advances, on the basis that the surety should perhaps take the benefit of the security with its obligation. Possibly the security would be apportioned rateably to the whole debt.

Consolidation against surety

The doctrine of consolidation permits a creditor, who holds two mortgages made by the same mortgagor, to refuse to allow the mortgagor to redeem one mortgage without redeeming the other. The right to consolidate will only exist if stipulated for: Law of Property Act 1925, s.93.

Under the general principle already discussed, a creditor should not be entitled to consolidate in that way as against a surety. There is a possible authority going in the opposite direction[43] although that decision appears to depend on the particular circumstances, where the surety knew that two separate mortgages were to be given for two loans, though he only granted one.

Where after the guarantee has been given, the creditor takes a security which is at once subject to consolidation, *e.g.* where there is a prior or simultaneous charge for another debt, the right of consolidation should apply against the surety. This is on the basis that the principle of preservation of securities for the benefit of the surety does not apply to securities which became subject to the doctrine of consolidation as soon as they were created.

Marshalling by surety for debt doubly secured

This problem arises where the guaranteed debt is secured by the mortgage of two funds, one of which is also subject to a

---

[41] *Dawson* v. *Bank of Whitehaven* (1877) 4 Ch.D.639 (reversed on another point 6 Ch.D.218); *Forbes* v. *Jackson* (1882) 19 Ch.D.615.

[42] *Forbes* v. *Jackson* (1882) 19 Ch.D.615 at 621.

[43] *Farebrother* v. *Wodehouse* (1856) 23 Beav.18 (Sir J. Romilly M.R.). The appeal was compromised. See also comments on the decision in *Re Kirkwood's Estate* (1878) 1 L.R.Ir.108; *Forbes* v. *Jackson* (1882) 19 Ch.D.615. See also *Nicholas* v. *Ridley* (1904) 1 Ch.192 at 196. In the previous edition of this work at p.219 it was considered highly inequitable that a surety could oust the right of consolidation.

second mortgage. If the surety pays the debt, he is compelled to marshal the securities in favour of the second morgagee. Thus if the proceeds of the fund upon which there are two mortgages are applied in satisfaction of the guaranteed debt, the second mortgagee will be entitled to the balance of the other fund, after satisfaction of the first mortgage, to the extent of the value of the fund mortgaged to him.[44]

Person charging property for debt of another

A person charging his own property to secure the debt of another who charges his own property for that debt occupies the position of a surety.[45] He is moreover entitled to the benefit of the security upon the property of the principal and is entitled to have the debt discharged out of the principal's property.[46]

Where several persons charged their properties by deposits of title deeds for the repayment of a company's debts to a person guaranteeing its overdraft, the mortgagors were entitled to have all the properties marshalled so as to cause any debt to fall rateably.[47]

Policies on life of principal debtor

A surety paying the debt is entitled to a policy on the life of a debtor if it has been provided as a security by or at the expense of the debtor in circumstances such that the policies are redeemable by the debtor and constitute a fund belonging to him in the hands of the creditor. However, if a creditor insures the life of a debtor on his own account he may keep and recoup upon the policies even though the debt is paid.[48]

Property wrongfully charged for the debt of another

A person whose property is wrongfully though validly, pledged by another to secure his own debt is entitled to have his property disencumbered out of any property of the debtor also

---

[44] *South* v. *Bloxam* (1865) 2 H. & M.457. *Cf. Dixon* v. *Steel* [1901] 2 Ch.602.

[45] See *e.g. Re Marley* [1976] 1 W.L.R. 952 (D.C.) where a father conveyed his property into the joint names of himself and his son so that it could be charged for the son's business debts. The father's position as a surety vis-à-vis the son's trustee in bankruptcy was conceded and a right of marshalling was held to exist as against the trustee.

[46] *Dixon* v. *Steel* [1901] 2 Ch.602. This type of suretyship has the advantage over a suretyship by covenant that the surety has a charge, from the date of execution of the relevant instruments, over the principal's property to secure his right of indemnity: *Re Marley, supra* at p.956 B.

[47] *Smith* v. *Wood* [1929] 1 Ch.14. Thus the release of any one of the charges or its subjection to a prior charge without the agreement of the other mortgagors would lead to their discharge.

[48] *Dalby* v. *India and London Life Assurance Co.* (1854) 15 C.B.365.

pledged for the same debt,[49] or at the expense of any surety who may have guaranteed the payment of that debt.[50]

Surety's right to securities arises on payment

A surety is only entitled to the securities held by the creditor on paying the debt. Admission of a proof in bankruptcy is not equivalent to payment for this purpose, so that the surety is not entitled to the creditor's securities merely on proof.[51] The surety, however, may tender the debt in return for the securities. If the creditor refuses to give the securities up, the surety may bring the debt into Court and sue to compel the creditor to assign the securities to him.[52]

As long as the creditor is fully paid, a surety who has only paid a part of the debt is still as against the principal entitled to the benefit of the creditor's securities.[53] For example, the trustee of a bankrupt surety, whose estate had paid a dividend to the creditor, would be entitled to a charge on any property mortgaged to the creditor by the principal after the creditor has realised the balance of his debt out of it,[54] and before any encumbrances subsequent to the creditor.

Surety's right to securities limited to indemnity

A surety's right to use securities given to the creditor by the principal is limited to the recoupment of the surety's indemnity against the principal. If the surety makes terms with the creditor and settles the debt for a lesser sum, and then obtains an assignment of the creditor's securities, he cannot recover more from the principal than he has actually paid.[55]

Abandonment or waiver of surety's right to securities

A surety paying the debt may abandon the securities to which he thereby becomes entitled to the debtor. Alternatively, the paying surety may leave the security to the creditor to use in respect of any further debt which it may cover, and if the

---

[49] *Ex p. Alston* (1868) L.R. 4 Ch. App.168.

[50] *Ex p. Salting* (1883) 25 Ch.D.148.

[51] *Ewart* v. *Latta* (1865) 4 Macq. 983 (H.L.); *Ex p. Turquand* (1876) 3 Ch.D.445. *Cf. Ex p. Brett* (1871) 6 Ch.App.838.

[52] *Goddard* v. *Whyte* (1860) 2 Giff.449; *Cf. Wodehouse* v. *Farebrother* (1856) 5 E. & B.277.

[53] *Gedye* v. *Matson* (1858) 25 Beav. 310. *i.e.* in order to recoup the indemnity due from the principal debtor.

[54] *Cf. Ewart* v. *Latta* (1865) 4 Macq.983 (H.L.).

[55] *Reed* v. *Norris* (1837) 2 My. & Cr. 361 following *ex p. Rushforth* (1805) 10 Ves.409 and *Butcher* v. *Churchill* (1808) 14 Ves.Jun.567. This rule now has statutory form in the proviso to s.5 Mercantile Law Amendment Act 1856. See Appendix 2.

payment was made with that intention the principal debtor cannot insist that the payment be applied in redemption of the security.[56] Thus a surety may find that the terms of the guarantee provide that he shall not have the benefit of the securities.[57] However, the terms often found in guarantees that the creditor may treat the surety as a principal debtor and that the surety should not be discharged by any giving of time or act or omission of the creditor which would normally discharge a surety, do not disentitle the surety to the creditor's securities if and when the surety pays.[58]

A question may arise as to whether the surety has waived his rights to enforce the creditor's security against the principal. The taking of a charge directly from the principal may possibly evince an intention to waive and disentitle the surety to the creditor's securities.[59] However, if the surety took the charge from the principal in ignorance of the security given to the creditor, he cannot be taken to have intended to waive a right he did not know of.[60] It may be necessary for there to be an express rather than an implied release.[61]

Agreement between principal and creditor as to securities

A stipulation between the creditor and the principal debtor that the surety may not have the benefit of the securities upon payment would seem to be inoperative.[62] It may be possible, however, to prevent the surety having the benefit of the securities by stipulating that they could only be resorted to if both the principal and the surety failed to pay.

5. Contribution between Co-Sureties

Where a co-surety pays the debt, or more than his proportion of it, and the principal is insolvent, the co-surety is entitled to contribution from his fellow co-sureties to equalise the burden. It makes no difference whether the co-sureties are bound jointly or severally or jointly and severally. Nor does it matter whether the co-sureties are bound by the same instrument or by separate instruments, whether in the same sum or different sums, whether at the same time or different times. Nor does it matter whether the surety paying the debt knows of the existence of

---

[56] *Waugh* v. *Wren* (1862) 11 W.R.244; 9 Jur.(N.S.) 365.
[57] *Midland Banking Co.* v. *Chambers* (1859) 4 Ch.App.398.
[58] *Re Kirkwood's Estate* (1878) 1 L.R.Ir.108.
[59] *Cooper* v. *Jenkins* (1863) 32 Beav.337.
[60] *Lake* v. *Brutton* (1856) 8 De G. M. & G. 440, 451, 452.
[61] *Brandon* v. *Brandon* (1859) 3 De G. & J.524.
[62] *Cf. Steel* v. *Dixon* (1881) 17 Ch.D.825.

any other sureties, since the rule of contribution does not depend upon agreement, express or implied, but upon an equity arising from the mere fact of the existence of co-sureties for the same debt owed to the same creditor.[63] The underlying principle of equity is that the creditors'remedies against the co-sureties should be applied so as to apportion the burden rateably. If the remedies have been applied otherwise the court will, by employing the remedies of the creditor or otherwise, correct the inequity as between the co-sureties.[64]

Where any of the co-sureties are insolvent, the contributions of the others are proportionately increased.[65]

Contributing co-sureties must be sureties in same degree

The equity depends upon the creditor's original ability (apart from any equity preventing him from doing so) to charge the co-surety from whom contribution is sought as much as the co-surety seeking contribution. Where this could not have been done there is no inequity to be remedied and no contribution. For example, where the surety's guarantee provides that he cannot be sued unless the other sureties made default, no right to contribution arises against him.[66] The surety in that position is in reality a "surety for the surety."[67]

In the case of a bill of exchange given as a security for a person's debt, whereas both the drawer and acceptor are sureties as regards the principal debtor, as between themselves the drawer is only surety for the acceptor and is in the absence of

---

[63] *Dering* v. *Lord Winchelsea* (1787) 1 Cox Eq. Cas.318; *Craythorne* v. *Swinburne* (1807) 14 Ves.160; *Re Ennis* [1893] 3 Ch.238.

[64] The use of the creditor's remedies to obtain contribution between co-sureties was always recognized in Roman Law: D.46.1.17; C.8.41.21. The Lex Apulia gave a direct right of contribution to a surety paying more than his proportion. However, Roman Law also gave co-sureties rights not fully established in English law to prevent the inequity of an unequal burden arising. The Lex Furia compelled the creditor in some cases to divide his demand amongst the sureties. Hadrian required a creditor to charge all co-sureties equally: G.3.121,122. The principles upon which the English law is based are stated in the following authorities: *Craythorne* v. *Swinburne* (1807) 16 Ves. at p.162 (argument of Sir S. Romilly judicially approved by Lord Eldon); *Stirling* v. *Forrester* (1821) 3 Bligh at p.590 (*per* Lord Redesdale); *Ex p. Stokes* (1848) De G. at p.622; *Hartley* v. *O'Flaherty* Beatty p.77, 78; *Duncan Fox & Co.* v. *North and South Wales Bank* (1880) 6 App.Cas. 1, 19; *Ward* v. *National Bank of New Zealand* (1883) 8 App.Cas. 755, 765. Goff and Jones, *The Law of Restitution* (2nd ed., 1978) consider that the principle of contribution is an illustration of the broader principle of unjust enrichment, at pp.211 *et seq.*

[65] *Peter* v. *Rich* (1629) 1 Ch.R.34; *Hole* v. *Harrison* (1673) 1 Ch.Ca.246; *Lawson* v. *Wright* (1786) 1 Cox Eq.Cas.275; *Hitchman* v. *Stewart* (1855) 3 Drew. 271; *Dallas* v. *Walls* (1873) 29 L.T.599; *Lowe* v. *Dixon* (1885) 16 Q.B.D.455; (Canada: *Re Price* (1978) 85 D.L.R.(3d) 554). The common law did not adjust the position to take insolvent co-sureties into account: *Batard* v. *Hawes* (1853) 2 E. & B. 287. Nor does Scottish law: *Buchanan* v. *Main* 3 F.215 (1900).

[66] *Re Denton* [1904] 2 Ch.178; *Craythorne* v. *Swinburne* (1807) 14 Ves.160.

[67] *Per* Lord Eldon in *Craythorne* v. *Swinburne* (1807) 14 Ves.160, referred as a "sub-surety" in Restatement, Security § 145 (1941).

contrary agreement entitled to throw the loss on him.[68] If, however, it can be shown that the parties who appear successively liable on the bill were intended as between themselves to be co-sureties in equal degree, contribution is recoverable by one against the other, irrespective of their places upon the bill.[69]

Where a "surety for the surety" is made to pay by the creditor, he can recoup himself from the surety.[70] The equities between them are not altered by the creditor's choice of whom he decided to sue.

If a surety pays off the creditor and demands the money from the debtor, who finds another surety, no right of contribution arises: the latter would have to pay the whole. The result may well be the same where the creditor, after the debt becomes due, presses the principal for payment and the debtor then finds a further surety,[71] unless the circumstances show that it was intended that the fresh surety would be co-ordinate with the liability of that of the existing guarantor and would not be that of a mere "surety for the surety," *i.e.* liable only upon the default of the original surety.

Time given to surety

The right to contribution is not affected by the fact that time has been given by the creditor to the claimant co-surety.[72]

Position at common law and in equity

It is doubtful whether the common law allowed any action for contribution between co-sureties prior to the beginning of the nineteenth century.[73] It was, however, enforceable in London by custom.[74] The common law courts eventually recognised the principle so as to permit an action for money paid to the use of the co-surety for contribution calculated by reference to a crude

---

[68] *Ex p. Hunter* 2 Gl. and J.7. In *Molsons Bank* v. *Korinsky* [1924] 4 D.L.R. 330 the indorser of the principal's promissory note payable to the bank was held not to be entitled to contribution from sureties of the sum ultimately due on the principal's account on the basis that he was a surety in a prior degree, following *Craythorne* v. *Swinburne* (1807) 14 Ves.Jun.160. See also the *Duncan Fox* case (1880) 6 App. Cas. 1 *per* Lord Blackburn at p.20.

[69] *Reynolds* v. *Wheeler* (1861) 10 C.B. (N.S.) 561; *Macdonald* v. *Whitfield* (1883) 8 A.C. 733; *Batson* v. *King* (1859) 4 H. and N.739.

[70] *Re Denton* [1904] 2 Ch.178. Lord Eldon in *Craythorne* v. *Swinburne* (1807) 14 Ves.160 treated the surety as being in the position of a principal debtor with regard to the "surety for the surety." In *Fox* v. *Royal Bank of Canada* (1975) 59 D.L.R. (3d) 258 such a sub-surety was upon payment held to be subrogated to the creditor's rights against the principal and the sureties, with no right on the part of the sureties to contribution against him.

[71] *Parsons* v. *Briddock* (1708) 2 Vern.608; *Armitage* v. *Baldwin* (1842) 5 Beav. 278.

[72] *Dunn* v. *Slee* (1817) 1 Moore 2. Nor does it matter that the payment from the claimant co-surety was exacted by the creditor upon a subsequent security given by that co-surety in aid of the creditor's remedies.

[73] Goff and Jones, *The Law of Restitution* (2nd ed., 1978) at p.212.

[74] *Offley and Johnson's Case* (1584) 2 Leon. 166.

division of the debt by the total number of sureties and not allowing for the insolvency of any co-surety.[75] In equity, however, the solvent sureties had to make good the contributions of those unable to pay.[76] Since the fusion of common law and equity in England in 1873, the rule of equity prevails throughout the English Courts, and the common law action for money paid to the use of the co-surety has fallen into disuse.[77]

Procedure

The proper course in England would now be to sue for contribution in the Chancery Division of the High Court, joining the co-sureties, and also the principal unless clearly insolvent. The rights of all can then be worked out in one inquiry.[78]

Insolvency of principal

It would seem right on principle that a surety should not have a contribution from a co-surety unless he can show that the principal debtor is insolvent or that there is some impediment in suing him.[79] It seems anomalous to permit an equitable remedy against co-sureties when recovery can be made against the principals thereby relieving all the co-sureties.[80]

Moreover, each co-surety joined might himself sue the principal, thereby multiplying actions unnecessarily.

The Court of Appeal has established the position that in an action for contribution between co-sureties the principal should be made a party unless it is proved or it can be inferred from the evidence that the principal is insolvent, or that there is other good reason why he should not be joined.[81]

Guarantees in varying amounts

It is important to distinguish between situations where different sureties are liable for the same debt but in different maximum sums, when contribution arises, and when different

---

[75] *Batard* v. *Hawes* (1853) 2 E. & B. 287.

[76] Goff and Jones, *op. cit.* at p.213 and cases cited at footnote 13.

[77] *Ibid.* at p.213 and footnote 17.

[78] *Lawson* v. *Wright* (1786) 1 Cox 275; *Hitchman* v. *Stewart* (1855) 3 Drew 271; *Hay* v. *Carter* [1935] Ch.397. For a form of order, see *Kent* v. *Abrahams* [1928] W.N.266.

[79] *Dering* v. *Earl of Winchelsea* (1787) 1 Cox 318. The insolvency will in many cases be inferable from the liquidation or bankruptcy of the principal debtor.

[80] But see *Cowell* v. *Edwards* (1800) 2 B. & P. 268.

[81] *Hay* v. *Carter* [1935] Ch.397. See also Goff and Jones *op. cit.* p.215. In both *Dering* v. *Winchelsea* and *Hay* v. *Carter* the insolvency of the principal debtor was inferable from the evidence before the court.

sureties are liable for different parts of the same debt, when it does not.[82]

The rule in suretyship cases where contribution arises, appears to be that sureties in varying amounts share the burden on a "maximum liability" basis in cases where the liabilities of the sureties are in limited amounts. Thus in *Ellesmere Brewery Co.* v. *Cooper*[83] there were four sureties, two at £50 each and two at £25 each. With a total liability of £48 it was assumed that the £50 sureties would bear £16 each and the £25 guarantors £8 each had they been held liable. The "independent liability" principle applicable, *e.g.* to indemnity insurance in England[84] would have divided liability between the two groups of sureties in the ratio 48:25.[85] A similar rateable method of division applies in suretyship cases where one of the sureties has unlimited liability, but the other's liability is in a limited amount.[85a]

Contributions varied by agreement

The right of contribution may be varied or even excluded by agreement,[86] although it is unsatisfactory to infer such an agreement in the absence of a clear stipulation.[87]

Where a co-surety has joined at the request of the other surety, it is a question of fact in each case on what terms one asked the other to join.[88] It has been said that a surety induced by another surety to join, cannot be required to contribute, especially where the inducing surety had taken a security for himself only[89] but that dictum is probably limited to a situation

---

[82] *Pendlebury* v. *Walker* (1841) 4 Y. & C. (Ex.) 424.

[83] [1896] 1 Q.B.75. To same effect see *Re McDonough* (1876) 10 Ir.Rep.Eq.269, where three sureties were liable up to £5,000, £3,000 and £1,000 respectively. As between them, the burden was to be shared in the proportion 5:3:1.

[84] *Commercial Union* v. *Hayden* [1977] 1 Q.B.804 (C.A.).

[85] In the U.S.A there is a division of opinion on this matter, but generally speaking the maximum liability principle is followed: see, *e.g. Malone* v. *Stewart* 235 Pa.99, 83A 607 (1912); *contra,* see, *e.g. Burnett* v. *Millsaps* 59 Miss. 333, 337 (1881). Where there are different groups of sureties or a group and an individual, bound in different amounts, the general rule in the U.S.A. is to divide the demand firstly between the groups on a maximum liability basis and then within each group on the basis of the available sureties in the group: *United States Fidelity & Guaranty Co.* v. *Naylor* 237 F.314 (1916).

[85a] *Naumann* v. *Northcote* (7th February 1978, unreported, C.A.: Transcript No.7835).

[86] *Swain* v. *Wall* (1641) 1 Ch. R.149. However, the judge who is said to have decided this case seems to have died in 1638 or 1639: see Goff and Jones, *The Law of Restitution* (2nd ed., 1978) at p.214, footnote 27. See also *Ellesmere Brewery Co.* v. *Cooper* [1896] 1 Q.B. 75; *Naumann* v. *Northcote, supra*.

[87] In *Swain* v. *Wall (supra)* the three sureties agreed amongst themselves that they could pay in thirds. The creditor exacted the whole sum from one. One was insolvent. Hutton J. is reported to have accepted the proposition that each co-surety had agreed to pay only a third and therefore only a third could be recovered by contribution, leaving the paying surety to bear two-thirds. This result defeats the equitable principle of equalisation of the burden, based on the notion that it should not matter which surety the creditor chooses to sue.

[88] *Done* v. *Walley* (1848) 2 Exch.198. And see *Lingard* v. *Bromley* (1812) 1 V. & B.114.

[89] *Per* Lord Kenyon in *Turner* v. *Davies* (1796) 2 Esp.478.

where the facts warrant the inference that the additional surety was asked to join on that basis. A surety can resist a claim for contribution on the basis of the verbal promise of the co-surety to indemnify him, and the Statute of Frauds cannot be used to present such a defence to contribution.[90]

Sureties for different debts of a principal in different combinations may agree to share equally in certain events any liability which may be enforced against any of them, ousting any right of contribution which might arise on any particular debt.[91]

A co-surety has a defence to an action for contribution by a surety who induced him to join by fraud, although the inducing surety need not disclose any interest in the money to be raised.[92]

If a surety pays with the aid of a stranger, the two will be considered as one person and entitled between them to contribution against a co-surety.[93]

Sureties for different debts

There is no co-suretyship and no contribution between sureties where sureties are bound for different debts. The same applies where a single debt is guaranteed in distinct parts by different sureties.[94]

Death of a surety

Where the surviving surety pays, the right to contribution exists against the deceased's surety's estate.[95] However, this right to contribution requires the obligation to have been several and not merely joint, unless there was something beyond the mere fact of co-suretyship from which an agreement that contribution should be payable out of the estate of a deceased surety may be inferred. At law the estate of a merely joint surety is discharged, and equity does not correct this by regarding the obligation as joint and several in the absence of special circumstances, *e.g.* mistake, partnership, prior extension of credit to the sureties where it was not the instrument that first created the liability.[96]

---

[90] *Rae* v. *Rae* (1857) 6 Ir.Ch.R.490.
[91] See *Arcedeckne* v. *Lord Howard* (1872) 27 L.T.194.
[92] *Mackreth* v. *Walmsley* (1884) 51 L.T.19.
[93] See *Arcedeckne* v. *Lord Howard* (1872) 27 L.T.194.
[94] See *Pendlebury* v. *Walker* (1841) 4 Y. & C. Ex.242; and *Cooke* v. *Twyman* (1823) Turn. & R.426; *cf. Collins* v. *Prosser* (1823) 1 B. & C.682; *Ellis* v. *Emmanuel* (1876) 1 Ex D.157.
[95] p.240 of the previous edition of this work is cited for this proposition by Goff and Jones, *The Law of Restitution* (2nd ed., 1978) at p.221, footnote 77.
[96] Goff and Jones, *op. cit.* at p.221 consider that a right of contribution may be available on the basis that there was a common obligation at some time in the past. They consider that in principle a contribution claim in equity should lie generally.

There is some authority, however, for saying that the survivors of a number of joint sureties have a right of contribution in respect of the liability surviving to them by reason of an implied contract with the deceased.[97] However, whilst an agreement binding the estate of a surety may often readily be inferred from the dealings of the parties, it will not necessarily be implied. A surety might well desire that his own liability should cease at death, even if that means that the co-surety's liability could cease in the same way. The court should consider in particular the question whether the surety's estate would have been expected to benefit from the continuing liability.

When the right to contribution arises

A surety has no right of contribution until he has paid a larger sum than his proportion of the debt then actually due to the creditor.[98] It is only then that the surety has a debt as against the co-surety which will support a petition in bankruptcy.[99]

Where the surety has paid less than his share, but it becomes more by reason of the creditor's recovery from the principal debtor, a right to contribution arises.[1]

A surety paying more than his share of what is then due cannot insist on contribution if a larger sum may later become due.[2] Similarly, a surety who has paid the whole interest but less than half the principal sum cannot recover in respect of the interest by treating it separately.[3]

Once a surety has paid his share, contribution can be claimed as often as, by reason of further payments by the surety or the principal, the amount paid becomes greater than the surety's

---

[97] In *Ashby* v. *Ashby* (1827) 7 B. & C.444, Bayley J. suggested that the paying surety could sue the deceased surety's executor for money paid to the use of the deceased as executor. However, it is difficult to see what benefit normally accrues to the deceased's estate from the payment unless Bayley J. was considering a situation where the assets of the estate were in some way bound by the debt. In *Prior* v. *Hembrow* (1841) 8 M. & W. 873 the cases where law would imply a contract on behalf of the deceased joint contractor that his executors should pay their proportion are described as those which "stand on the same footing as that of several persons jointly contracting for a chattel to be made or procured for the common benefit of all—the building of a ship, for instance, or the furnishing of a house—and as to which the executors of any party dying before the work is completed are by agreement to stand in the place of the party dying." If on the facts the suretyship provided a continuing benefit to the estate, *e.g.* it ensured the continuity of a loan to a company in which it had shares, one could see the analogy to chattel-acquiring contracts. In *Batard* v. *Hawes* (1853) 2 E. & B. 287, the dicta in *Ashby* v. *Ashby* were approved, but in that case the parties were not co-sureties.

[98] *Ex p. Gifford* (1802) 6 Ves.805; *Davies* v. *Humphreys* (1840) 6 M. & W.153; *Ex p. Snowdon* (1881) 17 Ch.D.44. In *Davies* v. *Humphreys* Parke B. felt that it might "be more convenient to require that the whole amount should be settled before the sureties should be permitted to call upon each other, in order to prevent multiplicity of suits."

[99] *Ex p. Snowdon* (1881) 17 Ch.D.44.

[1] *Davies* v. *Humphreys* (1840) 6 M. & W.153.

[2] *Stirling* v. *Burdett* [1911] 2 Ch.418.

[3] *Lever* v. *Pearce* (1888) W.N.105.

share.[4] Time begins to run under the Statute of Limitations in respect of each sum that might be claimed from the time the right to each portion arises.[4]

Payment without being sued

A surety may pay as soon as the demand becomes due and claim contribution.[5] If there is any doubt as to whether the sum is due, the surety should give notice to the co-sureties to defend, make terms or pay their proportions. If the co-sureties do not take any such action, the co-sureties will not be entitled to claim that the surety paid improperly.[6] The absence of notice permits the co-sureties to establish, if they can, that payment could have been resisted.[7] Contribution is of course not possible where a surety pays without being liable to the creditor.[8]

Claim before payment

Once judgment has been entered against a surety for more than his proportion, he has the right, if recovery cannot be made against the principal, to bring an action in equity joining the co-sureties and the creditor to compel the co-sureties to pay their proportions.[9] Even before judgment is obtained it is possible to bring such an action if the creditor has a right to immediate payment from the surety.[9] It has been suggested that there is a possible precondition that the creditor must be threatening to make the surety liable for more than his share.[10]

Securities given by co-surety to creditor

A surety is entitled in order to obtain contribution to any security given to the creditor by the co-surety.[11] Moreover, the creditor must not waste such securities.[12]

---

[4] *Davies* v. *Humphreys* (1840) 6 M. & W.153. See generally Chapter 10.

[5] *Pitt* v. *Purssord* (1841) 8 M. & W.538.

[6] *Duffield* v. *Scott* (1789) 3 Term Rep.374, approved in *Jones* v. *Williams* (1841) 7 M. & W. at p.501; *Pettmann* v. *Keble* (1850) 9 C.B.701.

[7] *Smith* v. *Compton* (1832) 3 B. & Ad.407.

[8] *Barry* v. *Moroney* (1837) 8 Ir.R.C.L.554; *Camberlege* v. *Lawson* (1857) 1. C.B. (N.S.) 709.

[9] *Wolmershausen* v. *Gullick* [1893] 2 Ch.514. For the U.S.A., see *Davies* v. *First National Bank* 86 Or.474, 161 P.93, 168 P.929 (1917). There it has also been suggested that a surety before payment may restrain a fraudulent conveyance by a co-surety: *Bowen* v. *Hoskins* 45 Miss.183 (1871); *Pashby* v. *Mandingo* 42 Mich.172 3 N.W.927 (1879). In Canada, it has been held that it is at least necessary that the surety should have been called on to pay more than his due: *Tucker* v. *Bennett* [1927] 2 D.L.R.42 *per* Orde J.A., at pp.47–48.

[10] See Goff and Jones, *The Law of Restitution* (2nd ed., 1978) at p.217 citing p.245 of the previous edition of this work.

[11] *Ex p. Crisp* (1744) 1 Atk.133 at p.135; *Greerside* v. *Benson* (1745) 3 Atk.248; *Stirling* v. *Forrester* (1821) 3 Bligh 575 at p.590 citing *Dering* v. *Lord Winchelsea* (1787) 2 B.& P.270; *Duncan Fox & Co.* v. *North and South Wales Bank* (1880) 6 App.Cas.1 *per* Lord Blackburn at p.19. s.5, Mercantile Law Amendment Act 1856 puts this rule into statutory form in England.

[12] *Margretts* v. *Gregory* (1862) 6 L.T.543.

Surety holding security or receiving payment from principal debtor

The surety's right to contribution from co-sureties is not affected by his having taken a bond for his security from the principal.[13] This is so even if the co-sureties are unaware of the security, if the surety only became a surety on the basis of having such a security and if it was agreed between the surety and the principal that the benefit of the security would not extend to the other sureties.[14] A security given by the principal to a surety to indemnify him against all liability in respect of his suretyship will in effect enure to the benefit of all the sureties until they are recouped in full, (or the security is exhausted).[15] If the surety gives up such a security, he loses *pro tanto* his right to contribution.[16]

The same principle appears to apply to a payment by the principal to the surety, which must be shared with the co-sureties,[17] whereupon the surety will aquire a fresh claim for indemnity from the principal debtor.

A paying surety who takes over securities from the creditor will have to allow for the securities in seeking contribution from co-sureties.[18] But where a surety insures the principal's life for the surety's benefit and pays the premiums himself, a co-surety cannot compel the surety to deliver up the policy.[19]

Surety consenting to time being given to the principal

A surety who agrees to time being given to the debtor loses, if the time is given, his right to contribution from any sureties who have not agreed to it, for they would then be released.[20]

---

[13] *Knight* v. *Hughes* (1828) 3 C. & P. 467. *Cf. Swain* v. *Wall* (1641) 1 Ch.149.

[14] *Steel* v. *Dixon* (1881) 17 Ch.D.825; *Re Arcedeckne, Atkins* v. *Arcedeckne* (1883) 24 Ch.D.709.

[15] *Berridge* v. *Berridge* (1890) 44 Ch.D.168.

[16] *Ramsey* v. *Lewis* 30 Barb. (N.Y.) 403 (1859).

[17] *Knight* v. *Hughes* (1828) 3 C. & P. 467; *Steel* v. *Dixon* (1881) 17 Ch.D.825.

[18] *Re Arcedeckne, Atkins* v. *Arcedeckne* (1883) 24 Ch.D.70.

[19] *Re Arcedeckne* (1883) 24 Ch.D.709 at 716, 717; *Re Albert Life Assurance Co.* (1870) L.R. 11 Eq.164 *per* Bacon V.C., at p.172.

[20] See *Way* v. *Hearn* (1862) 11 C.B. (N.S.) 774, 781, 782. This statement of the law in the previous edition of this work was approved by Lord J. in *Sword* v. *Victoria Super Service Ltd.* (1958) 15 D.L.R. (2d) 217. *Cf. Greenwood* v. *Francis* [1899] 1 Q.B. 312 where the giving time was authorised by the guarantee. Guarantees often contain stipulations permitting the creditor to give time wihout releasing any of the sureties. In Canada, it has been held that the release by a surety of principal's obligation to indemnity prevents that surety from seeking contribution from a co-surety who has thereby lost his right of indemnity: *Griffiths* v. *Wade* (1966) 60 D.L.R. (2d) 62, following the Massachussets decision of *Hobart* v. *Stone* 10 Pick.215 (1830).

Co-surety's counterclaim against creditor

A co-surety is fully liable to contribution to a paying surety regardless of any counterclaim the co-surety may have had against the creditor.[21]

Interest on contribution

A surety is entitled to charge interest[22] on the sum of contribution due as from the date or dates when his payments became in excess of his proportion.[23] It does not matter that the principal debt did not carry interest.[24] Moreover, the surety who has paid his share can insist on his co-sureties exonerating him from further interest accrued to the creditor on the shares which they should have paid.[25]

Costs

A surety can seek contribution in respect of costs incurred in reasonably resisting the creditor's claim.[26] This assumes that the proceedings were defended on grounds which would relieve the other co-sureties also, and not merely the defending surety on grounds personal to himself.[27]

---

[21] *Wilson* v. *Mitchell* [1939] 2 Q.B.869 citing p.139 of the last edition of this work and the cases of *Gillespie* v. *Torrance* 25 N.Y.306 (1862) and *Newton* v. *Lee* 139 N.Y.332 (1893) therein referred to. See *supra*, at p.103.

[22] *Lawson* v.*Wright* (1786) 1 Cox.275; *Hitchman* v.*Stewart* (1855) 3 Drewr. 271; *Ex p. Bishop* (1880) 15 Ch.D.400.

[23] Not necessarily the same as the dates of the payments: See *Davies* v. *Humphreys* (1840) 6 M. & W. 153.

[24] *Re Swan* (1869) 4 Ir.R.Eq.209.

[25] *Per* Wright J., *ex relatione* M. Mackenzie, December 1902.

[26] In *Wolmershausen* v. *Gullick* [1893] 2 Ch.514 at p.529, 530 Wright J. allowed contribution for costs incurred in resisting the creditor's claim, which had been thereby materially reduced. The contrary was suggested by Lord Tenterden in *Knight* v. *Hughes* (1828) 3 C. & P. 467, but see also *Kemp* v. *Finden* (1844) 12 M. & W. 421, *Tindall* v. *Bell* (1843) 11 M. & W. 228; *Broom* v. *Hall* (1859) 7 C.B. (N.S.) 503.

[27] See *Re International Contract Co., Hughes' Claim* (1872) L.R. 13 Eq.623 at p.624 *per* Wickens V.-C.; *South* v. *Bloxam* (1865) 2 H. & M.457.

CHAPTER 8

RELEASE OF THE SURETY BY DEALINGS WITH THE PRINCIPAL CONTRACT

Discharge of surety by release or giving time to principal

A surety is discharged by the creditor, without his consent, either releasing the principal debtor or entering into a binding arrangement with him to give him time. The ground upon which the surety is discharged being in both cases that his right at any time to pay the debt, and sue the principal in the name of the creditor, is interfered with.[1] In practice, guarantees often contain provisions attempting to exclude this rule.[2]

Basis of rule

The theory is that the creditor cannot place his remedies at the disposal of the surety without a breach of his arrangement with the principal not to sue him. To carry out that arrangement, it is necessary that the right of the surety to take action against the principal should be suspended.[3] And as this cannot be done without his consent, he is held discharged altogether.[4]

A surety is also discharged if the creditor agrees with the principal not to receive the money from the surety since this is inconsistent with the right of the surety to pay the debt and sue

---

[1] See *Nisbet* v. *Smith* (1789) 2 Bro.C.C. 579; *Samuell* v. *Howarth* (1817) 3 Mer. 272; *Orme* v. *Young* (1815) Holt N.P.C. 84; *Price* v. *Kirkham* (1864) 3 H. & C. 437, 442; *Bailey* v. *Edwards* (1864) 4 B. & S. 761, 771; *Swire* v. *Redman* (1876) 1 Q.B.D. 536. It is necessary carefully to distinguish the cases discussed in this chapter, from cases where the transaction amounts to a payment of the debt by the principal. For the importance of the distinction see *Perry* v. *National Provincial Bank* [1910] 1 Ch. 464.

The absurdity of the application of this rule with regard to agreements to give time, where the surety's interests are not harmed are pointed out by Glanville Williams in *Joint Obligations* (1949) at p. 124 and Cordozo in *Law and Literature* (1931) at p. 51 and in *The Nature of the Judicial Process* (1932), pp. 153–154. Manitoba (R.S.M. 1970 M–120) and Saskatchewan (R.S.S. 1965 C. 73) have legislated to limit the surety's defence in such cases to the extent of his prejudice. The same change is suggested by the Law Reform Commission of British Columbia in its Report on Guarantees of Consumer Debts (1979) in respect of 'consumer' transactions.

[2] See, *e.g.* Appendix 1. The South Australian Law Reform Committee in its 39th Report (1976) has proposed that this type of provision be made void, either in any event or if not drawn to the surety's attention and explained to him.

[3] See *per* Lord Eldon C.J. in *English* v. *Darley* (1800) 2 B. & P., at p. 62: *per* Best C.J. in *Philpot* v. *Briant* (1828) 4 Bing. 717 at p. 719; *Ex p. Gifford* (1802) 6 Ves. 805; *Nevile* v. *Glendinning* (1816) 7 Taunt. 126; *Davies* v. *Stainbank* (1855) 6 De G.M. & G. 679, 689, 696; *North* v. *Wakefield* (1849) 13 Q.B. 536, 541; *Webb* v. *Hewitt* (1857) 3 K. & J. 438, 442: *Bateson* v. *Gosling* (1871) L.R. 7 C.P. 9, 14; *Cragoe* v. *Jones* (1873) L.R. 8 Ex. 81, 83.

[4] See *Combe* v. *Woolf* (1832) 8 Bing. 156, 163.

the principal.[5] It has been held by a majority in the Court of Appeal that the doctrine has no application where the surety has agreed with the principal not to require him to pay until the surety is himself sued; but this view, though not formally overruled, was questioned in the House of Lords in the same case.[6]

Doctrine does not apply to quasi-sureties

The doctrine releasing a surety when time is given to a principal debtor does not apply to persons not sureties but who merely occupy positions of secondary liability.[7]

Actual damage to surety not material

The surety is discharged however short may have been the time given, and whether or not the arrangement in fact operated to the advantage or disadvantage of the surety.[8] An analogy with the cases on variations might have suggested an exception where it is clear without enquiry[9] that the matter is not substantial or can only be beneficial to the surety.[10]

Sureties contracting as principals but where one is a surety

The rule as to the effect of giving time is not confined to sureties contracting as such, but extends to those who undertake what is in form a principal liability, but is in fact only assumed to secure the consideration for another. Such persons are released, if the creditor gives time or releases the principal, after notice of the true relations of the parties, whether he had that notice at the time of taking the security or not. For example, a person who gives a bond or promissory note for the debt of another, or who becomes a party, either as acceptor or as indorser, to a bill of exchange for the accommodation of another, in order that the other may obtain money upon it, is released if

---

[5] *Oriental Financial Corporation* v. *Overend Gurney & Co.* (1871) L.R. 7 Ch.App. 142 at p. 152; (1874) L.R. 7 H.L. 348 at p. 358.

[6] *Rouse* v. *Bradford Banking Co.* [1894] 2 Ch. 32; [1894] A.C. 586.

[7] *Way* v. *Hearn* (1862) 11 C.B.(N.S.) 774. *British Airways* v. *Parish* [1979] 2 Lloyd's Rep. 361 (director liable for company's debt because name of company misdescribed contrary to s.108, Companies Act 1948). Nor does it apply to a surety who undertakes to be liable as a principal: *Reade* v. *Lowndes* (1857) 23 Beav. 361.

[8] *Rees* v. *Berrington* (1798) 2 Ves. 540; *Bowmaker* v. *Moore* (1819) 3 Price 214; 7 Price 223; *Samuell* v. *Howarth* (1817) 3 Mer. 272; *Oakley* v. *Pasheller* (1836) 4 C. & F. 207, 224, 233; *Bailey* v. *Edwards* (1864) 4 B. & S. 761; *Wilson* v. *Lloyd* (1873) L.R. 16 Eq. 60, 71; *Polak* v. *Everett* (1876) 1 Q.B.D. 669; *Holme* v. *Brunskill* (1878) 3 Q.B.D. 495, 505. *Ward* v. *National Bank of New Zealand* (1883) 8 A.C. 755, 763; *Re Darwen and Pearce* [1927] 1 Ch. 178, 183–185.

[9] *Holme* v. *Brunskill* (1878) 3 Q.B.D. 495.

[10] *National Bank of Nigeria Ltd.* v. *Awolesi* [1964] 1 W.L.R. 1311, P.C.; *Hydro-Electric Power Commission* v. *Fidelity Insurance Co.* (1937) 4 D.L.R. 626; *Bell* v. *National Forest Production Ltd.* (1964) 45 D.L.R. (2d) 249; 47 W.W.R. 449; *Nelson Fisheries Ltd.* v. *Boese* [1975] 2 N.Z.L.R. 233.

the holder, after notice of these facts, gives time to the principal debtor or person accommodated. This applies even though in the case of a bill the accommodation party may upon the bill appear to be liable in a prior degree to the party accommodated, as where he is acceptor and the party accommodated the drawer.

Debtors originally principals may become sureties

The doctrine extends, further, even to those who, having contracted as and being in fact principals, afterwards by arrangement with another principal become sureties as between themselves and that other, if the creditor before the time is given, has notice of that fact.[11] A partner, therefore, who retires taking a covenant from the continuing partners that they will pay the debts and indemnify him, becomes a mere surety to such of the creditors of the firm as have notice of the dissolution deed.[12] A proviso in that deed to the effect that he is not to be entitled to call upon the continuing partners to pay off the debts so long as he is kept indemnified does not apparently deprive him of his discharge if the time is given to the continuing partners.[13] But the rule under discussion has no application to cases where the relation of principal and surety does not exist, but one person indemnifies another against loss which may accrue from credit given to another.[14]

Delay no discharge

A surety is only discharged if a binding agreement is made between the creditor and the principal that time shall be given to the principal. Mere delay, therefore, by the creditor in suing the principal does not discharge the surety.[15] It is the surety's business to see whether the principal pays, and not that of the creditor.[16]

---

[11] *Rouse* v. *Bradford Banking Company* [1894] 2 Ch. 32 A.C. 586; *Goldfarb* v. *Bartlett* [1920] 1 K.B. 639.

[12] *Rouse* v. *Bradford Banking Company, supra.*

[13] See *Rouse* v. *Bradford Banking Co.* [1894] A.C. 586. The House of Lords was evidently of this opinion and would have overruled the opinions to the contrary expressed in the Court of Appeal [1894] 2 Ch. 32. But *cf. Oakford* v. *The European and American Steam Shipping Co. Ltd.* (1863) 1 H. & M. 182.

[14] See *Way* v. *Hearn* (1862) 11 C.B.(N.S.) 774.

[15] *Shepherd* v. *Beecher* (1725) 2 P.W. 288; *Ex p. Mure* (1788) 2 Cox 63, 74; *Walwyn* v. *St. Quentin* (1797) 1 B. & P. 652; *Wright* v. *Simpson* (1802) 6 Ves. 714 at p. 734; *Trent Navigation Co.* v. *Harley* (1808) 10 East 34; *Goring* v. *Edmunds* (1829) 6 Bing. 94; *Brickwood* v. *Anniss* (1814) 5 Taunt 614; *Orme* v. *Young* (1815) Holt N.P.C. 84; *Perfect* v. *Musgrave* (1818) 6 Price 111; *Bell* v. *Banks* (1841) 3 M. & Gr. 258; *Eyre* v. *Everett* (1826) 2 Russ. 381; *Heath* v. *Key* (1827) 1 Y. & J. 434; *Clarke* v. *Wilson* (1838) 3 M. & W. 208; *Price* v. *Kirkham* (1864) 3 H. & C. 437.

[16] *Wright* v. *Simpson* (1802) 6 Ves. 714 at p. 734. This is also the view of the case-law in most states of the U.S.A. However, the doctrine in *Pain* v. *Packard* 13 Johns. 174, 7 Am.Dec. 369 (1816) adopted by the Courts of three states and by statute in a number of others holds that it is a defence for a surety to show (a) that he urged the creditor to proceed against the principal; (b) the principal was then solvent; (c) the creditor could by proceeding have recovered; (d) the principal is now insolvent and the creditor cannot now collect. See also Restatement, Security § 130 (1941).

Although a surety is not discharged by the mere failure of the creditor to press for payment, even though this may prejudice the surety,[17] it is equally clear that a binding agreement to give time discharges the surety even though, as often happens, he suffers no harm.[18]

Forms of giving time

It is immaterial what form the giving time takes, so long as there is a binding agreement by the creditor to suspend his rights. Thus, agreeing to take payment by instalments,[19] taking a bill or note payable on a future day,[20] accepting a new bill in lieu of payment,[21] renewing a promissory note,[22] or obtaining judgment by consent with a stay of execution beyond the date when in the regular course judgment could have been obtained,[23] discharges the surety. An agreement to accept the proceeds of the sale of ships at sea and of others then about to be built[24] is a giving of time. But taking a security for the payment of a debt at a future time, with the reservation of the right to proceed at any time upon the original demand, does not discharge the surety.[25] Equally, taking a bill of sale for the debt does not affect the liability of the surety, even though the property assigned is not to be seized until after a certain time, if the personal liability of the debtor is not postponed.[26]

Where a mortgage, in which the defendant had joined as a surety, was assigned, and a new covenant entered into by the mortgagor with the assignee to pay the amount together with further advances at a future day, it was held that this put an end to the right to sue on the covenant in the first mortgage, and that the surety was therefore discharged, notwithstanding that the "full benefit of the covenants" in the first mortgage was expressed to be assigned.[27] So where a mortgage was taken for a debt already secured by an accommodation acceptance with a covenant for payment at a later date, the acceptor was discharged.[28] But where it was intended that the promissory

---

[17] *e.g.* if the principal becomes insolvent: *Trent Navigation Co.* v. *Harley* (1808) 10 East 34.
[18] *Petty* v. *Cooke* (1874) L.R. 6 Q.B. 790 at p. 795 (Blackburn J.).
[19] *Clarke* v. *Henty* (1838) 3 Y. & C. Ex. 187. And see *Tyson* v. *Cox* (1823) T. & R. 395.
[20] *Rees* v. *Berrington* (1795) 2 Ves. 540; *Samuell* v. *Howarth* (1817) 3 Mer. 272.
[21] *Goldfarb* v. *Bartlett* [1920] 1 K.B. 639.
[22] *Provincial Bank of Ireland* v. *Fisher* (1919) 2 Ir. R. 249.
[23] *Whitfield* v. *Hodges* (1836) 1 M. and W. 679; *Croft* v. *Johnson* (1814) 5 Taunt. 319.
[24] *Davies* v. *Stainbank* (1855) 6 De G.M. & G. 679.
[25] *Lindsay* v. *Lord Downes* (1840) 2 Ir. Eq. R. 307. And see *Pearl* v. *Deacon* (1857) 24 Beav. 186; 1 De G. & J. 461.
[26] *Twopenny* v. *Young* (1824) 3 B. & C. 208; but *cf. Searles* v. *Finch* (1891) 7 T.L.R. 253.
[27] *Bolton* v. *Buckenham* [1891] 1 Q.B. 278.
[28] *Munster and Leinster Bank* v. *France* (1889) 24 L.R.Ir. 82.

note of the debtor and sureties, and also a mortgage by the
debtor and others, should be taken, and that the promissory note
should be collateral to the mortgage, the sureties in the
promissory note were not discharged by the taking of the
mortgage, though it contained a covenant by the debtor to pay at
a later date.[29]

The receipt of interest before it is due amounts to a contract
not to sue for the principal till the date arrives when that
interest would have been payable, and is therefore a giving of
time and discharges the surety,[30] unless it is part of an
understanding that, not withstanding the payment in advance,
the right to sue is reserved.[31]

Binding agreement necessary

In order that there may be a giving of time so as to discharge a
surety, there must be an agreement legally binding to that
effect.[32] Therefore, if a further security is given by the principal
which may induce the creditor to forbear, this does not discharge
the surety if the creditor does not bind himself to forbear.[33] Nor
does any obligation merely binding on the honour of the
creditor.[34] Where there was an overdraft for £50,000 for which a
surety was liable, and the principal requested the bank to allow
it to be increased to £53,046 until March 14, to which the bank
assented, it was held in the House of Lords that the only legal
effect of this was to oblige the bank to honour drafts up to that
amount till March 14, and that the bank did not contract not to
claim the £50,000 before that day; consequently the surety was
not discharged.[35] A mere promise by the debtor of interest,[36] or
of interest at an increased rate[37] if the debt is not pressed,
followed by payment accordingly, does not show there has been
such a giving of time as to discharge the surety, because it
remains optional with the creditor whether in order to earn the
interest he should let the debt run on. In the same way, if the
agreement is to give time provided certain things are done by
the debtor, which he does not do, the surety is not discharged.
For example, where the debtor was to give a bill and goods for

---

[29] *Boaler* v. *Mayor* (1865) 19 C.B.(N.S.) 76.

[30] *Blake* v. *White* (1835) 1 Y. & C. Eq. 420.

[31] *Rayner* v. *Fussey* (1859) 28 L.J.Ex. 132.

[32] See *per* Lord Eldon in *Samuell* v. *Howarth* (1817) 3 Mer. 272, at p. 278; *Heath* v. *Key* (1827) 1 Y.
and J. 434.

[33] *Bell* v. *Bankes* (1841) 3 M. & Gr. 258.

[34] *Ladbrook* v. *Hewett* (1832) 1 Dowl. 488. And see *Tucker* v. *Laing* (1856) 2 K. & J. 745.

[35] *Rouse* v. *Bradford Banking Co.* [1894] A.C. 586; reversing on this point the Court of Appeal
[1892] 2 Ch. 32.

[36] *Arundel Bank* v. *Goble* cited in *Philpot* v. *Briant* (1828) 4 Bing. 717 at p. 721.

[37] *York City and County Banking Co.* v. *Bainbridge* (1880) 43 L.T. 732.

the balance due, and he gave a bill but not the goods, the taking of the bill was held to be conditional and there was no discharge of the surety.[38] Similarly where time was promised if £100 was sent by return of post, but only £80 was sent.[39]

If the creditor merely intimates to the debtor that he will accept a composition if the other creditors do, and promises to hold his hand while the debtor approaches them, this is no binding agreement to give time, and the surety is not discharged.[40]

The same result will follow if a creditor signs an agreement to take a composition provided all the other creditors come in and they do not come in.[41] If, however, the proviso is only to operate by way of defeasance on failure to carry out certain arrangements, and in the meantime the creditor is debarred from suing, the surety will be discharged.[42] A promise by the creditor not to enforce the debt for a certain time, if arrears of interest and expenses were paid up, is not binding because of lack of consideration and does not discharge the surety.[43]

Remedy against principal must be actually postponed

A surety is not discharged unless the remedy against the principal is, in a practical sense, postponed. Thus if an action is commenced against the principal and judgment agreed on terms that no execution issues until a day earlier than judgment could have been obtained in the usual course of the courts, the surety is not discharged.[44] And even where it is agreed that if instalments are regularly paid the stay of execution is to continue beyond that period, the surety is not discharged if default is made in the payment of an instalment (so that the whole becomes due) before that period expires.[45]

Giving time in respect of one of several debts

Where a surety is liable for several distinct debts, duties or obligations, time given in respect of one of them, the position of

---

[38] *Vernon* v. *Turley* (1836) 1 M. & W. 316.
[39] *Badnall* v. *Samuel* (1817) 3 Price 521.
[40] *Brickwood* v. *Anniss* (1814) 5 Taunt. 614.
[41] See *Lewis* v. *Jones* (1825) 4 B. & C. 506.
[42] *Bailey* v. *Edwards* (1864) 4 B. & S. 761.
[43] *Tucker* v. *Laing* (1856) 2 K. & J. 745. However, consideration should be given to the possible application of equitable estoppel applying so as to make the promise binding: see *Central London Property Trust Ltd.* v. *High Trees House Ltd.* [1947] K.B. 130, and the subsequent cases on "equitable estoppel".
[44] *Ladbrook* v. *Hewitt* (1832) 1 Dowl. 488; *Hulme* v. *Coles* (1827) 2 Sim. 12; *Whitfield* v. *Hodges* (1836) 1 M. & W. 679; *Jay* v. *Warren* (1824) 1 C. & P. 532.
[45] *Price* v. *Edmunds* (1829) 10 B. & C. 578; *Bowsfield* v. *Tower* (1812) 4 Taunt. 456; *Croft* v. *Johnson* (1814) 5 Taunt. 319.

the surety with regard to the remainder not being altered, will not discharge the surety as to the remainder. In *Croydon Commercial Gas Co.* v. *Dickinson*[46] where the principal had contracted to buy the by-products of a gas company, and there was a surety for payment of the price monthly, and time was given in respect of one month's supply, it was held in the Court of Appeal[47] that the surety was discharged only as to that monthly payment, as his position in reference to the contract as a whole was not varied, though the effect of the arrangement was to cause the indebtedness to acumulate. Similar considerations apply when the guarantee is for the performance of several duties[48] or distinct contracts.[49] Where there was a continuing guarantee for the price of the goods to be supplied, and an amount having become due, time was given in respect of that amount without prejudice to the creditor's rights in respect of future supplies, it was held that the surety remained liable in respect of future supplies.[50] However, the giving of time, followed by an agreement to take instalments and a variation of the terms of the principal debt has been held to release a surety, not only as to the payments for which time had been given, but as to the whole debt. The circumstances were such that what had been done "directly or by its consequences wholly altered the situation of the surety."[51] A surety for the payment of the premiums on a policy deposited by a debtor with his creditor was held discharged by the creditor releasing the debtor from his personal liability upon the original debt, and agreeing to look only to the policy.[52]

Power to give credit may be implied

A guarantee for the price of goods supplied involves the usual trade credit being given, and this will not discharge the surety as a giving of time.[53] It seems, too, that the creditor is entitled to give, not merely the usual trade credit, but the credit usual as between him and the debtor[54] on the theory the surety ought to

---

[46] (1876) 1 C.P.D. 707; (1876) 2 C.P.D. 46; See also *Davies* v. *Stainbank* (1855) 6 De G.M. & G. 679, 689; *Provincial Bank* v. *Cussen* (1886) 18 L.R.Ir. 382; cf. *Midland Motor Showrooms* v. *Newman* [1929] 2 K.B. 256.
[47] (1876) 2 C.P.D. 46.
[48] *Skillet* v. *Fletcher* (1867) L.R. 1 C.P. 217; (1867) 2 C.P. 469.
[49] *Harrison* v. *Seymour* (1866) L.R. 1 C.P. 518.
[50] *Bingham* v. *Corbett* (1864) 34 L.J.Q.B. 37; the principal paid the amount in respect of which time had been given.
[51] *Per* Sir John Leach V.-C. in *Eyre* v. *Bartrop* (1818) 3 Madd. 221.
[52] *Lowes* v. *Maugham* (1884) C. & E. 340.
[53] *Samuell* v. *Howarth* (1817) 3 Mer. 272; *Combe* v. *Woolf* (1832) 8 Bing. 156; *Allan* v. *Kenning* (1833) 9 Bing. 618; *Re Fox, Walker and Co., ex p. Bishop* (1880) 15 Ch.D. 400 (C.A.).
[54] *Simpson* v. *Manley* (1831) 2 C. & J. 12; *Combe* v. *Woolfe* (1832) 8 Bing. 156; *Howell* v. *Jones* (1834) 1 C.M. & R. 97 at p. 107.

inquire into the nature of the dealings before he assents to guarantee. It is probably a question in each case what latitude it was fairly in the contemplation of the surety to allow to the creditor under the circumstances. The surety would clearly not be bound to allow any dealings which he would not expect might naturally take place.[55] But the creditor cannot allow a long time to elapse and then give the agreed or trade credit, for this is in effect granting more than that credit.[56]

Time given expiring before surety's liability arises

Where the liability of the surety is only to come into being upon the happening of a condition (*e.g.* after demand), he is not discharged by time having been given, where it has expired before his liability arose.[57] An agreement by the creditor with a stranger[58] or with another surety[59] to give time to the principal does not discharge the surety.

Time given after payment by surety

If a surety, on being applied to, pays part of the debt in satisfaction of the whole of his liability, and the creditor afterwards releases the debtor, the surety has no ground of complaint, because his right of action against the debtor in respect of the payment made has already attached and is not interfered with.[60]

Time given after surety undertakes principal liability

Where, on being applied to, the surety gives a fresh undertaking to pay, by way of a note of his own[61] or a covenant by himself,[62] or makes an arrangement by which the creditor is to obtain satisfaction from securities provided by the surety[63] he may be held to have come under a principal liability to pay. In that case he will not be discharged by dealings between the creditor and the original principal.

---

[55] *Cf. Lee v. Jones* (1864) 17 C.B.(N.S.) 482 at p. 503.

[56] *Cf. Holl v. Hadley* (1828) 5 Bing. 54; *Combe v. Woolfe* (1832) 8 Bing. 156. And see *Howell v. Jones* (1834) 1 C.M. & R. 97.

[57] *Prendergast v. Devey* (1821) 6 Madd. 124. See S.C. at law, *sub nom. Davey v. Prendergrass* (1821) 5 B. & Ald. 187, 190.

[58] *Frazer v. Jordan* (1857) 8 E. & B. 303; following *Lyon v. Holt* (1839) 5 M. and W. 250.

[59] *Clarke v. Birley* (1889) 41 Ch.D. 422. *Cf. Cross v. Sprigg* (1850) 2 Mac. & G. 113.

[60] *Reade v. Lowndes* (1857) 23 Beav. 361, 367, 368. And see *Ex p. Bishop* (1880) 15 Ch.D. 400, 407, 415.

[61] *Hall v. Hutchons* (1830) 3 M. & K. 426.

[62] *Defries v. Smith* (1862) 10 W.R. 189.

[63] *Reade v. Lowndes* (1857) 23 Beav. 361.

Time given after judgment against surety

It has been held[64] that time given to the principal after judgment against both the surety and the principal does not discharge the surety, and there seems no difference between this case and the case of judgment recovered against the surety only. But where joint and several judgment has been obtained against both principal and surety, and one of them is actually released, both are discharged on the ordinary principles applicable to judgments.[65]

Reservation of remedy against surety

The doctrine under which a surety is discharged by an agreement on the part of the creditor either not to sue, or to give time to the principal debtor, does not apply if it is made a condition of the agreement that the rights of the creditor to sue or receive the money from[66] the surety are reserved. The principle upon which the surety is released rests on the basis that if the surety is not released he will be able to sue the principal for indemnity and that will be a fraud on the principal.[67] Where the creditor reserves rights against the surety, in the agreement with the principal, the principal knows that he will be exposed to a claim by the surety for indemnity and the surety is therefore not discharged.[68] This being the principle upon which the reservation operates, it is unnecessary that the surety should be a party to or have notice of it.[69]

Reservation incompatible with actual release

Where, however, the creditor actually releases the principal, there is no room for any reservation of remedies against the surety.[70] Similarly no such reservation can have effect where

---

[64] *Re A Debtor* [1913] 3 K.B. 11. See also *Pole* v. *Ford* (1816) 2 Chit. 125; *Bray* v. *Manson* (1841) 8 M. & W. 668; *Jenkins* v. *Robertson* (1854) 2 Drew. 351. See references at footnote 1, *supra*.

[65] *Re E.W.A.* [1901] 2 K.B. 642.

[66] See *Philpot* v. *Briant* (1828) 4 Bing. 717, 719; *Oriental Financial Corporation* v. *Overend, Gurney and Co.* (1871) L.R. 7 Ch.App. 142, 152; 7 H.L. 348, 358. The Law Reform Commission of British Columbia in its Report on Guarantees of Consumer Debts (1979) suggested that such reservations be prevented in the case of "consumer" guarantees.

[67] *Per* Mellish J. in *Nevill's Case* (1870) 6 Ch.App. 43 at p. 47.

[68] *Ex p. Glendinning* (1819) Buck. 517; *Ex p. Gifford* (1802) 6 Ves. 805; *Boultbee* v. *Stubbs* (1811) 18 Ves. 20; *Kearsley* v. *Cole* (1846) 16 M. & W. 128; *Nichols* v. *Norris* (1831) 3 B. & Ad. 41, note; *North* v. *Wakefield* (1849) 13 Q.B. 536, 541; *Price* v. *Barker* (1855) 4 E. & B. 760; *Bailey* v. *Edwards* (1864) 4 B. & S. 761, 774; *Webb* v. *Hewitt* (1857) 3 K. & J. 438, 442; *Bateson* v. *Gosling* (1871) L.R. 7 C.P. 9, 14; *Cragoe* v. *Jones* (1873) L.R. 8 Ex. 81, 83, 84. *Muir* v. *Crawford* (1875) L.R. 2 H.L.Sc. 456. *Cf. Bellingham* v. *Freer* (1837) 1 Moo.P.C. 333.

[69] See *Webb* v. *Hewitt* (1857) 3 K. & J. 438, 442.

[70] See *Commercial Bank of Tasmania* v. *Jones* [1893] A.C. 313, 316; *Webb* v. *Hewitt* (1857) 3 K. & J. 438. And *cf. Bolton* v. *Buckenham* [1891] 1 Q.B. 278.

another debtor is accepted in the place of the debtor guaranteed.[71] But the presence of such a reservation is frequently a reason for construing words of release (if the intention absolutely to put an end to the debt is not apparent)[72] as a mere covenant not to sue,[73] in which case no such repugnancy arises.[74]

However, if there is no doubt as to the intention absolutely to extinguish the debt, it is a release, and any sureties or co-debtors are discharged.[75] In *Metropolitan Bank of England* v. *Coppee*[76] it seems to have been assumed that the withdrawal of execution under a *fi. fa.* discharged the surety *in toto*. A similar result will follow from a withdrawal of a bankruptcy petition on terms.[77] It may, however, be that the true principle of these decisions is not that discussed in this chapter, but that the transaction amounted to an accord and satisfaction which is equivalent to the payment of the debt.[78]

Accepting from principal composition outside bankruptcy law discharges surety

Since *Ex p. Smith*[79] it has been settled that a voluntary composition outside the bankruptcy law giving time to the debtor or reducing his liability discharges the surety: unless there is in the deed a reservation of the remedies against sureties.[80] In that case the debtor remains open at the suit of the surety to the original demand of the creditor, notwithstanding the provisions for giving time or reducing the debt which the deed may contain.[81] In such cases the operation of the deed,

---

[71] *Commercial Bank of Tasmania* v. *Jones* [1893] A.C. 313, 316. See, however, as to this case, *Perry* v. *National Provincial Bank* [1910] 1 Ch. 464; and contrast *Bradford Old Bank* v. *Sutcliffe* [1918] 2 K.B. 833.

[72] See *Webb v. Hewitt* (1857) 3 K. & J. 438, 442.

[73] *Solly* v. *Forbes* (1820) 2 B. & B. 38; *Thompson* v. *Lack* (1846) 3 C.B. 540; *North* v. *Wakefield* (1849) 13 Q.B. 536; *Price* v. *Barker* (1855) 4 E. & B. 760; *Willis* v. *De Castro* (1858) 4 C.B.(N.S.) 216; 27 L.J.C.P. 243; *Keyes* v. *Elkins* (1864) 5 B. & S. 240; *Muir* v. *Crawford* (1875) L.R. 2 H.L. Sc. 456; *Hooper* v. *Marshall* (1869) L.R. 5 C.P. 4; *Bateson* v. *Gosling* (1871) L.R. 7 C.P. 9; *Re Armitage, ex p. Good* (1877) 5 Ch.D. 46; *Duck* v. *Mayeu* [1892] 2 Q.B. 511.

[74] *Kearsley* v. *Cole* (1846) 16 M. & W. 128 at p. 136; *Price* v. *Barker* (1855) 4 E. & B. 760, 777; *Owen* v. *Homan* (1851) 4 H.L.C. 997, 1037; *Muir* v. *Crawford* (1875) L.R. 2 H.L.Sc. 456; *Jones* v. *Whitaker* (1887) 57 L.T. 216; *Cole* v. *Lynn* [1942] 1 K.B. 142.

[75] *Cheetham* v. *Ward* (1797) 1 B. & P. 630; *Nicholson* v. *Revill* (1836) 4 A. & E. 675; *Gholson* v. *Savin* 137 Ohio St. 551, 31 N.E. (2d) 858 (1941).

[76] (1895) 12 T.L.R. 129, 258. Cf. *Mayhew* v. *Crickett* (1818) 2 Swanst. 185; *Williams* v. *Price* (1824) 1 S. & S. 581.

[77] *Re E.W.A.* [1901] 2 K.B. 642.

[78] See *Perry* v. *National Provincial Bank* [1910] 1 Ch. 464.

[79] (1789) 3 Bro.C.C. 1, followed in *Ex p. Wilson* (1805) 11 Ves. 410; *Ex p. Glendinning* (1819) Buck. 517; *Ex p. Carstairs* (1820) Buck. 560; *Lewis* v. *Jones* (1825) 4 B. & C. 506; *Cragoe* v. *Jones* (1873) L.R.8 Ex. 81.

[80] *Ex p. Glendinning* (1819) Buck. 517; *Ex p. Carstairs* (1820) Buck. 560; *Kearsley* v. *Cole* (1846) 16 M. & W. 128; *Bateson* v. *Gosling* (1871) L.R. 7 C.P. 9.

[81] *Kearsley* v. *Cole* (1846) 16 M. & W. 128; *Close* v. *Close* (1853) 4 De G.M. & G. 176; *Green* v. *Wynn* (1868) L.R. 4 Ch. 204; *Re Whitehouse* (1887) 37 Ch.D. 683.

though containing words of release, is often held to be that of a covenant not to sue only.[82] But where all the property of the debtor was assigned absolutely to a creditor in consideration of a release and the payment by that creditor of a composition to all the others, this was held a release notwithstanding a reservation of the remedies against a surety.[83] And where the creditor made a secret bargain with the principal that he should be paid in full, notwithstanding the composition (the effect of this being, on ordinary principles, that the creditor could thereafter claim against the principal neither the debt nor the composition), the surety was held discharged, notwithstanding a reservation in composition deed of remedies against him.[84]

Contributories in winding-up of company

Where the holder of shares at the date of the winding-up of a company agreed with the liquidator, under sanction of the court, that upon paying certain sums and surrendering all his interest in the company he should be discharged from all calls, with a proviso that nothing in the agreement should prejudice the right of another liquidator against any other contributories, whether as past or present members or otherwise, it was held that a former holder of the same shares was not discharged.[85] And in such a case the former holder being made liable can recover over against his transferee, notwithstanding the agreement.[86]

Composition under bankruptcy laws

Where the composition is under bankruptcy laws no question of the reservation of remedies against sureties can arise. The debtor is absolutely released, even as against the surety, by the effect of the Statute.[87] A release or indulgence to the principal as part of an arrangement or composition under the Bankruptcy Act 1914 does not discharge a surety whether the creditor votes

---

[82] *Green* v. *Wynn* (1868) L.R. 4 Ch. 204; *Bateson* v. *Gosling* (1871) L.R. 7 C.P. 9; *Re Whitehouse* (1887) 37 Ch.D. 683; *Bateson* v. *Gosling* (1871) L.R. 7 C.P. 9.

[83] *Webb* v. *Hewitt* (1857) 3 K. & J. 438. And see *Muir* v. *Crawford* (1875) L.R. 2 H.L.Sc. 456, 459. Even where there is an absolute release under a voluntary composition, the reservation of remedies against sureties may perhaps not be, from every point of view, nugatory. If any of the creditors party to the arrangement were secured by guarantees, they might, so far as the sureties' rights were concerned, retain them by the consent of the sureties. But it might be considered that such retention of such securities would be a fraud upon the other creditors and void (see *Mawson* v. *Stock* (1801) 6 Ves. 300; *Davidson* v. *McGregor* (1841) 8 M. & W. 755; *Bateson* v. *Gosling* (1871) L.R. 7 C.P. 9, 14. But cf. *Lewis* v. *Jones* (1825) 4 B. & C. 506 at p. 516, note; *Thomas* v. *Courtnay* (1817) 1 B. & Ald. 1), and the provisions preserving the remedies against sureties might be designed to negative this contention.

[84] *Mayhew* v. *Boyes* (1910) 103 L.T. 1 (C.A.).

[85] *Nevill's Case* (1870) L.R. 6 Ch.App. 43.

[86] *Roberts* v. *Crowe* (1872) L.R. 7 C.P. 629.

[87] *Hooper* v. *Marshall* (1869) L.R. 5 C.P. 4; *Ex p. Jacobs* (1875) L.R. 10 Ch.App. 211. Now s.16(20), Bankruptcy Act 1914.

for it or not,[88] upon the principle that such release is the act of the law.[88] Nor, where the principal is a company, does the adoption of a scheme of arrangement under section 206 of the Companies Act 1948 affect the liability of sureties.[89] The position is that the surety cannot complain of what is not the act of the creditor, but the act of the law; and the debtor cannot complain, because he is entirely free by the discharge, and the liability of the surety does not mean a recourse against himself.[90] Such recourse cannot be preserved and the doctrine of the reservation of remedies against sureties is wholly inapplicable.[91] Nor can the surety who has not paid the debt in any way interfere with the dealings of the creditor with the bankrupt under the statutes.[92] His right is, upon the bankruptcy law being invoked, to pay off the creditor and intervene in his place in the proceedings.[93] But if, by an arrangement outside the Bankruptcy Acts, a debtor is expressed to be discharged as if he had been adjudged bankrupt and discharged in bankruptcy, but without any express reservation of remedies against sureties, the latter, unless they consented, are discharged, for a discharge in bankruptcy is a discharge from the demand even at the suit of the surety, and this if produced by the voluntary act of the creditor, must discharge the surety.[94]

Discharge of principal in bankruptcy, dissolution of a corporation and disclaimer

A discharge of the principal in the ordinary course after adjudication in bankruptcy does not affect the liability of the surety. This is now expressly provided by enactment,[95] but it was also so held before.[96] The position is the same when the principal is a corporation and it is dissolved.[97] It has, however,

---

[88] *Ex p. Jacobs* (1875) L.R. 10 Ch. App. 211, overruling *Wilson* v. *Lloyd* (1873) L.R. 16 Eq. 60, and following *Megrath* v. *Gray* (1874) L.R. 9 C.P. 216. See also *Ellis* v. *Wilmot* (1874) L.R. 10 Exch. 10; *Ex p. Wilson* (1805) 11 Ves. 410; *Provincial Bank* v. *Cussen* (1886) 16 L.R.Ir. 382. And *cf. English* v. *Darley* (1800) 2 B. & P. 61 at p. 62; *Browne* v. *Carr* (1831) 7 Bing. 508.

[89] *Re London Chartered Bank of Australia* [1893] 3 Ch. 540, decided under the Joint Stock Companies Arrangement Act 1870. *Cf. Mortgage Insurance Corporation* v. *Pound* (1894) 64 L.J.Q.B. 394; 65 L.J.Q.B. 129 (H.L.). See also *Dane* v. *Mortgage Insurance Corporation* [1894] 1 Q.B. 54.

[90] *Ex p. Jacobs* (1875) L.R. 10 Ch.App. 211 at p. 214; *Cragoe* v. *Jones* (1873) L.R. 8 Ex. 81.

[91] See *Ex p. Jacobs* (1875) L.R. 10 Ch.App. 211 at p. 214; *Re London Chartered Bank of Australia* [1893] 3 Ch. 540; *Dane* v. *Mortgage Insurance Corporation* [1894] 1 Q.B. 54.

[92] *Browne* v. *Carr* (1831) 7 Bing. 508; *Ellis* v. *Wilmot* (1874) L.R. 10 Exch. 10.

[93] *Browne* v. *Carr* (1831) 7 Bing. 508; *Ellis* v. *Wilmot* (1874) L.R. 10 Exch. 10.

[94] *Cragoe* v. *Jones* (1873) L.R. 8 Exch. 81.

[95] Bankruptcy Act 1914, s.28(4), replacing Bankruptcy Act 1883, s.30(4). The corresponding section, s.50, of the earlier Bankruptcy Act 1869, did not mention sureties.

[96] See *English* v. *Darley* (1800) 2 B. & P. at p. 62; *Ex p. Jacobs* (1875) L.R. 10 Ch.App. at p. 213. Nor of course does the occurence of the bankruptcy itself discharge the surety, except in certain special situations: see, *e.g. Re Moss* [1905] 2 K.B. 307 (distinguished in Canada: *Bank of Montreal* v. *McFatridge* (1958) 14 D.L.R. (2d) 552; aff'd (1959) 17 D.L.R. (2d) 557).

[97] *Re Fitzgeorge, ex p. Robson* [1905] 1 K.B. 462.

been held by the Court of Appeal in *Stacey* v. *Hill*[98] that a disclaimer by a trustee in bankruptcy of a lease discharges a surety for the rent, and the result is the same although the lessee may have sublet before his bankruptcy.[99] A disclaimer by a liquidator under section 323 of the Companies Act 1948 would seem to have the same effect.[1] The dissolution of a lessee principal who is a corporation without assigning the lease has in this respect the same effect as a disclaimer, as thereby the reversion is accelerated.[2]

A surety for the upkeep of a policy of insurance on the life of the principal pledged to the creditor to secure the debt is discharged if the creditor values the policy and proves in the bankruptcy of the principal for the balance.[3] On the other hand, a surety for the payment of interest until repayment of the principal has been held not to be discharged by the dissolution of the principal, who was a corporation.[4] It would have been different if the obligation had been to pay interest so long as the principal may remain due.[5]

What reservation of remedies effectual

In order to prevent an agreement for giving time from discharging the sureties, it must be so worded as to show that it was intended only to apply to suits for the benefit of the creditor, and to except from its operation suits at the instance of sureties and on their behalf.[6] And this exception must be unqualified. Therefore, where time was given to the debtors to enable them to carry out certain proposals, and the remedy against the sureties was reserved in the event of the proposals not being carried out, the sureties were discharged, because till that event was determined the creditor could not without breach of contract allow the surety to sue the debtors.[7] In the same way, if the

---

[98] [1901] 1 Q.B. 660. This decision seems difficult to reconcile either with the terms of the Bankruptcy Act 1883 s.55, now re-enacted by the Bankruptcy Act 1914, s.54 or with the decisions on previous Acts: see *Smythe* v. *North* (1872) L.R. 7 Ex. 242; *Ex p. Walton* (1881) 17 Ch.D. 746; *Ex p. East and West India Dock Co.* (1881) 17 Ch.D. 759; *Harding* v. *Preece* (1882) 9 Q.B.D. 281; *East and West India Dock Co.* v. *Hill* (1883) 22 Ch.D. 14; (1884) 9 A.C. 448. See also *Tuck* v. *Fyson* (1829) 6 Bing. 321.

[99] *Morris and Sons* v. *Jeffreys* (1932) 148 L.T. 56; *Re Lennard* [1934] Ch. 235; *Re Wells* [1933] Ch. 29.

[1] *Re Katherine et Cie.* [1932] 1 Ch. 70.

[2] *Hastings Corporation* v. *Letton* [1908] 1 K.B. 378.

[3] *Re Moss* [1905] 2 K.B. 307.

[4] *Re Fitzgeorge, ex p. Robson* [1905] 1 K.B. 462.

[5] *Re Moss* [1905] 2 K.B. 307. See also *Re Forster*, unreported, but referred to [1919] 2 Ch. at p. 159. In *Re Moss* the surety was released because on the wording employed, there ceased upon the bankruptcy to be any sums due from the principal which the surety had guaranteed. The bankruptcy of the principal does not normally of itself release a surety: see *Bank of Montreal* v. *McFatridge* (1958) 14 D.L.R. (2d) 552, aff'd (1959) 17 D.L.R. (2d) 557, where *Re Moss* was distinguished.

[6] *Bailey* v. *Edwards* (1864) 4 B. & S. 761, *per* Blackburn J. at p. 774.

[7] *Bailey* v. *Edwards* (1864) 4 B. & S. 761.

arrangement with the principal is express that he shall have the respite in any case, a reservation of rights against sureties might be rejected as repugnant.[8]

Assent of surety to composition

A surety will remain liable even if there is no reservation of his liability on the face of a composition deed, release, or agreement in writing not to sue, where it was made at his request and with his agreement to remain liable notwithstanding,[9] at any rate unless it is shown that the agreement was kept secret from the other creditors.[10] In such a case the liability of the surety must be without recourse to the principal. It was laid down generally in *Ex p. Glendinning*[11] that a reservation of rights against a surety on a release to the principal must appear on the face of the release.[12] This rule, however, can apparently only apply where the reservation is to be given effect to as a term of the contract with the principal debtor.[13] If the continuance of the liability of the surety is assented to by the surety, this can be proved dehors the instrument.

Guarantee authorising giving of time

The surety remains bound where either the guarantee authorises the indulgence which has been given to the principal,[14] or the surety has assented to it at the time,[15] or even upon hearing of it afterwards has ratified it or promised to pay notwithstanding.[16] Where a guarantee expressly provides that the creditor may give time or enter into a composition with the debtor, the right of the creditor against the surety remains by virtue of that clause, whether the latter is precluded from

---

[8] See *Webb* v. *Hewitt* (1857) 3 K. & J. 438; *Wilson* v. *Lloyd* (1873) L.R. 16 Eq. 60 (overruled on the main point in *Ex p. Jacobs* (1875) L.R. 10 Ch. App. 211).

[9] *Davidson* v. *McGregor* (1841) 8 M. & W. 755; *Poole* v. *Willats* (1869) L.R. 4 Q.B. 630.

[10] *Davidson* v. *McGregor* (1841) 8 M. & W. 755.

[11] (1819) Buck 517.

[12] See, too, *Lewis* v. *Jones* (1825) 4 B. & C. 506; *Wyke* v. *Rogers* (1852) 1 De G.M. & G. 408. But *cf. Pring* v. *Clarkson* (1822) 1 B. & C. 14.

[13] See the note to *Lewis* v. *Jones* (1825) 4 B. & C. 506 at pp. 515, 516; *Smith* v. *Winter* (1838) 4 M. & W. 454; *Davidson* v. *McGregor* (1841) 8 M. & W. 755.

[14] See *Cowper* v. *Smith* (1838) 4 M. & W. 519; *Union Bank of Manchester* v. *Beech* (1865) 3 H. & C. 672; *Perry* v. *National Provincial Bank* [1910] 1 Ch. 464. *Cf. Rouse* v. *Bradford Banking Co.* [1894] 2 Ch. 32; [1894] A.C. 586. Such provision is common. See forms in Appendix 1.

[15] *Clark* v. *Devlin* (1803) 3 B. & P. 363; *Tyson* v. *Cox* (1823) T. & R. 395; *Davidson* v. *McGregor* (1841) 8 M. & W. 755. *Ex p. Harvey* (1854) 4 De G.M. & G. 881; *Atkins* v. *Revell* (1860) 1 De G.F. & J. 360.

[16] *Mayhew* v. *Crickett* (1818) 2 Swanst. 185; *Smith* v. *Winter* (1838) 4 M. & W. 454. The reference in the judgments in the latter case to the assent being given was held so to allege. *Mayhew* v. *Crickett* shows that the assent would have been effectual, though given later.

having any remedy over against the debtor or not.[17] The result is the same as in cases where the surety, though he remains liable himself, is prevented by the bankruptcy law from recovering over against the principal.[18] Where a surety guaranteed payments to be made within fourteen days from the close of each month, unless the creditor "should by writing allow a longer time for payment," it was held that this did not enable the creditor to enlarge the time for a payment after the fourteen days had expired, and the liability had attached.[19]

Compositions amounting to payment by the principal

There is, however, a distinction between compositions which operate merely as a discharge of the principal debtor and compositions where there is an accord and satisfaction of the debt or part of the debt. Thus in *Perry* v. *National Provincial Bank*[20] the plaintiff as surety mortgaged certain property to the defendants to secure the principal's overdraft. The mortgage deeds provided that the defendants should be at liberty to compound with the principal without affecting their rights against the plaintiff. Subsequently, the principal being insolvent, a company was formed to acquire the principal's property, and the defendants agreed to take debentures from that company at the rate of 25 shillings worth of debentures for every pound of debt not secured by mortgages of the principal's own property in full satisfaction of their whole claim against the principal. It was held by the Court of Appeal that this transaction amounted to payment by the principal of that portion of the debt in respect of which the debentures had been issued, and that the plaintiff's property was not liable in respect of that portion of the debt; but that as to the residue of the debt, there had been no payment but merely a discharge of the principal under a composition, and that therefore the plaintiff's property remained liable.

Surety not discharged by loss of recourse to principal, unless due to act or omission of creditor contrary to duty to surety

A guarantee is not put an end to by reason of the debt becoming unenforceable against the principal by reason of

---

[17] *Cowper* v. *Smith* (1838) 4 M. & W. 519; *Union Bank of Manchester* v. *Beech* (1865) 3 H. & C. 672.
[18] *Hooper* v. *Marshall* (1869) L.R. 5 C.P. 4.
[19] *Croydon Gas Co.* v. *Dickinson* (1876) 1 C.P.D. 707; (1876) 2 C.P.D. 46.
[20] [1910] 1 Ch. 464.

matters happening subsequently, unless it is due to an act or omission of the creditor contrary to his duty to the surety.[21] Thus a surety is liable though the claim against the principal be barred by the Statute of Limitations,[22] or by reason of the bankruptcy of the principal.[23]

Since the discharge of a surety by time given to the principal rests upon the basis that it is against good faith for the creditor to make such an arrangement, where the creditor in good faith receives payment from the principal, which payment is afterwards set aside as a fraudulent preference, the surety is not discharged. However, the effect is that his right to intervene is suspended, for the creditor could not have refused to accept the payment.[24] Where the creditor releases the surety on the representation of the surety (resulting from the fraud of the debtor but unknown to the surety) that the debt is covered by a security which the debtor has given to the creditor, the creditor, when the fraud is discovered, is entitled to set aside the release, though in the meantime, of course, the surety's right of recourse to the debtor has been in abeyance.[25] Where a contractor for works by fraud obtained a certificate of completion from the engineer, and was paid his retention money, the surety was not released.[26] This was on the basis that a surety cannot claim to be discharged on the ground that his position has been altered by the conduct of the creditor where that conduct has been caused by a fraudulent act or omission against which the surety guaranteed him.[27]

Where the creditor promised the principal without consideration that time would be allowed him for payment, and the surety, hearing this, abandoned a negotiation to get the money raised elsewhere for the principal, it was held that the surety was not discharged, though circumstances which had arisen in the meantime had made it impossible for that negotiation to be renewed.[28] Unless he has been misled by the creditor, a surety cannot escape from his guarantee by reason that, in the belief that there was nothing outstanding upon it, he has given up a right of indemnity over against a third party.[29]

---

[21] Similarly in the U.S.A., mere inaction, even if it results in the claim being unenforceable, *e.g.* by reason of the Statute of Limitations does not release a surety: *Fidelity & Casualty Co. of New York* v. *Lackland* 175 Va. 178. 8 S.E. (2d) 306 (1940); *Manchester Savings Bank* v. *Lynch* 151 Minn. 349, 186 N.W. 794 (1922).

[22] *Carter* v. *White* (1883) 25 Ch.D. 666.

[23] *Bank of Montreal* v. *McFatridge* (1958) 14 D.L.R. (2d) 552, aff'd. (1959) 17 D.L.R. (2d) 557.

[24] *Pritchard* v. *Hitchcock* (1843) 6 M. & Gr. 151; *Petty* v. *Cooke* (1871) L.R. 6 Q.B. 790.

[25] *Scholefield* v. *Templer* (1859) 4 De G. & J. 429.

[26] *Kingston-upon-Hull* v. *Harding* [1892] 2 Q.B. 494.

[27] *Ibid. per* Bowen L.J., at p. 504.

[28] *Tucker* v. *Laing* (1856) 2 K. & J. 745.

[29] *Oxley* v. *Young* (1796) 2 H.Bl. 613.

Death of a debtor bound jointly

If a surety contracts jointly only with his principal or another surety, and the surety dies before the principal or the co-surety, his estate will be discharged.[30] However, a promise by such a surety in his lifetime to pay the debt himself in consideration of the joint demand being forborne might be enforceable against his estate.[30]

Giving time to principal under disability

It has never been decided, nor has the point apparently ever been discussed, whether a surety for a person under disability is discharged by the creditor purporting to give time to the so-called principal. It is certain that, whether the so-called surety is in theory to be held liable as a principal or by way of estoppel,[31] he has in fact, no recourse against the principal. Thus he has the enjoyment of none of those rights against the principal which are held infringed by the creditor giving time, and may therefore be said to have no cause to complain. On the other hand, if the basis of his liability is that he is estopped from setting up the disability of the principal, the creditor, perhaps, should likewise take no advantage of that circumstance. The rule discharging the surety where time is given does not depend upon the proof of actual damage to the surety; and he could urge that he might, notwithstanding the disability, have got the debt paid by or on behalf of the principal had his position not been weakened by the indulgence of the creditor. It would not be difficult to imagine cases of real hardship to a surety under such circumstances. But, as an absolute rule of law, the principle by which a surety is discharged by time being given to the principal is perhaps not likely to receive any extension.

Rescission of contract by creditor upon repudiatory breach by principal debtor

Where the victim of a repudiatory breach exercises his right to treat the contract as rescinded, this does not amount to a fresh agreement or to any variation so as to discharge the surety for the defaulting party's performance.[32] In this situation, the guarantor's obligation does not cease but is transmuted by

---

[30] *Cf. Jones* v. *Beach* (1851) 2 De G.M. & G. 886; *Brookes* v. *Stuart* (1839) 1 Beav. 512. For criticism of this rule see Glanville Williams, *Joint Obligations* (1949), p. 63 *et seq.* where exceptions are also discussed.

[31] See *ante,* Chap. 1 and Chap. 4, part 1.

[32] *Moschi* v. *Lep Air Services Ltd.* [1973] A.C. 331 (H.L.). The rescinding party was merely exercising a right conferred by the original contract.

operation of law into an obligation to compensate the creditor for the loss suffered by the breach.[33] A discharge of the guarantor in this situation would mean the creditor would lose the guarantor when he most needed him.[34]

A guarantor is not released in such a situation even where arguably the acceptance of the repudiation seems detrimental to the position of the creditor or surety.[35]

---

[33] The House of Lords in *Moschi's Case* (*supra*) referred to the previous edition of this work (p. 143) with approval for the proposition that the guarantor's obligation was to see that the debtor paid or performed his obligations to the creditor (Lord Diplock at p. 348C, Lord Kilbrandon at p. 359B). Upon the guarantor's failure to perform this primary obligation there arose a secondary obligation on the guarantor to pay the amount of the creditor's loss (Lord Diplock p. 351B).

[34] *Moschi's Case* (*supra*) *per* Lord Simon at p. 355C.

[35] In *Chatterton* v. *MacLean* [1951] 1 All E.R. 761 the acceptance of the hirer's repudiation by a creditor under a hire-purchase agreement meant that he lost the right to repossess the vehicle hired. The guarantor was not released. For the position in England under the Consumer Credit Act see *post*, p.231.

CHAPTER 9

LOSS OF SECURITIES AND CO-SURETIES

General principles

Since a surety is entitled to contribution from every co-surety, and to the benefit of every security held by the creditor, an allowance must always be made to the surety for every right of contribution or security lost by the fault of the creditor. The relief to which he is entitled in this respect is, however, of a different kind from that which is accorded him where his remedies upon the principal obligation itself are interfered with. Unless the obtaining of a co-surety or a security is a condition, express or implied, of his undertaking the liability of a surety, he is not discharged absolutely, but is only entitled to an allowance commensurate with the value of the protection lost to him. In *Carter* v. *White*[1] Cotton L.J. said:

"The principle is this: that if there is a contract express or implied that the creditor shall aquire or preserve any right against the debtor, and the creditor deprives himself of the right which he has stipulated to aquire, or does anything to release any right which he has, that discharges the surety; but where there is no such contract, and he only has a right to perfect what he has in his hand, which he does not do, that does not release the surety unless he can show that he has received some injury in consequence of the creditor's conduct."

In such an event the surety is only released *pro tanto*. A similar principle applies to the release of or failure to obtain co-sureties.

Where instrument of suretyship reveals security

Where the instrument which the surety signs reveals that a certain security has been or is to be given, or a certain co-surety

---

[1] (1884) 25 Ch.D. 666, 670. See also *Dale* v. *Powell* (1911) 105 L.T. 291. A similar principle is generally accepted in the U.S.A., see *e.g. Morton* v. *Dillon* (1894) 90 Va. 592, 19 S.E. 654 and in Canada see *Rose* v. *Aftenberger* (1969) 9 D.L.R. (3d) 42. However, Manitoba (R.S.M. 1970 M–120) and Saskatchewan (R.S.S. 1965 C. 73) have legislated to limit the surety's defence to the extent of his prejudice. The Law Reform Commission of British Columbia in its Report on Guarantees of Consumer Debts (1979) has suggested a similar change in the case of "consumer" guarantees. For an unsuccessful attempt to exclude this principle by a clause in a guarantee, see: *Dowling* v. *Ditanda* (1975) 236 E.G. 485.

has joined or is to join, he is only liable, as surety, for a principal liability so secured or so additionally guaranteed. And if the security is not taken or after being taken is surrendered, or the co-surety does not join or after joining is released, the surety first named is not bound. Thus a surety for performance of covenants in a deed granting land with rent reserved was held discharged from liability for rent in arrear by the grantor accepting a reconveyance of the land, notwithstanding that the land was not worth the annual rent for which the surety was liable, and that the reconveyance was therefore a relief to the surety.[2] Similarly, a surety who guarantees performance of a contract for works by joining as surety in the instrument constituting the contract is discharged absolutely if the owner prematurely advances the retention money to the contractor,[3] or does not insure the works according to the contract.[4] A surety joining as such in a deed by which the debtor agreed to pay a certain sum, and gave a charge on book debts to cover it, was, upon the release of the charge, liberated *in toto* without reference to the value of the debts.[5] Where a debtor assigned a policy to his creditor by way of security for the debt, engaging to pay the premiums, and the latter engagement was guaranteed by a surety, and the creditor subsequently released the debtor from his personal liability for the original debt, looking only to the policy, it was held that the surety was discharged.[6] Where a surety agreed to join the principal in a joint and several bond on having a counter-bond, and the principal never executed the bond, though he gave the counter-bond, the surety was held entitled to have the bond given up and cancelled.[7] But where a surety executed a bond from the form of which it appeared that the principal was to execute it too, and on the faith that he would do so, and the principal never did so, but executed an agreement under seal which gave the creditor the same remedy as the bond would have done, it was held that the surety was bound.[8] Where sureties covenanted to make good the deficiency which should remain after the realisation of certain securities recited to be held by the creditor, and it turned out that one of those securities had never been aquired, it was held that the sureties were discharged, and that they were not estopped by the

---

[2] *Lord Harberton* v. *Bennett* (1829) Beatt. 386, 389.
[3] *General Steam Navigation Co.* v. *Rolt* (1858) 6 C.B.(N.S.) 550 *cf. Kingston-upon-Hull* v. *Harding* [1892] 2 Q.B. 494.
[4] *Watts* v. *Shuttleworth* (1861) 7 H. & N. 353.
[5] *Polak* v. *Everett* (1876) 1 Q.B.D. 669; *Smith v. Wood* [1929] 1 Ch. 14; *Cp. Burke* v. *Rogerson* (1866) 14 L.T. 780. (U.S.A. see: *Foerderer* v. *Moors* 91 F. 476 (C.A. Pa. 1898)).
[6] *Lowes* v. *Maughan* (1884) 6 C. and E. 340.
[7] *Bonser* v. *Cox* (1841) 4 Beav. 379.
[8] *Cooper* v. *Evans* (1867) L.R. 4 Eq. 45.

recital.[9] Sureties for the payment of future calls on shares will be discharged if, on non-payment by the holders, the company, as it is entitled to do, forfeits the shares, since by such act the sureties lose the lien on the shares which they would have on payment.[10]

Guarantee showing intended co-surety

On similar principles a surety is not bound if the instrument, when signed by him, is drawn in a form showing himself and another or others as intended joint and several guarantors, and any intended surety does not sign.[11] It is immaterial by whom the instrument was prepared,[12] or whether the surety omitted was solvent or not.[13] In such cases the creditor must show that the surety consented to dispense with the execution of the document by the other or others.[14] The rule is an equitable one, and is applicable even though the surety who has executed did not execute as an escrow, and is consequently bound at law.[15] The principle is, that the arrangement to which the surety consented to become a party has been left incomplete, and has, in equity, never become binding upon him. He is entitled, therefore, to have the instrument given up to be cancelled, and not merely to have relief to the extent of the contribution which the other surety might have been compelled to pay in his relief.[16] Thus if a surety only signs for a smaller amount than the form of the instrument indicated he was to sign for, the sureties who signed before him are discharged.[17] And the further result has been held to follow in such a case, inasmuch as the surety who signed for the reduced amount himself only agreed to be liable if the other sureties were also liable, their release, owing to the alteration introduced by him, indirectly liberates him too.[17]

---

[9] *Coyte* v. *Elphick* (1874) 22 W.R. 541.

[10] *Re Darwen and Pearce* [1927] 1 Ch. 176.

[11] *Evans* v. *Brembridge* (1852) 2 K. & J. 174: (on appeal) 8 De G.M. & G. 100. *Hansard* v. *Lethbridge* (1892) 8 T.L.R. 346 (C.A.) *Fitzgerald* v. *McCowan* (1898) 2 Ir.R.1; *National Provincial Bank* v. *Brackenbury* (1906) 22 T.L.R. 797.

[12] *Hansard* v. *Lethbridge* (1892) 8 T.L.R. 346 (C.A.).

[13] *Fitzgerald* v. *McCowan* (1898) 2 Ir.R.I.

[14] *Hansard* v. *Lethbridge* (1892) 8 T.L.R. 346. This decision in the Court of Appeal settles the law. See, however, *Cumberlege* v. *Lawson* (1857) 1 C.B.(N.S.) 709; *Coyte* v. *Elphick* (1874) 22 W.R. 541, 543, 544. The rule may operate harshly upon the creditor where the joinder of the other surety was a matter really insisted on by him and afterwards waived, and was never, in fact, made a point of by the surety who signed first. See *Traill* v. *Gibbons* (1861) 2 F. & F. 358; *Horne* v. *Ramsdale* (1842) 9 M. & W. 329.

[15] *Evans* v. *Brembridge* (1852) 2 K. & J. 174; (on appeal: 8 De G.M. & G. 100). And see *Elliott* v. *Davis* (1800) 2 B. & P. 338; *Cumberlege* v. *Lawson* (1857) 1 C.B.(N.S.) 709; *Underhill* v. *Horwood* (1804) 10 Ves. 209 at pp. 225, 226.

[16] See *per* Wood V.C in *Evans* v. *Brembridge* (1852) 2 K. & J. 174 at p. 185.

[17] *Ellesmere Brewery Co.* v. *Cooper* [1896] 1 Q.B. 75.

The right of a surety to his discharge upon this principle would apparently not be affected by the fact that he has, by some independent arrangement between himself and the intended co-surety, obtained a right over against him; for he is entitled to insist that the latter should become liable to the creditor by the same instrument as himself or one equivalent to it.[18]

Securities and co-sureties existing at the same time

The mere circumstance that, at the time when the surety became bound, there exists, to the knowledge of the surety, another surety for the same debt, or a security available to the creditor which is collateral, and the surrender of which does not, therefore, alter the contract itself, performance of which is guaranteed, does not necessarily establish that it is an implied term of the contract of suretyship that this protection shall remain for the benefit of the surety so as to bring the case within the principle cited from *Carter* v. *White*.[19] The maintenance of such protection must in such cases be expressly made a condition.

Existing co-sureties

Thus, to take the cases relating to co-sureties, it has been held that mere knowledge by the surety who signed that the creditor is insisting on having the additional liability of another surety will not suffice,[20] even though in his own mind the surety signing relied upon it,[21] and still less the mere existence of the co-surety at the time when the surety seeking relief became bound.[22]

Existing securities

The same rule holds in the case of securities. In *Taylor* v. *Bank of New South Wales*,[23] a surety guaranteed bank advances "on the faith of" a mortgage securing such advances. The Privy Council held that the surety was entitled to allege that the creditor had mishandled part of the mortgaged property. However, even if the surety had made out such an allegation he would not have been entirely discharged. The principle is that

---

[18] See *Bonser* v. *Cox* (1841) 4 Beav. 379; *Cooper* v. *Evans* (1867) L.R. 4 Eq. 45.
[19] (1884) 25 Ch.D. at p. 670; *ante*, p. 180.
[20] *Traill* v. *Gibbons* (1861) 2 F. & F. 358.
[21] See *Cumberlege* v. *Lawson* (1857) 1 C.B.(N.S.) 709; *Dallas* v. *Walls* (1873) 29 L.T. 599.
[22] *Ward* v. *National Bank of New Zealand* (1883) 8 App.Cas. 755 (see the plea at p. 759).
[23] (1886) 11 App.Cas. 596.

where the creditor has by his own act, rendered unavailable part of the security to the benefit of which the surety was entitled, and the latter is only discharged *pro tanto*.[24]

There is, however, a dictum of Blackburn J. in *Polak* v. *Everett*[25] to the effect that the surety is discharged absolutely if the creditor abandons rights which he held "when the surety entered into the suretyship," or, as the Law Journal reports it,[26] "rights which the surety acquires under the original bargain," as opposed to "rights acquired by him under some subsequent collateral security." This passage, does not, it is submitted, lay down the principle that the surety impliedly contracts for collateral securities merely because they exist when he becomes bound.[27] This would be at variance with *Ward* v. *National Bank of New Zealand*.[28]

Where Act of Parliament requires several sureties

If, under Act of Parliament, a bond is required to be taken with two sureties, and it is taken with one only, it is not therefore void at law.[29] Nor, if it was not drawn in a form to indicate that a second surety was to join, would it apparently be voidable in equity.[30]

Release of a co-surety whose liability was a condition

If a surety, whose liability is an essential condition of the liability of another surety, signs the instrument, but is afterwards released, or becomes entitled to his discharge by virtue of any equitable principle,[31] the other surety is discharged in the same way as if the first had never become bound.[32]

Rules applicable to joint debtors

Where the sureties have become jointly or jointly and severally bound, and one is released absolutely, the other is discharged at common law and independently of the equitable

---

[24] *Pearl* v. *Deacon* (1857) 24 Beav. 186; 1 De G. & J. 461. For the facts see the report in Beavan.

[25] (1876) 1 Q.B.D. 669 at p. 676. *Cf. Rainbow* v. *Juggins* (1880) 5 Q.B.D. 138, 142.

[26] 45 L.J.Q.B. 365 at p. 373.

[27] This was the basis upon which in *Newton* v. *Chorlton* (1853) 10 Hare 646, the general right of a surety to securities was explained. But the reasoning in that case cannot be considered as law. See *Pledge* v. *Buss* (1860) Johns. 663.

[28] (1883) 8 App.Cas. 755 (see the plea at p. 759). See also *R.* v. *Fay* (1878) 4 L.R.Ir. 606.

[29] *Peppin* v. *Cooper* (1819) 2 B. & Ald. 431.

[30] *Cf. Bank of Ireland* v. *Beresford* (1818) 6 Dow. 233.

[31] *Ellesmere Brewery Co.* v. *Cooper* [1896] 1 Q.B. 75.

[32] *Ward* v. *National Bank of New Zealand* (1883) 8 App.Cas. 755 at p. 765; *Evans* v. *Brembridge* (1855) 2 K. & J. 174 at p. 185; *Ellesmere Brewery Co.* v. *Cooper* [1896] 1 Q.B. 75.

rule now under consideration, upon the principle that the discharge of one joint debtor discharges all.[33] The principle applies, moreover, if one surety is released after joint and several judgment against the two.[34]

Release of persons analogous to co-sureties

Where several persons charge their properties by the deposit of title deeds with the repayment of any sum due from a company to one guaranteeing its overdraft, and the title deeds of one depositor are subsequently released, all the others are absolutely discharged on the principle that the release affects the right to have all the properties marshalled so as to cause the debt to fall rateably.[35]

Express stipulation for another surety

Even where it does not appear from the form of the instrument signed by a surety that others are to join also, the surety signing will be discharged if it was orally made a condition that another should join and he does not, or after joining is released.[36]

Express stipulation for security

Where, again, the surety expressly stipulates for a security, the taking or maintaining of it according to the stipulation is an essential condition of his liability.[37]

Conduct of creditor causing loss of security

A surety is not discharged absolutely by the loss of a security or co-surety, even if stipulated for by him, unless that loss is

---

[33] *Nicholson* v. *Revill* (1836) 4 A. & E. 675. So judgment against one of two co-sureties bound jointly used to put an end to the right of action against the other; but not judgment on a cheque given by one for the joint debt. *Wegg-Prosser* v. *Evans* [1895] 1 Q.B. 108. But see now in England the Civil Liability (Contribution) Act 1978, s.3 which prevents judgment against one joint debtor releasing another joint debtor: see Appendix 2.

[34] *Re E.W.A.* [1901] 2 K.B. 692. For criticism, see Glanville Williams, *Joint Obligations* (1949), pp. 117, 135–137; Cardozo, *Law and Literature* (1931), p. 51.

[35] *Smith* v. *Wood* [1929] 1 Ch. 14. Lord Hanworth M.R., and Sankey L.J., treated the case as determined by authorities which establish that the surety is released where the creditor has varied the principal obligation. *Cf.* the reasons given by Russell L.J., who also points out, at p. 31, that the deeds returned to the depositor had not been released from the charge, but had been subjected to a prior charge of £600.

[36] *Leaf* v. *Gibbs* (1830) 4 C. & P. 466; *Traill* v. *Gibbons* (1861) 2 F. & F. 358; *Barry* v. *Moroney* (1873) 8 Ir.R.C.L. 554; Exch. Ch. reversing C.P. 7 Ir.R.C.L. 110. See *Stirling* v. *Forrester* (1821) 3 Bligh 575; *Coope* v. *Twynam* (1823) T. and R. 426 at p. 429; *Dallas* v. *Walls* (1873) 29 L.T. 599; *Ex p. Harding* (1879) 12 Ch.D. 557, 564; *Ward* v. *National Bank of New Zealand* (1883) 8 App.Cas. 755, 765.

[37] *Watson* v. *Alcock* (1853) 1 Sm. & G. 319; (on appeal: 4 De G.M. & G. 242). The security being under seal, this defence had failed at law. See *Parker* v. *Watson* (1853) 8 Exch. 404. *Cf.* also *Jephson* v. *Maunsell* (1847) 10 Ir.Eq.R. 38, 132.

brought about either by the wilful act of the creditor or by his neglect to take some step which the surety had stipulated he should take.[38] Where the creditor, by neglecting to comply with the Ships Register Acts, lost the benefit of the assignment of two ships recited in the surety bond, the surety was only discharged *pro tanto*.[39] Similarly, where he neglected to give notice of an equitable assignment by way of security[40] to register a bill of sale,[41] or to value a security in bankruptcy,[42] although in each case the security was part of the surety's contract. Where a surety joined in a contract for the execution of works which the creditor was to insure, the surety was discharged absolutely by his omission to insure.[43] Whenever the obtaining of a security or the liability of another as co-surety is an essential term of the surety's contract, of course the mere omission by the creditor to do so discharges the last-named surety.[44]

Mere neglect may give rise to discharge pro tanto

Where the question is not of the absolute discharge of the surety, but merely of an allowance *pro tanto* in respect of the loss of a security, or of a right of contribution, the distinction between a wilful act of abandonment and a mere negligent omission disappears. With regard to securities, whenever taken, the creditor, is chargeable in relief of the surety with everything which, but for his wilful neglect or default, he might have recovered by means of the security.[45] Where the creditor by wilful negligence wasted goods upon which he had a bill of sale a security for the debt, so that they did not realise the full value,

[38] *Polak* v. *Everett* (1876) 1 Q.B.D. 669, 672; *Carter* v. *White* (1883) 25 Ch.D. 666, 670; *Rainbow* v. *Juggins* (1880) 5 Q.B.D. 138, 422; *R.* v. *Fay* (1878) 4 L.R.Ir. 606; *Re Darwen and Pearce* [1927] 1 Ch. 176, at p. 187.

[39] *Capel* v. *Butler* (1825) 2 S. and S. 457.

[40] *Strange* v. *Fooks* (1863) 4 Giff. 408. In Scotland, the negligence of a creditor in allowing a third party to obtain priority over the security was held to discharge the surety: *Fleming* v. *Thomson* (1826) 2 W. & S. 277 (H.L.) (Sc.).

[41] *Wulff* v. *Jay* (1872) L.R. 7 Q.B. 756.

[42] *Rainbow* v. *Juggins* (1880) 5 Q.B.D. 138, 422.

[43] *Watts* v. *Shuttleworth* (1861) 5 H. & N. 235; 7 H. & N. 353.

[44] *Bonser* v. *Cox* (1841) 4 Beav. 379; *Coyte* v. *Elphick* (1874) 22 W.R. 541; *Evans* v. *Brembridge* (1855) 2 K. & J. 174; (on appeal: 8 De G.M. & G. 100); *Hansard* v. *Lethbridge* (1892) 8 T.L.R. 346.

[45] *Capel* v. *Butler* (1825) 2 S. & S. 457; *Strange* v. *Fooks* (1863) 4 Giff. 408; *Mutual Loan Fund* v. *Sudlow* (1858) 5 C.B. (N.S.) 449; *Wulff* v. *Jay* (1872) L.R. 7 Q.B. 756; *Polak* v. *Everett* (1876) 1 Q.B.D. 669, 675; *Rainbow* v. *Juggins* (1880) 5 Q.B.D. 138; *Taylor* v. *Bank of New South Wales* (1886) 11 App.Cas. 596. For a similar principle in the U.S.A. see, *e.g.* the cases on failure to perfect securities by registration, such as *Shraepel* v. *Shaw* 3 N.Y. 445 (1850); *Sullivan* v. *State* 59 Ark. 47; 26 S.W. 194 (1894); *Redlon* v. *Heath* 59 Kan. 255, 52 P. 862 (1898). However, certain other types of inactivity have been held to have no effect on the surety's liability, *e.g.* failure to insure the mortgaged property: *Willard* v. *Welch* 94 App. Div. 179, 88 N.Y.S. 173 (1904) and failure to defend an action to remove the creditor's mortgage: *Wasson* v. *Hodshire* 108 Ind. 26, 8 N.E. 621 (1886). In Canada it has been held that a creditor has a duty to a surety to exercise due diligence in preserving and enforcing a security: *Provincial Bank of Canada* v. *P.E.I. Lending Authority* (1959) D.L.R. (3d) 446.

the surety was discharged to the extent of the waste.[46] So, also, if the creditor destroys the security by the exercise of a paramount right, *e.g.* by distraining for rent furniture mortgaged to secure the advance guaranteed by the surety, the latter is entitled to a discharge *pro tanto*.[47] But giving a further advance on the security does not discharge the surety, for his right is not interfered with.[48]

Creditor's duty to surety

It may be that in some situations the creditor's liability to suffer for his neglect in dealing with securities is limited by the concept of duty towards the surety. In *Barclays Bank Ltd.* v. *Thienel*,[49] Thesiger J., appears to have been of the opinion that a creditor holding a security from the principal debtor had no duty to the surety to exercise reasonable care to obtain the best price available for the security.[50] This view seems difficult to reconcile with previous authority. It may be that the actual decision in *Thienel's Case* turned on the clause in the bank's guarantee excluding any duty. The decision on that clause may in future also be open to question in the general run of cases, since such a clause could be held unreasonable and void in England under the provisions of section 2 of the Unfair Contract Terms Act 1978, which limits the ability of a party to contract out of liability for negligence.[50a]

Loss of security only avails surety, if by act or omission of creditor

The loss of a security must, if it is to relieve the surety to any extent, be due to some act or omission of the creditor. He is not bound to preserve securities at his peril.[51] Thus in *Wheatley* v. *Bastow*[52] a solicitor by the unauthorised use of the names of the parties in a case got hold of a fund court over which the creditor had a security. It was held that the surety was not discharged,

---

[46] *Mutual Loan Fund* v. *Sudlow* (1858) 5 C.B.(N.S.) 449. *Cf. Margrett* v. *Gregory* (1862) 10 W.R. 630.
[47] *Pearl* v. *Deacon* (1857) 24 Beav. 186; 1 De G. and J. 461.
[48] *York City and County Banking Co.* v. *Bainbridge* (1880) 43 L.T. 732.
[49] (1978) 247 E.G. 385. *Cf. Mercantile Credit Co.* v. *Edge* (unreported, C.A., June 13, 1969, Transcript No. 221), which may suggest that a creditor has a duty to obtain the best price reasonably obtainable for a security, at least for the purpose of calculating the true balance due from the surety.
[50] Refusing to apply the principle of *Cuckmere Brick Co.* v. *Mutual Finance Ltd.* [1971] Ch. 949 in this context. *Barclays Bank Ltd.* v. *Thienel* appears to have been followed in *Latchford* v. *Beirne Incorporated* (1981) 131 N.L.J. 856 (Milmo J.) where it was held that a receiver under a debenture had no duty to the company's surety to obtain full market value in selling company property. In Canada, it has been held that a creditor holding a chattel mortgage has no duty to prevent the principal rendering the mortgage void by transportation to a different jurisdiction; *Household Finance Corp.* v. *Foster* [1949] 1 D.L.R. 840; [1949] O.R. 123. But see *Provincial Bank of Canada* v. *P.E.I. Lending Authority* (1975) 59 D.L.R. (3d) 446.
[50a] See Appendix 2.
[51] In the civil law the loss must be *culpa*. See *McDonald* v. *Bell* (1840) 3 Moo.P.C. 315.
[52] 7 De G.M. & G. 261.

just as if a pledge had been stolen. Similarly, where a creditor surrenders to the trustees in bankruptcy of the principal debtor securities which he could not successfully have retained, the surety was not relieved.[53]

Where debt is assigned

A surety is not discharged if the debt and guarantee are assigned and he receives no notice of the assignment,[54] nor if the creditor assign the debt and no notice of the assignment is given by the assignee either to the surety or to perfect the assignee's title to a security.[54] In such a case the assignor remains the only creditor known to the parties, and if any payment is made upon the security or by the surety to the original creditor, the assignee is bound by it, and no harm can be suffered by the surety.[54]

Sale of part of security in due course of management

A sale by a mortgagor, with the consent of the mortgagee, of some live stock mortgaged with a run, the mortgagor being in possession, and the sale being in the due course of management, does not affect the liability of a surety for the mortgagor who became bound on the faith of the mortgage.[55]

Relief by discharge of co-surety to extent of contribution

The relief to which a surety is entitled where the creditor releases a co-surety is (putting aside the special cases where he is thereby discharged absolutely upon principles already discussed) limited to the extent of the contribution he could have claimed from the surety released.[56] Since a surety has no right to contribution until he has paid more than his share,[57] he remains liable to the extent of that share despite the release of a co-surety.[58] Where two independent sureties each guarantee a floating account to the extent of a certain sum, the release of one

---

[53] *Hardwick* v. *Wright* (1865) 35 Beav. 133. Contrast a voluntary surrender of a security to the debtor himself: *Rose* v. *Aftenberger* [1970] 1 O.R. 547.

[54] *Wheatley* v. *Bastow* (1855) 7 De G.M. & G. 261; *Bradford Old Bank* v. *Sutcliffe* [1918] 2 K.B. 833. It would apparently make no difference even if as between the principal and the creditor the transaction amounted to a novation (*ibid*): *sed quaere*.

[55] *Taylor* v. *Bank of New South Wales* (1886) 11 App.Cas. 596. In Australia, it has been held that the mere fact of sale of property comprised in a bill of sale given by the principal as security for a loan does not operate to discharge the guarantor of the loan: *Tooth and Co.* v. *Lapin* (1936) 53 N.S.W.W.N. 224.

[56] *Ex p. Gifford* (1802) 6 Ves. 805; *Ward* v. *National Bank of New Zealand* (1883) 8 App.Cas. 755: *Re Wolmershausen* (1890) 62 L.T. 541: *Stirling* v. *Forrester* (1821) 3 Bligh 575.

[57] See *ante*, p. 158.

[58] *Ex p. Gifford* (1802) 6 Ves. 805; *Ward* v. *National Bank of New Zealand* (1883) 8 App.Cas. 755.

will not relieve the other at all if the balance owing is more than the aggregate amount of the two guarantees.[59] If a surety guaranteeing a particular part of the debt is released, that does not relieve in any respect a surety engaged for a different part.[60]

Release of one surety after payment by another

If a surety has already paid more than his share before the co-surety is released, he will not apparently be entitled to a return of the excess, for his right to contribution is vested and not interfered with.[61]

Application of payments by principal where one surety has been released

If one of two sureties is discharged without any reservation of rights against the other, the creditor is, it seems, to be treated as having taken upon himself the position of the surety discharged.[62] On this basis the creditor should give, and possibly receive, as the discharged surety would have done, credit for the proper proportion of any payment made by the principal in relief of the guarantors. The sum borne by the surety not discharged is therefore (where each surety is liable for half the total debt) half the debt left after the payment by the principal.[63] This was the order in *Stirling* v. *Forrester*.[64] But any payment made by the surety discharged may be applied by the creditor in discharge of that share of the liability which the surety discharged would have borne, and as to which the other surety is relieved. This is involved in the decision in *Ex p. Gifford*,[65] where the surety undischarged unsuccessfully contended that, though he had not paid more than his share, he was entitled to a proportion of the composition paid by the other.

Where remedy of creditor against co-surety is statute-barred

There is no reason for suggesting that the liability of a surety is affected by the circumstance that time has run under the Statutes of Limitation in favour of a co-surety.[66] And the latter will doubtless remain open to the demand of the former for

---

[59] *Ward* v. *National Bank of New Zealand* (1883) 8 App.Cas. 755, at p. 766.
[60] See *Coope* v. *Twynam* (1823) T. & R. 426; *Pendlebury* v. *Walker* (1841) 4 Y. & C. Ex. 424; and see *Stirling* v. *Forrester* (1821) 3 Bligh 575, *per* Lord Eldon at p. 592.
[61] See *Reade* v. *Lowndes* (1857) 23 Beav. 361, 367, 368.
[62] See *per* Lord Redesdale in *Stirling* v. *Forrester* (1821) 3 Bligh 575, 590.
[63] See *ante*, p. 160.
[64] (1821) 3 Bligh 575.
[65] (1802) 6 Ves. 805.
[66] See as to the effect of time running in favour of the principal, *post*, pp.193, 194, 197.

contribution,[67] although as against the demand of the creditor he has a defence.

Giving time to co-sureties

It has never been suggested that a surety is discharged by time being given to a co-surety. The doctrine which prevails where time is given to the principal seems wholly inapplicable. At the same time it would seem an injustice if a creditor after bargaining to give time to a surety were to be allowed while that time is running to sue another surety for more than his share, or even to accept it from him, and so turn him for contribution upon the surety to whom time has been given.[68] And if this is so, and the former surety could prove that he has been damnified by the delay (as, for instance, by the other surety in the meantime becoming insolvent), it is possible that he ought to be allowed the amount of this damage. But the point seems never to have arisen.

Discharge of surety with reservation of rights against others

A discharge of a surety with a reservation of the creditor's rights against co-sureties operates to preserve intact the right of the latter, when sued, to have contribution from the first surety, notwithstanding the so-called discharge.[69] And it was pointed out by Lord Eldon in *Ex p. Gifford*[70] that a discharge on these terms is a much more real advantage to a co-surety than to a principal debtor; the principal will, notwithstanding his discharge, be had recourse to as soon as any surety is made to pay anything; but a co-surety who has obtained such a qualified discharge is safe until some other surety pays more than his share. However, when a creditor surrenders his right of proof in the bankruptcy of a surety, reserving his rights against another surety, the latter will be entitled to an allowance to the extent of the sum by which he would have been relieved had the creditor's right of proof been exercised.[71] A release of a co-surety with a reservation of a right to sue another co-surety, such right to be exercised for the benefit of the co-surety released, is equivalent to an absolute release.[72]

---

[67] See *Wolmershausen* v. *Gullick* [1893] 2 Ch. 514.

[68] See *ante,* p. 162.

[69] It requires clear words to reserve rights against the co-sureties: a release of one surety with a reservation against sureties and persons liable to pay the released party's debts proved ineffective in *Liverpool Corn Trade Association* v. *Hurst* [1936] 2 All E.R. 309 since on a literal reading the co-sureties did not come within those categories.

[70] (1802) 6 Ves. 805. See, too *Commercial Bank of Australia* v. *Official Assignee* [1893] A.C. 181.

[71] *Re Wolmershausen* (1890) 62 L.T. 541.

[72] *Hallet* v. *Taylor* (1921) 6 Ll.L.R. 417.

Where surety entitled to relief expressly promises to pay

If a surety entitled to equitable relief owing to the release of a co-surety or a security afterwards expressly promises to pay notwithstanding, this promise would appear to be binding and not open to objection as being without consideration.[73]

[73] *Mayhew* v. *Crickett* (1818) 2 Swanst. 185.

CHAPTER 10

STATUTES OF LIMITATION

1. *As to Claims against a Surety*

When time begins to run

Time begins to run under the Statutes of Limitations[1] in favour of a surety from the date of the accrual of the cause of action; that is to say from the date on which the surety may hve been sued.[2] Where there are successive breaches, the time runs anew in respect of each breach, from the time when it occurred, so that the remedy against the surety may be barred in respect of earlier breaches, but remain available as to later ones. And this will apply even in the case of a bond.

Where a surety is only liable to pay after demand,[3] time does not begin to run till after it has been made.[4]

In *Wright* v. *New Zealand Farmers Co-operative Association of Canterbury Ltd.*[5] the Privy Council held that under the guarantees there involved, the repayment of every debit balance was guaranteed as it was constituted from time to time by the excess of total debits over total credits, and therefore the time which had expired since any individual debt was incurred was immaterial, and the period of limitation could run only from the time at which the balance guaranteed and sued for had been constituted.

---

[1] The Limitation Acts 1939 to 1980. The relevant rules are: actions founded on simple contract cannot be brought after six years following accrual of the cause of action (s. 5 of the 1980 Act); where a loan is made which contains no specific date for repayment and does not effectively make the obligation to repay conditional on demand or the occurrence of some other event, time will only begin to run under s. 5 when the creditor makes a demand in writing for repayment (s. 6) except that where a debtor enters into a "collateral obligation" to pay the amount of the debt (*e.g.* a promissory note as security, but not, it is submitted, a guarantee) either on or before a fixed or determinable date, or effectively on demand, time will run against the creditor from the date of making the loan (s. 6(2)); actions upon a specialty (*i.e.* contract or other obligation contained in a document under seal) cannot be brought after 12 years from the accrual of the cause of action (s. 8); the limitation period for claiming contribution under the Civil Liability (Contribution) Act 1978 is two years. (s. 10); and the general period of limitation relating to mortgages or other charges on property (whether real or personal) is 12 years (s. 20).

[2] *Colvin* v. *Buckle* (1841) 8 M. & W. 680: *Holl* v. *Hadley* (1835) 2 A. & E. 758.

[3] See *ante*, p. 115.

[4] *Hartland* v. *Jukes* (1863) 1 H. & C. 667; *Re Brown* [1893] 2 Ch. 300.

[5] [1939] A.C. 439 The Privy Council expressed no views on the correctness of *Parr's Banking Co.* v. *Yates* [1898] 2 Q.B. 460 which had suggested that in the case of a continuing guarantee, a cause of action arises as at the date of each advance, *sed quaere. Cf. Hartland* v. *Jukes, supra,* not cited in *Parr's* case.

Where a guarantee is given in consideration of forbearance to sue the debtor, time commences to run not later than when the time of forbearance expires; and this if not defined will be a reasonable time.[6] Where the surety is not to be liable till after measures taken against the debtor, a reasonable time for taking these measures must elapse before time begins to run against the surety.[7] When the surety was to become liable in the event of pending transactions with the principal showing a certain result, time was held to run as soon as all the facts were ascertained on which an adjustment could have been made; notwithstanding that, owing to disputes and litigation, no such adjustment had been made until long afterwards.[8]

Application of legacy by creditor to surety to statute-barred liability

The executors of the creditor are entitled to apply in payment of the debt a legacy left to the surety by their testator, even though an action to recover the debt would be statute-barred.[9]

Interest

Interest expressly guaranteed is recoverable, if it has accrued within six years, though the principal money is statute-barred.[10]

Surety for mortgage debt

The obligation of a surety for a mortgage debt who gives a separate bond is not statute-barred until after the lapse of 12 years.[11] Whether this is also the case where the surety joins in the covenant in a mortgage deed is not definitely settled. The question arose, but was not finally dealt with in *Re Frisby*.[12]

Where principal alone protected by statute

A surety, whose liability is not itself barred by any statute of limitation, remains liable, notwithstanding that the remedy

---

[6] See *Henton* v. *Paddison* (1893) 68 L.T. 405.
[7] *Holl* v. *Hadley* (1835) 2 A. & E. 758.
[8] *Colvin* v. *Buckle* (1841) 8 M. & W. 680.
[9] *Coates* v. *Coates* (1864) 33 Beav. 249.
[10] *Parr's Banking Co.* v. *Yates* [1898] 2 Q.B. 460; *Wright* v. *New Zealand Farmers Co-operative Association of Canterbury Ltd.* [1939] A.C. 439; Limitation Act 1980 s. 29(6).
[11] Limitation Act 1980, s. 20. Formerly the limitation period prescribed by the Real Property Limitation Act 1874, s. 8 was 20 years. *Re Powers* (1885) 30 Ch.D. 291 Cf. *Re Wolmershausen* (1890) 62 L.T. 541; *Barnes* v. *Glenton* [1899] 1 Q.B. 885.
[12] (1889) 43 Ch.D. 106. See also *Barnes* v. *Glenton, supra.*

against the principal may be barred.[13] Thus, where securities were deposited to secure payment of bills, and the bills became statute-barred, the charge remained.[14]

Effect of payment or acknowledgment by principal

The effect upon the running of time under the Statutes of Limitations in favour of a surety of a payment or acknowledgment by the principal must be considered to some extent with reference to the statutory provision which, in the particular case, applies to the liability of the surety.

Surety by simple contract

In the Limitation Act 1623, which formerly applied to sureties liable by simple contract, there was no provision making time run afresh after a payment or acknowledgment; and the doctrine that a payment or acknowledgment interrupts the running of the Act rested upon the theory that it was evidence of a new promise to pay. Therefore a payment or acknowledgment by one person, unless the circumstances were such that it must have been regarded as payment for another, could not keep alive the remedy against that other. There appeared to be nothing in the relation of principal and surety itself which made payment or acknowledgment by the principal binding as a payment or acknowledgment by the surety.[15] Before Lord Tenterden's Act,[16] either a payment or any other acknowledgment by a principal liable jointly with the surety, or jointly and severally, would have prevented time running in favour of the surety, on the principle that a payment or acknowledgment by one joint debtor was a payment or acknowledgment by all.[17] This was altered as regards an acknowledgment by Lord Tenterden's Act, and as regards a payment by the Mercantile Law Amendment Act 1856. By section 14 of the latter Act it was provided that no co–debtor should lose the benefit of the Statutes by reason only

---

[13] *Carter* v. *White* (1883) 25 Ch.D. 666. But *cf. Re Powers* (1885) 30 Ch.D. 291 at pp. 295, 297. This question is considered by the British Columbia Law Reform Commission Report on Consumer Guarantees (1979) where it is recommended that a guarantor should be able to rely on the principal debtor's defence. *Semble* such may already be the position in British Columbia itself. See British Columbia Limitations Act S.B.C. 1975 (c. 37), s. 9(1).

[14] *Carter* v. *White, supra.* See also *Manning* v. *Phelps* (1854) 10 Exch. 59. *Cf. Re Powers, supra,* where Cotton L.J. at 295 seems to imply that a bond conditioned for the payment of a mortgage debt would only remain enforceable so long as the rights of the mortgagee are not barred by the Statute of Limitations. See also *Re Frisby* (1890) 43 Ch.D. 106. Therefore payment by the principal debtor will interrupt the running of the limitation period on the contract of guarantee, *Cf. Re Thomson* [1927] 2 D.L.R. 254.

[15] See *Re Wolmershausen* (1890) 62 L.T. 541; *Henton* v. *Paddison* (1893) 68 L.T. 405.

[16] Statute of Frauds Amendment Act 1828. See Appendix 2.

[17] *Whitcomb* v. *Whiting* (1781) 2 Dougl. 652.

of payment by any principal, interest or other money by another co-debtor. And in *Cockrill* v. *Sparkes*,[18] it was held that payment of a composition by a principal debtor to the creditor with the assent of the surety, such assent being given with a view only of preventing the surety being discharged by the acceptance of the composition, and not amounting to any acknowledgment by the surety, was a "payment only" within this section, and that the remedy against the surety was statute-barred.

Now the effect of these provisions as reproduced in sections 29(5), 29(6) and 31 of the Limitation Act 1980 is to make time run afresh in the case of an acknowledgment of debt and not to create a fresh cause of action.[19] Subject to part payments of interest being treated as payments in respect of the principal debt,[20] after the limitation period is extinguished, any acknowledgment or payment subsequently made will not create a fresh cause of action.[21] Section 31 of the 1980 Act applies the provisions of section 29 to persons other than the acknowledgor or maker of the part payment in particular cases. Subsections 31(6) and (7) provide respectively that an acknowledgment of a debt shall bind the acknowledgor and his "successors" but not other persons[22] and that a payment made in respect of any debt shall bind all persons liable in respect of the debt or claim. Therefore part payment of a debt by the principal debtor will cause a re-accrual of the limitation period against the surety[23] and payment of interest by a surety will make time run against the principal debtor.[24]

Surety by mortgage

The period of limitation for actions to recover moneys secured by a mortgage or charge to recover proceeds of the sale of land is in general twelve years,[25] which is the period also applicable to specialties.[26] A period is reckoned from the date when the right to receive the money accrued.[27]

---

[18] (1863) 1 H. & C. 699; *Re Powers* (1885) 30 Ch.D. 291, 295; *Re Wolmershausen* (1890) 62 L.T. 541; *Bradford Old Bank* v. *Sutcliffe* [1918] 2 K.B. 833, 839, 848. And *cf. Henton* v. *Paddison* (1893) 68 L.T. 405.

[19] *Bush* v. *Stevens* [1963] 1 Q.B. 1. Note, too, s. 30 of the Act providing for the formalities regarding acknowledgments and part payments and dealing with questions of agency. See *Wright* v. *Pepin* [1954] 1 W.L.R. 635.

[20] s. 29(6).

[21] s. 29(7).

[22] "Successor" is defined in s. 31(9) for present purposes as a person on whom the liability in respect of the debt or claim may "devolve" whether on death or bankruptcy or disposition of property and would not therefore appear to include a surety.

[23] See *Re Powers* (1885) 30 Ch.D. 291.

[24] See *Re Seager's Estate* (1857) 26 L.J. Ch. App. 809.

[25] Limitation Act 1980, s. 20.

[26] Limitation Act 1980, s. 8. For a review of the law prior to the Limitation Act 1939 see the 3rd edition of this work at pp. 301–305.

[27] Limitation Act 1980, s. 20(1)–(4).

If in a mortgage deed the mortgagor and surety jointly and severally covenant for repayment of the mortgage debt, the above provisions will not apparently apply to an action against the surety.[28]

As has been seen, under the Limitation Acts 1939 to 1980 the period of limitation is postponed where the proper person either makes a payment in respect of a debt, or acknowledges the claim.[29] And in neither case will the part payment be treated as a fresh promise to pay.[30]

Effect of payment or acknowledgment by co-surety

The effect of part payment or acknowledgment by a co-surety upon the running of the statute in favour of a surety will apparently be the same as—at least it cannot be greater than—the effect of part payments or acknowledgments by the principal.

2. As to Claims by the Surety Against the Principal

When time begins to run

A surety has ordinarily six years from the time when payment was made by him in which to sue the principal, there being before payment no breach of the contract of indemnity.[31] Thus the right over of an accommodation acceptor against the drawer is not barred till six years from payment by him of the bill.[32] But time begins to run against an indorser, whose remedy is upon the bill, in favour of the drawer, as soon as the bill is dishonoured.[33] If a principal expressly covenants with a surety,

---

[28] *Re Frisby* (1889) 43 Ch.D. 106; *Re Powers* (1885) 30 Ch.D. 291. See also *Re Wolmershausen* (1890) 62 L.T. 541 at p. 544 *per* Stirling J. At p. 303 of the 3rd edition it was pointed out that there exists a distinction between those cases where, by virtue of one bond or covenant, several persons claiming under the obligor or covenantor, or their property, are all liable to the debt (see *e.g. Roddam* v. *Morley* (1857) 1 De G. & J. 1; *Dibb* v. *Walker* |1893| 2 Ch. 429; *Barclay* v. *Owen* (1889) 60 L.T. 220) and the case of a surety by several bond or covenant, where there are in effect two debtors. See *Re Powers* (1885) 30 Ch.D. 291 at p. 295 *per* Cotton L.J. Nor does the case of a bond or covenant for payment of money by another appear to be affected by the considerations applicable where a mortgage is given by a surety, and is expressed to be redeemable on payment by the principal and the latter makes payments on account of the mortgage money or interest, which payments will keep the mortgage alive. See *Lewin* v. *Wilson* (1886) 11 App.Cas. 639. Further where a surety has given a mortgage of his property expressed to be redeemable upon payment by the principal, payments by the latter will keep alive the remedy of the creditor against the land under s. 31(2) of the Limitation Act 1980. But note that s. 31(2) makes no reference to acknowledgments.

[29] Limitation Act 1980, s. 29(5) and (7). See text in preceding section.

[30] *Ibid. Re Powers* (1885) 30 Ch.D. 291; *Re Frisby* (1889) 43 Ch.D. 106.

[31] *Considine* v. *Considine* (1846) 9 Ir. L.R. 400; *Angrove* v. *Tippett* (1865) 11 L.T. 708. If a surety satisfies a debt which has become statute-barred as against him, he cannot recover the money from the principal: *Re Morris* |1922| 1 I.R. 81 and 136.

[32] *Angrove* v. *Tippett, supra.*

[33] *Webster* v. *Kirk* (1852) 17 Q.B. 944.

not only to indemnify him, but positively to pay the debt at the due date, there is a breach if the debt is not paid as soon as the due date is reached, and the statute begins to run from that moment.[34]

Time runs separately in respect of each payment by surety

A right of action against the principal accrues to a surety *toties quoties* for every amount he pays under the guarantee and he can therefore only recover from the principal such payments as have been made within six years before action.[35]

It follows from what has already been said that the principal may remain liable at the suit of the surety after he has obtained a defence founded on the statute against the creditor, and this apparently even though the creditor does not sue the surety till after the principal debt is barred.[36]

3. As to Claim by a Surety against a Co-Surety

When time begins to run

The right of a surety to recover contribution from a co-surety does not stand upon quite the same footing as his right to recover over against the principal. No claim for contribution accrues till a surety has paid more than his share of what is unpaid by the debtor,[37] or perhaps, if his estate is being administered by the court, from the time that his liability is ascertained.[38] As soon as the surety has paid his share he can sue his co-sureties *toties quoties* for every further payment made by him.[39]

If a surety more than six years before action has paid a portion of the debt not exceeding his share, and the principal has paid the residue within six years, the limitation period will not run from the payment by the surety but from the payment of the residue by the principal, if until the latter date the surety has not paid more than his share.[40]

In an action for contribution, there can be recovered not half what the plaintiff has paid within six years, but the whole

---

[34] *Carr* v. *Roberts* (1833) 5 B. & Ad. 78.
[35] *Davies* v. *Humphreys* (1840) 6 M. & W. 153, 167.
[36] See *Wolmershausen* v. *Gullick* [1893] 2 Ch. 514.
[37] *Ex p. Gifford* (1802) 6 Ves. 805; *Ex p. Snowdon* (1881) 17 Ch.D. 44. *Gardner* v. *Brooke* (1897) 2 I.R. 6. Note the provisions of Limitation Act 1980, s. 10 providing a two year limitation period in respect of the right to recover contribution under s. 1 of the Civil Liability (Contribution) Act 1978.
[38] See *Wolmershausen* v. *Gullick* [1893] 2 Ch. 514; *Robinson* v. *Harkin* [1896] 2 Ch. 415.
[39] *Davies* v. *Humphreys* (1840) 6 M. & W. 153, 169.
[40] *Davies* v. *Humphreys, supra.*

amount, whenever paid, that has been paid by the plaintiff in excess of his share, provided that nothing be recovered in respect of what has been in excess for more than six years.

Where claim by creditor against co-surety is statute-barred

The right of a surety to contribution from a co-surety is apparently not affected by the circumstance that at the time of his suing for contribution, the right of the creditor to recover from the co-surety is statute-barred,[41] nor even that such right was so barred when the creditor sued the surety who seeks contribution, inasmuch as this would not seemingly affect the liability of the last-named surety. It may be open to question however, whether, where the sureties are bound by separate instruments, and the right to contribution rests entirely on their common though independent liability,[42] one of them paying at a time when the other had become protected by the statute, would be entitled to contribution. At any rate, it would hardly seem reasonable that there should be contribution if the surety paying had (as might happen) only become surety after the other had obtained the protection of the Limitation Acts.

Whether statute can ever run against surety before payment

It is submitted that the existence of a right in the surety before payment to take equitable proceedings to compel the principal or a co-surety to pay, as the case may be, the whole or the proper proportion of the debt, can have no affect on the time when the statute begins to run against him. The statute would seem to have no direct application to a claim in that form; and if the surety pays and immediately afterwards sues principal or co-surety for money paid, it is hard to see how a defence founded on the statute could be supported by evidence that more than six years before proceedings might have been taken *quia timet* in equity. Where, however, a surety before payment sued a co-surety who resisted the claim on the ground that as against him the creditor's claim was statute-barred, Wright J. said that even if the statute could begin to run against the plaintiff before payment, at any rate it did not run till the plaintiff's liability, which had been disputed, was ascertained.[43]

---

[41] See *Wolmershausen* v. *Gullick* [1893] 2 Ch. 514.
[42] See *ante*, p. 189.
[43] See *Wolmershausen* v. *Gullick* [1893] 2 Ch. 514.

CHAPTER 11

BANKRUPTCY

1. *Rights of Creditor in Bankruptcy of Principal*

Giving credit in the creditor's proof

In proving in the principal's bankruptcy, the creditor must give credit for anything received before proof from the surety, whether by payment or by realisation of a security provided by the surety.[1] Similarly, where the surety is also bankrupt, any dividend declared out of the surety's estate even though unpaid, must be given credit for when the creditor proves in the principal's estate.[2]

Where the creditor, in order to liquidate a debt owed to him by the surety on his own account, realised a security deposited by the surety on both accounts and carried the balance to a suspense account, it was held that this was not a receipt by the creditor of the balance so as to reduce his proof in the principal's estate.[3]

Creditors without surety have no right in equity to compel creditors who have a surety to proceed against the surety.[4]

The creditor who holds a guarantee is not a "secured creditor"

The rules as to valuing and surrendering securities held by the creditor do not apply to a guarantee or to a charge on the property of a third person.[5] It makes no difference to this that the surety has a security on the principal's estate.[6]

If the principal has pledged to the creditor bills on which third parties are liable to the principal, reserving to himself the right to redeem them this is a security upon the principal's property

---

[1] *Cooper* v. *Pepys* (1741) 1 Atk. 107; *Ex p. Wildman* (1750) *ibid.* 109; *Ex p. Royal Bank of Scotland* (1815) 19 Ves. 310; *Ex p. Leers* (1802) 6 Ves. 644; *Ex p. Tayler* (1857) 1 De. G & J. 302; *Ex p. Egyptian Commercial and Trading Co.* (1868) L.R. 4 Ch.125; *Re Oriental Commercial Bank* (1868) L.R. 6 Eq. 582; *Ex p. Joint Stock Discount Co.* (1871) L.R. 6 Ch. App. 455; *Ex p. Gilbey* (1878) 8 Ch.D. 248.
[2] *Ex p. Leers* (1802) 6 Ves. 644.
[3] *Ex p. Watson* (1815) 42 L.T. 516.
[4] *Ex p. Kendal* (1811) 17 Ves. 514.
[5] *Ex p. Parr* (1811) 1 Rose 76; *Ex p. Goodman* (1818) 3 Madd. 373; *Ex p. Biddulph* (1849) 3 De. G. & S. 587; *Ex p. Shepherd* (1841) 2 M.D. & De. G. 204.
[6] *Midland Banking Co.* v *Chambers* (1869) L.R. 7 Eq. 179; 4 Ch. App. 398. *Cf. Re Melton* [1918] 1 Ch. 37.

which must be valued or surrendered.[7] However, bills indorsed and transferred to the creditor need not be valued or surrendered,[8] unless it can be shown that despite the indorsement, the transaction was intended to be merely a deposit.[9] The creditor need never value bills in his hands accepted for the principal's accommodation, since possession of such bills is not a security on any property of the principal. The principal has none of the bills and the acceptor is merely a surety.[10]

Subsequent bankruptcy of the principal who has entered into a composition guaranteed by sureties

Where the principal defaults in the terms of a composition and becomes bankrupt, the creditor can prove for the full amount of the debt, allowing for anything received from the principal or the surety under the composition.[11] The creditor is not confined to the amount unpaid in the composition, even though a surety for one instalment may have paid and may not be entitled to recover the payment.[12]

Where the principal and the surety are both bankrupt

The creditor can prove against each for the full amount owing at the date of proof and can take and keep dividends limited to a total of 100p in the £.[13] A creditor who is owed a number of debts guaranteed by different sureties, is limited to keeping 100p in the £ in respect of each debt. He cannot attempt to accumulate dividends beyond that limit in order to achieve 100p in the £ on the aggregate indebtedness.

The rule in Ex p. Waring[14]

Property which is in a bankrupt's possession for a specific purpose is not normally available for division among the creditors. Thus where the principal and the surety are both bankrupt and the principal has deposited with the surety security in respect of the debt, a creditor of the principal is

---

[7] *Ex p. Rushforth* (1805) 10 Ves. at p.419; *Ex p. Twogood* (1812) 19 Ves. at p.232; *ex p. Britten* (1833) 3 D. & Ch. 35; *Ex p. Schofield* (1879) 12 Ch.D. 337.
[8] See *Ex p. Schofield* (1879) 12 Ch.D. at pp. 347, 348.
[9] See note 7, *ante.*
[10] *Ex p. Schofield* (1879) 12 Ch.D. 337, 348.
[11] *Ex p. Gilbey* (1878) 8 Ch.D. 248.
[12] *Ibid.*
[13] *Ex p. Rushforth* (1805) 10 Ves. at p. 417; *Cooper* v. *Pepys* (1741) 1 Atk. 107; *Ex p. Wildman* (1750) *ibid.* 109; *Ex p. Royal Bank of Scotland* (1815) 19 Ves. 310; *Re Blakeley* (1892) 9 Morr. 173; *Ex p. Turquand* (1876) 3 Ch.D. 445, 450.
[14] (1815) 19 Ves. 345.

entitled to have the security applied in the discharge of the principal's debt.[14] This is not because the creditor has any lien or equity but in order to work out the equities between the two insolvent estates. The security having been realised for the creditor's benefit, he is then entitled to prove in the surety's bankruptcy for the balance of the debt. An alternative solution has been found in Scotland, where the creditor is restricted to proving in the surety's bankruptcy and the surety's estate can indemnify itself out of the security in respect of the dividends paid to the creditor.[15]

2. *Rights of Creditor in the Bankruptcy of a Surety*

Proof

The creditor clearly has a right of proof for any amount due and payable by the surety at the date of the receiving order. Proof in the surety's estate is reduced by any receipts, realisation of securities or receipt of dividends from the principal's estate.[16] Where several sureties are jointly and severally liable for the whole debt, the creditor may prove in the bankruptcy of one for the whole amount owing at the time of the receiving order without giving credit for sums received from other sureties between the receiving order and proof, providing that in all he does not recover more than 100p in the £.[16a]

The creditor who receives a security from some of a number of sureties is not obliged to apply it to reduce his proof in the bankruptcy of another surety. This is so even though the security was a deposit of money in a suspense account which the creditor could at any time apply for the payment of the debt.[17]

No allowance for co-surety or collateral securities

The creditor can prove for the full amount without having to make over any collateral securities, since the surety's right to these arises only on payment in full.[18] The creditor may also prove even though he has given up his remedy against a co-surety.[19] However, in that case the dividends are limited to the amount which the surety would have had to bear, allowing

---

[15] *Royal Bank of Scotland* v. *Commercial Bank of Scotland* (1882) 7 App. Cas. 366, 387.
[16] *Re Blakeley* (1892) 9 Morr. 173.
[16a] *Re Houlder* [1929] 1 Ch. 205. See also *Ulster Bank* v. *Lambe* [1966] N.I. 161.
[17] *Commercial Bank of Australia* v. *Official Assignee* [1893] A.C.181.
[18] *Ewart* v. *Latta* (1865) 4 Macq. H.L. 983.
[19] *Ex p. Gifford* (1802) 6 Ves. 805.

for the contribution from the released co-surety which has been lost.[20]

Bankruptcy of the surety from whom nothing is yet due

The creditor can under the Bankruptcy Act 1914 prove in the bankruptcy of the surety in respect of this contingent debt in practically every case,[21] though the estimate of the amount may often be very difficult.

3. *Rights of a Surety in the Bankruptcy of the Principal*

Proof generally

Payments made by the surety to the creditor and dividends paid in the surety's bankruptcy to the creditor can, provide no double proof results, be proved for in the principal's bankruptcy.[21]

Under s.30(3) of the Bankruptcy Act 1914, the surety can prove against every claim, present or future, certain or contingent.[22] By s.28(2) the principal is similarly protected in respect of such claims upon his discharge

The surety's right of proof is however subject to the rule against double proof: the surety cannot prove if the creditor is proving for the debt himself. However, if the creditor proves in the principal's bankruptcy and once he has been paid from all sources 100p in the £, the surety will then be entitled to the benefit of the creditor's proof so as to receive future dividends to the extent the surety's recouping himself such part of the 100p as he may have paid.[23]

Thus if the surety and the principal are both bankrupt, no proof can be made on behalf of the surety's estate in the principal's bankruptcy in respect of dividends declared out of the surety's estate after proof by the creditor in the principal's estate.[24] But once the situation arises that the creditor receives 100p in the £ from the aggregate dividends paid out of the surety's and the principal's estate, the surety's estate can claim the benefit of future dividends receivable as a result of the creditor's proof.[25]

---

[20] *Ibid.*

[21] See *Hardy* v. *Fothergill* (1888) 13 App.Cas. 351; *Wolmershausen* v. *Gullick* [1893] 2 Ch. 514; *Re Fitzgeorge* [1905] 1 K.B. 462; Bankruptcy Act 1914, s.30(3).

[22] See also *Ex p. Reader,* (1819) Buck 381.

[23] In the U.S.A., this is described as the result of the surety's subrogation to the creditor's rights: *American Surety Co. of New York* v. *Bethlehem National Bank* 314 U.S. 314, 62 S. Ct.226, 86 L. Ed.241 (1941).

[24] *Ex p. European Bank* (1871) L.R. 7 Ch. App. 99.

[25] *Re Whitehouse* (1887) 37 Ch.D. 683.

In *Ex p. Whittaker*[26] it was left open whether a surety for a present liquidated debt could prove before payment, but it was held that any such proof would be in respect of a contingent debt.

History of proof

Before the Bankruptcy Act 1809, the surety could only prove (and the bankrupt receive his discharge) in respect of money actually paid by the surety to the creditor before the principal's bankruptcy.[27] If the surety paid the whole debt after the creditor had proved, the surety became entitled to the benefit of the creditor's proof.[28] If the surety paid the debt after the bankruptcy but before the creditor's proof, the creditor could not prove[29] and the surety was wholly deprived of the benefit of any dividend in the principal's bankruptcy, while the bankrupt did not receive a discharge from the surety's claim. The Courts of Equity intervened to permit the surety to pay the money into court and compel the creditor to prove before exacting payment from the surety.[30]

It was then provided by section 8 of the Bankruptcy Act 1809 as re-enacted in section 52 of the Bankruptcy Act 1825 and in section 173 of the Bankruptcy Act 1849 that where the surety paid after the commencement of the bankruptcy, he was entitled to the benefit of the creditor's proof, or if the creditor had not proved he could prove in his own name, but not disturbing past dividends.

Prior to the Bankruptcy Act 1914, if the surety paid part only of the debt after the principal's bankruptcy but before proof by the creditor, neither the surety nor the creditor could prove in respect of that part; the creditor could not prove because he had received payment, the surety because he had paid after bankruptcy and not in full discharge of the debt. The principal remained liable to the surety after the principal's discharge from bankruptcy. However, under section 30 of the Bankruptcy Act 1914 the surety can in principle prove in such a case, since it is a debt to which the bankrupt became subject before his discharge by reason of an obligation incurred prior to the receiving order.

The only other situation in which the 1914 Act may have

---

[26] (1891) 3 W.R.400.

[27] *Taylor* v. *Mills* (1777) 2 Cowp. 525; *Paul* v. *Jones* (1787) 1 Term Rep. 599; *Howis* v. *Wiggins* (1792) 4 T.R.714.

[28] *Ex p. Rushforth* (1805) 10 Ves. 409, and at pp. 417, 419 (Lord Eldon); *Wright* v. *Morley* (1805) 11 Ves. at p.23.

[29] *Cooper* v. *Pepys* (1741) 1 Atk 107; *Ex p. Royal Bank of Scotland* (1815) 2 Rose 197; *Ex p. Leers* (1802) 6 Ves. 644; *Ex p. Taylor* (1857) I De. G. & J. 302.

[30] See *Ex p. Tayler* (1857) 1 De. G. & J. 302 *per* Turner L.J., at p.308; *Wright* v. *Simpson* (1802) 6 Ves. at p.734; *Ex p. Rushforth* (1805) 10 Ves. at p.414; *Philips* v. *Smith* referred to 10 Ves. at p.412.

expanded the surety's right to prove is where the creditor permanently covenants not to sue the principal, while reserving his remedy against the surety. The surety may now be entitled to have his contingent liability valued even though he could not prove for the whole amount as a liquidated sum.[31]

Under the Bankruptcy Act 1914, where the creditor has proved, the surety's only right upon payment to the creditor is to stand, wholly or partly, in the place of the creditor for dividends,[32] and the surety will only have this right if the creditor has been paid in full.[33] If the surety holds a security upon the principal's estate, the surety's ability to benefit from the creditor's proof in the principal's estate is limited to the sum by which the debt (or its guaranteed part), exceeds the security. If the creditor proves and takes dividends for the whole debt and the surety realises the security, the surety will have to restore to the estate the amount by which the dividends paid exceed the dividends which would have been paid to the surety on the amount by which the debt was greater than the value of the security.[34] Where, however, the creditor by the terms of the guarantee can take all dividends from the principal's estate and hold the surety liable to the full extent of the guarantee, proof by the creditor does not affect any security held by the surety over the principal's estate.[35]

Set off

Where a guarantee was entered into before the principal's bankruptcy, the surety, if he is called upon to pay the debt after the bankruptcy and does pay, is nevertheless not entitled to set off such payment against debts due from him to the principal.[36] Such set-off would now be under section 31 of the Bankruptcy Act 1914. Where the surety has made no actual payment to the creditor, he certainly cannot set off his contingent liability as at the date of the receiving order against debts due to the principal. This is despite the fact that the surety's debt arises out of

---

[31] *Ex p. Whittaker* (1891) 39 W.R. 400.

[32] See *Re Pyke* (1910) 55 S.J. 109. He may also have the right to prove for interest in certain circumstances.

[33] *Ex p. Turquand* (1876) 3 Ch.D.445. It was held in that case that debentures issued to creditors under a scheme of arrangement by a company formed under the scheme to take over the business of the debtors were to be treated as dividends, and that a surety who had only paid part of the debt was not therefore entitled to a proportion of them. In the U.S.A., in *U.S.* v. *National Surety Co.* 254 U.S. 73, 41 S. Ct.29,65 L.Ed. 143 (1920) it was held that a surety paying only part of the debt did not become subrogated to the creditor's preferential claim in the principal's bankruptcy.

[34] *Baines* v. *Wright* (1885) 15 Q.B.D. 102; 16 Q.B.D. 330.

[35] *Midland Banking Co.* v. *Chambers* (1869) L.R. 7 Eq.179; 4 Ch. App. 398; *Re Melton* [1918] 1 Ch. 37; *Re Lennard* [1934] Ch. 235.

[36] *Re Hawkins* (unreported, Walton J., February 2, 1978). But see *Jones* v. *Mossop* (1844) 3 Hare 568, 571. *Re Hawkins* is based on the "double-proof" rule in *Re Fenton, infra*, and the "relevant date" principle in *Re A Debtor* (No. 66 of 1955), *Re Waite* [1956] 1 W.L.R. 1226.

mutual dealings and is a provable debt. This is decided by the case of *Re Fenton*[37] on the basis that such a set-off would infringe the rule against double proof, since it was always open to the creditor to prove.

Re Waite

In *Re Waite*[38] the principal claimed to set off a debt owed to him by the surety against a judgment obtained by the surety's trustee in bankruptcy enforcing the surety's right to be indemnified by the principal against sums paid by the surety as guarantor of debts owed by the principal. No set-off was allowed in respect of payments made after the relevant date of the bankruptcy (the date of the receiving order), that being the date at which the respective rights of the parties are crystallised.

Payment by the surety with notice of act of bankrupty

Where the surety gives a guarantee for the debts of the principal with notice of an availble act of bankruptcy by the principal, it seems that the surety cannot prove in the principal's bankruptcy for contribution in respect of monies paid to the creditor.[39] This is so, even though the principal debt was incurred before the act of bankruptcy and therefore the creditor could have proved if the surety had not paid.

Interest

The surety cannot prove in the principal's bankruptcy for money paid by the surety to the creditor as interest on the principal debt accrued due after the commencement of the bankruptcy where the debt was payable at the date of the bankruptcy.[40] Where, however, the debt is payable at a future date with interest in the meantime, the surety is entitled to value his liability for interest at the rate for which he is liable and to prove for and take full dividends on that value, and also to prove for the principal as a present debt subject to a rebate of 5 per cent. on the dividends calculated from the declaration of the dividend to the date when the debt would have been payable.[41]

---

[37] [1931] 1 Ch. 85.
[38] *Re A Debtor* (No. 66 of 1955) [1956] 1 W.L.R. 1226.
[39] *Farhall* v. *Farhall* (1871) 7 Ch. App. 123.
[40] *Re International Contract Co. Hughes' Claim* (1872) L.R. 13 Eq.623.
[41] *Re Browne and Wingrove, Ex p. Ador* [1891] 2 Q.B.574. See also *Re Evans* (1897) 4 Manson 114.

Where the principal and surety are partners[42]

In *Lacey* v. *Hill*[43] a partner in a banking firm deposited in a separate account at the bank money received by him as treasurer of a public body. Another partner was surety for the treasurer's responsibilities to the public body. The partnership became bankrupt, although the separate estate of the surety was solvent. The separate estate of the surety was not allowed to prove against the separate estate of the treasurer, since the dividend would have gone to enlarge the assets of the joint estate, which was in reality primarily liable for the money deposited.

Proof by persons in positions analogous to suretyship

The principles applicable to proof by sureties should extend to all persons in analogous positions, *i.e.* where a person is secondarily liable under a liability for which another person is also liable, whether or not the former is strictly speaking a surety. Early examples are of an accommodation acceptor,[44] drawer[45] or indorser[46] of a bill of exchange, and also a retired partner[47] or solvent partner paying the whole partnership debt[48] and an executor liable for the default of a co-executor.[49] Examples of cases where the suretyship analogy has not been applied include an undertenant whose goods were distrained for rent due from his immediate lessor,[50] and a lessee who incurred expenses by reason of the non-observance of covenants by the assignee.[51]

4. *Rights of surety in Bankruptcy of Co-surety Proof in Co-surety's Bankruptcy*

The surety can in principle prove in respect of his future claim against a co-surety.[52] However, the rule against double proof

---

[42] For an extensive treatment of bankruptcy as it affects partnership generally, see Chap.27 of *Lindley on Partnership* (14th ed., 1979).

[43] (1872) L.R. 8 Ch. App.441.

[44] *Stedman* v. *Martinnant* (1811) 13 East. 427; *Cf. Filbey* v. *Lawford* (1841) 3 M. & Gr. 468. But where the surety paid off the creditor's promissory note prior to the Receiving Order he was held to be able to prove for interest between payment and the receiving order by reason of section 5 of the Mercantile Law Amendment Act 1856; *Re Evans* (1897) 76 L.T. 530.

[45] *Ex p. Lobbon* (1810) 17 Ves. 334.

[46] *Haigh* v. *Jackson* (1838) 3 M. & W. 598.

[47] *Wood* v. *Dodgson* (1813) 2 M. & S. 195.

[48] *Ex p. Yonge* (1814) 3 V. & B. 31,40; *Ex p. Watson* (1815) 4 Madd 477; *Aflalo* v. *Foudrinier* (1829) 6 Bing. 306.

[49] *Lincoln* v. *Wright* (1841) 4 Beav. 427.

[50] *Hoare* v. *White* (1857) 3 Jur. (N.S.) 445.

[51] *Hardy* v. *Fothergill* (1888) 13 App.Cas. 351.

[52] *Wolmershausen* v. *Gullick* |1893| 2 Ch. 514.

will prevent the surety from proving in respect of the surety's liability for sums for which the creditor cannot be debarred from proving. The surety, however, has the right to stand in the creditor's place for dividends as he did under the 1869 Act[53] (under which the surety could not prove for his own contingent claim).

Rights of the surety to benefit of the creditor's proof in co-surety's estate

Where a co-surety is bankrupt and the creditor proves for the whole debt, if the surety pays the creditor more than the surety's share, the surety (or his trustee in bankruptcy) is entitled, once the creditor is paid 100p in the £, to the benefit of the creditor's proof. The surety may use the creditor's proof to take dividends up to the amount of the surety's right to contribution.[54]

If, however, the creditor has not proved, when the surety pays and then proves in his own right for contribution, it seems that proof can only be made in respect of the amount which could be recovered as contribution.[55] Where the surety pays the debt he should always see that proof is made on the estate of any insolvent co-surety in the name of the creditor for the whole debt. This right is confirmed by section 5 of the Mercantile Law Amendment Act 1865.[56]

5. *Surety's Equity of Exoneration*

Where the surety and principal charge their properties for the principal's debt, the surety's equity to have the debt paid out of the principal's property before the surety's property is resorted to, is effective against the principal's trustee in bankruptcy. In *Re Marley*,[57] the bankrupt's father had conveyed his property into the joint names of himself and his son so that it could be charged for the son's business debts. It was conceded that the father was only a surety.[58] However, the trustee in bankruptcy argued that since the father had not paid the debt prior to the bankruptcy it was too late for him to acquire a charge over the bankrupt's property.[59] It was held that the original charging of the jointly owned property immediately gave the father a charge

---

[53] *Ex p. Stokes* (1848) De G. 618.
[54] *Ex p. Stokes* (1848) De G. 618; *Re Parker, Morgan v. Hill* [1894] 3 Ch. 400.
[55] *Re Parker, Morgan v. Hill* [1894] 3 Ch. 400.
[56] *Ibid.*
[57] [1976] 1 W.L.R. 952.
[58] At p. 955 A.
[59] At p. 955 B-C.

upon the bankrupt's property.[60] Upon any sale of the property the father had as a result a right to insist that the bankrupt's property bore the creditor's demand in priority to the father's property.[61]

6. *Spouse's Equity of Exoneration*

Where either spouse is bankrupt and the other spouse has lent or entrusted money or other property to the bankrupt spouse for the purpose of any trade or business of the bankrupt spouse, the lending or entrusting spouse's proof is deferred.[62] There is, however, a difference between the provisions in that in the case of a bankrupt husband not only is the wife's proof deferred but the money or property lent or entrusted by the wife to the husband is to be "treated as assets of his estate."[63]

The provision concerning the husband's bankruptcy is taken from section 3 of the Married Womens' Property Act 1882,[64] which in *Re Cronmire*[65] was held by the Court of Appeal to have no application to cases where the wife charged her "separate estate" for the bankrupt husband's debt. Nevertheless it has been held[66] that in a case involving a joint charge of jointly owned property for the husband's business purposes that the corresponding provision contained in section 36(2) of the Bankruptcy Act 1914 ruled out any application of a wife's claim to an equity of exoneration.[67]

It would seem that where a wife charges her property to secure money for the husband's purposes, this can, if the wife is to be regarded as only secondarily liable, be seen as a "lending"[68] and that it may be regarded as a "lending" falling foul of section 36(2) of the Bankruptcy Act 1914.[66] In that case, the bankrupt's wife will not be entitled to exoneration, since, if the equity applied, she would in effect be repaid her "loan"[66] in priority to the other creditors rather than after them.

---

[60] At p. 956 B, following *Gee* v. *Liddell* [1913] 2 Ch.62 at p.73 (Warrington J).

[61] At p. 956 C.

[62] s.36, Bankruptcy Act 1914.

[63] s.36(2), Bankruptcy Act 1914. See also *Williams and Muir Hunter on Bankruptcy* (19th ed., 1979), pp. 165, 166, 235.

[64] Repealed by the Law Reform (Married Women and Tortfeasors) Act 1935, Sched. 2.

[65] [1901] 1 Q.B. 480.

[66] In *Re Woodstock* [1980] C.L.Y. 148, *Re Cronmire* was not cited. Walton J. also doubted the application of the wife's equity of exoneration in modern social conditions.

[67] The same point occurred in *Re Berry* [1978] 2 N.Z.L.R. 373 but on the facts there it proved unnecessary for the Court of Appeal in New Zealand to decide it. See also in Australia *Davis* v. *MacKenna* (1930) 43 C.L.R. 448, esp. 491.

[68] *Paget* v. *Paget* [1898] 1 Ch. 470 at p. 474–75 (Lindley M.R.).

CHAPTER 12

WINDING UP AND RECEIVERS

Effect of section 317 of the Companies Act 1948

By section 317 of the Companies Act 1948, the rules obtaining in bankruptcy as to the debts provable, and as to the valuation of annuities and future and contingent liabilities are to be observed in the winding-up of insolvent companies. Every company liable by way of guarantee, and every company for which a guarantee has been given, would seem, therefore, if wound up and insolvent, to be open at the instance of the creditor or the surety respectively, to the same proof as might have been made against its assets had it been an individual adjudged bankrupt. This includes the rules as to set-off and reference should be made to Chap. 11 on this point.

Disclaimer

The disclaimer provisions in section 323 of the Companies Act 1948, have removed some of the difficulties that previously existed when applying the bankruptcy rules in a winding-up.[1] Thus, where the lessee was a company, and the lessor refused in the winding-up to accept the surrender of an onerous lease, his only right was to prove for any rent due and bring in a claim for future rents.[2] He was unable to have a dividend on the estimated value of the future rent set aside or impounded.[3] In such a case the liquidator can now disclaim and the lessor prove in the liquidation for the injury sustained.[4]

Rent may come to be paid during a winding-up by a person secondarily liable to pay it. That person will therefore be entitled to be indemnified by the company and if the rent would have ranked as an expense of the winding-up, if the liquidator of the assignee had paid it himself, the person paying the rent will be subrogated to the landlord's right to be indemnified out of the company's assets. The amount of his indemnity claim against

---

[1] *Re Westbourne Grove Drapery Co.* (1877) 5 Ch.D. 248 at 253; *Re New Oriental Bank* |1895| 1 Ch. 753 at 756.
[2] *Re New Oriental Bank, supra; Re London and Colonial Co.* (1868) L.R. 5 Eq. 561.
[3] *Re London and Colonial Co., supra; Re Westbourne Grove Drapery Co.* (1877) 5 Ch.D. 248.
[4] Companies Act 1948, s. 323(7); *Re Katherine et Cie.* |1932| 1 Ch. 70; *Warnford Investments Ltd.* v. *Duckworth* |1979| Ch. 127; |1978| Conv. 256. For the rights of landlords in a winding-up, including the right to prove for rent accruing after liquidation see generally, *Palmer's Company Law* (22nd ed., 1976), Volume 1 at pp. 921 *et seq.*

the company will rank as a pre-preferential expense in the winding-up.[5]

If leave to disclaim is granted, a guarantor of the rent is apparently discharged,[6] and for this reason a liquidator has been refused leave to disclaim an onerous lease, since to have allowed the disclaimer would have deprived the lessor of his rights against the surety, who was solvent.[7]

Company not insolvent

The section will not apply where the company being wound up is not insolvent. In that case the creditor would apparently have the right to have impounded, before any money is distributed amongst the *shareholders* a sum sufficient to answer, if invested at interest, any ascertained payments that will become due, such as future instalments of rent.[8]

It would seem reasonable that, if the creditor did not avail himself of any such right, the surety who would be certain to have to pay, the company being about to be dissolved and the assets distributed to the shareholders, ought to have such rights. Whether the creditor could claim any similar right in respect of future liabilities, as for breaches of covenants to repair, must be treated as open. The question arose in *Gooch* v. *London Banking Association*,[9] but the case was compromised. It was suggested in argument that the company impliedly agreed to maintain capital to answer the liabilities assumed by the covenants,[10] and that the lessor could claim a sum as for breach of this agreement. If so, perhaps a surety for the company could in some cases take the same position.

It would appear that, if the surety for a company in liquidation but not insolvent has the rights above-mentioned against the company, the creditor would have similar rights against a surety company in the same position. In the cases upon leases cited above, no allowance seems to have been made for possible payments by assignees of the lease. In either case, as the money would only be impounded, and would be released if no

[5] *Re Downer Enterprise Ltd.* [1974] 1 W.L.R. 1460.

[6] *Stacey* v. *Hill* [1901] 1 Q.B. 600; *Morris* v. *Sims & Jeffreys* (1932) 148 L.T. 56; *Re Katherine et Cie* [1932] 1 Ch. 70. Where the company in liquidation is an assignee of the lease, the original lessee, although for some purposes in a position anologous to that of a surety, is not released by the disclaimer. See *Warnford Investments Ltd.* v. *Duckworth* [1979] Ch. 129.

[7] *Re Katherine et Cie, supra. Cf.* position of a trustee in bankruptcy, who might become personally liable if no disclaimer is granted.

[8] *Oppenheimer* v. *British & Foreign, etc., Bank* (1877) 6 Ch.D. 744; *Gooch* v. *London Banking Association* (1885) 32 Ch.D. 41 *Cf. Re Telegraph Construction Co.* (1870) L.R. 10 Eq. 384.

[9] *Supra.* See also *James Smith & Sons* v. *Goodman* [1936] 1 Ch. 216 at pp. 227, 235.

[10] *Cf. per* Jessel M.R. in *Re National Funds Assurance Co.* (1878) 10 Ch.D. 118, 127.

payment became due, no ultimate injustice would be done to the company by the omission to make such allowance.

Preferential payments

A surety for a company's rates may, as to payment, stand in the place of the payee,[11] and will be entitled in the winding-up to their right of preferential payment under section 319 of the Companies Act 1948.[12]

Effect of liquidation

As in the case of bankruptcy, the liquidation of a company will not release the surety for a company's obligations.[13]

Effect of receivership

There is no reason to suppose that the appointment out of court of a receiver by a debenture-holder even in the case of an insolvent company, would have the consequence of discharging a surety.

It has been held that a receiver appointed by a debenture holder of a company owes no duty of care[14] to the guarantor of the company's indebtedness to realise the assets of the company in relation to which he is appointed, at a fair market value, on the basis that any such duty is only owed to the company, and not to individual creditors or shareholders.

Liability for mutual guarantees

In *Ford & Carter Ltd.* v. *Midland Bank Ltd.*[15] the question arose as to whether the plaintiff company in liquidation had entered into a pre-existing mutual guarantee with five other related companies. The authorised signatures of the plaintiff company were added to a document containing the signatures given on behalf of the related companies but no fresh signatures were sought from the previous party to the guarantees. The

---

[11] *Re Lampleigh Iron Ore Co.* [1927] 1 Ch. 308.
[12] *Ibid.*
[13] *Re Fitzgeorge* [1908] 1 K.B. 462. In *Re London Chartered Bank of Australia* [1893] 3 Ch. 540 there is the suggestion that the liquidation of a company had the same effect on a surety's liability as would the bankruptcy of an individual.
[14] *Latchford* v. *Beirne* [1981] 3 All E.R. 705, applying *Barclays Bank Ltd.* v. *Thienel* (1978) 247 E.G. 385 where no such duty of care was held to exist as between the creditor and the surety. Both these decisions appear to fail to apply the principle that a duty arises in situations of sufficient proximity: see *Cuckmere Brick Co. Ltd.* v. *Mutual Finance Ltd.* [1971] Ch. 949, in the case of mortgagee and mortgagor. See also Farrar (1975) J.B.L. 23.
[15] (1979) 129 N.J.L. 543 (H.L.).

House of Lords rejected the arguments first, that as a matter of construction the initial mutual liability could automatically and unilaterally extend to a fresh signatory, albeit a member of the same corporate group, and secondly in reversing the view of the Court of Appeal, that the liability of the other companies had been incurred through the agency of an officer common to all companies. The House of Lords stressed that whenever creditors became involved, as in this case, the separate legal existence of the companies in the group had to be respected.

CHAPTER 13

BILLS OF EXCHANGE AND NEGOTIABLE INSTRUMENTS

1. *General*

The drawer of an ordinary bill of exchange is not, strictly speaking, a surety for the acceptor, who will remain primarily liable, although the position of a person liable on a bill is clearly analogous to that either of principal debtor or surety to the holder.[1]

Bills of Exchange and the Statute of Frauds

Difficulties have frequently arisen under the Statute of Frauds when a bill of exchange has merely been indorsed with the name of a person other than the drawee, and to whom the bill has not been negotiated, as guarantor for the acceptor. To a holder in due course both by the law merchant[2] and by virtue of section 56 of the Bills of Exchange Act 1882,[3] such a person incurs the liabilities of an indorser and no question of the Statute of Frauds arises. Similarly, it appears that if a bill so indorsed is otherwise properly completed, such an indorser is liable to the drawer on default by the acceptor.[4] Oral evidence is admissible to show that the indorsee put his signature to the bill with the intention of being liable as guarantor to the drawer of payments by the acceptor.[5] If, on the other hand, the evidence is insufficient to establish this,[6] or the bill was incomplete when indorsed and the circumstances are such that section 20 of the Bills of Exchange Act does not apply, then an attempt to render the indorser liable apart from the law merchant and the Bills of

---

[1] See *Re Conley* [1938] 2 All E.R. 127, 131 *per* Lord Greene M.R., citing *Duncan Fox & Co.* v. *North & South Wales Bank* (1880) 6 App. Cas. 1. See *supra*, p. 5 and generally *Byles on Bills of Exchange* (24th ed., 1979), Chap. 33. See also *Horne* v. *Rouquette* (1878) 3 Q.B.D. 514, 518 *per* Brett L.J.

[2] *Steele* v. *M'Kinlay* (1880) 5 App. Cas. 754 at 769, 782; *McDonald* v. *Nash* [1924] A.C. 625 at 632, 650.

[3] *McDonald* v. *Nash, supra.* s. 56 provides that where a person signs a bill otherwise than as drawer or acceptor, he thereby incurs the liability of an indorser to a holder in due course. For a discussion on the continental *aval*, see below at p. 217.

[4] *McDonald* v. *Nash, supra; McCall* v. *Hargreaves* [1932] 2 K.B. 423. *Cf. Singer* v. *Elliott* (1888) 4 T.L.R. 524.

[5] *Steele* v. *M'Kinlay* (1880) 5 App. Cas. 754; *MacDonald* v. *Whitfield* (1883) 8 App. Cas. at 749; *McDonald* v. *Nash, supra; Elliott* v. *Bax-Ironside* [1925] 2 K.B. 301.

[6] *Steele* v. *M'Kinlay, supra.*

Exchange Act will fail, unless there is writing to satisfy the Statute of Frauds.[7]

Where a bill is indorsed by the drawer and by his indorsee back again to the drawer, it may be shown by oral evidence that the intermediate party indorsed as surety so as to enable the indorsee, though himself also the drawer, to sue such indorser— a right which he would not have if the indorser had been holder of the bill.[8] Similarly where the payee indorses to the drawer for the same purpose.[9]

Consideration

On the same principle whereby the granting of credit will be sufficient consideration for a guarantee to secure a further debt which may in the future be due,[10] the obtaining of bill stamps and drawing bills thereon will be sufficient consideration to support a guarantee of bills to be drawn.[11]

Accommodation bills

It has already been noted[12] that the rights of a surety depend not upon contract but upon notice, and that even notice given to the creditor after the contract has been entered into is sufficient. On this principle, an accommodation party to a bill of exchange is, from the time when the relation to the parties is notified to the holder, entitled to be regarded as surety only for the party accommodated, notwithstanding that upon the bill he is liable in a prior degree to the other, as where a bill is accepted for the accommodation of the drawer.[13]

---

[7] *Jenkins* v. *Coomber* [1898] 2 Q.B. 168; *Shaw* v. *Holland* [1913] 2 K.B. 15. It is extremely difficult, if not impossible, to reconcile these two cases and *Singer* v. *Elliott* (1888) 4 T.L.R. 524 with the decisions as to the filling up of an incomplete bill indorsed by way of guarantee under s. 20 of the Bills of Exchange Act 1882 in *Glenie* v. *Bruce-Smith* [1908] 1 K.B. 268; *Re Gooch* [1921] 2 K.B. 593; *Bernardi* v. *National Sales Corporation* [1931] 2 K.B. 188; *McCall* v. *Hargreaves* [1932] 2 K.B. 423. It is submitted, following the opinion of Goddard J. in the last named case that *Jenkins* v. *Coomber* and *Shaw* v. *Holland, supra,* are no longer good law. This appears to be borne out by *Yeoman Credit Ltd.* v. *Gregory* [1963] 1 W.L.R. 343. See *Byles, op. cit.,* at pp. 168 *et seq.* especially at 171, 172, where the problem is extensively discussed.

[8] *Wilkinson* v. *Unwin* (1881) 7 Q.B.D. 736. See also *Re Gooch, supra; Yeoman Credit Ltd.* v. *Gregory, supra.*

[9] *Holmes* v. *Durkee* (1883) C.B. & E. 23.

[10] See *supra.,* p. 9.

[11] *Bluck* v. *Gompertz* (1852) 7 Exch. 862.

[12] See *supra* at p. 3.

[13] *Oriental Finance Corporation* v. *Overend Gurney & Co.* (1874) L.R. 7 H.L. 348. See too *Davies* v. *Stainbank* (1855) 6 De G. M. & G. 679; *Pooley* v. *Harradine* (1857) 7 E. & B. 431; *Greenough* v. *McLelland* (1860) 30 L.J.Q.B. 15. The recognition of accommodation bills was much regretted by many judges, including Lord Eldon. See *Bank of Ireland* v. *Beresford* (1818) 6 Dow. 233; *Ex p. Glendinning* (1819) Buck. 517; and *Cf. Fentum* v. *Pocock* (1813) 5 Taunt. 192; *Nichols* v. *Norris* (1831) 3 B. & Ad. 41, note; *Harrison* v. *Courtauld* (1832) 3 B. & Ad. 36.

An accommodation party to a bill is defined by section 28(1) of the Bills of Exchange Act 1882 as a person who has signed a bill as drawer, acceptor or indorser, without receiving value therefor, and for the purpose of lending his name to some other person. Section 28(2) provides that he will be liable on a bill to a holder for value and that it is immaterial, when such holder took the bill that he knew such party to be an accommodation party or not.[14] The underlying intention to a transaction whereby one party signs without consideration for the accommodation of another is that the latter should be at liberty to raise money, *e.g.* by negotiating the bill, but should be in a position to meet the bill if called on at maturity.[15] By virtue of the foregoing provisions in the 1882 Act, a bill will only be a true accommodation bill when the accommodation party signs as acceptor and not in any other capacity.[16] If the party who is accommodated is in default in failing to provide funds to meet the bill at maturity, he must indemnify the acceptor or any other party compelled to pay the holder.[17]

A holder who has made advances on an accommodation bill without discounting it outright, with or without notice, can recover no more than the amount of the advances[18]; although, if the accommodation party is bankrupt, the holder, if he took without notice, can prove for the full amount and take dividends to the extent of his advances.[19] This rule applies where the bill has been indorsed to the creditor as security for a debt, and rests upon the principle that the excess would be recovered only for the indorser or depositor who, as the party accommodated, would have no right to recover anything.[20]

---

[14] See generally *Oriental Finance Corporation* v. *Overend Gurney & Co., supra,* affirmed *sub. nom. Overend Gurney & Co. (Liquidators)* v. *Oriental Finance Corporation (Liquidators)* (1874) L.R. 7 H.L. 348.

[15] *Sleigh* v. *Sleigh* (1850) 5 Exch. 514. See the discussion in *Byles, op. cit.,* at pp. 221, 222.

[16] *Scott* v. *Lifford* (1808) 1 Camp. 246. The maker of an accommodation note will on similar principles be a surety. See *Bechervaise* v. *Lewis* (1872) L.R. 7 C.P. 372.

[17] The acceptor will also enjoy the right to benefit from securities belonging to the party accommodated in the hands of the holder. See *Bechervaise* v. *Lewis, supra; cf. Duncan Fox & Co.* v. *North and South Wales Bank* (1880) 6 App. Cas. 1. The indemnity may be extended to include the rights of an action fought unsuccessfully against the holder. See *Bagnall* v. *Andrews* (1830) 7 Bing. 217 at 222 *per* Tindal C.J. *Cf. Beech* v. *Jones* (1848) 5 C.B. 696. See also *Garrard* v. *Cottrell* (1847) 10 Q.B. 679; *Hammond & Co.* v. *Bussey* (1887) 20 Q.B.D. 79. For the manner in which the indemnity is enforced, see *Sleigh* v. *Sleigh* (1850) 5 Exch. 514 and *Re Fox Walker & Co., Ex p. Bishop* (1880) 15 Ch.D. 400.

[18] *Wiffen* v. *Roberts* (1795) 1 Esp. 261. (Note however the caution expressed by *Byles, op. cit.,* at p. 191 on this decision.); *Smith* v. *Knox* (1880) 3 Esp. 46; *Charles* v. *Marsden* (1808) 1 Taunt. 224; *Simpson* v. *Clarke* (1835) 2 C.M. & R. 342; *Ex p. Newton* (1880) 16 Ch.D. 330. Quite apart from the provisions of s. 28(2) of the 1882 Act, it is no defence to an action upon an accommodation bill that it was negotiated when overdue, unless the negotiation was a fraud upon the accommodation party. *Charles* v. *Marsden, supra; Sturtevant* v. *Ford* (1842) 4 M. & G. 101; *Re Overend Gurney & Co., Ex p. Swan* (1868) L.R. 8 Eq. 344.

[19] *Ex p. Newton, supra.*

[20] *Ibid.* at p. 336.

Contribution

Two or more persons agreeing to becoming parties to an instrument for the accommodation of a third party will be treated as co-sureties entitled to contribution *inter se* irrespective of the order of priority of their names on the instrument.[21] Further an accommodation party will be entitled to contribution from another such party even though he was unaware of the latter's capacity when he became such a party.[22]

Discharge[23]

Generally the holder of a bill of exchange need not actively or diligently pursue the acceptor, but if he extinguishes or suspends his right of action against the acceptor, or contracts with the latter so to do, the drawer and indorsers will be released, in the absence of agreement to the contrary, *e.g.* where it is agreed that judgment is to be given to the holder in the case of default, on the same terms as those to which he would otherwise have been entitled, the drawer is not released.[24]

A covenant not to sue the acceptor will generally discharge the drawer and indorsers, unless such agreement is made without consideration.[25] Similarly, an acceptor, known only by the holder to be a surety, will be released if the holder gives time to the party accommodated.[26]

The taking of a fresh bill from the acceptor in lieu of a dishonoured bill will similarly discharge the other parties, unless it is given as a second or collateral security.[27]

However, no release of the indorser will be effected if he consents to it,[28] and this will be so if the consent is expressed or can be inferred after the state of facts giving rise to the release.[29]

---

[21] *Reynolds* v. *Wheeler* (1861) 30 L.J.C.P. 350 approved in *Macdonald* v. *Whitfield* (1883) 8 App. Cas. 733; *Godsell* v. *Lloyd* (1911) 27 T.L.R. 383; *Lacombe* v. *Labonté* (1920) Q.R. 59 S.C. 17. Note too *Dering* v. *Winchelsea* (1880) 2 B. & P. 270; *Mayhew* v. *Crickett* (1818) 2 Swanst. 185 for the general rules regarding contribution showing that there will still be mutual contribution even though the same debt be secured by different instruments executed by different sureties.

[22] *Reynolds* v. *Wheeler, supra.* See the other cases cited in the preceding note.

[23] See generally Chap. 8 where several of the cases cited there involve the rights of holders of bills, *e.g. Moss* v. *Hall* (1850) 5 Ex. 46; *Philpot* v. *Briant* (1828) 4 Bing. 717; *Clarke* v. *Birley* (1888) 41 Ch.D. 422.

[24] *Kennard* v. *Knott* (1842) 4 M. & G. 474; *Michael* v. *Myers* (1843) 6 M. & G. 702. Cf. *Rayner* v. *Fussey* (1859) 28 L.J. Exch. 132. See also *Abrey* v. *Crux* (1869) L.R. 5 C.P. 37.

[25] See, *e.g. Arundel Bank* v. *Goble* (1816) 2 Chit. 364; *Clarke* v. *Birley* (1888) 41 Ch.D. 422.

[26] See *Re Acraman, ex p. Webster* (1847) De G. 414.

[27] *Gordon* v. *Calvert* (1828) 4 Russ. 581; *Calvert* v. *Gordon* (1828) 7 B. & C. 809. See also *Twopenny* v. *Young* (1824) 3 B. & C. 208; *Bedford* v. *Deakin* (1818) 2 B. & Ald. 210.

[28] See, *e.g. Clark* v. *Devlin* (1803) 3 B. & P. 363.

[29] See, *e.g. Stevens* v. *Lynch* (1810) 12 East. 38. Cf. *Withall* v. *Masterman* (1809) 2 Camp. 179.

Aval

In continental systems, a stranger to a bill can undertake liability as a guarantor by signing it. This is known as an *aval* and is not recognised in English law.[30]

The Statute of Frauds requires guarantees in English law to be in writing.[31] Moreover an *aval* is a security which passes with the bill and therefore breaches the necessity in English law to have privity between the surety and the creditor.

However, as has already been discussed above, section 56 of the Bills of Exchange Act 1882 imposes the liability of an indorser upon a stranger signing a bill regardless of the question of the Statute of Frauds.

The equivalent of section 56 in Canada has been held in *Robinson* v. *Mann*[32] to have introduced the principle of the *aval* into English law.[33] In Australia in *Ferrier* v. *Stewart*[34] the equivalent provision of section 56 of the English statute was held to make a stranger liable where she had indorsed the bill at the payee's insistence, the latter subsequently indorsing his name both above and below hers. The stranger was estopped from denying either that she was an indorser or that the payee was a holder in due course.[35]

2. *Cross Acceptances and Bankruptcy*

Specific exchange of acceptances

The simple case of one accommodation bill does not differ from an ordinary guarantee: namely, the accommodating party, even though he may be an acceptor of the bill, is entitled as between himself and the party accommodated to have it taken up by the latter and be indemnified against his liability upon it. However, where two parties enter into a specific exchange of accommodation acceptances, each acceptance is regarded as being the consideration for the other, and each acceptor is bound to pay his own acceptance, his remedy being against the drawer on the

[30] *Per* Lord Blackburn in *Steele* v. *M'Kinlay* (1880) 5 App. Cas. 754, 772, citing *Jackson* v. *Hudson* (1810) 2 Camp. 447, 448. See also *Moti & Co.* v. *Cassim's Trustee* [1924] A.D. 720 (South Africa). In South Africa, Roman-Dutch law recognises the principle of the *aval*. See generally Cowen, *Law of Negotiable Instruments in South Africa* (1966), Chap. 13; the Geneva Convention (*Uniform Law on Bills of Exchange and Promissory Notes*: Convention No. 3313: Geneva, June 7, 1930) upon which continental and some other systems are based and which expressly provides for *avals* in Chapter IV, Articles 30, 31 and 32.

[31] See generally Chapter 3.

[32] (1901) 31 S.C.R. 484.

[33] At p. 486. See also *Grant* v. *Scott* (1919) 59 S.C.R. 227, 230 and see discussion in Byles, *op. cit.*, pp. 172 *et seq.*

[34] (1912) 15 C.L.R. 32.

[35] See to similar effect in New Zealand *Cook* v. *Fenton* (1892) 11 N.Z.L.R. 505; *Erickssen* v. *Bunting* (1901) 20 N.Z.L.R. 388.

other bill and not as surety in the bill accepted.[36] It was finally settled that the drawer holding the bill accepted by the other party might prove in the bankruptcy of the acceptor, provided the counter acceptance was taken up.[37]

Acceptances not specifically exchanged

Where, however, two parties have mutually accommodated each other, but have not specifically exchanged acceptances, one in consideration of the other, all the bills must be treated as strictly accommodation bills, and the acceptor paying any of them can prove upon the footing that he has made such payment as surety.[38]

Double bankruptcy

Where acceptances for mutual accommodations have been exchanged between two persons both of whom are bankrupt, neither trustee can prove against the other estate in respect of any of such bills which may have remained in the hands of the bankrupt whose estate he represents, until the holders of all the bills have been paid in full. This is so even though, by reason of the unequal negotiation of bills by the two parties, greater damage arises out of the accommodation transactions to one estate than to the other.[39]

This rule also applies to prevent a proof being made on behalf of the estate of a bankrupt who has given accommodation acceptances (which have been discounted and are outstanding) against the estate of the drawer of other accommodation bills on a third party given by that drawer to the acceptor of the first-named accommodation bills in exchange for such acceptances.[40]

The rule in Ex p. Walker

The basis of this rule, as set out in the previous paragraph, appears to be that the only ascertainable debt which could arise

---

[36] *Rolfe* v. *Caslon* (1795) 2 H.Bl. 571; *Cowley* v. *Dunlop* (1798) 7 Term Rep. 565; *Buckler* v. *Buttirant* (1802) 3 East 72.

[37] See *Re Bowness and Padmore* (1789) 1 Cooke's *Bankruptcy Laws* (8th ed.), 183; *Ex p. Rawson* (1821) Jac. 274 *per* Lord Eldon at 278. The history of this development is set out at pp. 329–330 of the third edition of this work. See also Byles, *op. cit.* at pp. 394–396.

[38] See *Ex p. Read* (1822) 1 Gl. & J. 224.

[39] *Ex p. Walker* (1798) 4 Ves. 373; *Ex p. Earle* (1801) 5 Ves. 833.

[40] *Ex p. Solarte* (1832) 2 D. & Ch. 261 explained in *Ex p. Solarte* (1834) 3 D. & Ch. 419. Note too *Sarratt* v. *Austin* (1811) 4 Taunt 200. Byles, *op. cit.*, at p. 395 suggests that s. 30(3) of the Bankruptcy Act 1914 may enable a party to prove a bill not yet due as a contingent debt even though his own counter-bill remains undue and unpaid.

between the parties out of the mutual accommodation transactions is in respect of the balance which would result if both parties remained solvent and the bills duly met and accounts adjusted.[41] Otherwise the proportion in which the liability will fall on the two estates will depend upon the respective dividends which they may pay, resulting in a possible double proof, *i.e.* a proof by the party accommodating, in addition to a proof by the holders of the bills. Proof should therefore be allowable only in respect of any balance outstanding as between the parties or bills actually paid.[42]

Where one estate shows a surplus

In *Ex p. Rawson*[43] it was stated by Lord Eldon that in the event of there being a surplus upon the estate suffering less than the other, owing to the accommodation given, the rule in *Ex p. Walker*[44] would not apply but relief would be given to the other estate out of the surplus.[44]

Rule inapplicable except in cases of cross-accommodation

The rule in *Ex p. Walker* will also not apply where one party only has given accommodation paper[45] and secondly where the person that seeks to prove is not the same as the person who made the arrangement for the exchange of acceptances.[46]

Where A gave B his own accommodation acceptances and B then indorsed them to C in exchange for acceptances of C, and all three became bankrupt, it was held that, though no proof could be made on behalf of the estate of C against the estate of B[47] (with whom he had made the exchange) as indorser of the acceptances of A in the hands of C at the date of his bankruptcy, this did not prevent such proof being made against the estate of A, the acceptor, even though first there had been cross-acceptances by B to A, which were outstanding, and secondly dividends were kept in hand pending the final adjustment of the equities between the three estates.[47]

---

[41] Lord Eldon who argued *Ex p. Walker* (1798) 4 Ves. 373 before Lord Loughborough, who in turn applied the rule in *Ex p. Earle* (1801) 5 Ves. 833, said later that none of the counsel in the case understood the judgment. See *Ex p. Rawson* (1821) Jac. 274 at p. 278.

[42] See *Ex p. Read* (1822) 1 Gl. & J. 224; *Ex p. Macredie* (1873) L.R. 8 Ch. 533.

[43] (1821) Jac. 274.

[44] (1798) 4 Ves. 373. Except in the case of a surplus, Lord Eldon did not question the rule in *Ex p. Walker* and it was further followed in *Ex p. Solarte* (1834) 3 D. & Ch. 419 and *Ex p. Laforest* (1833) 2 D. & Ch. 199.

[45] *Ex p. Metcalfe* (1805) 11 Ves. 404.

[46] *Ex p. Cama* (1874) L.R. 9 Ch. App. 686, 689. See also *Ex p. Macredie* (1873) L.R. 8 Ch. 535, 539.

[47] See *Ex p. Solarte* (1832) 2 D. & Ch. 261 explained in *Ex p. Solarte* (1834) 3 D. & Ch. 419. *Cf. Ex p. Metcalfe* (1805) 11 Ves. 404.

The estate of a bankrupt indorser may stand in the place of the holder, after the latter has received 100p in the £, for any future dividends upon the estate of the acceptor to the extent of dividends already paid to the holder by the estate of the indorser, even though the bill was received by the indorser from a previous holder in exchange merely for his own acceptance given to that holder.[48]

Proof on bills of exchange generally

If a bill is indorsed by a debtor as security for the debt the indorsee can prove in the bankruptcy of the acceptor for the full amount of the bill, even though less may be owing to him from the indorser.[49] This is true, at any rate if he took without notice, even though the bill was accepted for accommodation,[49] or, if for value, even though, as between drawer and acceptor, less than the full amount of the bill would be recoverable.[50] If one person, to secure the debt of another, accepts or indorses a bill direct to the creditor, no more can be proved against his estate than the amount of the debt secured.[51]

If an accommodation bill is indorsed to his creditor by the party accommodated, the creditor having notice that it was an accommodation bill, it may be that the creditor can only prove against the party accommodating for the amount due to him from the indorser.[52] If the benefit of a guarantee for payment of a promissory note is transferred with the note, the transferee cannot prove in the bankruptcy of the guarantor but he can claim that the amount of the guarantee be brought into the account between the parties to it, and he can stand in the place of the transferor in respect of any balance found due to him to the extent of the guarantee.[53]

---

[48] *Ex p. Greenwood* (1834) Buck. 237.

[49] *Ex p. Moxham* (1802) 6 Ves. 449; *Ex p. Philips* (1840) 1 M.D. & De G. 232; *Ex p. Newton* (1880) 16 Ch. D. 330.

[50] *Ex p. Newton, supra.*

[51] *Ex p. Reader* (1819) Buck 381.

[52] See *Ex p. Gomersall* (1875) 1 Ch. D. 137, at p. 142. This in substance would be the same case as *Ex p. Reader, supra. Ex p. Newton* (1880) 16 Ch. D. 330 does not deal with such a case to which it is probable that the dicta in the Gomersall case were confirmed. The latter case really turned on the fact that the bills were, to the knowledge of the holder, issued fraudulently in contemplation of bankruptcy by both drawer and acceptor. See same case in the House of Lords, *sub nom. Jones* v. *Gordon* (1887) 2 App. Cas. 616.

[53] *Re Barrington* (1804) 2 Sch. & Lef. 112. Cf. *Re Barned's Banking Co.* (1871) L.R. 6 Ch. 388.

CHAPTER 14

LANDLORD AND TENANT

Continuation of liability

In the case of a business tenancy protected under Part II of the Landlord and Tenant Act 1954, most of the contractual terms survive the contractual termination date of the lease.[1] However, unless the contrary is specifically agreed, the surety's obligations will end at the contractual termination date.[2] This applies to future rent or breaches of the lease, but the surety remains liable for past breaches.

Where the landlord gives notice to quit and then withdraws it with the tenant's consent, this gives rise to a new lease under which the surety under the old lease is not liable.[3]

Disclaimer

A disclaimer by a trustee in bankruptcy or a liquidator of a lease held by the principal debtor releases the surety[4] from the date of the disclaimer. Liability remains in respect of rent or other liabilities accruing due prior to that date. The surety may, if he considers the lease to have potential value, seek to have it vested in him.[5]

Although the original lessee, if he has assigned the lease, may be thought of as being in a position analogous to that of a surety for the liabilities under the lease,[6] he is not discharged by a disclaimer by the assignee's trustee in bankruptcy or liquidator.[7]

---

[1] s.24, Landlord and Tenant Act 1954; *Bolton Engineering Ltd.* v. *Graham and Sons Ltd.* |1957| 1 Q.B. 159.

[2] *Junction Estates Ltd.* v. *Cope* (1974) 27 P. & C.R. 482 (McKenna J.).

[3] *Giddens* v. *Dodd* (1856) 3 Drew 485; *Tayleur* v. *Wildin* (1868) L.R. 3 Exch. 303. See p. 58, *ante*.

[4] *Stacey* v. *Hill* |1901| 1 K.B. 660 (C.A.); *D. Morris and Sons Ltd.* v. *Jeffrey's* (1932) 148 L.T. 56; *Re Katherine et Cie. Ltd.* |1932| 1 Ch. 70. In the case of a winding-up, this may be a factor persuading the court to refuse leave to disclaim. In a bankruptcy, unlike winding-up, the lease vests in the trustee and he is exposed to possible personal liability if the requisite disclaimer is refused. Therefore the release of the surety is not likely to lead to a refusal of leave to disclaim. See pp. 209, 210, *ante*.

[5] See s. 54, Bankruptcy Act 1914; Companies Act 1948, s.323 (6).

[6] *Re Russell* (1885) 29 Ch. D. 254; *Baynton* v. *Morgan* (1888) 21 Q.B.D. 101; (1888) 22 Q.B.D. 74.

[7] *Warnford Investments* v. *Duckworth* |1979| Ch. 127. See also *Harding* v. *Preece* (1882) 9 Q.B.D. 281.

Revocation of guarantee

The surety under a lease cannot normally revoke his guarantee, since the consideration has moved once and for all.[8] However, in the case of a weekly tenancy it has been held that the guarantee is revocable.[9]

In the case of, *e.g.* a yearly tenancy, the surety may face the unenviable prospect of indeterminate liability if neither party to the lease wishes to give notice. It is an undecided question here whether the surety can compel the termination of the principal liability by requiring the giving of notice under the lease. Clearly a surety should attempt to require express provision for this.

Discharge by variation of principal liability

A surety is discharged by any material variation in the principal obligation. Materiality is often difficult to judge in this context and the surety may well be held to be discharged if the variation is capable of being material without being put to proof of materiality.

In *Holme* v. *Brunskill* [10] the surety guaranteed the redelivery of a flock of sheep let with a farm. Later, the landlord accepted the surrender of one field and made a small reduction in rent. The Court of Appeal by a majority held that the variation discharged the surety, since it could not without inquiry be said to be incapable of prejudicing the surety, and the question of materiality could not be litigated.[11]

Construction

The lease may provide a convenant by the surety that the tenant will pay the rent on the due dates and that if the tenant failed to make payment, the surety would have to pay (a) after default for n days by the tenant and (b) "on demand." Such words are construed so as to (i) override the general words of liability and to (ii) make the period of default by the tenant and the demand upon the surety preconditions of the surety's liability.[12]

---

[8] *Lloyd's* v. *Harper* (1880) 16. Ch. D. 290 at p. 319. See pp. 62, 63 *ante.*
[9] *Wingfield* v. *De St. Croix* (1919) 35 T.L.R.432.
[10] (1878) 3 Q.B.D. 495.
[11] Brett L.J. dissented on the basis that a variation not violating a specific condition of the suretyship must be proved to be material to effect a discharge. The jury at the trial had found the variation to be immaterial.
[12] *Sicklemore* v. *Thistleton* (1817) 6 M. & S. 9.

Securities held by landlord

By the rule of equity and under section 5 of the Mercantile Law Amendment Act 1856, the paying surety is entitled to any remedies and any securities held by the landlord over the tenant and his property in order to enforce the surety's right to contribution. However, the landlord's right to distrain for rent has been held to be neither one of the "remedies of the creditor" nor a "security" within the section.[13] On the other hand, a surety for the performance of convenants in a lease is entitled to be recouped out of the land in respect of payments made on account of rent.[14]

Rent review

A surety for rent seems to have no right to participate in a rent review. It is submitted that the surety should be permitted to compel the tenant to participate in the review or to allow the surety to participate in the tenant's name. An express term to this effect in the lease would clearly be desirable from the surety's point of view.

Relief from forfeiture

A surety for rent in the ordinary way has no right to seek relief from forfeiture, and again a clause enabling him to act in the principal's name may be desirable. A similar result has been achieved where the lessee agreed with the surety that the lessee would if called upon execute a mortgage of the lease. This was held to be an agreement for an underlease within section 146(5) of the Law of Property Act 1925 enabling the surety to apply for relief from forfeiture.[15]

Discharge of other party's liability

Where one person may be forced to discharge a liability which belongs primarily to another party, there will on recognised principles[16] be a right of reimbursement sometimes thought of as being akin to suretyship. For example, where a sub-lessee is compelled to pay sums to the head lessor in respect of rent due from the intermediate landlord, the sub-lessee may deduct such sums from his rent to the intermediate landlord.[17] Moreover, it

---

[13] *Re Russell* (1885) 29. Ch. D. 254.
[14] *Lord Harberton* v. *Bennett* (1829) Beat. 386.
[15] *Re Good's Lease* [1954] 1 W.L.R. 309.
[16] See Goff and Jones, *The Law of Restitution* (2nd ed., 1978), Chap. 12; p. 134, *ante*.
[17] *Carter* v. *Carter* (1829) 7 L.J. (O.S.) C.P.141.

would seem that a person in the sub-lessee's position can claim to be subrogated to the head landlord's securities and rights against the intermediate landlord.[18] In *Re Downer Enterprises Ltd.*[19] a lease was assigned to the plaintiff and then by him on to a company which went into liquidation. The plaintiff upon paying the arrears of rent, was held entitled to be subrogated to the landlord's right, in the circumstances of the case, to have part of the arrears paid out of the company's assets as an expense of the winding-up. This was because as between the plaintiff and the company, the company was ultimately liable.[20]

Mesne profits

A guarantor of rent and the performance of a lessee's covenants will not be held liable for mesne profits, or in general matters arising after the termination of the lease.[21] Nevertheless, he will be held liable for breach of a covenant to yield up possession.[22]

Privity

There must be privity of contract between a creditor and a surety in order to make the latter liable. Accordingly, where guarantors covenanted with a lessor and its "successors and assigns," this was not held to enable the lessor to sue without an assignment of the benefit of the guarantee.[23]

Non-disclosure

Although bound to give truthful answers to questions put to him regarding a tenant for whom a surety is taken,[24] the lessor is under no positive duty to disclose material facts affecting the tenant's reliability, *e.g.* the fact that the tenant still owed rent to the lessor from a previous tenancy,[25] unless the circumstances are such that the surety might naturally have expected those facts not to rise.[26]

---

[18] *Re Downer Enterprises Ltd.* [1974] 1 W.L.R 1460, *per* Pennycuick J. at p.1468 C.

[19] [1974] 1 W.L.R. 1460.

[20] Pennycuick J. [1974] 1 W.L.R. at p.1468 considered that the principles enunciated in *Duncan Fox and Co.* v. *North and South Wales Bank* (1880) 6 App. Cas. 1 by Lord Selborne at p.10 and Lord Blackburn at p.19 applied not only to guarantees but to any situation of primary and secondary liability, "primary" meaning ultimate liability.

[21] *Associated Dairies* v. *Pierce* (1981) 259. E.G. 562.

[22] *Ibid.*

[23] *Sacher Investments Pty. Ltd.* v. *Forma Stereo Consultants Pty. Ltd.* [1976] 1 N.S. W.L.R. 5, and see p. 71, *ante.*

[24] See pp. 122, 123, *ante.*

[25] *Roper* v. *Cox* (1882) 10 L.R. Ir. 200.

[26] See p. 123, *ante.*

Chapter 15

BUILDING CONTRACTS[1]

A guarantee may relate to the performance of any party to the building contract. The standard form of building contract such as the JCT form does not provide for sureties, so that typically a guarantee will be a collateral document, *e.g.* some sort of "bond." As in other types of guarantees the need for writing is present unless the surety's promise can be construed as an indemnity undertaking primary liability.[2]

Non-disclosure

The employer's duty (if any) on the making of any implied representation to the surety, *e.g.* as to the nature of contracted works to be performed or the prevailing conditions, depends on the particulars of each transaction.[3] The guarantor is said to look, in the usual situation, no further than the skill and experience of the contractor[3] and there is no duty on the employer to reveal difficulty in the terrain.

Extent of liability

In the case of a guarantee of the contractor's performance, the surety's liability will in normal circumstances be interpreted to cover only the building works and not any other, albeit related, transactions with the employer, *e.g.* a loan to enable the contractor to carry out or complete the works.[3] The situation may be otherwise where the surety knows of the related transaction, *e.g.* where it is made a term of the building contract or is contained in a collateral document which accompanies it. Again, where a surety guarantees the building work his guarantee is not normally construed so as to extend to the consequences of the contractor's fraud.[4] However, the contrac-

---

[1] See also Keating, *Building Contracts* (4th ed. 1978), especially p.130–134.

[2] *Lakeman* v. *Mountstephen* (1874) L.R. 7 H.L. 17.

[3] *Trade Indemnity Co.* v. *Workington Harbour and Dock Board* [1937] A.C.1 (H.L.). With regard to the question of the fitness of the site, the employer does not normally warrant this to the contractor: see *Appleby* v. *Myers* (1867) L.R. 2 C.P. 651. The court may imply a term for further payments where the difficult nature of the site requires further work.

[4] *Kingston-upon-Hull* v. *Harding* [1892] 2 Q.B. 494 (C.A) The guarantors guaranteed that the contractors would "well and truly" execute the contract and this was held to apply to a situation where the certificate of completion was obtained by fraudulent concealment of defects.

tor's fraud is not necessarily a defence for the surety, if on the true construction of the guarantee the guaranteed liability has arisen.[4]

Completion of performance

The usual rule is that when the principal debtor has completed his performance the surety is discharged. In building terms the performance may be "complete" but the building contract may require the architect to certify certain stages of completion by means of certificates, *e.g.* as in the JCT form. Where a building contract, unlike the JCT form, does not specify any stages of certified completion, actual completion may be taken as complete performance by the contractor of the principal obligation so as to discharge the surety.[5] Where the building contract specifies certain stages of certified completion but the guarantee is silent as to which stage is meant, it is submitted that the Final Certificate should be taken as the stage of complete performance for the purpose of the guarantee.

Discharge otherwise than by completion

It occurs from time to time that the building contract determines, not according to the provisions of the agreement, but by a repudiatory breach by one party accepted by the other. This type of determination will not release the surety of the repudiating party who remains liable for the losses caused by the repudiation.[6] Nor is a surety of a contractor bound by the contractor fraudulently obtaining such a certificate.[7]

Another possible cause of the discharge of a surety for the contractor other than by performance is where there has been some material non-disclosure by the employer which alters the nature or an important quality of the work to be executed, *e.g.* where the employers failed to disclose that the supervision of the work was to be shared with the surveyor of an outside party.[8] However, where the contract itself anticipates possible difficulties, *e.g.* by warning the contractor itself to make proper inspections of the site, unexpected difficulties arising from the nature of the site may not enable a surety to treat himself as discharged.[9]

---

[5] *Lewis* v. *Hoare* (1881) 44 L.T. 66 (H.L.).
[6] *Moschi* v. *Lep Air Services Ltd* [1973] A.C. 331 (H.L).
[7] *Kingston-upon-Hull* v. *Harding* [1892] 2 Q.B. 494 (C.A.).
[8] *Stiff* v. *Eastbourne Local Board* (1869) 20 L.T. 339.
[9] *Trade Indemnity Co.* v. *Workington Harbour and Dock Board* [1937] A.C. 1 (H.L.).

As in other situations, conduct by the creditor which pre-
judices the surety's position will discharge the surety.[10] For
example, a surety for a contractor will be discharged where the
employer has a contractual duty but fails to carry it out, *e.g.* a
duty to superintend the work[11] or to insure the works against
fire.[12] Moreover, where the building contract provides for the
retention of sums which act both as security for completion and
as a form of pressure upon the contractor, a premature payment
to the contractor without his surety's consent will discharge the
surety.[13]

A surety may also be released by variations in the contractual
obigations agreed between the employer and contractor without
the surety's consent, *e.g.* an extension of the contractual time for
performance.[14] It should be remembered here that a standard
form building contract will normally make express provision for
extensions of time.

Guarantee of employer's payments

Where a surety guarantees payment by the employer of the
contract price, the contractor in the absence of provision for
stage payments cannot normally recover against the surety
unless he can show entire completion.[15] However, in a case
where guarantors guaranteed payment for the building works
by instalments, and the employers failed to make payment,
giving the contractors the right to rescind, which they exercised,
the guarantors were held liable to pay the accrued instalment.[16]
The guarantors had contended that the contractor's rescission
terminated the contract and destroyed their right to recover the
instalment as opposed to recovery of damages. They argued
moreover that such damages were not recoverable under the
guarantee as sums "due or to become due" under the contract.
The House of Lords rejected these arguments on the basis that
(a) the instalment accrued due prior to rescission was recoverable from the employer and therefore due under the guarantee,
alternatively (b) the object of the guarantee was to enable
recovery of the instalment irrespective of the position between
the contractors and employers.

---

[10] *Kingston-upon-Hull* v. *Harding* [1892] 2 Q.B. 494.
[11] *Ibid.*
[12] *Watts* v. *Shuttleworth* (1861) 7 H. & N.353.
[13] *Calvert* v. *London Dock Co.* (1838) 2 Keen 638, 7 L.J. Ch. 90.
[14] *Rees* v. *Barrington* (1795) 2 Ves. Jun. 540; *Harrison* v. *Seymour* (1866) L.R. 1 C.P. 518.
[15] *Eshelby* v. *Federated European Bank Limited* [1932] 1 K.B. 432 (C.A.).
[16] *Hyundai Heavy Industries Co. Ltd.* v. *Papadopoulos* [1980] 1 W.L.R. 1129 (shipbuilding
contract).

Procedure

Where the surety has entered into a bond for a contractor's performance, as soon as the contractor commits a breach, the employer can sue the surety and claim judgment for the whole amount of the bond, as long as some damage occasioned by the breach can be shown.[17] Execution can only issue for the amount of damages proved, but the judgment remains as security for the recovery of damages for future breaches.[18] If the initial action fails, future actions can be brought in respect of the same breach, albeit supported by different evidence.[19]

---

[17] *Workington Harbour & Dock Trade* v. *Trade Indemnity Co. Ltd. (No. 2).* [1938] 2 All E.R. 101 (H.L.) *per* Lord Atkin at p. 105 E.
[18] *Ibid.* p. 105 E–F.
[19] *Ibid.* p. 105 F–H.

CHAPTER 16

CONSUMER CREDIT

Introduction

The Consumer Credit Act 1974[1] has been enacted to reflect the fact that in many modern commercial contexts, the notion of freedom of contract is more imaginary than real. Without abolishing the discrepancy in bargaining power it has imposed certain formalities and standards of disclosure which must be satisfied to render a transaction enforceable.

Definitions

Continuing the tradition laid down in earlier hire purchase legislation, the 1974 Act makes no distinction between contracts of guarantee and contracts of indemnity.[2] "Security" is defined in section 189(1) as:

" . . . a mortgage, charge, pledge, bond, debenture, indemnity, guarantee, bill, note or other right provided by the debtor or hirer, or at his request (express or implied), to secure the carrying out of the obligations of the debtor or hirer under the agreement."

A surety is defined as one by whom any security as above defined is provided or the person to whom his rights and duties in relation to the security have passed by assignment or operation of law.[3] This is a widely drawn definition and can obviously include not only guarantors and indemnifiers, but even the debtor or hirer himself.

---

[1] For the background to the Act see the Report of the Committee on Consumer Credit (The Crowther Report) Cmnd. 4596 (1974), and generally Guest & Lloyd, *The Encyclopaedia of Consumer Credit Law* (1975). Not all the Act's provisions are in force at the date of this edition. Note too the increasing importance of distinguishing between commercial and consumer guarantees as to which see, *e.g.* British Columbia Law Refom Commission Report on Guarantees of Consumer Debts 1979 ("British Columbia Report"). So-called recourse agreements are excluded from the British Columbia Report. The relevant sections of the 1974 Act are set out in Appendix 2.

[2] See *e.g.* Hire Purchase Act 1965. Note s. 113(7) of the Act which ensures that where a debtor or hirer is for example, a minor, any contract of indemnity will not be unenforceable merely by reason of his minority, as if it would be if it were a contract of guarantee. See *ante*, p.70.

[3] s. 189(1) of the Act.

Scope of the Act

The Act regulates the supplying of credit not exceeding £5,000 to individuals (including sole traders and partnerships) in the form of so-called consumer credit agreements[4] and consumer hire agreements.[5] The Act also imposes a system of licensing in respect of credit and hire businesses dealing with such agreements.[6] It further regulates the form and content of such agreements[7] and modifies the common law rules in respect of those to whom notice of withdrawal may be given and the consequences of withdrawal.

Formal requirements

The Act does not however affect or modify the basic formal requirements that guarantees be evidenced in writing and signed by the surety or his agent, but it does require the creditor under a regulated agreement for fixed sum credit[8] or running-account credit[9] and the owner under a regulated consumer hire agreement in relation to which a security as defined in the Act is required, after receiving a request in writing to that effect from a surety as well as payment of the statutory fee, to give the latter a statement of the account as between himself and the debtor or hirer, in the same terms as the statement given to the debtor or hirer.[10] The creditor or owner must also give the surety first a copy of the executed agreement if any, and any other document referred to in it, and a copy of the security instrument, if any.[11] Any failure to comply will prevent the creditor from enforcing the security and will after one month's default, constitute a criminal offence.[12] Non-commercial agreements are exempt.[13]

The creditor or owner of a regulated agreement must also in the same way, give to the debtor or hirer a copy of any security instrument[14] executed in relation to the agreement *after* the making of the agreement.

---

[4] Defined in s. 8 of the Act.

[5] Defined in s. 15 of the Act, *e.g.* ordinary domestic rental agreements.

[6] See Part III of the Act (see ss. 21 *et seq.*).

[7] See ss. 60 *et seq.* of the Act. *Cf.* the recommendations of the British Columbia Report.

[8] Defined in s. 10(1) and 189(1) of the Act, *e.g.* bank loans or hire purchase transactions.

[9] *Ibid., e.g.* bank overdrafts, shop budget accounts or credit cards.

[10] ss. 107–109 of the Act. For the requirements regarding the contents of such statements, see ss. 77 *et seq.* of the Act.

[11] *Ibid.*

[12] *Ibid.*

[13] Defined in s. 189(1) of the Act as not made by a creditor or owner in the course of a business carried on by him.

[14] Defined and prescribed by ss. 105, 189(1) of the Act.

Termination

Section 98(1) of the Act provides that a creditor or hirer is not entitled to terminate a regulated agreement except by or after giving the debtor seven days' notice of the termination, but that section will not apply to termination by reason of any breach by the debtor or hirer of the agreement.[15] In cases of breach, a default notice must be served. Section 76(1) provides that a creditor or owner is not entitled to enforce a term of a regulated agreement by (a) demanding earlier payment of any sum, or (b) recovering possession of any goods or land, or (c) treating any right conferred on the debtor or hirer by the agreement as terminated, restricted or deferred, except by or after giving the debtor or hirer not less than seven days' notice of his intention to do so. Copies of notices under section 76(1) and 98(1)[16] must be served on any surety.[17] Failure to comply means that the security is enforceable against the surety on an order of the court only.[18]

Surety's right to security instrument

The surety is also naturally entitled to receive a copy of the security instrument. Section 105 provides that when the document is presented or sent for the purposes of being signed by him or on his behalf, there must also be presented or sent a copy of the document. He is also entitled to receive a copy of the executed credit or hire agreement. Rules regarding the time at which a copy must be given to him are also set out in section 105 and depend generally on whether the security is provided after or at the time when the regulated agreement is made. Failure to supply such copies means that the security instrument is not properly executed.[19]

Section 105(7) of the Act provides some relief for the surety at the discretion of the court should a "security" not be expressed in writing or be otherwise improperly executed, but does not set out the relevant considerations which ought to be taken into account in exercising that discretion.[20]

---

[15] s. 98(6) of the Act.
[16] The need for and content of a default notice are set out in ss. 87, 88 *et seq.* of the Act.
[17] s. 111(1) of the Act.
[18] s. 111(2) of the Act. Note s. 127 of the Act which deals with enforcement orders which may be imposed by the court in cases of infringement including failure to comply with s. 111, *supra*. s. 173 forbids contracting out of the protection afforded by the Act.
[19] s. 105(4) (*d*) of the Act.
[20] The British Columbia Report, as to which see n. 1, *supra*, recommends that any judicial determination be conducted on an "objective" basis to ascertain whether the guarantor ought not to have been misled by any formal irregularities.

Disclosure

The question of disclosure in guarantees is dealt with in detail elsewhere,[21] but the Consumer Credit Act 1974 imposes no specific duty of disclosure on either creditor or principal debtor to ensure for example that the guarantor is acquainted with whatever other indebtedness the debtor may have or indeed with every term of the principal transaction[22] either before or during the currency of the guarantee.

Ineffective securities

Section 106 of the Act provides that where under any provision of the Act that Section is applied to any security provided in relation to a regulated agreement then:

(a) The security, so far as it is so provided, shall be treated as never having effect[23];

(b) any property lodged with the creditor or owners solely for the purposes of the security as so provided shall be returned by him forthwith;

(c) the creditor or owner shall take any necessary action to remove or cancel an entry in any register, so far as the entry relates to the security as so provided; and

(d) any amount received by the creditor or owner on realisation of the security shall, so far as it is referrable to the security agreement, be repaid to the surety.[24]

---

[21] See Chap. 5.

[22] *Cf.* British Columbia Consumer Protection Act S.B.C. 1977. s. 12 of that Act is discussed in the British Columbia Report, which recommends that a consumer guarantee be treated as one *uberrimae fidei.*

[23] See also *Orakpo* v. *Manson Investments Ltd.* [1978] A.C. 95 which effectively frustrated an attempt to assert an unpaid vendor's lien by way of subrogation in the case of a security made unenforceable by the Money Lendors Act 1927. The 1927 Act has now been repealed and replaced by the 1974 Act.

[24] Examples of where s. 106 of the Act would apply to a security include where a regulated agreement is cancelled under s. 69(1) or terminated under s. 91, where a court dismisses an application for an order under s. 65(1) for the enforcement of an improperly executed agreement. See generally Guest & Lloyd, *op. cit.*

CHAPTER 17

PERFORMANCE BONDS

Nature of bonds

Performance or guarantee bonds[1] are here dealt with given their increasing importance in modern commerce, especially in construction and international sales contracts where they represent the means whereby surety companies or banks will guarantee performance in accordance with the provisions of the requisite contract.

A performance bond[2] will also act as an assurance of the financial stability of the contractor and is a means of ensuring total execution of the contract should he fail to perform whether through his own default or not. A distinction is in practice drawn between performance bonds issued by surety companies and those issued by banks or other financial institutions. In the case of the former, there is a guarantee in the event of the contractor's failure causing loss; in the case of the latter there is often an undertaking to pay money, in the event of breach or in certain cases upon presentation of certain documents or even upon a mere formal demand.

A performance bond is an undertaking given by a bank, insurance company or other party (the guarantor) at the request of a tenderer or contractor (the principal or seller) to a party inviting the tender or entering into a contract of purchase (the beneficiary or buyer) whereby the guarantor undertakes in the event of default by the seller in the performance of the

---

[1] *Cf.* usage in the United States where the term "surety bond" is frequently given to an indemnity granted by a surety company which undertakes in effect to perform the contract, as distinct from merely making payment in the event of non-performance by a contractor. See generally McNeill Stokes, *International Construction Contracts* (New York; McGraw Hill, 1980). Bid bonds are given at the pre-tender stage and advance payment bonds are for the due repayment as the work proceeds of advance payments made to secure plant or equipment or for financing purposes. Other types of bonds include, *e.g.* in building cases, maintenance, materials and labour bonds.

[2] The practice of bonding grew out of the relationship of master and servant and the desire of the former to safeguard his secrets or goods from being stolen or passed on to another employer. In due course buyers, in the sense used later in the text, who awarded large contracts out of public funds became concerned to ensure first that bidders for such contracts had sufficient technical and financial ability to undertake the property involved and further that the contracts would subsequently be fulfilled satisfactorily in accordance with their terms and conditions. Moreover a buyer might want to be certain that any payment made to a contractor was used for the purposes of the contract and not, for example, as part of a contractor's working capital. These various forms of undertakings or assurances have come to be known as bid bonds, performance bonds and advance payment bonds respectively and as suggested in the text the term "Guarantee Bond" can be used in respect of any one of these entities. Specimen bonds are contained in Appendix 1.

latter's obligations under the tender or contract to pay the buyer up to a limit of a stated sum of money or to arrange for performance of the relevant obligations under the tender or contract.

The transaction therefore involves agreement first between the guarantor and buyer (the guarantee or bond), secondly between seller and buyer (the contract of sale or purchase) and thirdly between guarantor and seller (the counter-indemnity). Normally the contract of sale will precede the issue of the bond, followed by the execution of the counter-indemnity.[3] The nature of the undertaking given by the guarantor is sometimes described as "conditional" since he will only pay the buyer on condition that the latter proves or establishes default by the seller.[4]

Unconditional bonds

The risks incurred by a seller in providing unconditional bonds, however,[5] have been illustrated in four recent English decisions. In *R. D. Harbottle (Mercantile) Ltd.* v. *National Westminster Bank Ltd.*[6] performance bonds providing security to Egyptian buyers for the fulfilment by the plaintiffs, who were English sellers, of the latter's obligations under various contracts for the supply of goods were taken with Egyptian banks. The bonds provided payment would be made on first demand by the buyers without proof of any breach of contract by the plaintiffs or any other safeguard against abuse by the buyers. Kerr J. in discharging interim injunctions against *inter alia* the English bank which confirmed the latter's guarantees stated:[7]

> "It is only in exceptional cases that the courts will interfere with the machinery of irrevocable obligations assumed by banks. They are the life-blood of international commerce. Such obligations are treated as collateral to the underlying rights and obligations between the merchants at either end of the banking chain. Except possibly in clear cases of fraud

---

[3] Except in the case of a bid bond, where there will probably be no executed contract of sale. For an illustration of the operation of a performance bond and counter-indemnity in the context of a building contract see *General Surety & Guarantee Co. Ltd.* v. *Francis Parker Ltd.* (1977) 6 Build. L.R. 16 *per* Donaldson J. This case shows that in any case of ambiguity a bond will not be construed so as to be enforceable without proof of default in the discharge of the bonded obligation.

[4] This is to be contrasted with so-called unconditional bonds discussed in the authorities referred to in the text below. Such bonds are commonly used abroad, especially in the Middle East where the guarantor is required to pay the buyer on first demand without any need by the latter to prove any default by the seller.

[5] See footnote 4 *supra*.

[6] [1978] Q.B. 146.

[7] At p. 155G.

of which the banks have notice, the courts will leave the merchants to settle their disputes under the contracts by litigation or arbitration as available to them or stipulated in the contracts."

On the facts the result appears to have been inevitable given the manner in which the plaintiffs had there agreed to enter into the particular commitments.[8] In various passages in his judgment[9] Kerr J. suggests that only "established frauds" would be a sufficient reason not to pay,[10] but there is little guidance on the kind of evidence required to establish this concept.

In *Howe-Richardson Scale Co. Ltd.* v. *Polimex-Cekop*[11] and *Edward Owen Engineering Ltd.* v. *Barclays Bank International Ltd.*[12] English suppliers again entered into contracts for the supply of goods to be paid by irrevocable letters of credit confirmed by their English banks. In both cases it was a condition precedent to the execution of such contracts first that the buyers had to establish a letter of credit in the suppliers' favour and further that the suppliers had to provide the buyers with unconditional performance bonds, as to which first requirement for differing reasons the buyers failed to open the requisite letters of credit on each supplier refusing to proceed with its contract on the basis of non-performance by each buyer resulting in the latter calling in the bonds. Interim injunctions were again sought by the suppliers to restrain their respective banks from paying out under the bonds and the English banks succeeded in the Court of Appeal in the *Howe-Richardson* case in resisting the granting of any such injunction and in the *Edward Owen* decision, in discharging an injunction previously preventing them from paying a Libyan bank and seller the amount stipulated under the bond.

In the latter case[13] Lord Denning M.R. characterised per-

---

[8] The learned judge adopted a similar approach to the so-called "conclusive evidence" provision in the counter-guarantee given by the plaintiffs to their own English bank, applying *Bache & Co. (London) Ltd.* v. *Banques Vernes* [1973] 2 Lloyd's Rep. 431.

[9] See, *e.g.* p. 155F and 155G. *Cf. Edward Owen Engineering Ltd.* v. *Barclays Bank International Ltd.* [1978] 1 Lloyd's Rep. 166 at pp. 172, 173, *per* Lord Denning M.R. and Browne L.J.

[10] The only defendant before the Court in the *Harbottle* case was the plaintiffs' own bank in England, against whom there was no allegation of fraud. See also *Discount Records Ltd.* v. *Barclays Bank* [1975] 1 W.L.R. 315. Making a demand in order to put financial pressure upon the contractor will probably not be held to be fraud enabling the court to intervene. See *Wood Hall Ltd.* v. *The Pipeline Authority* (1979) 53 Austr. L.J. Rep. 487.

[11] [1978] 1 Lloyd's Rep. 161.

[12] [1978] 1 Lloyd's Rep. 166. In the U.S., see *Szteyn* v. *J. Henry Schroder* 31 N.Y.S. (2d.) 631 (1941). See also *Emerson Electric Industries Controls* v. *Bank of America* (Court of Appeal Transcript 79442, July 10, 1979) (alleged frustration of sale contract held not to affect implementation of bond).

[13] At p. 171. See generally Gutteridge and Megrah, *The Law of Bankers' Commercial Credits* (6th ed. 1979).

formance bonds as "virtually promissory notes on demand." He added[14]:

> "So long as the Libyan customs make an honest demand, the banks are bound to pay: and the banks will rarely, if ever, be in a position to learn whether the demand is honest or not. . . . All this leads to the conclusion that the performance guarantee stands on a similar footing to a letter of credit. A bank which gives a performance guarantee must honour the guarantee according to its terms . . . The bank must pay according to its guarantee, on demand, if so stipulated, without proof or conditions. The only exception is when there is a clear fraud of which the bank has notice."[15]

In *Intraco Ltd.* v. *Notis Shipping Corporation*[16] the Court of Appeal applied the *Howe-Richardson* to a situation where the purchasers of a ship tried to restrain the sellers from calling for payment from the bank under the bond for part of the purchase price. Without proof of fraud, the court held payment could not be stopped by attempting to restrain the sellers from calling upon the bond. However, Parker J. was willing to grant a *Mareva*[17] injunction freezing the proceeds of the bonds. The Court of Appeal discharged the *Mareva* injunction on the basis that the bond was payable in Greece and not within the jurisdiction.[18]

The risk inherent in agreeing to the issue of unconditional bonds is therefore that the bond may be unfairly called by the beneficiary and yet there may be no adequate redress under the contractual terms of the transaction which gave rise to the bond.[18a]

It is suggested that such a risk can be minimised by the inclusion of clauses designed, for example, first to prevent any claim being met by the guarantor unless accompanied by a court or arbitration award[19] in a party's favour, secondly to specify the precise documentation required to accompany claims by the

---

[14] *Ibid.* at p. 171.

[15] Browne L.J. at p. 173 stated that the fraud had to be "very clearly established".

[16] [1981] 2 Lloyd's Rep. 256.

[17] [1975] 2 Lloyd's Rep. 509, C.A.

[18] Donaldson L.J. said that since a bank guarantee is to be treated as cash when a bank pays and the cash is received by the beneficiary, it should be subject to the same restraints as any other of his cash assets.

[18a] It is not possible to imply a term that the bond will only be called upon, where there is reasonable and just cause to complain of default, *State Trading Corp. of India Ltd.* v. *E. D. & F. Man (Sugar) Ltd.* (July 17, 1981, C.A., unreported, Transcript No. 81307) *per* Lord Denning M.R. An honest belief on the part of the buyer permits him to call on the bond.

[19] *e.g.* by reference to the I.C.C. (International Chamber of Commerce) Rules of Conciliation and Arbitration. For an example of a claim under I.C.C. Rules see *Dalmia Dairy Industries Ltd.* v. *National Bank of Pakistan* [1978] 2 Lloyd's Rep. 223.

beneficiary,[20] and thirdly to stress the importance of the bond being returned to the guarantor on a definite expiry date.[21]

Article 9 of the I.C.C. Uniform Rules for Contract Guarantees[22] assumes that the bond will provide for documentary proof for a claim in default of which an arbitral or court award will be required for the bond to be called. Article 9 may be excluded by agreement. Article 5 assumes the provision of an expiry date for the bond and Article 6 provides for the return of a guarantee which ceases to be valid.

---

[20] This appears to a principal reason as to why many banks object to using conditional bonds.
[21] Even if the buyer accepts the expiry date of the date for returning the bond he may well, as was shown in the *Harbottle* case, insist on the validity date being extended by threatening to call on the bond if such extension is not granted.
[22] 1st edition, (1978) I.C.C. Publication No. 325.

CHAPTER 18

STAMP DUTY

There is no longer any statutory requirement for the memorandum of a guarantee not under seal to be subject to stamp duty.[1]

However, insofar as guarantees under seal are concerned, a duty of 50p is imposed[2] but ad valorem duty will not be payable.[3] In any event *ad valorem* duty is not payable upon a guarantee within the heading[4] "Mortgage, Bond, Debenture, Covenant, etc.," since it is not "the only or principal or primary security for the repayment of money," as required by paragraph 1 of that heading.[5]

A guarantee requiring stamping should be stamped prior to execution, although it may be stamped later on certain terms.[6] Section 14(4) of the Stamp Act 1891 provides that an instrument of guarantee executed in the United Kingdom or relating to any property or matter situate or done or to be done there is not, save in criminal proceedings, available for any purpose whatever, and cannot be given in evidence, unless stamped according to the law in force at the time of its execution.[6]

---

[1] *i.e.* by the Stamp Act, s. 1., Sched. 1, "Agreement or any Memorandum of an Agreement, etc.," now repealed; see Finance Act 1970, s. 32(a), Sched. 7, para. 1(2)(a).

[2] *Ibid.* Sched. 1, "Deed of any kind whatsoever, etc."; Decimal Currency Act 1969, s. 10(1).

[3] *Ibid.* Sched. 1, "Bond for securing the payment etc." but now abolished by Finance Act 1971, s. 64; "Covenant for securing the payment etc."; "Mortgage, Bond, Debenture, Covenant, etc." A guarantee in respect of periodical payments, whether made under seal or bond will not attract duty by reference to Sched. 1, "Bond, Covenant or Instrument etc."

[4] *Ibid.* see Sched. 1.

[5] *I.R.C.* v. *Henry Ansbacher & Co.* [1963] A.C. 191. The whole amount of duty payable under paragraph (2) of the same heading on any instrument being a collateral additional or substituted security must not exceed 50p. Note however the effect of s. 63, Finance Act 1963. See generally Sergeant and Sims, *Stamp Duties and Capital Duty* (7th ed., 1977), especially at p. 177.

[6] See Stamp Act 1891, s.15; Finance Act 1895, ss.15 and 19; Finance Act 1962, s.30(1). Note *Haigh* v. *Brooks* (1840) 10 A. & C. 309; on appeal *sub nom. Brooks* v. *Haigh Co.* (1840) 10 A. & E. 323. *quaere* whether this decision that a guarantee could be produced in evidence, even though unstamped, would now be correct.

Appendix 1

SPECIMEN FORMS

DRAFT BID BOND

To: The Buyer

Dear Sirs,

At the request of   (hereinafter referred to as
"X") We (insert name of Bank) .... of (insert Bank's
address) . . . . hereby undertake to pay to you subject as hereinafter provided such amount as may be claimed by you in writing up
to £ . . . . (insert maximum figure) in respect of X's tender
dated . . . . for . . . . (insert description of project)
valid for a period of . . . . . . (insert number of days or months) (hereinafter referred to as "the Tender") on the occurrence of either of
the following events:-

(1) Where you have indicated in writing your willingness to enter
    into a contract with X (hereinafter referred to as "the Contract")
    either on the terms of the Tender or on such modified terms as
    may have been agreed between you and X and X has indicated
    to you that it does not wish to sign or otherwise enter into the
    Contract, or
(2) Where you have signed the Contract with X and where the
    Contract would have otherwise come into force except only
    for X's failure to provide any Performance Guarantee or Bond
    required in connection therewith by the times and on the con-
    ditions stipulated in the Contract.

Provided that no such amount shall become due and payable by us
under this Guarantee:-

(1) Where the aggregate amount claimed exceeds £ . . . .
                                         (insert maxium figure)
(2) More than one month after the validity period of the Tender
    has expired, unless we have been notified by X that the period
    of validity of the Tender has been extended.
(3) Unless your written claim shall have been received by us
    accompanied by the following documents:

    (a) In the circumstances provided for under (1) above a copy
        certified by a Notary Public of your written indication to

239

enter into the Contract with X together with evidence of X's indication not to sign or otherwise enter into the Contract.

(b) In the circumstances provided for under (2) above a copy, certified by a Notary Public, of the signed Contract together with evidence that you have fulfilled all your obligations precedent to the coming into force of the Contract and that the Contract would have come into force but for X's failure as aforesaid.

Our liability hereunder shall cease and terminate on whichever of the following events first occurs, upon which event this Guarantee shall be returned to us for cancellation:-

(1) When we have paid to you the amount of £ . . . .
(insert maximum figure)

(2) when you have awarded the contract to another company or organisation or have indicated to X that the Tender will not be accepted or have otherwise indicated that no contract will be placed with any tenderer, whichever occurs the earlier.

(3) One month after the validity period of the Tender (including any agreed extension thereof) has expired unless before that time we have received your written claim satisfying the conditions set out above.

This Guarantee and any claims arising hereunder shall be governed in all respects by English law and any disputes in connection therewith shall be submitted to arbitration in accordance with the Rules of Conciliation and Arbitration of the International Chamber of Commerce in Paris.

Yours faithfully, etc.

DRAFT PERFORMANCE BOND

To: The Buyer

Dear Sirs

At the request of   (hereinafter referred to as "X") We (insert name of Bank) of . . . . (insert Bank's address) hereby undertake to indemnify you against all claims, costs and damages which you have necessarily incurred as a direct consequence of failure by X to fulfil in accordance with its terms any of its obligations under the contract signed between yourselves and X dated . . . . (hereinafter referred to as "the Contract") by paying to you subject as hereinafter provided such amount as may be claimed by you in writing in respect thereof.

This Guarantee shall not become effective unless and until we have been notified by X in writing that all conditions precedent otherwise required to bring the Contract into force have been fulfilled.

This Guarantee shall not in any event exceed £ . . . . (insert maximum figure) and shall be reduced proportionately as follows upon completion of the following phases of the Contract as provided thereunder:

Phase of Contract	Percentage Reduction in Guarantee
e.g. (Factory Acceptance) (Provisional Acceptance)	

Provided that no such amount shall become due and payable by us under this Guarantee:-

(1) Where the aggregate amount claimed exceeds £ . . . . (insert maximum figure).

(2) Where notification of your intention to make a claim has been received by us later than . . . . or . . . . or . . . . (insert dates respectively one month after which a Factory Acceptance Certificate or Provisional Acceptance or Final Acceptance Certificate is required to be issued as appropriate) in respect of any amount exceeding £ . . . . or £ . . . . or £ . . . . (insert reduced figures as appropriate).

(3) Unless your written claim shall be accompanied by one of the following documents:

(a) A signed admission by X of its failure as aforesaid and agreement to the amount claimed, or

(b) A copy, certified by a Notary Public, of a Court or Arbi-

trator's award in your favour made in accordance with
accordance with Clause . . . . of the Contract.

Our liability hereunder shall cease and terminate on whichever of the
following events first occur, upon which event this Guarantee shall
be returned to us for cancellation.

(1) When we have paid to you the maximum amount for which we
are liable hereunder.
(2) If the Contract is terminated by you otherwise than for reasons
of X's default.
(3) On . . . . (insert date), being one month after the date
provided in the Contract for Final Acceptance) unless before
that date we have received notification of your intention to
make a claim.

This Guarantee and all claims arising hereunder shall be governed in
all respects by English law and any dispute in connection therewith
shall be submitted to arbitration in accordance with the Rules of
Conciliation and Arbitration of the International Chamber of Commerce in Paris.

Yours faithfully, etc.

DRAFT ADVANCE PAYMENT BOND

To: The Buyer

Dear Sirs

In consideration of your paying to   (hereinafter referred to as "X") the sum of £ . . . . due to them under Clause . . . . of their contract with you dated . . . . (hereinafter referred to as "the Contract") We (insert name of Bank) of (insert Bank's address) hereby guarantee that in the event of any failure on the part of X to deliver the equipment or carry out the work for which they are responsible under the Contract in accordance with its terms we shall, subject as hereinafter provided, pay you the amount of all claims, costs and damages which you have necessarily incurred as a direct consequence of such failure up to but not exceeding the amount paid to X under the said Clause.

Provided that no such amount shall become due and payable by us under this Guarantee:-

(1) Where the aggregate amount claimed exceeds £ . . . . (insert maximum figure).

(2) Where any shipments made or services rendered under the Contract exceed £ . . . . (insert maximum figure) and X has provided us with invoices or shipping documents, certified by a Notary Public, to that value;

(3) Where notification of your intention to make a claim has been received by us not later than . . . . (insert date one month after which shipments are to be made or services rendered as appropriate).

(4) Unless your written claim shall be accompanied by one of the following documents:-

   (a) A signed admission by X of its failure aforesaid and agreement to the amount claimed.

   (b) A copy, certified by a Notary Public, of a Court or Arbitrator's award in your favour made in accordance with Clause . . . . of the Contract.

Our liability hereunder shall cease and terminate on whichever of the following events first occurs, upon which event this Guarantee shall be returned to us for cancellation:-

(1) When we have paid to you the maximum amount for which we are liable hereunder.

(2) If the Contract is terminated by you otherwise than for reasons of X's default.

(3) On . . . . (insert date one month after which shipments are to be made or services rendered, as appropriate) unless before that date we have received notification of your intention to make a claim.

This Guarantee and all claims arising hereunder shall be governed in all respects by English law and any disputes in connection therewith shall be submitted to arbitration in accordance with the Rules of Conciliation and Arbitration of the International Chamber of Commerce in Paris.

Yours faithfully, etc.

DRAFT INDIVIDUAL GUARANTEE

To   Limited

In consideration of   (hereinafter called "the Bank") making or continuing advances or otherwise giving credit or affording banking facilities for as long as the Bank may think fit to

of

(hereinafter called "the Principal") I the undersigned

hereby agree to pay and satisfy to the Bank on demand all and every the sum and sums of money which are now or shall at any time be owing to the Bank anywhere on any account whatsoever whether from the Principal solely or from the Principal jointly with any other person or persons or from any firm in which the Principal may be a partner including the amount of notes or bills discounted or paid and other loans credits or advances made to or for the accommodation or at the request either of the Principal solely or jointly or of any such firm as aforesaid or for all moneys for which the Principal may be liable as surety or in any other way whatsoever together with in all the cases aforesaid all interest discount and other Bankers' charges including legal charges occasioned by or incident to this or any other security held by or offered to the Bank for the same indebtedness or by or to the enforcement of any such security.

Provided always that the total liability ultimately enforceable against me under this guarantee shall not exceed the sum of

pounds together with interest thereon as well after as before any judgment at the rate of two per cent. per annum above the published base rate of the Bank for the time being provided that such rate plus the two per cent. be equal to or exceed five per cent. and at all other times at the rate of five per cent. per annum from the date of demand by the Bank upon me for payment

This Guarantee shall not be considered as satisfied by any intermediate payment or satisfaction of the whole or any part of any sum or sums of money owing as aforesaid but shall be a continuing security and shall extend to cover any sum or sums of money which shall for the time being constitute the balance due from the Principal to the Bank upon any such account as hereinbefore mentioned.

This Guarantee shall be binding as a continuing security on me my executors administrators and legal representatives until the expiration of three calendar months after I or in case of my dying or becoming under disability my executors administrators or legal representatives shall have given to the Bank notice in writing to discontinue and determine the same

In the event of this Guarantee ceasing from any cause whatsoever to be binding as a continuing security on me or my legal representatives the Bank shall be at liberty without thereby affecting their rights hereunder to open a fresh account or accounts and to continue any then existing account with the Principal and no moneys paid from time to time into such such account or accounts by or on behalf of the Principal and subsequently drawn out by the Principal shall on settlement of any claim in respect of this Guarantee be appropriated towards or have the effect of payment of any part of the moneys due from the Principal at the time of this Guarantee ceasing to be so binding as a continuing security or of the interest thereon unless the person or persons paying in such moneys shall at the time in writing direct the Bank specially to appropriate the same to that purpose

Any admission or acknowledgement in writing by the Principal or by any person authorised by the Principal of the amount of indebtedness of the Principal to the Bank and any judgment recovered by the Bank against the Principal in respect of such indebtedness shall be binding and conclusive on and against me my executors and administrators in all Courts of Law and elsewhere

The Bank shall be at liberty without thereby affecting their rights against me hereunder at any time to determine enlarge or vary any credit to the Principal to vary exchange abstain from perfecting or release any other securities held or to be held by the Bank for or on account of the moneys intended to be hereby secured or any part thereof to renew bills and promissory notes in any manner and to compound with give time for payment to accept compositions from and make any other arrangements with the Principal or any obligants on bills notes or other securities held or to be held by the Bank for and on behalf of the Principal

This Guarantee shall be in addition to and shall not be in any way prejudiced or affected by any collateral or other security now or hereafter held by the Bank for all or any part of the moneys hereby guaranteed nor shall such collateral or other security or any lien to which the Bank may be otherwise entitled or the liability of any person or persons not parties hereto for all or any part of the moneys hereby secured be in anywise prejudiced or affected by this present Guarantee. And the Bank shall have full power at their discretion to give time for payment to or make any other arrangement with any such other person or persons without prejudice to this present

Guarantee or any liability hereunder. And all moneys received by the Bank from me or the Principal or any person or persons liable to pay the same may be applied by the Bank to any account or item of account or to any transaction to which the same may be applicable.

Although my ultimate liability hereunder cannot exceed the limit hereinbefore mentioned yet this present Guarantee shall be construed and take effect as a guarantee of the whole and every part of the principal moneys and interest owing and to become owing as aforesaid and accordingly I am not to be entitled as against the Bank to any right of proof in the bankruptcy or insolvency of the Principal or other right of a surety discharging his liability in respect of the principal debt unless and until the whole of such principal moneys and interest shall have first been completely discharged and satisfied. And further for the purpose of enabling the Bank to sue the Principal or prove against his estate for the whole of the moneys owing as aforesaid or to preserve intact the liability of any other party the Bank may at any time place and keep for such time as they may think prudent any moneys received recovered or realised hereunder to and at a separate or suspense account to the credit either of me or of such other person or persons or transaction if any as they shall think fit without any intermediate obligation on the part of the Bank to apply the same or any part thereof in or towards the discharge of the moneys owing as aforesaid or any intermediate right on my part to sue the Principal or prove against his estate in competition with or so as to diminish any dividend or other advantage that would or might come to the Bank or to treat the liability of the Principal as diminished

I have not taken in respect of the liability hereby undertaken by me on behalf of the Principal and I will not take from the Principal either directly or indirectly without the consent of the Bank any promissory note bill of exchange mortgage charge or other counter-security whether merely personal or involving a charge on any property whatsoever of the Principal whereby I or any person claiming through me by endorsement assignment or otherwise would or might on the bankruptcy or insolvency of the Principal and to the prejudice of the Bank increase the proofs in such bankruptcy or insolvency or diminish the property distributable amongst the creditors of the Principal. And as regards any such counter-security as aforesaid which I may have taken or may take with such consent as aforesaid the same shall be a security to the Bank for the fulfilment of my obligations hereunder and shall be forthwith deposited by me with them for that purpose

The Bank shall so long as any moneys remain owing hereunder

have a lien therefor on all moneys now or hereafter standing to my credit with the Bank whether on any current or other account

If it shall so happen that the name of the Principal hereinbefore inserted shall be that either of a firm or of a limited company or other corporation or of any committee or association or other unincorporated body any of the printed provisions hereinbefore contained which shall be primarily and literally applicable to the case of a single and individual Principal only shall be construed and take effect so as to give the Bank hereunder a guarantee for the moneys owing from such firm and every member thereof or from such limited company or corporation or committee or association or other unincorporated body as identical or analogous as may be with or to that which would have been given for the moneys owing from a single individual if the Principal had been a single individual. And any moneys shall be deemed to be so owing notwithstanding any defect informality or insufficiency in the borrowing powers of the Principal or in the exercise thereof which might be a defence as between the Principal and the Bank And further in the case of a firm this Guarantee shall be deemed to be a continuing Guarantee of all moneys owing on any such account as hereinbefore mentioned from the persons or person carrying on business in the name of or in succession to the firm or from any one or more of such persons although by death retirement or admission of partners or other causes the constitution of the firm may have been partially or wholly varied. And in the case of a limited company or other corporation any reference to bankruptcy shall be deemed to be a reference to liquidation or other analogous proceeding and the moneys owing as aforesaid and hereby guaranteed shall be deemed to include any moneys owing in respect of debentures or debenture stock of such limited company or other corporation held by or on behalf of the Bank. This Guarantee shall be in addition to and not in substitution for any other Guarantee for the Principal given by me to the Bank The expression "The Bank" wherever used herein includes and extends to their successors and assigns **In witness** whereof I have hereunto set my hand this day of   One thousand nine hundred and

Witness to the signature of

Name and
Address of
Witnesses

The full
address and
the professio
or business o
the Guaranto
must be adde

DRAFT JOINT AND SEVERAL GUARANTEE

To   Limited

In consideration of   (hereinafter called "the Bank") making or continuing advances or otherwise giving credit or affording banking facilities for as long as the Bank may think fit to

of

(hereinafter called "the Principal") **We the undersigned**

jointly and severally hereby agree to pay and satisfy to the Bank on demand all and every the sum and sums of money which now are or shall at any time be owing to the Bank anywhere on any account whatsoever whether from the Principal solely or from the Principal jointly with any other person or persons or from any firm in which the Principal may be a partner including the amount of notes or bills discounted or paid and other loans credits or advances made to or for the accommodation or at the request either of the Principal solely or jointly or of any such firm as aforesaid and all moneys for which the Principal may be liable to the Bank as surety or in any other way whatsoever together with in all cases aforesaid all interest discount and other Bankers' charges including legal charges occasioned by or incident to this or any other security held by or offered to the Bank for the same indebtedness or by or to the enforcement of any such security

Provided always that the liability ultimately enforceable against us jointly or against each of us separately under this Guarantee shall not exceed in the aggregate the sum of

pounds together with interest thereon as well after as before any judgment at the rate of two per cent. per annum above the published base rate of the Bank for the time being provided that such rate plus the two per cent. be equal to or exceed five per cent. and at all other times at the rate of five per cent. per annum from the date of demand by the Bank upon us for payment

This Guarantee shall not be considered as satisfied by any intermediate payment or satisfaction of the whole or any part of any sum or sums of money owing as aforesaid but shall be a continuing security and shall extend to cover any sum or sums of money which shall for the time being constitute the balance due from the Principal to the Bank upon any such account as hereinbefore mentioned

This Guarantee shall be binding as a continuing security on us and each of us our and each of our executors administrators and legal representatives until the expiration of three calendar months after each of us or in case of all or any of us dying or becoming under disability the executors administrators or legal representatives of the person or persons so dying or becoming under disability shall have given to the Bank notice in writing to discontinue and determine the same

In the event of this Guarantee ceasing from any cause whatsoever to be binding as a continuing security on us or any of us our or any of our legal representatives the Bank shall be at liberty without thereby affecting their rights hereunder to open a fresh account or accounts and to continue any then existing account with the Principal and no moneys paid from time to time into any such account or accounts by or on behalf of the Principal and subsequently drawn out by the Principal shall on settlement of any claim in respect of this Guarantee be appropriated towards or have the effect of payment of any part of the moneys due from the Principal at the time of this Guarantee ceasing to be so binding as a continuing security or of the interest thereon unless the person or persons paying in such moneys shall at the time in writing direct the Bank specially to appropriate the same to that purpose

Any admission or acknowledgement in writing by the Principal or by any person authorised by the Principal of the amount of indebtedness of the Principal to the Bank and any judgment recovered by the Bank against the Principal in respect of such indebtedness shall be binding and conclusive on and against us and each of us and each of our executors and administrators in all Courts of Law and elsewhere

The Bank shall be at liberty without thereby affecting their rights against us or any of us hereunder at any time to determine enlarge or vary any credit to the Principal to vary exchange abstain from perfecting or release any other securities held or to be held by the Bank for or on account of the moneys intended to be hereby secured or any part thereof to renew bills and promissory notes in any manner and to compound with give time for payment to accept compositions from and make any other arrangements with the Principal or any obligants on bills notes or other securities held or to be held by the Bank for and on behalf of the Principal. The Bank shall also be at liberty to release or discharge any of us from the obligations of this Guarantee or to accept any composition from or make any other arrangements with any of us without thereby releasing or discharging the other or others of us or otherwise prejudicing or affecting the rights and remedies of the Bank against the other or others of us

This Guarantee shall be in addition to and shall not be in any way prejudiced or affected by any collateral or other security now or hereafter held by the Bank for all or any part of the moneys hereby guaranteed nor shall such collateral or other security or any lien to which the Bank may be otherwise entitled or the liability of any person or persons not parties hereto for all or any part of the moneys hereby secured be in anywise prejudiced or affected by this present security And the Bank shall have full power at their discretion to give time for payment to or make any other arrangement with any such other person or persons without prejudice to this present Guarantee or the liability of us or any of us hereunder And all moneys received by the Bank from us or any of us or the Principal or any person or persons liable to pay the same may be applied by the Bank to any account or item of account or to any transaction to which the same may be applicable

Although the ultimate liability hereunder cannot exceed the limit hereinbefore mentioned yet this present Guarantee shall be construed and take affect as a guarantee of the whole and every part of the principal moneys and interest owing and to become owing as aforesaid and accordingly neither we nor any of us shall be entitled as against the Bank to any right of proof in the bankruptcy or insolvency of the Principal or other right of a surety discharging his liability in respect of the principal debt unless and until the whole of such principal moneys and interest shall first have been completely discharged and satisfied And further for the purpose of enabling the Bank to sue the Principal or prove against his estate for the whole of the moneys owing as aforesaid or to preserve intact the liability of any other party the Bank may at any time place and keep for such time as they may think prudent any moneys received recovered or realised from us or any of us hereunder to and at a separate or suspense account to the credit of us or any of us or of such other person or persons or transaction if any as they shall think fit without any intermediate obligation on the part of the Bank to apply the same or any part thereof in or towards the discharge of moneys owing as aforesaid or any intermediate right on the part of us or any of us to sue the Principal or prove against his estate in competition with or so as to diminish any dividend or other advantage that would or might come to the Bank or to treat the liability of the Principal as diminished

We have not nor have any of us taken in respect of the liability hereby undertaken by us and each of us on behalf of the Principal and we will not nor will any of us take from the Principal either directly or indirectly without the consent of the Bank any promissory note bill of exchange mortgage charge or other counter-security whether merely personal or involving a charge on any property whatsoever of the Principal whereby we or any of us or any person claiming through us or any of us by endorsement assignment or otherwise would or might on the bankruptcy or insolvency of the Principal and to the prejudice of the Bank increase the proofs in such bankruptcy or insolvency or diminish the property distributable amongst the creditors of the Principal. And as regards any such counter-security as aforesaid which we may have taken or may take with such consent as aforesaid the same shall be a security to the Bank for the fulfilment of our obligations hereunder and shall be forthwith deposited by us with them for that purpose

The Bank shall so long as any moneys remain owing hereunder have a lien therefor on all moneys now or hereafter standing to the credit of us or any of us with the Bank their successors or assigns whether on any current or other account

If it shall so happen that the name of the Principal hereinbefore inserted shall be that either of a firm or of a limited company or other corporation or of any committee association or other unincorporated body any of the printed provisions hereinbefore contained which shall be primarily and literally applicable to the case of a single and individual principal only shall be construed and take effect so as to give the Bank hereunder a guarantee for the moneys owing from such firm and every member thereof or from such limited company or corporation or committee or association or other unincorporated body as identical or analogous as may be with or to that which would have been given for the moneys owing from a single individual if the Principal had been a single individual And any moneys shall be deemed to be so owing notwithstanding any defect informality or insufficiency in the borrowing power of the Principal or in the exercise thereof which might be a defence as between the Principal and the Bank And further in the case of a firm this Guarantee shall be deemed to be a continuing Guarantee of all moneys owing on any such account as hereinbefore mentioned from the persons or person carrying on business in the name of or in succession to the firm or from any one or more of such persons although by death retirement or admission of partners or other causes the constitution of the firm may have been partially or wholly varied And in the case of a limited company or other corporation any reference to bankruptcy shall be deemed to be a reference to liquidation or other analogous proceeding and the moneys owing as aforesaid and hereby guaranteed shall be deemed to include any moneys owing in respect of debentures or debenture stock of such limited company or other corporation held by or on behalf of the Bank This Guarantee shall be in addition to and not in substitution for any other Guarantee for the Principal given by all or any of us to the Bank The expression "the Bank" wherever used herein includes and extends to their successors and assigns

In witness whereof we have hereunto set out hands this   day of   One thousand nine hundred and

Witnesses to the signatures of   }

Names and
Addresses of
Witnesses   }

The full
address and
the profession
or business of
each Guaran-
tor must be
added.

DRAFT/COMPOSITE JOINT AND SEVERAL GUARANTEES BY SEVERAL COMPANIES

In consideration of (hereinafter called "the Bank") making or continuing advances or otherwise giving credit or affording banking facilities for as long in any and every case as the Bank may think fit to any or all of us **we**

Insert names of guarantor companies (minimum three) and rule up any blank space thereafter

have agreed to create by this Agreement as many separate and independent guarantees as there are parties hereto (apart from the Bank) each in the succeeding clauses hereof whereby the liabilities of each and every one of us to the Bank are guaranteed by the others of us and accordingly the expression "the Principal" shall mean and apply to the particular one of us for whose liabilities such a guarantee as aforesaid is hereby created and references to "this security" shall be references to the guarantee hereby created for the liabilities of the Principal

1. **We hereby jointly and severally agree** to pay and satisfy to the Bank on demand all and every the sum and sums of money which now are or shall at any time be owing to the Bank anywhere on any account whatsoever whether from the Principal solely or from the Principal jointly with any other person or persons or from any firm in which the Principal may be a partner including the amount of notes or bills discounted or paid and of loans credits or advances made to or for the accommodation or at the request either of the Principal solely or jointly or of any such firm as aforesaid and all moneys for which the Principal may be liable as surety (otherwise than as surety under this Agreement) or in any way whatsoever together with in all the cases aforesaid all interest commission discount and other Bankers' charges including legal charges occasioned by or incident to this or any other security held by or offered to the Bank for the same indebtedness or by or to the enforcement of any such security together with interest on all such moneys from the date of demand by the Bank upon us for payment as well after as before any judgment at the rate of two per cent. per annum above the

published base rate of the Bank for the time being provided that such rate plus the two per cent. be equal to or exceed five per cent. and at all other times at the rate of five per cent. per annum

2. This security shall not be considered as satisfied by any intermediate payment or satisfaction of the whole or any part of the moneys owing as aforesaid and shall be a continuing security until the expiration of three calendar months after all of us shall have given (whether at the same or different times) notice to the Bank in writing to discontinue and determine this security

3. In the event of this security ceasing pursuant to the last preceding clause hereof to be binding on all of us as a continuing security or ceasing from any cause whatsoever to be binding on any of us as such security this security shall (but without prejudice to its remaining binding on any other or others of us as a continuing security) be a security for all moneys then owing or contingently owing or which may become owing in respect of any transaction previously entered into or undertaken by the Bank and the Bank shall be at liberty without thereby affecting its rights hereunder to open and to operate a fresh account or accounts and/or to continue any then existing account and no moneys paid from time to time into any such account or accounts shall on satisfaction of any claim in respect of this security be appropriated to or have the effect of payment of any part of the moneys owing or contingently owing or which might become owing as aforesaid when this security ceased to be so binding unless the person or persons paying in such moneys shall at the time in writing direct the Bank specially to appropriate the same to that purpose

4. Any admission or acknowledgement in writing by the Principal or by any person authorised by the Principal of the amount of indebtedness of the Principal to the Bank and any judgment recovered by the Bank against the Principal in respect of such indebtedness shall be binding and conclusive on and against us and each of us in all Courts of Law and elsewhere

5. The Bank shall be at liberty without thereby affecting its rights against us or any of us hereunder at any time to determine enlarge or vary any credit to the Principal to vary exchange abstain from perfecting or release any other securities held or to be held by the Bank for or on account of the moneys intended to be hereby secured or any part thereof to renew bills and promissory notes in any manner and to give time for payment to accept any composition from and make any other arrangements with the Principal or any obligants on bills notes or other securities held or to be held by the

Bank for and on behalf of the Principal. The Bank shall also be at liberty at any time to release or discharge any of us from the obligations of this security and to give time for payment to accept any composition from or make any other arrangements with any of us without thereby releasing or discharging the other or others of us or otherwise prejudicing or affecting the rights and remedies of the Bank against the other or others of us

6. This security shall be in addition to and shall not be in any way prejudiced or affected by any collateral or other security now or hereafter held by the Bank for all or any part of the moneys intended to be hereby secured nor shall such collateral or other security or any lien to which the Bank may be otherwise entitled or the liability of any person or persons not parties hereto for all or any part of such moneys be in anywise prejudiced or affected by this present security And the Bank shall have full power at their discretion to give time for payment to accept any composition from and make any other arrangements with any such other person or persons without prejudice to this security or the liability of us or any of us hereunder And all moneys received by the Bank from us or any of us or the Principal or any person or persons liable to pay the same may be applied by the Bank to any account or item of account or to any transaction to which the same may be applicable

7. Whether or not this security has ceased as against any or all of us to be a continuing security and the liability hereunder enforceable against us or any of us has been limited accordingly this security shall be construed and take effect as a security for the whole and every part of the moneys owing as aforesaid and accordingly neither we nor any of us shall be entitled as against the Bank to any right of proof in the liquidation of the Principal or other right of a surety discharging his liability unless and until the whole of such moneys shall first have been completely paid and satisfied And further for the purpose of enabling the Bank to enforce any remedies against the Principal or prove in the liquidation of the Principal for the whole of such moneys or to preserve intact the liability of any other person the Bank may at any time place and keep for such time as it may consider expedient any moneys received recovered or realised from us or any of us hereunder or from any such other person to and at a separate or suspense account to the credit of us or any of us or of such other person or transaction if any as the Bank shall think fit without any intermediate obligation on its part to apply the same or any part thereof in or towards the discharge of the moneys owing as aforesaid or any intermediate right on the part of us or any of us to sue the Principal or prove in the liquidation of the Principal in competition with or so as to diminish any dividend or other advantage

that would or might come to the Bank or to treat the liability of the Principal as diminished

8. We have not nor have any of us taken in respect of the liability hereby undertaken by us and each of us on behalf of the Principal and we will not nor will any of us take from the Principal either directly or indirectly without the consent of the Bank any promissory note bill of exchange mortgage charge or other counter-security whether merely personal or involving a mortgage or charge on any property whatsoever of the Principal whereby we or any of us or any person claiming through us or any of us by endorsement assignment or otherwise would or might on the liquidation of the Principal and to the prejudice of the Bank increase the proofs in such liquidation or diminish the property distributable amongst the creditors of the Principal And as regards any such counter-security as aforesaid which we may have taken or may take the same shall be a security to the Bank for the fulfilment of our obligations hereunder and shall be fothwith deposited with the Bank for that purpose

9. In addition to all rights of set off conferred by law and without prejudice to any lien any moneys now or hereafter standing to the credit of any of us solely or of any or all of us jointly with the Bank whether on current or other account shall at the discretion of the Bank be liable to be set off against our liabilities hereunder

10. Any moneys shall be deemed to be owing as aforesaid notwithstanding any defect informality or insufficiency in or absence of the powers of the Principal or in the exercise thereof which might be a defence as between the Principal and the Bank

11. A party hereto shall have no liability under this security in respect of moneys owing to the Bank by the Principal being moneys applied or utilised by the Principal either for any purchase or subscription of such party's shares (or those of any holding company of such party) or by way of financial assistance direct or indirect for the purpose of or in connection with any such purchase or subscription but this provision shall not prejudice or affect the liability in respect of such moneys of any of us other than such party

If the whole or any part of this Agreement be now or hereafter unenforceable against one or more of us for any reason whatsoever the **Agreement** shall nevertheless be and remain fully binding upon and enforceable against the others or other of us as if it had been made by the Bank only with such others or other of us but to secure the liabilities of each and every one of us to the Bank

In Witness whereof one Director of each of the Companies party hereto (other than the Bank) duly authorised in this behalf (as the Secretary or another Director of his Company hereby certifies by his signature hereto) by a Resolution passed by his Board of Directors on or before the date hereof has hereunto set his hand this   day of   One thousand nine hundred and

[SIGNATURES AND SEALS]

SELECTED STATUTES

Statute of Frauds 1677

(29 Car. 2, c.3)

Promises and agreements by parol

4.— [. . .] no action shall be brought [. . .] whereby to charge the defendant upon any special promise to answer for the debt, default or miscarriages of another person [. . .] unless the agreement upon which such action shall be brought, or some memorandum or note thereof, shall be in writing and signed by the party to be charged therewith, or some other person thereunto by him lawfully authorised.

Statute of Frauds Amendment Act 1828

(Lord Tenterden's Act)

(9 Geo 4, c.14)

Action not maintainable on representations of character, etc., unless they may be in writing signed by the party chargeable

6.—No action shall be brought whereby to charge any person upon or by reason of any representation or assurance made or given concerning or relating to the character, conduct, credit, ability, trade, or dealings of any other person, to the intent or purpose that such other person may obtain credit, money, or goods upon, unless such representation or assurance be made in writing, signed by the party to be charged therewith.

Mercantile Law Amendment Act 1856

(19 & 20 Vict. c. 97)

Consideration for guarantee need not appear by writing

3.—No special promise to be made by any person [. . .] to answer for the debt, default, or miscarriage of another person, being in writing, and signed by the party to be charged therewith, or some other person by him thereunto lawfully authorized, shall be deemed invalid to support an action, suit, or other proceeding to charge the person by whom such promise shall have been made, by reason only that the consideration for such promise does not appear in writing, or by necessary inference from a written document.

A surety who discharges the liability to be entitled to assignment of all securities held by the creditor

5.—Every person who, being surety for the debt or duty of another, or being liable with another for any debt or duty, shall pay such debt or perform such duty, shall be entitled to have assigned to him, or to a trustee for him, every judgment, specialty, or other security which shall be held by the creditor in respect of such debt or duty, whether such judgment, specialty, or other security shall or shall not be deemed at law to have been satisfied by the payment of the debt or performance of the duty, and such person shall be entitled to stand in the place of the creditor, and to use all the remedies, and, if need be, and upon a proper indemnity, to use the name of the creditor, in any action, or other proceeding, at law or in equity, in order to obtain from the principal debtor, or any co-surety, co-contractor, or co-debtor, as the case may be, indemnification for the advances made and loss sustained by the person who shall have so paid such debt or performed such duty, and such payment or performance so made by such surety shall not be pleadable in bar of any such action or other proceeding by him : provided always, that no co-surety, co-contractor, or co-debtor, shall be entitled to recover from any other co-surety, co-contractor, or co-debtor, by the means aforesaid, more than the just proportion to which, as between those parties themselves, such last-mentioned person shall be justly liable.

Bills of Exchange Act 1882

(45 & 46 Vict. c. 61)

Stranger signing bill liable as indorser

56.—Where a person signs a bill otherwise than as a drawer or acceptor, he thereby incurs the liabilities of an indorser to a holder in due course.

Consumer Credit Act 1974

(1974 c. 39)

PART II

CREDIT AGREEMENTS, HIRE AGREEMENTS AND LINKED TRANSACTIONS

Consumer credit agreements

8.—(1) A personal credit agreement is an agreement between an individual ("the debtor") and any other person ("the creditor") by which the creditor provides the debtor with credit of any amount.

(2) A consumer credit agreement is a personal credit agreement by which the creditor provides the debtor with credit not exceeding £5,000.

(3) A consumer credit agreement is a regulated agreement within the meaning of this Act if it is not an agreement (an "exempt agreement") specified in or under section 16.

Meaning of credit

9. (1) In this Act "credit" includes a cash loan, and any other form of financial accommodation.

(2) Where credit is provided otherwise than in sterling it shall be treated for the purposes of this Act as provided in sterling of an equivalent amount.

(3) Without prejudice to the generality of subsection (1), the person by whom goods are bailed or (in Scotland) hired to an individual under a hire-purchase agreement shall be taken to provide him with fixed-sum credit to finance the transaction of an amount equal to the total price of the goods less the aggregate of the deposit (if any) and the total charge for credit.

(4) For the purposes of this Act, an item entering into the total charge for credit shall not be treated as credit even though time is allowed for its payment.

Running-account credit and fixed-sum credit

10.—(1) For the purposes of this Act—

(*a*) running-account credit is a facility under a personal credit agreement whereby the debtor is enabled to receive from time to time (whether in his own person, or by another person) from the creditor or a third party cash, goods and services (or any of them) to an amount or value such that, taking into account payments made by or to the credit of the debtor, the credit limit (if any) is not at any time exceeded; and

(*b*) fixed-sum credit is any other facility under a personal credit agreement whereby the debtor is enabled to receive credit (whether in one amount or by instalments).

(2) In relation to running-account credit, "credit limit" means, as respects any period, the maximum debit balance which, under the credit agreement, is allowed to stand on the account during that period, disregarding any term of the agreement allowing that maximum to be exceeded merely temporarily.

(3) For the purposes of section 8 (2), running-account credit shall be taken not to exceed the amount specified in that subsection ("the specified amount") if-

(*a*) the credit limit does not exceed the specified amount; or

(*b*) whether or not there is a credit limit, and if there is, notwithstanding that it exceeds the specified amount,—

    (i) the debtor is not enabled to draw at any one time an amount which, so far as (having regard to section 9 (4)) it represents credit, exceeds the specified amount, or

    (ii) the agreement provides that, if the debit balance rises above a given amount (not exceeding the specified amount), the rate of the total charge for credit increases or any other condition favouring the creditor or his associate comes into operation, or

    (iii) at the time the agreement is made it is probable, having regard to the terms of the agreement and any other relevant considerations, that the debit balance will not at any time rise above the specified amount.

Restricted-use card and unrestricted-use credit

11.—(1) A restricted-use credit agreement is a regulated consumer credit agreement—

(*a*) to finance a transaction between the debtor and the creditor, whether forming part of that agreement or not, or

(*b*) to finance a transaction between the debtor and a person (the "supplier") other than the creditor, or

(*c*) to refinance any existing indebtedness of the debtor's, whether to the creditor or another person, and "restricted-use credit" shall be construed accordingly.

(2) An unrestricted-use credit agreement is a regulated consumer credit agreement not falling within subsection (1), and "unrestricted-use credit" shall be construed accordingly.

(3) An agreement does not fall within subsection (1) if the credit is in fact provided in such a way as to leave the debtor free to use it as he chooses, even though certain uses would contravene that or any other agreement.

(4) An agreement may fall within subsection (1) (*b*) although the identity of the supplier is unknown at the time the agreement is made.

Debtor-creditor-supplier agreements

12. A debtor-creditor-supplier agreement is a regulated consumer credit agreement being--
   (*a*) a restricted-use credit agreement which falls within section 11 (1) (*a*), or
   (*b*) a restricted-use credit agreement which falls within section 11 (1) (*b*) and is made by the creditor under pre-existing arrangements, or in contemplation of future arrangements, between himself and the supplier, or
   (*c*) an unrestricted-use credit agreement which is made by the creditor under pre-existing arrangements between himself and a person (the "supplier") other than the debtor in the knowledge that the credit is to be used to finance a transaction between the debtor and the supplier.

Debtor-creditor agreements

13. A debtor-creditor agreement is a regulated consumer credit agreement being—
   (*a*) a restricted-use credit agreement which falls within section 11 (1) (*b*) but is not made by the creditor under pre-existing arrangements, or in contemplation of future arrangements, between himself and the supplier, or
   (*b*) a restricted-use credit agreement which falls within section 11 (1) (*c*), or
   (*c*) an unrestricted-use credit agreement which is not made by the creditor under pre-existing arrangements between himself and a person (the "supplier") other than the debtor in the knowledge that the credit is to be used to finance a transaction between the debtor and the supplier.

Linked transactions

19.—(1) A transaction entered into by the debtor or hirer, or a relative of his, with any other person ("the other party"), except one for the provision of security, is a linked transaction in relation to an actual or prospective regulated agreement (the "principal agreement") of which it does not form part if—

    (*a*) the transaction is entered into in compliance with a term of the principal agreement; or

    (*b*) the principal agreement is a debtor-creditor-supplier agreement and the transaction is financed, or to be financed, by the principal agreement; or

    (*c*) the other party is a person mentioned in subsection (2), and a person so mentioned initiated the transaction by suggesting it to the debtor or hirer, or his relative, who enters into it—

        (i) to induce the creditor or owner to enter into the principal agreement, or

        (ii) for another purpose related to the principle agreement, or

        (iii) where the principal agreement is a restricted-use credit agreement, for a purpose related to a transaction financed, or to be financed, by the principal agreement.

  (2) The persons referred to in subsection (1) (*c*) are—

    (*a*) the creditor or owner, or his associate;

    (*b*) a person who, in the negotiation of the transaction, is represented by a credit-broker who is also a negotiator in antecedent negotiations for the principal agreement;

    (*c*) a person who, at the time the transaction is initiated, knows that the principal agreement has been made or contemplates that it might be made.

  (3) A linked transaction entered into before the making of the principal agreement has no effect until such time (if any) as that agreement is made.

  (4) Regulations may exclude linked transactions of the prescribed description from the operation of subsection (3).

PART VIII

SECURITY

General

Form and content of securities

  105.—(1) Any security provided in relation to a regulated agreement shall be expressed in writing.

  (2) Regulations may prescribe the form and content of documents ("security instruments") to be made in compliance with subsection (1).

(3) Regulations under subsection (2) may in particular—

(*a*) require specified information to be included in the prescribed manner in documents, and other specified material to be excluded;

(*b*) contain requirements to ensure that specified information is clearly brought to the attention of the surety, and that one part of a document is not given insufficient or excessive prominence compared with another.

(4) A security instrument is not properly executed unless—

(*a*) a document in the prescribed form, itself containing all the prescribed terms and conforming to regulations under sub-section (2), is signed in the prescribed manner by or on behalf of the surety, and

(*b*) the document embodies all the terms of the security, other than implied terms, and

(*c*) the document, when presented or sent for the purpose of being signed by or on behalf of the surety, is in such state that its terms are readily legible, and

(*d*) when the document is presented or sent for the purpose of being signed by or on behalf of the surety there is also pre-sented or sent a copy of the document.

(5) A security instrument is not properly executed unless—

(*a*) where the security is provided after, or at the time when, the regulated agreement is made, a copy of the executed agree-ment, together with a copy of any other document referred to in it, is given to the surety at the time the security is pro-vided, or

(*b*) where the security is provided before the regulated agree-ment is made, a copy of the executed agreement, together with a copy of any other document referred to in it, is given to the surety within seven days after the regulated agreement is made.

(6) Subsection (1) does not apply to a security provided by the debtor or hirer.

(7) If—

(*a*) in contravention of subsection (1) a security is not expressed in writing, or

(*b*) a security instrument is improperly executed,

the security, so far as provided in relation to a regulated agreement, is enforceable against the surety on an order of the court only.

(8) If an application for an order under subsection (7) is dismissed (except on technical grounds only) section 106 (ineffective securities) shall apply to the security.

(9) Regulations under section 60 (1) shall include provision requir-ing documents embodying regulated agreements also to embody any

security provided in relation to a regulated agreement by the debtor or hirer.

Ineffective securities

106.—Where, under any provision of this Act, this section is applied to any security provided in relation to a regulated agreement, then, subject to section 177 (saving for registered charges)—

(a) the security, so far as it is so provided, shall be treated as never having effect;

(b) any property lodged with the creditor or owner solely for the purposes of the security as so provided shall be returned by him forthwith;

(c) the creditor or owner shall take any necessary action to remove or cancel an entry in any register, so far as the entry relates to the security as so provided; and

(d) any amount received by the creditor or owner on realisation of the security shall, so far as it is referable to the agreement, be repaid to the surety.

Duty to give information to surety under fixed-sum credit agreement

107.—(1) The creditor under a regulated agreement for fixed-sum credit in relation to which security is provided, within the prescribed period after receiving a request in writing to that effect from the surety and payment of a fee of 15 new pence, shall give to the surety (if a different person from the debtor)—

(a) a copy of the executed agreement (if any) and of any other document referred to in it;

(b) a copy of the security instrument (if any); and

(c) a statement signed by or on behalf of the creditor showing, according to the information to which it is practicable for him to refer,—

　(i) the total sum paid under the agreement by the debtor,

　(ii) the total sum which has become payable under the agreement by the debtor but remains unpaid, and the various amounts comprised in that total sum, with the date when each became due, and

　(iii) the total sum which is to become payable under the agreement by the debtor, and the various amounts, comprised in that total sum, with the date, or mode of determining the date, when each becomes due.

(2) If the creditor possesses insufficient information to enable him to ascertain the amounts and dates mentioned in subsection (1) (c) (iii), he shall be taken to comply with that sub-paragraph if his statement under subsection (1) (c) gives the basis on which, under the regulated agreement, they would fall to be ascertained.

(3) Subsection (1) does not apply to—

(*a*) an agreement under which no sum is, or will or may become, payable by the debtor, or

(*b*) a request made less than one month after a previous request under that subsection relating to the same agreement was complied with.

(4) If the creditor under an agreement fails to comply with subsection (1)—

(*a*) he is not entitled, while the default continues, to enforce the security, so far as provided in relation to the agreement; and

(*b*) if the default continues for one month he commits an offence.

(5) This section does not apply to a non-commercial agreement.

Duty to give information to surety under running-account credit agreement

108.—(1) The creditor under a regulated agreement for running-account credit in relation to which security is provided, within the prescribed period after receiving a request in writing to that effect from the surety and payment of a fee of 15 new pence, shall give to the surety (if a different person from the debtor)—

(*a*) a copy of the executed agreement (if any) and of any other document referred to in it;

(*b*) a copy of the security instrument (if any); and

(*c*) a statement signed by or on behalf of the creditor showing, according to the information to which it is practicable for him to refer,—

    (i) the state of the account, and

    (ii) the amount, if any, currently payable under the agreement by the debtor to the creditor, and

    (iii) the amounts and due dates of any payments which, if the debtor does not draw further on the account, will later become payable under the agreement by the debtor to the creditor.

(2) If the creditor possesses insufficient information to enable him to ascertain the amounts and dates mentioned in subsection (1) (*c*) (iii), he shall be taken to comply with that sub-paragraph if his statement under subsection (1) (*c*) gives the basis on which, under the regulated agreement, they would fall to be ascertained.

(3) Subsection (1) does not apply to—

(*a*) an agreement under which no sum is, or will or may become, payable by the debtor, or

(*b*) a request made less than one month after a previous request under that subsection relating to the same agreement was complied with.

(4) If the creditor under an agreement fails to comply with subsection (1)—

(*a*) he is not entitled, while the default continues, to enforce the security, so far as provided in relation to the agreement; and

(*b*) if the default continues for one month he commits an offence.

(5) This section does not apply to a non-commercial agreement.

Duty to give information to surety under consumer hire agreement

109.—(1) The owner under a regulated consumer hire agreement in relation to which security is provided, within the prescribed period after receiving a request in writing to that effect from the surety and payment of a fee of 15 new pence, shall give to the surety (if a different person from the hirer)—

(*a*) a copy of the executed agreement and of any other document referred to in it;

(*b*) a copy of the security instrument (if any); and

(*c*) a statement signed by or on behalf of the owner showing, according to the information to which it is practicable for him to refer, the total sum which has become payable under the agreement by the hirer but remains unpaid and the various amounts comprised in that total sum, with the date when each became due.

(2) Subsection (1) does not apply to—

(*a*) an agreement under which no sum is, or will or may become, payable by the hirer, or

(*b*) a request made less than one month after a previous request under that subsection relating to the same agreement was complied with.

(3) If the owner under an agreement fails to comply with subsection (1)—

(*a*) he is not entitled, while the default continues, to enforce the security, so far as provided in relation to the agreement; and

(*b*) if the default continues for one month he commits an offence.

(4) This section does not apply to a non-commercial agreement.

Duty to give surety copy of default etc. notice

111.—(1) When a default notice or a notice under section 76 (1) or 98 (1) is served on a debtor or hirer, a copy of the notice shall be served by the creditor or owner on any surety (if a different person from the debtor or hirer).

(2) If the creditor or owner fails to comply with subsection (1) in the case of any surety, the security is enforceable against the surety (in respect of the breach or other matter to which the notice relates) on an order of the court only.

112. [. . .] regulations may provide for any matters relating to the sale or other realisation, by the creditor or owner, of property over which any right has been provided by way of security in relation to an actual or prospective regulated agreement, other than a non-commercial agreement.

Act not to be evaded by use of security

113.—(1) Where a security is provided in relation to an actual or prospective regulated agreement, the security shall not be enforced so as to benefit the creditor or owner, directly or indirectly, to an extent greater (whether as respects the amount of any payment or the time or manner of its being made) than would be the case if the security were not provided and any obligations of the debtor or hirer, or his relative, under or in relation to the agreement were carried out to the extent (if any) to which they would be enforced under this Act.

(2) In accordance with subsection (1), where a regulated agreement is enforceable on an order of the court or the Director only, any security provided in relation to the agreement is enforceable (so far as provided in relation to the agreement) where such an order has been made in relation to the agreement, but not otherwise.

(3) Where—

(a) a regulated agreement is cancelled under section 69 (1) or becomes subject to section 69 (2), or

(b) a regulated agreement is terminated under section 91, or

(c) in relation to any agreement an application for an order under section 40 (2), 65 (1), 124 (1) or 149 (2) is dismissed (except on technical grounds only), or

(d) a declaration is made by the court under section 142 (1) (refusal of enforcement order) as respects any regulated agreement,

section 106 shall apply to any security provided in relation to the agreement.

(4) Where subsection (3) (d) applies and the declaration relates to a part only of the regulated agreement, section 106 shall apply to the security only so far as it concerns that part.

(5) In the case of a cancelled agreement, the duty imposed on the debtor or hirer by section 71 or 72 shall not be enforceable before the creditor or owner has discharged any duty imposed on him by section 106 (as applied by subsection (3) (a)).

(6) If the security is provided in relation to a prospective agreement or transaction, the security shall be enforceable in relation to the agreement or transaction only after the time (if any) when the agreement is made; and until that time the person providing the security shall be entitled, by notice to the creditor or owner, to require that section 106 shall thereupon apply to the security.

(7) Where an indemnity is given in a case where the debtor or hirer is a minor, or is otherwise not of full capacity, the reference in subsection (1) to the extent to which his obligations would be

enforced shall be read in relation to the indemnity as a reference to the extent to which they would be enforced if he were of full capacity.

(8) Subsections (1) to (3) also apply where a security is provided in relation to an actual or prospective linked transaction, and in that case—

(a) references to the agreement shall be read as references to the linked transaction, and

(b) references to the creditor or owner shall be read as references to any person (other than the debtor or hirer, or his relative) who is a party, or prospective party, to the linked transaction.

Definitions

189.—(1) In this Act, unless the context otherwise requires—

"consumer credit business" means any business so far as it comprises or relates to the provision of credit under regulated consumer credit agreements;

[. . .]

"creditor" means the person providing credit under a consumer credit agreement or the person to whom his rights and duties under the agreement have passed by assignment or operation of law, and in relation to a prospective consumer credit agreement, includes the prospective creditor;

[. . .]

"debtor" means the individual receiving credit under a consumer credit agreement or the person to whom his rights and duties under the agreement have passed by assignment or operation of law, and in relation to a prospective consumer credit agreement includes the prospective debtor;

[. . .]

"executed agreement" means a document, signed by or on behalf of the parties, embodying the terms of a regulated agreement, or such of them as have been reduced to writing;

"exempt agreement" means an agreement specified in or under section 16;

[. . .]

"goods" has the meaning given by section 62 (1) of the Sale of Goods Act 1893;

[. . .]

"hire-purchase agreement" means an agreement, other than a conditional sale agreement, under which—

(a) goods are bailed or (in Scotland) hired in return for periodical payments by the person to whom they are bailed or hired, and

(b) the property in the goods will pass to that person if the terms of the agreement are complied with and one or more of the following occurs

    (i) the exercise of an option to purchase by that person,

    (ii) the doing of any other specified act by any party to the agreement,

    (iii) the happening of any other specified event.

"hirer" means the individual to whom goods are bailed or (in Scotland) hired under a consumer hire agreement, or the person to whom his rights and duties under the agreement have passed by assignment or operation of law, and in relation to a prospective consumer hire agreement includes the prospective hirer;

"individual" includes—a partnership or other unincorporated body of persons not consisting entirely of bodies corporate;

[. . .]

"payment" includes tender;

[. . .]

"prescribed" means prescribed by regulations made by the Secretary of State;

[. . .]

"regulated agreement" means a consumer credit agreement, or consumer hire agreement, other than an exempt agreement, and "regulated" and "unregulated" shall be construed accordingly;

"regulations" means regulations made by the Secretary of State;

"security", in relation to an actual or prospective consumer credit agreement or consumer hire agreement, or any linked transaction, means a mortgage, charge, pledge, bond, debenture, indemnity, guarantee, bill, note or other right provided by the debtor or hirer, or at his request (express or implied), to secure the carrying out of the obligations of the debtor or hirer under the agreement;

"security instrument" has the meaning given by section 105 (2);

"supplier" has the meaning given by section 11 (1) (*b*) or 12 (*c*) or 13 (*c*) or, in relation to an agreement falling within section 11 (1) (*a*), means the creditor, and includes a person to whom the rights and duties of a supplier (as so defined) have passed by assignment or operation of law, or (in relation to a prospective agreement) the prospective supplier;

"surety" means the person by whom any security is provided, or the person to whom his rights and duties in relation to the security have passed by assignment or operation of law;

Unfair Contract Terms Act 1977

(1977 c. 50)

Negligence liability

2.—(1) A person cannot by reference to any contract term or to a

notice given to persons generally or to particular persons exclude
or restrict his liability for death or personal injury resulting from
negligence.

(2) In the case of other loss or damage, a person cannot so exclude
or restrict his liability for negligence except in so far as the term or
notice satisfies the requirement of reasonableness.

(3) Where a contract term or notice purports to exclude or restrict
liability for negligence a person's agreement to or awareness of it is
not of itself to be taken as indicating his voluntary acceptance of any
risk.

[*Section 11 and Schedule 2 do not apply in terms to section 2.
However, in considering the test of reasonableness for the purposes
of section 2 it might be helpful to consider the guidelines set out in
Schedule 2 by analogy.*]

The "reasonableness" test

11.—(1) In relation to a contract term, the requirement of reasonableness for the purposes of this Part of this Act, section 3 of the
Misrepresentation Act 1967 and section 3 of the Misrepresentation
Act (Northern Ireland) 1967 is that the term shall have been a fair
and reasonable one to be included having regard to the circumstances
which were, or ought reasonably to have been, known to or in the
contemplation of the parties when the contract was made.

(2) In determining for the purposes of section 6 or 7 above whether
a contract term satisfies the requirement of reasonableness, regard
shall be had in particular to the matters specified in Schedule 2 to
this Act; but this subsection does not prevent the court or arbitrator
from holding, in accordance with any rule of law, that a term which
purports to exclude or restrict any relevant liability is not a term of
the contract.

(3) In relation to a notice (not being a notice having contractual
effect), the requirement of reasonableness under this Act is that it
should be fair and reasonable to allow reliance on it, having regard to
all the circumstances obtaining when the liability arose or (but for
the notice) would have arisen.

(4) Where by reference to a contract term or notice a person seeks
to restrict liability to a specified sum of money, and the question
arises (under this or any other Act) whether the term or notice
satisfies the requirement of reasonableness, regard shall be had in
particular (but without prejudice to subsection (2) above in the case
of contract terms) to—

    (*a*) the resources which he could expect to be available to him for
        the purpose of meeting the liability should it arise; and

    (*b*) how far it was open to him to cover himself by insurance.

(5) It is for those claiming that a contract term or notice satisfies the requirement of reasonableness to show that it does.

SCHEDULE 2

"GUIDELINES" FOR APPLICATION OF
REASONABLENESS TEST

The matters to which regard is to be had in particular for the purposes of sections 6 (3), 7 (3) and (4), 20 and 21 are any of the following which appear to be relevant—

(a) the strength of the bargaining positions of the parties relative to each other, taking into account (among other things) alternative means by which the customer's requirements could have been met;

(b) whether the customer received an inducement to agree to the term, or in accepting it had an opportunity of entering into a similar contract with other persons, but without having to accept a similar term;

(c) whether the customer knew or ought reasonably to have known of the existence and extent of the term (having regard, among other things, to any custom of the trade and any previous course of dealing between the parties);

(d) where the term excludes or restricts any relevant liability if some condition is not complied with, whether it was reasonable at the time of the contract to expect that compliance with that condition would be practicable;

(e) whether the goods were manufactured, processed or adapted to the special order of the customer.

Civil Liability (Contribution) Act 1978

(1978 c. 47)

Entitlement to contribution

1. (1) Subject to the following provisions of this section, any person liable in respect of any damage suffered by another person may recover contribution from any other person liable in respect of the same damage (whether jointly with him or otherwise).

(2) A person shall be entitled to recover contribution by virtue of subsection (1) above notwithstanding that he has ceased to be liable in respect of the damage in question since the time when the damage occurred, provided that he was so liable immediately before he made

or was ordered or agreed to make the payment in respect of which the contribution is sought.

(3) A person shall be liable to make contribution by virtue of subsection (1) above notwithstanding that he has ceased to be liable in respect of the damage in question since the time when the damage occurred, unless he ceased to be liable by virtue of the expiry of a period of limitation or prescription which extinguished the right on which the claim against him in respect of the damage was based.

(4) A person who has made or agreed to make any payment in bona fide settlement or compromise of any claim made against him in respect of any damage (including a payment into court which has been accepted) shall be entitled to recover contribution in accordance with this section without regard to whether or not he himself is or ever was liable in respect of the damage, provided, however, that he would have been liable assuming that the factual basis of the claim against him could be established.

(5) A judgment given in any action brought in any part of the United Kingdom by or on behalf of the person who suffered the damage in question against any person from whom contribution is sought under this section shall be conclusive in the proceedings for contribution as to any issue determined by that judgment in favour of the person from whom the contribution is sought.

(6) References in this section to a person's liability in respect of any damage are references to any such liability which has been or could be established in an action brought against him in England and Wales by or on behalf of the person who suffered the damage; but it is immaterial whether any issue arising in any such action was or would be determined (in accordance with the rules of private international law) by reference to the law of a country outside England and Wales.

Assessment of contribution

2.—(1) Subject to subsection (3) below, in any proceedings for contribution under section 1 above the amount of the contribution recoverable from any person shall be such as may be found by the court to be just and equitable having regard to the extent of that person's responsibility for the damage in question.

(2) Subject to subsection (3) below, the court shall have power in any such proceedings to exempt any person from liability to make contribution, or to direct that the contribution to be recovered from any person shall amount to a complete indemnity.

(3) Where the amount of the damages which have or might have been awarded in respect of the damage in question in any action brought in England and Wales by or on behalf of the person who suffered it against the person from whom the contribution is sought was or would have been subject to—

(*a*) any limit imposed by or under any enactment or by any agreement made before the damage occurred;

(*b*) any reduction by virtue of section 1 of the Law Reform (Contributory Negligence) Act 1945 or section 5 of the Fatal Accidents Act 1976; or

(*c*) any corresponding limit or reduction under the law of a country outside England and Wales;

the person from whom the contribution is sought shall not by virtue of any contribution awarded under section 1 above be required to pay in respect of the damage a greater amount than the amount of those damages as so limited or reduced.

Proceedings against persons jointly liable for the same debt or damage

3. Judgment recovered against any person liable in respect of any debt or damage shall not be a bar to an action, or to the continuance of an action, against any other person who is (apart from any such bar) jointly liable with him in respect of the same debt or damage.

Successive actions against persons liable (jointly or otherwise) for the same damage

4. If more than one action is brought in respect of any damage by or on behalf of the person by whom it was suffered against persons liable in respect of the damage (whether jointly or otherwise) the plaintiff shall not be entitled to costs in any of those actions, other than that in which judgment is first given, unless the court is of the opinion that there was reasonable ground for bringing the action.

INDEX

277